T0271208

Monetary Transmission in Diverse Economies

The transmission mechanism of monetary policy explains how monetary policy works – which variables respond to interest rate changes, when, why, how, how much and how predictably. It is vital that central banks and their observers, worldwide, understand the transmission mechanism so that they know what monetary policy can do and what it should do to stabilise inflation and output. The volume sets out different aspects of the transmission mechanism. Some chapters scrutinise the relevance of practical issues such as asymmetries, recent structural changes and estimation errors using data on the USA, the euro area and developing countries. Other chapters focus on modelling crucial aspects such as productivity, the exchange rate and the monetary sector. These issues are counterpointed by contributions that analyse contemporary monetary policy in Japan and the UK.

DR LAVAN MAHADEVA is an adviser at the Centre for Central Banking Studies at the Bank of England.

PROFESSOR PETER SINCLAIR is Director of the Centre for Central Banking Studies at the Bank of England.

Monetary Transmission in Diverse Economies

Edited by
LAVAN MAHADEVA AND
PETER SINCLAIR

CAMBRIDGE
UNIVERSITY PRESS

CAMBRIDGE
UNIVERSITY PRESS

University Printing House, Cambridge CB2 8BS, United Kingdom

Cambridge University Press is part of the University of Cambridge.

It furthers the University's mission by disseminating knowledge in the pursuit of education, learning and research at the highest international levels of excellence.

www.cambridge.org
Information on this title: www.cambridge.org/9780521813464

© Lavan Mahadeva & Peter Sinclair 2002

First published 2002, 2003
First paperback edition 2011

A catalogue record for this publication is available from the British Library

ISBN 978-0-521-81346-4 Hardback
ISBN 978-0-521-01325-3 Paperback

Contents

Contents

Figures

Tables

Contributors

FABIO ARAUJO *Central Bank of Brazil.*

DERICK BOYD *University of East London.*

JAGJIT S. CHADHA *Clare College, Cambridge University.*

K. ALEC CHRYSTAL *City University, London; formerly, Bank of England.*

PAULO SPRINGER DE FREITAS *Central Bank of Brazil.*

LAVAN MAHADEVA *Centre for Central Banking Studies, Bank of England.*

GUY MEREDITH *International Monetary Fund; formerly, Executive Director (Research), Hong Kong Monetary Authority.*

PAUL MIZEN *University of Nottingham.*

MARCELO KFOURY MUINHOS *Central Bank of Brazil.*

V. ANTON MUSCATELLI *Department of Economics, University of Glasgow.*

EDWARD NELSON *Research Adviser, Monetary Policy Committee, Bank of England; and Research Affiliate, Centre for Economic Policy Research.*

CHARLES NOLAN *Department of Economics, University of Durham; formerly, Department of Economics, University of Reading.*

GERT PEERSMAN *Bank of England; formerly, Ghent University.*

PETER SINCLAIR *Director, Centre for Central Banking Studies, Bank of England; and University of Birmingham.*

FRANK SMETS *European Central Bank; Centre for Economic Policy Research; and Ghent University.*

RON SMITH *Birkbeck College London.*

CARMINE TRECROCI *University of Brescia.*

KAZUO UEDA *The Bank of Japan.*

PETER WESTAWAY *Bank of England.*

Acknowledgements

All the papers in this book are the outcome of a conference held at the Centre for Central Banking Studies, Bank of England, 19–23 June 2000 on the theme of the Transmission Mechanism of Monetary Policy.

Our particular thanks go to Lucy Clary and Lorraine Yuille for their accomplished editorial assistance. We would also like to thank Paul Robinson and Gabriel Sterne for commenting on earlier drafts. We are grateful to Nedalina Divena (Editorial Services, Annapolis, Md) for her editing and to Tony Ison for his administrative help. Any mistakes remain our own and the views contained in the introduction and each chapter represent the authors themselves as individuals and are not attributable to the Bank of England in particular or to any of the institutions for which they work.

URL disclaimer

The publisher has used its best endeavours to ensure that the URLs for external websites referred to in this book are correct and active at the time of going to press. However, the publisher has no responsibility for the websites and can make no guarantee that a site will remain live or that the content is or will remain appropriate.

1 Introduction: the transmission mechanism and monetary policy

Lavan Mahadeva and Peter Sinclair

The transmission mechanism of monetary policy explains how monetary policy works – which variables respond to interest rate changes, when, why, how, how much and how predictably. This broadens to the issue of what monetary policy can do and what it should do to offset the effects of disturbances on inflation.

This volume sets out how the transmission mechanism is analysed for the purpose of informing monetary policy. The chapters that follow tackle different aspects of how a central bank can build a good working understanding of the transmission mechanism of monetary policy. In this introduction, we summarise how this understanding relates to the forecast apparatus and models employed, along with practical difficulties to be overcome. We highlight two key aspects of the monetary transmission mechanism – the monetary sector and the exchange rate – and conclude by summarising the key elements of current good practice.

1.1 How does the central bank analyse the transmission mechanism?

A central bank's interest in the transmission mechanism of monetary policy arises from the fact that it takes time for monetary policy to exert its maximum impact on inflation.[1] A central bank has to know how to position its interest rate *now* to keep inflation *in the future* close to its target, while avoiding any excessive destabilisation of output. It also has to form some view about what might happen to inflation and output over this intervening period (see Blinder, 1998; Budd, 1998).

If resources permitted, the central bank would be continually constructing and revising a comprehensive quantitative picture of the transmission mechanism of monetary policy over the policy horizon of, say, one or two years. Ideally, the monetary policy forecast would encompass much more than just predicted outcomes for inflation and output. It would include the following elements:
1. A set of *models* of the transmission mechanism with an explanation of how each model can be consistent with the others.

2. A set of *values for the underlying processes* that drive the forecast. These values are not just the exogenous variables but also the parameters and the off-model adjustments to endogenous variables. In the 1999 version of the Bank of England's macroeconometric model, for example, inventories as a ratio of GDP are determined by an exogenous de-stocking trend that partly accounts for innovations in integrated production processes and stock management techniques (Bank of England, 1999b, p. 50). In principle, this trend can be altered in the forecast, for example to reflect a view that the technical change has run its course, leaving the inventory–output ratio at a new constant equilibrium. The coefficient on any variable in the equation can also be thought of as a driving process; there may be good evidence to suggest that the firm's behaviour has altered, shifting the elasticities from their past values (Bank of England, 1995, p. 24).[2] Inventories could also be affected by other factors outside those in the equation. These factors could still be allowed to influence the inventory forecast as off-model adjustments.

3. Assumptions about *the policy reaction function*. What economic data do the central bank's policy decisions respond to, and how? What are the public's expectations of that policy reaction function?

4. By combining 1, 2 and 3, *the predicted out-turns* for inflation and output as well as for any other endogenous variable that can be matched against data when they become available.

5. Since forecasts can be wrong, *an appreciation of why previous forecasts turned out wrong* and what that could mean for the future forecast.

Inflation-targeting central banks, and many others too, make their views about what is likely to happen over this horizon explicit.[3] The reason is that credibility can be acquired and retained through the provision of transparent explanations, by publishing an inflation report or a forecast, for example (Mishkin and Posen, 1997; Bernanke et al., 1999; Chortareas et al., 2001).

The information presented becomes important if the central bank's view over this horizon is formed to *explain* and not just to *inform* policy. The public can become party to the uncertainties associated with the transmission mechanism. Higher moments, such as the risks and variances, would be quantified and published along with the expected forecast values. The presentation becomes an account of how the forecast depends on the interpretation of the current set of data. The weight attached to individual data series in determining forecasted inflation and output is not constant; it varies from policy round to policy round as new information comes to light (Svensson, 1999).

How is this understanding of the transmission mechanism over the future horizon to be built? For the purposes of illustration, we can split the construction of this forecast into the following stages:[4]

1. Formulate various hypotheses about how the driving processes (exogenous variables, residual adjustments and parameters) are developing and will develop.

2. Test the hypotheses against each other, comparing how they match up to theory and data. This testing can be done in two stages. Each hypothesis would first be cast into a theoretically consistent model. Then the predictions of this model would be compared with recent data. The most favoured hypotheses provide the expected values (and also the associated probability distribution of outcomes) of the driving processes in the forecast.

3. Calculate the implications for inflation and output using a model. These implications are conditional on assumptions about both the policy reaction and the expectations of this policy reaction.

4. Derive the optimal policy response that would return inflation to target without incurring unsatisfactory output losses.[5]

The key in specifying the driving processes – step 1 – is establishing how they might deviate in the future from their past behaviour. Shocks to the driving processes ultimately originate in shifts to the parameters that shape the preferences of agents, the micro-structure of markets, technological developments or endowments. The categories of agents whose preferences can shift are investors, borrowers, consumers, workers, firms and the monetary and fiscal authorities. The micro-structure of markets where goods, services, financial and non-financial assets, factors of production and information are traded can also change. Technological developments can arise in the production of goods, services, financial and non-financial assets, working capital (physical and human), inputs and information. Finally changes can occur in the endowments of natural resources, technical progress and the size of the working population, all of which are typically taken to be exogenous but not, of course, necessarily constant over time. A shock can also arise from changes in population composition, because different cohorts or groups may vary in preferences and constraints.

Once we have located an underlying cause, we still have to determine other dimensions of each shock. To begin with, the time path of the underlying disturbance needs specification. Is it permanent or temporary? If temporary, does it die off gradually or sharply? As shocks affect different sectors of the economy in different ways, does a sectoral or disaggregated model tell us significantly more about monetary policy implications than an aggregate model?[6] For open economies, the international dimension of shocks can be crucial. The implications of a disturbance can differ greatly, depending on whether it occurs only at home or is mirrored in the country's trading partners or capital partners abroad.

Can the shock be satisfactorily understood in isolation or is it related to other concurrent developments? Even if two disturbances have the same underlying cause, this relationship need not be an explicit part of the model used to forecast inflation. Consider an IT improvement that is skill biased, not only raising the overall level of productivity but also shifting demand from unskilled to skilled labour. We can capture how this skill-biased IT shock hits the economy in a model that disaggregates skilled and unskilled labour markets.

But, in more aggregate models, we could also combine an 'adjustment' to the wage equation with an exogenous shift to the time profile of technical progress.

No single methodology or model can convincingly analyse all shocks in this degree of detail. One solution is to build our picture of the transmission mechanism from individual studies covering different aspects of individual shocks. As an example, Peersman and Smets' contribution to this volume (chapter 2) explores how a common monetary policy tightening affects the euro area and how it depends on the economic cycle. Their findings are an important step in quantifying the money transmission mechanism of the region as a whole.

By introducing a common monetary shock into the models for growth of eight euro-area countries,[7] Peersman and Smets estimate that monetary policy exerts a significantly stronger effect when the euro area is in recession compared with a boom. Although the asymmetry varies among the countries sampled, on average it seems to be only two-fifths as strong in an expansion as in a recession. The authors explain that asymmetric monetary policy transmission could come about because economic conditions influence the sensitivity of consumption and investment decisions to monetary policy shocks through the extension of credit to constrained borrowers and investors. An alternative explanation is that nominal prices were stickier in expansionary than in disinflationary episodes (Ball and Mankiw, 1994). Other research by Peersman and Smets (Peersman and Smets, 2000b) isolates and tests the credit-availability effect on data disaggregated by sector, which could be more revealing. These findings are relevant for euro-area monetary policy. More generally, they remind us that shocks are not always linear in effect. Linearisation is a convenient assumption since the effects of each shock will then be independent of other events. Each shock can be judged in isolation and the effects of different shocks can then be summed to give us an aggregate picture of the transmission mechanism. Although linearity may often be a sufficiently close approximation,[8] the policy implications derived from linear models can sometimes be misleading. Furthermore, the interaction of a set of shocks makes their combined impact differ from that resulting from adding their effects one by one.

In this book, as elsewhere, a wide variety of models and approaches are now used to analyse shocks in such detail. But the tools at our disposal, and the models on which they are based, are consistent with the following two tenets:

- The economy converges towards a long-run state in which prices are fully flexible in nominal terms. The long-run state is described by an adapted neoclassical model in which the adaptations allow for rigidities in *real* prices that prevent the markets for goods and factors of production from fully clearing.[9]
- In the short run, the nominal prices of goods, inputs and assets are not fully flexible. New Keynesian phenomena, which arise chiefly because of menu costs, imply some degree of predetermination in nominal prices.[10] Any shock

to a nominal variable (for example, a surprise monetary policy action) will not be accompanied by an instantaneous complete adjustment to all other nominal variables. Relative prices, and hence real quantities, will not always be at the values they would take if all nominal prices were flexible – nominal shocks have temporary real effects. The scale of the real effects arising from nominal rigidities is in part determined by the real rigidities (Ball and Romer, 1991). So, even if monetary policy-makers cannot affect these underlying long-run market failures, the need to research them can still exist.

Models of the transmission mechanism that are grounded on this consensus can be labelled as 'IS–LM plus Phillips curve' descriptions of the economy. As the name implies, any model of this class can be summarised into a simple aggregate structure comprising only an IS curve, a policy rule and a Phillips curve[11] after many simplifying assumptions[12] are made.

1.2 How can we derive the policy implications?

To give policy advice, the driving processes, and the 'IS–LM plus Phillips curve' models in which they are couched, are combined. One way of combining is to ask whether the underlying shock implies any movements in the *real rate of interest*, assuming that the nominal interest rates and the expectations of it are constant.[13] A large enough forecasted fall (rise) in the real interest rate, when the nominal rate is unchanged, would imply that inflation will shift above (below) its target. If so, nominal interest rates would have to change.

No matter how this is done, when a response is called for, the path for setting interest rates depends on the temporary output losses and the preferences of the central bank concerning these costs. The output losses arise from both the original shock and the policy response to it. A major enterprise of monetary policy then becomes to identify the implications for the real interest rate and for real output of any shock, and to ensure that these estimates are correctly conditional on unchanged policy.

A popular scheme for deriving the policy implications of shocks has been to classify them into demand- and supply-side shocks, on the basis of what they imply for real output. Given constant expectations of monetary policy, inflationary demand-side shocks are associated with a rise in temporary output that leaves long-run or potential output unaffected, whereas inflationary supply-side shocks are associated with a fall in potential output with actual output falling or constant. Monetary policy should react to the shocks that are identified as inflationary on the demand side, whereas it is likely to respond to supply-side shocks only if the inflationary threat outweighs the output costs of responding. If the output implications of a shock are visible before its inflationary impact, this 'demand- versus supply-side' scheme can, in principle, serve as an early warning system for monetary policy.[14]

To put this into practice, the monetary policy-maker must be able to separate the output consequences of a shock into the changes in the potential value on the one hand and the changes in the output gap (actual output minus potential output) on the other. The relevant concept of potential output for monetary policy purposes here is the output that would arise at each moment in time if all nominal prices were flexible (McCallum and Nelson, 1999b; McCallum, 2000a,b). To apply this theory to the measurement of the current output gap, it is necessary to estimate what would determine output if prices were flexible: the counterfactual 'flexible-price' values of inputs into production, real rigidities (such as the factors that determine structural unemployment) as well as exogenous technical progress. Data that would determine the flexible-price value of inputs may be hard to come by. The flexible-price rate of unemployment, for example, is determined by structural factors such as workers' reservation wage rates and their bargaining power (see, for example, Layard, Nickell and Jackman, 1991, and Nickell, 1996). The data we have on the real unemployment benefit and union density can serve as a poor proxy for these deep structural factors. The importance of these theories has to be balanced with the implications of theories that link the flexible-price rate of unemployment to the actual rate of unemployment, such as hysteresis models (Cross, 1995; Ball, 1999a). Many researchers have relied instead on measures of potential output that employ only a few broad assumptions about the cyclical nature of potential output series compared with the output gap series. These measures tend to use only a single time series for output.[15]

As an alternative, Chadha and Nolan (chapter 3 in this volume) use a micro-founded model of the UK economy to give us a broad feel for what drives potential output in the 'flexible-price' economy. Their model departs from standard real business cycle models because firms are allowed to vary the intensity of utilisation of their existing capital stock, at the cost of wearing it down more quickly. The effect is to allow firms more leeway in investment; they can bunch investment decisions because they know that the capital they do have can be made to work harder.

Following a persistent series of total factor productivity (TFP) shocks, the authors show how variable capital utilisation makes investment less correlated with current output and more correlated with future output; investment anticipates underlying productivity improvements. The 'speeding up' of investment also reflects the fact that this is a model of an open economy and capital can be borrowed from abroad.

They further find that, in either of the standard real business cycle or varying capacity utilisation models, the difference between the real interest rate of the flexible-price artificial economies and the observed actual real interest rate seems to play a statistically significant role in explaining UK inflation and output outcomes. These results demonstrate that the flexible-price behaviour of important variables – not just investment but also the real rate of interest – can differ from the smooth processes typically assumed by popular detrending methods, and it can be of interest to monetary policy to explore why.

1.3 What makes a good model for analysing the transmission mechanism?

With the aim of deriving the policy implications of shocks, central banks have long been active in the production of models of the transmission mechanism. These models vary in scope, ranging from single-variable indicators to large-scale macroeconometric models. Whatever the nature of the model of the transmission mechanism, three criteria are traditionally held important in determining a good model for monetary policy purposes.

(a) The model should forecast inflation and output, accurately and robustly, in the face of structural breaks (Clements and Hendry, 1998, 1999).

(b) The model should accurately identify and be correctly conditional on policy reactions, making it immune to the Lucas critique (Bernanke and Mihov, 1998; Banerjee, Hendry and Mizon, 1996).

(c) The model should be estimated on and refer to data that are available and reliable.

Deriving working models that fulfil all three criteria satisfactorily in practice has proved difficult. Later on, we will therefore suggest that transparency has been an additional, important criterion for a good central bank model.

History is cluttered with examples of unreliable forecasts of macroeconomic variables, with such failures afflicting many types of models (Zarnowitz, 1992). The problem is that, although we acknowledge that a model must predict well, how can we assess this predictive capacity when constructing it?

It would seem sensible to choose models that display a good fit and satisfy all the necessary diagnostics indicating a robust specification. But problems arise when the structural breaks – defined as 'permanent large shifts' in the transmission mechanism 'occurring intermittently' (Banerjee, Hendry and Mizon, 1996) – are prevalent. The presence of structural breaks implies that a model passing all these tests on past data need not necessarily forecast the future well (Hendry and Doornik, 1997; Clements and Hendry, 1998, 1999).

Boyd and Smith's paper (chapter 4 in this volume) asks why we have failed to find reliable estimates of the monetary transmission mechanism. The authors' approach is novel. Across a panel data set of annual observations on 60 developing countries, the authors estimate a simple model of the monetary transmission mechanism comprising an IS curve, a trade balance equation, a purchasing parity equation for the exchange rate and a Phillips curve. Their purpose was *not*, however, to produce an average estimate of the transmission mechanism across these countries, but rather to see what we can learn from the wide cross-country differences in the estimates of the parameters.

By comparing the aggregate panel estimates with individual country-specific estimates, the authors show that the dispersion in parameter values is very broad across the countries they sample. They conclude that this diversity seems too large to be attributed to international differences in the transmission mechanism; the process of estimation itself seems to impart biases. What could be the root cause here? The authors suggest that errors in measuring unobservable variables, such as potential output, largely explain why our estimates of the transmission mechanism are so unreliable. These biases appear to vary so much across countries that we should adapt the data, theory and techniques to fit the country-specific circumstances if we are to improve the performance of our estimated models of the transmission mechanism. In their words, more 'tender loving care' is needed.

Structural breaks create additional hazards if they are related to monetary policy. Inaccurate policy advice can be produced from models that are incorrectly conditional on policy reactions; that is, models that do not satisfy condition (b). With this motivation, Muscatelli and Trecroci (chapter 5) look for recent shifts in the transmission mechanism in the USA and the UK that have been caused by changes in monetary policy institutions. More credible monetary policy frameworks in the United Kingdom and the United States may have lowered inflation and, at the same time, made it less volatile. In turn, a more predictable environment may have encouraged firms and workers to establish price and wage contracts in nominal terms. Stickier nominal prices would have slowed down the pass-through of nominal shocks, such as exchange rate changes (Taylor, 2000). Causality could also run in the opposite direction. Changes in the monetary transmission mechanism, such as lower and less volatile global inflation expectations, may have reduced the output cost of anti-inflationary policies in individual countries. These two hypotheses are not necessarily exclusive; an improvement in one country's monetary policy framework may have made it easier for its trading partners to stabilise their own domestic inflation, and vice versa.

Working with postwar US and UK data, Muscatelli and Trecroci test whether changes in monetary policy setting have led to changes in an aggregate demand relationship that determines output and an aggregate supply relationship that determines inflation.[16] They find that, after 1984, it is the inflation equation and not the aggregate demand relationship that appears to have been affected by policy changes in the United States. Both equations seem to have been affected in the United Kingdom over the same period. To estimate the scale and timing of any shift in policy institutions that may have caused this change in the transmission mechanism, the authors estimate a Bayesian (and hence time-varying) vector autoregression (VAR) of the transmission of interest rates, inflation and output gap shocks onto the variables themselves.[17] These time-varying estimates of the responses of the interest rate to shocks suggest that changes in policy reaction function took place in the 1990s for both countries. The responses of UK and US inflation to a shock in the output gap and of UK output to the interest rate shock also seem to have been heightened, albeit gradually, in line with their preliminary findings. These estimates of the interaction between the transmission mechanism and monetary policy in recent years suggest that the Lucas critique is still relevant to estimates of the transmission mechanism, even if it is less visible when inflation is low and stable.

The final requirement of a good model – to be intimate with reliable data – could mean trying to avoid too many unverifiable or unstable parameter calibrations that transport us from the data to the model's forecasts. One example of a family of models that has been well directed to its available data set is the models belonging to the monetary framework of the International Monetary Fund (IMF) (Polak, 1998).[18] The objective of the IMF framework for model design was to forecast what changes in a nation's current economic environment (especially those arising from exports and bank credit) imply for the sustainability of the balance of trade. The approach has proved remarkably influential and durable. From its inception in the 1950s to this day, it continues to perform a key role in the analysis that builds up to the conditionality of IMF borrowing in many countries on IMF programmes.

As Polak (1998) explains, its success may owe much to its simplicity. At the centre of the model is a simple structure that avoids the need to rely excessively on econometric estimates of coefficients from poor-quality data or on theoretical assumptions that may not be valid. To implement the framework, it is not necessary to estimate much more than the nominal income elasticity of the demand for money and parameters for the export and import equations.[19] Inflation and GDP are determined elsewhere but, given the environment to which the framework is applied, the risk of inconsistency is not great. Most of the countries with IMF programmes have fixed exchange rates; prices are therefore determined from abroad. Also, with nominal prices flexible, real output is often dominated by supply-side developments.

1.4 How can these difficulties in modelling the transmission mechanism affect monetary policy in practice?

Kazuo Ueda (chapter 6 in this volume) draws from his experience as a member of the Bank of Japan's policy board to provide a vivid real-world example of the difficulties in understanding the transmission mechanism. From 1998 to 2000, the Japanese economy was in recession, with the overnight call interest rate below 0.5% and prices falling or close to falling. The Bank of Japan lowered the policy rate very close to zero in February 1999; shortly afterwards it announced its commitment to keep the rate at these levels until deflation concerns were alleviated. Ueda's paper analyses this zero interest rate policy, commonly called the ZIRP.

Ueda suggests that the ZIRP had some favourable effect at the time; by committing to a fixed short-term rate for some length of time, the Bank of Japan was able to hold down longer rates and reduce unhelpful uncertainties at the longer end of the yield curve. To have fully exploited the benefits of a ZIRP, however, it would have been necessary to formalise the conditions for terminating it. These conditions could then be made explicit as part of the monetary signal. The conditions for ending the ZIRP could only have been derived if it were possible to assess, with reasonable accuracy, how the transmission mechanism was evolving at that time. The continuing financial crisis and the widespread threat of bankruptcy made it difficult to say confidently where potential output was and where it was heading. Another key parameter, the sensitivity of consumption and investment to the real interest rate, may also have shifted from previous estimates as a result of the credit crunch. Ueda's example illustrates just how serious the measurement difficulties that commonly bedevil monetary policy implementation can, on occasion, become.

Nelson's discussion in chapter 7 of the recent and historical difficulties in understanding the UK monetary transmission mechanism makes an interesting comparison with Ueda's contribution. Other commentators have suggested that the combination of high inflation and high unemployment in the UK from 1965 to 1975 came about because, in policy circles, the view was that permanent improvements in the level of employment could be achieved at the cost of higher rates of inflation. Nelson disagrees. His review of the historical debate shows that influential policy-makers at that time were sceptical of such a systematic trade-off in the UK Phillips curve and became even more so by the early 1970s when evidence against an exploitable trade-off accumulated. He argues that the consensus centred on two views: the coefficient of the output gap in the Phillips curve was too *small* to support such a trade-off, and monetary policy was not very important in determining inflation.[20] In the mid-1970s, these premises led to a situation in which the primary task delegated to monetary policy was to maintain aggregate demand and employment, with the control of inflation left to prices and incomes policies.

Later, the importance of monetary policy in determining UK inflation became ever more firmly established. In 1997, it was enshrined in the instrument-independence of the Bank of England. In parallel, research was redirected towards a better understanding of the transmission of monetary policy to inflation. Perhaps the domestic channels of monetary policy could be best traced through a structural model. In a closed economy setting, that structure would connect the short-run real interest rates to aggregate demand in an IS curve, and then aggregate demand to inflation via the GDP output gap in a Phillips curve.

Nelson shows how estimates of how real interest rates affect real GDP growth in the UK report coefficients that are significant, but with signs that are opposite to what would be predicted by standard IS–LM models! After weighing up the evidence for the many possible explanations for this puzzle, Nelson's preferred explanation for the failure to reproduce a theoretically consistent IS curve is that some other important influences on consumption, such as real asset yields, are omitted (Meltzer, 1995). As for the Phillips curve stage of this transmission, Nelson stresses that the measurement of potential output is an important constraint that we have to overcome. Together, Nelson's and Ueda's contributions show that the most problematic aspects of understanding the transmission mechanism apply widely, although the scale of the problems and what is at stake may vary across national borders and over history.

1.5   What are the implications of practical difficulties for monetary policy modelling?

Structural breaks, measurement errors and policy identification problems appear to pose real challenges for the analysis of the transmission mechanism. These recurrent problems may explain why the degree of accuracy with which we can forecast inflation and output one or two years ahead remains modest despite great technological advances in the tools and data at the economist's disposal (Zarnowitz, 1992; Wallis, 1989). Point forecasts are too uncertain for the publication of forecast numbers for output and inflation by themselves to be a reliable means of acquiring credibility. But central bank forecasts have survived and even thrived in what appears to be a harsh environment. This situation suggests that other outputs of forecast production confer internal benefits to the central bank beyond the simple acquisition of an accurate picture of the economic future.

Smith (1998) and Westaway (1995) explain that one of the main advantages of producing a forecast with a model is that it allows policy-makers to explore different scenarios. If models are used flexibly, beliefs and judgements can be integrated and made consistent with econometric information. Although alternative strategies exist, producing a forecast with structural models seems to be an efficient way of processing the data into stories about the underlying shocks – information that can then be relayed to the public.

A simple model, adapted from Clarida, Galí and Gertler (1999) and Cecchetti (2000), helps to explain the benefits of identifying and communicating the source of shocks. As in Bean (1998), the transmission mechanism for a closed economy is cut down to just two equations: aggregate demand and aggregate supply. In the aggregate demand equation (1.1), output (measured relative to its potential), y, is a function of the (policy-determined) real interest rate, r, and a demand-side shock, d:

$$y = -br + d. \tag{1.1}$$

In the aggregate supply equation (1.2), inflation, π, is a function of the expectation of current inflation by the public based on their information sets, π^e, the output gap and a supply-side shock, s. This formula captures the concept that inflationary surprises cause output to rise above potential.

$$\pi = \pi^e + cy + s. \tag{1.2}$$

The role of monetary policy is captured by a loss function (L) for the monetary policy-maker, in equation (1.3).

$$2L = (y)^2 + \lambda(\pi - \pi_L)^2. \tag{1.3}$$

The policy-maker influences the real interest rate to minimise the weighted average of the output gap volatility and the volatility of inflation about its long-run rate (π_L).[21] As in Blinder (1998), King (1996) and Clarida, Galí and Gertler (1999), no average bias exists in the central bank's preferences towards a positive output gap. The central bank knows of the demand and supply shocks only with some error. The demand shock, as measured by the central bank, is d'. The 'control' error in the demand shock is then $d - d'$. Analagously, $s - s'$ is the control error on the supply side. The public's understanding of the underlying demand and supply shocks is cloaked by noise from both control errors and transparency errors. The transparency errors, denoted by $s' - s''$ and $d' - d''$ respectively, depend on how willing and able the central bank is to make the public privy to its understanding of the shocks.

Both parties form rational expectations and neither the public nor the central bank behaves strategically.[22] The problem can then be solved to yield the output gap, inflation rate, real rate of interest and inflation expectations as functions of the underlying shocks and the control and transparency errors (see the appendix). Equation (1.4) describes the solution for the output gap and table 1.1 summarises the solutions for the other variables:

$$y = -\frac{s}{c} + \frac{(s' - s'')}{c(1 + \lambda c^2)} + \left(d - d' - \frac{s - s'}{c}\right). \tag{1.4}$$

In our simple model without inflation stickiness, both the rates of inflation and output are independent of the demand shock, because the real rate of interest can be adjusted without cost to offset these shocks as soon as they arise (Cecchetti, 2000). A supply shock that is inflationary will lower output to the extent that prices are sticky (the parameter c is finite), because the real rate of interest

Table 1.1 *The effect of supply and demand shocks on the output gap, inflation and expected inflation, decomposed into the underlying shock, a transparency error and a control error*

Effect	Control errors in		Transparency errors in		Underlying shock in	
	Demand shocks	Supply shocks	Demand shocks	Supply shocks	Demand shocks	Supply shocks
On the output gap	+	+	0	+	0	−
On the actual inflation gap $(\pi - \pi_L)$	+	−	0	−	0	+
On the real interest rate	−	+	0	−	+	+
On the expected inflation gap $(\pi^e - \pi_L)$	0	−	0	−	0	+

will have to rise to deal with its inflationary impact. The supply shock raises inflation directly and indirectly. The indirect influence results from a combined rise in expected inflation and an offsetting fall in the output gap.

In our set-up, the central bank wants to improve its understanding of the transmission mechanism. Imperfect measurement of the demand and supply shocks by the central bank and public – control errors – create further volatility in the output gap as well as inflation. Control errors about supply shocks affect inflation through excess output volatility and unstable inflation expectations. Fuzziness surrounding demand shocks feeds through to inflation via output only. If a supply control error is more likely to be associated with a demand control error of the opposite sign, the negative covariance would add further to output and inflation volatility, as can be seen in equation (1.4). Why might the central bank's errors in measuring supply and demand shocks be negatively related? One reason could be that the output data that the central bank uses to identify these shocks are noisy. Following the process similar to that described earlier in this chapter, the central bank would identify supply and demand shocks by applying what data it has on output, inflation and expected inflation to its understanding of the transmission mechanism to recover the supply and demand shock. But if output and inflation expectations data were poorly measured, all things being equal, excessively relying on the imperfect data means that a positive supply shock is more likely to be incorrectly identified as a negative demand shock, and vice versa (see the appendix to this chapter).

The output gap signal could be distorted by measurement errors in the data on actual output (Orphanides et al., 1999) and by the uncertainties – emphasised by many contributors to this volume – in measuring its potential value.

Here, transparency errors in supply, but not those in demand, also add to volatility. Transparency errors in demand are not important for either inflation or output, because the central bank is able to offset the impact of these shocks on both output and inflation simultaneously with a flexible inflation process. It does not matter whether or not the public is made aware of this.[23] Transparency errors in supply do matter, however. Because supply shocks drive inflation and the output gap in opposite directions, the central bank is unable to achieve its goals for both inflation and output by either raising or cutting interest rates. The less the public knows about supply shocks, the more unstable inflation expectations become and the more active real interest rates must be.

In practice, there may be limited scope for a central bank to reduce control and transparency errors. The message from our simple framework is that the central bank would always choose to reduce such errors if possible. In more complicated models in which the central bank targets a positive gap (on average), or where agents are in the process of learning, there could be gains from not being transparent since an incentive exists for the central bank to cheat the public.[24] Our simple model demonstrates only that imperfect understanding and transparency about both the *scale* and *nature* of shocks to the transmission mechanism can potentially play a malignant role in inflation and output volatility.

1.6   Putting this approach into practice

To put this approach into perspective, we discuss the application of two important aspects of the transmission mechanism: the monetary sector and the exchange rate.

1.6.1   The monetary sector

Westaway's contribution (chapter 8) was based on a speech he gave to kick-start the discussion for the conference held at the Centre for Central Banking Studies in June 2000. In his speech, as well as in his chapter in this volume, he set out some of the key issues in policy-related work on the transmission mechanism. One of Westaway's questions was, 'What role can money play in the transmission mechanism?' One answer is that quantities of money, in aggregate or in disaggregate, could serve as an indicator for other unobservable variables – such as expected asset prices. Going beyond its role as an indicator, there are many other reasons why, at least in theory, money could play a causal role in the transmission mechanism. Aggregate demand could be influenced by real money balances directly, or the transmission of policy to market interest rates could be effected through credit market imperfections or wealth effects, for example. *Quantifying* this active role for money, however, requires us to estimate how exactly it interacts with consumption and investment. To answer Westaway's question, monetary policy-makers need to explore ways of modelling the monetary sector.

In part, a central bank's interest in monetary variables reflects the fact that monetary data are home-grown from the central bank's own survey. Monetary data also help the central bank keep track of its other responsibilities (financial stability, market operations and possibly banking supervision) in addition to monetary stability. Despite these advantages, problems of the type that we have highlighted (structural breaks and difficulties in conditioning on the policy re-action) have made it notoriously difficult to use monetary aggregates to predict inflationary components of shocks. Because financial portfolios can be adjusted with great facility, investors can easily move funds, for example, to react to pol-icy announcements and potential productivity improvements. A consequence is that the volumes and prices of monetary variables become ever more sensitive to underlying shocks and expectations.

Chrystal and Mizen (chapter 9) explore one promising route to extract the information on these variables from monetary data. They model the flows of loans and credit from one sector to another in the United Kingdom and ask if these credit flows have any information content for monetary policy above that of money in aggregate. Given that money flows are partly endogenous, they are determined jointly with the prices and volumes of goods and assets and the associated rates of interest (Papademos and Modigliani, 1990; Friedman and Kuttner, 1993). Customers of the banking sector transact primarily over deposits and loans; each category of customer and the banks themselves also have another set of economic decisions to make. Flows to and from banks into these sectors may tell us about agent's present and future actions.

Firms have to choose investment in: physical capital; dividend payments; the issue or the buy-back of equity or commercial paper; the employment and utilisation of other inputs; their cash balances; and the price of their output. The personal sector chooses its demand for bank loans and deposits jointly with its supply of labour, consumption of goods and services, asset holdings and transaction balances. Other important counterparties are the central bank, which determines its monetary operations and its policy objectives, and the government agency that determines its net issue of bonds if there is a separation of debt management. The banking sector itself has decisions to make over its reserves at the central bank, borrowing from the interbank market, holdings of commercial bonds and equity, and stock of government bonds.[25]

Chrystal and Mizen estimate a dynamic model of the sectoral flows between the UK banking sector, the personal sector, the non-financial corporate sector and non-bank financial institutions in the UK.[26] Many results confirm that this sectoral model contains information that would be lost on aggregation. One interesting example is that non-bank financial institutions[27] seem to be very active in supplying funds for investment by firms, to the extent that their lending would affect real investment even if it were matched by a rise in non-bank financial institutions' liabilities. These non-bank financial institutions' long-run decisions to lend appear to be dominated by their view of the economic conditions of their customers (earnings and wealth). Supply factors (such as credit spreads) have more of a temporary effect. Combining these results, non-bank financial institutions may constitute a balance sheet channel for monetary policy to affect aggregate demand through wealth (Bernanke and Gertler, 1995).

Importantly, Chrystal and Mizen model the transaction costs incurred when transferring money from one sector. Transaction costs arise because lending and borrowing are associated with risks – the information on which is not shared equally by both parties. There may be market solutions (such as insurance schemes, collateral, monitoring agencies) to resolve these market failures. But these solutions are costly to activate. Interestingly, these transaction costs may be related to the variables that are informative about the forecast. For example, the insurance costs of a loan may be sensitive to expectations about aggregate demand; transaction costs can fall with the expected realised value of some assets (through collateral).

Because not all assets act as collateral, transaction costs may give rise to imperfect substitution in the demand for and supply of the different components of the monetary aggregates and other assets.[28] Assets and liabilities are traded by consumers to maximise expected lifetime consumption (plus bequests) and by firms and banks to maximise expected firm value. Ultimately, the differences in degree of substitutability of assets depend on the costs of transferring them into consumption. One way of modelling this scenario is to distinguish the real value set aside for consumption (C_t) from the realised consumption $(\widehat{C}_t)$.

We can write:

$$\widehat{C}_t = T\left(X_t^1, \ldots, X_t^N\right), \quad \text{for the } N \text{ assets.}$$

The technology that transforms planned consumption into realised consumption depends on how the consumption activity is purchased; i.e. through which asset or liability. This formulation recognises that different transaction costs are associated with different sources of wealth. Some wealth components (such as those that can be collateralised) are complementary in reducing the transaction costs of transferring other components.[29] If the technology were linear, there would be no transactions costs as in a standard model. Substituting the transaction cost function into aggregate consumption in the utility function implies that the demand for different components of wealth can also be modelled as imperfect substitutes in utility (Clower, 1984).

The information content of monetary variables depends on this substitutability. If two assets are always viewed by any group of agents as perfect substitutes, the interest rate will be equalised once adjusted for the expected change in asset price and the relative transaction costs of turning assets into consumption. Even here, the information derived from data on these assets may help us understand the transmission mechanism. One important reason is that nominal interest rate differentials can be used to forecast expected asset prices. Asset prices may explain goods prices just as the uncovered interest rate parity (UIP) model explains expected exchange rate depreciation. Similarly, the spread between two bonds that differ only in their maturity should reflect the expected path of real interest rates on the short-term bond until the maturity date of the long bond. In addition, interest rate differentials may tell us about per unit value transaction costs – whether they depend on expectations of the monetary cycle, for example.

A second source of information about the transmission mechanism is the relative *volumes* of these assets. Even if the rates of return are equalised, relative volumes tell us about the decisions of other agents who do not regard the assets as substitutes. For example, even if borrowers consider loans from domestic banks to be identical to loans from foreign banks, the *relative* supply of these loans could provide information about loan providers' expectations of domestic versus foreign macroeconomic conditions.

1.6.2   Exchange rates

The exchange rate is often blamed for the forecast failure of models of the transmission mechanism in an open economy. This blame reflects the perception not only that exchange rate shocks are large relative to other shocks, but also that the exchange rate is pervasive in the open economy's transmission mechanism. Muinhos, de Freitas and Araujo's paper (chapter 10) on the Brazilian exchange rate provides an example of how the central bank might assess different models of the exchange rate.

The authors evaluate the different exchange rate models in terms of their implications for impulse responses to different shocks. Given a recent history of fixed exchange rates in Brazil, the data sample is too brief to judge the ability of models to forecast the exchange rate over the long term. Drawing from the discussion on transparency, the central bank is also interested in models with three characteristics: emphasis on reliable data; visibility of the role its own policy plays in the forecast; and transparency. Checking that impulse responses conform to commonsense or theoretical priors is one in the set of criteria typically used to accept or reject policy models.[30]

The authors compare how two exchange rate relationships perform against each other when placed in a small structural model of Brazil made up of an IS curve, a Phillips curve, a Taylor rule and trade equations. The first exchange rate relationship – a random walk with monetary surprises (RWMS) – combines UIP with the assumption that the expected change in the exchange rate is white noise. A risk premium term is determined by the public sector borrowing rate and a current account. The second method – called UIP plus fundamentals – determines the exchange rate according to UIP, with a terminal condition that is consistent with purchasing power parity as determined by the model-consistent expectations.[31]

One interesting difference between the models emerges in their response to a shock to the IS curve. Under the random walk with monetary surprises, the real exchange rate returns to equilibrium slowly, whereas in the UIP plus fundamental model the convergence is more rapid. The primary feedback that brings the real exchange rate back to equilibrium in the RWMS model is an appreciation effect pushing GDP below potential (by creating a trade deficit) and hence reducing inflation in the Phillips curve. In the UIP plus fundamentals model, the influence of the long-run real exchange rate as a terminal condition brings the real exchange rate quickly back to equilibrium.

Researchers have explored different models of the exchange rate because the UIP has been overwhelmingly rejected in the numerous empirical trials to which it has been subjected.[32] Underpinning this rejection was the presumption that, if UIP were to hold, the correlation between the ex post UIP residual (the actual exchange rate depreciation minus the interest rate differential) and the interest rate differential itself had to be much closer to zero than the significant positive values that were commonly estimated (Fama, 1984).

Meredith provides many arguments in chapter 11 to explain why these tests may not provide sufficient (or even necessary) grounds for excluding UIP from the model of the transmission mechanism of an open country with a free-floating exchange rate. His key insight is that the estimated equation of the exchange rate on which this inference is based may not be correctly conditioned on monetary policy. Using model-based experiments, he proves that, even when UIP holds, a positive correlation could arise because the interest rate differential is correlated with the unmeasured risk premium. Interest rates become related to risk if monetary policy smooths out exchange rate fluctuations, for example.[33] The UIP's holding over long horizons (Chinn and Meredith, 1998) is, therefore, consistent with its empirical rejection at shorter maturities, if we accept that these risk premium shocks are relatively larger and more short lived than other shocks.

Meredith explains that UIP does not imply a strict relationship between the exchange rate and interest rates. Even when UIP holds, a widening in the interest rate differential will not always lead to an appreciation. The UIP relationship (without a risk premium) specifies that the current exchange rate level will depend on the current interest rate differential, the expected path of the interest rate differential and a terminal value for the nominal exchange rate. All of these determinants of the exchange rate level – not just the current interest rate differential – may shift in response to shocks that are hitting the economy; for example, the terminal exchange rate can depend on the expected long-run differences in growth both at home and abroad and the elasticity of substitution between domestic and foreign goods. Meredith's paper shows that when we assess the behaviour of the exchange rate we should be aware of its place within the broader transmission mechanism. The UIP example reminds us that underlying shocks need to be properly understood if we are forecasting for monetary policy.

1.7 Conclusion

Central banks' forecasts generate predictions for inflation and output. They can also provide transparent explanations of monetary policy. Producing a forecast seems to be an efficient way to organise and update a working understanding of the transmission mechanism.

To extract these internal and external benefits from the monetary policy forecast, we need a stylised numerical representation of the future transmission mechanism as a set of models. Forecasting the transmission mechanism, with or without models, is a challenge because economies are always evolving. And shifts in the transmission mechanism can cause shifts in monetary policy and be caused by it. As Muscatelli and Trecroci have shown, we can still gather useful monetary policy advice providing we use the appropriate tools.

One of the messages from the papers by Boyd and Smith, Nelson, Ueda and Westaway is that measurements of unobservable variables, such as potential output, present a major challenge to the monetary policy-makers of many different countries. We cannot shy away from trying to discover what drives potential output and, more generally, the flexible-price values of other key variables. We have to distinguish the underlying shocks using data on variables that may have changing flexible-price values. Chadha and Nolan have demonstrated that unobservable developments in the flexible-price value of variables need not necessarily be smooth and predictable.

Our models will never be perfect descriptions of the economy. Yet transparency could still have particular use when the nature of the underlying shocks in the transmission mechanism – including the scale of the uncertainty and risks associated with their expected or modal (most likely) values – is exposed.[34] To enhance transparency in this sense, the forecast could reveal the inputs and inner machinations of the forecast as well as its outputs. Outside observers would then appreciate the assumptions and calibrations that drive the monetary policy decision (including the possible measurement errors) and the relative contributions of different sources of evidence.

A detailed diagnosis of shocks is crucial here. One symptom to check for is whether the transmission of policy reactions depends on the state of the business cycle, as in Peersman and Smets' example of the euro area. Ueda's paper suggests that the transmission of monetary policy when Japan is mired in recession differs from estimates derived from other, more stable, historical periods. Chrystal and Mizen's emphasis on the *sectoral* flows of credit and spending is one way to explore this further; the transmission of monetary impulses within their framework is linked to expectations of a firm's profitability and workers' future income streams, both of which can shift downwards in a recession.

It is also important not to underestimate the benefit from establishing the timing and persistence of shocks. Meredith's and Muinhos, de Freitas and Araujo's papers both stress that exchange rate responses to different shocks can vary depending on the source and duration of the underlying shock. Not all exchange rate movements merit the same policy reaction; we need to establish how long lived the shock is and through which channel it affects the exchange rate. There are costs to getting the timing wrong. Research by Batini and Haldane (1999), among others, shows that setting interest rates to return inflation to target levels either too quickly or too slowly can destabilise both output and inflation.[35] If uncertainty exists about the timing and duration of shocks, there will be a trade-off in the risks of incurring long-term versus short-term policy errors. For example, by choosing to adjust the interest rate actively, the risks of long-term persistent misalignments of real interest rates are minimised at the cost of incurring short-term errors.

The data set that helps us characterise shocks in detail can be very variable in its frequency, degree of disaggregation and available sample size. Much of this information is not readily amenable to standard econometric techniques. Incorporating this varied information into one model would make that model too complex and threaten transparency. Many practitioners are, therefore, becoming pluralistic. Several user-friendly models are used to inform the forecast. Each model is purpose built to handle a different set of shocks and is often focused on a particular data set (Whitley, 1997; Kohn, 2000). The criteria for validating and selecting models take centre stage in a pluralistic approach, because the emphasis is on understanding and evaluating the differences among the many models in the central bank's stable. Transparency is as important a criterion for the process of validating the model as it is for choosing the model. Transformations used to derive the predictions on which the model is tested should be explicable and reproducible. Decisions about what evidence is needed to discriminate between rival explanations of the state of the monetary economy could and should embrace the public.

How then is the information from different models to be combined both consistently and in a transparent manner? An overarching conceptual framework, such as the 'IS–LM plus Phillips curve paradigm', is needed here. The real variables would be unaffected by monetary decisions in the long run, but other calibrations (particularly short-term adjustments) can be quantified with an open mind by combining theory and data. An effective way to ensure consistency with this paradigm would be to place a standard quarterly macroeconomic model at the core of the forecast production. This model would be adjusted explicitly and revised continually to incorporate relevant information from its satellite sources.

Much can be revealed about the underlying shocks and the strengths and weaknesses of different models by dissecting recent forecast errors.[36] Working with structural models rather than their reduced-form representations means that overall forecast errors can be attributed usefully to underlying shocks. Although there are risks in over-relying on theory, a structural model is better suited to explain what went wrong with the previous forecast (Smith, 1998; Diebold, 1998).

The data that are most relevant vary from country to country. For this reason, we should not expect to see the same method applied to all economies. For example, Basu and Taylor (1999) point out that the persistence of output gap measures should depend on the stickiness of prices. Countries with quicker nominal price adjustment, measured by a speedier exchange rate pass through, should have more short-lived output gaps. Our methods of measuring potential output should not impose the same degree of smoothness for all countries, as acknowledged by Coe and McDermott (1996).

Monetary policy mistakes can cause enormous economic damage. The past is imperfectly reported; the future is unknowable; key relationships linking economic variables rarely stand still. Maintaining price stability, and stabilising the macroeconomy more generally, are daunting responsibilities for all central banks. A thorough, up-to-date grasp of the transmission mechanism for monetary policy is essential. Without it, the central bank will not understand the effects of its actions. Without it, the risks of policy errors are vastly increased. If the central bank is open to the outside world and certain about what it expects, why it is doing what it is doing, and why and how its previous forecasts were mistaken, the various disturbances that confront it should be much less injurious.

Countries' monetary transmission mechanisms do not only evolve in complex ways – they differ, too. So do their central banks' experiences, which all of us can learn from. Their actions affect each other's economies. In today's interdependent world, everyone – central bankers, financial market participants and observers, economists, employees and shareholders – can benefit from greater knowledge about how prices and livelihoods are affected by monetary policy decisions at home and abroad. We hope that this volume will extend and deepen this knowledge, in central banks and elsewhere.

Appendix

The closed economy is summarised by an aggregate demand curve (1A.1) and an aggregate supply curve (1A.2):

$$y = -br + d; \tag{1A.1}$$
$$\pi = \pi^e + cy + s. \tag{1A.2}$$

π is the current inflation rate; π^e is the public's expectation of the current inflation rate, based on its information set at time t; y is the deviation of output from its flexible-price level; r is the real rate of interest; and d and s are demand and supply shocks, respectively. All variables other than inflation and interest rate are measured in natural logarithms.

Substituting 1A.1 into 1A.2 gives

$$\pi = \pi^e - cbr + cd + s. \tag{1A.3}$$

The objectives of the central bank are summarised in the following loss function:

$$L = 0.5(y)^2 + 0.5\lambda(\pi - \pi_L)^2. \tag{1A.4}$$

There are no uncertainties in the objectives of the central bank.

Information

At each moment in time, both the public and the central bank are aware of the model's parameters and the *past* history of shocks. The central bank's ability to measure the current values of demand and supply shocks, however, is imperfect and is subject to random *control* errors, written as $d - d'$ and $s - s'$ respectively. These errors are white noise. The public's knowledge of the demand and supply shocks at time t is subject not only to these control errors but also to white noise *transparency* errors, written as $d' - d''$ and $s' - s''$, respectively.

Both the public and the central bank form rational expectations; hence the control error for demand (respectively, supply) is uncorrelated both with the demand (respectively, supply) shock itself and with the transparency error for demand (respectively, supply) shock. Neither the central bank nor the public behaves strategically.

Substituting (1A.1) and (1A.3) into (1A.4), and conditioning on the information set of the central bank, gives:

$$L = 0.5(-br + d')^2 + 0.5\lambda(\pi^e - cbr + cd' + s' - \pi_L)^2. \tag{1A.5}$$

Minimising with respect to the rate of interest gives us a first-order condition with respect to the real interest rate, taking inflation expectations as determined by underlying shocks.

$$0 = -b(-br + d') - cb\lambda(\pi^e - cbr + cd' + s' - \pi_L). \tag{1A.6}$$

Rearranging, we have:

$$-(b^2 + \lambda c^2 b^2)r = -b(d') - cb\lambda(\pi^e + cd' + s' - \pi_L)$$

$$r = \frac{1}{(b + \lambda c^2 b)}((1 + c^2\lambda)d' + c\lambda(\pi^e - \pi_L) + c\lambda s'). \qquad (1A.7)$$

To solve for expected inflation, we substitute for the real rate of interest from (1A.7) into (1A.3) and condition on the public's information set:

$$\pi^e = \pi^e + \frac{-c}{(1 + \lambda c^2)}((1 + c^2\lambda)d'' + c\lambda(\pi^e - \pi_L) + c\lambda s'')$$
$$\quad + cd'' + s''$$

$$0 = \frac{-c}{(1 + \lambda c^2)}((1 + c^2\lambda)d'' + c\lambda(\pi^e - \pi_L) + c\lambda s'') + cd'' + s''$$

$$\pi^e = \pi_L - \frac{s' - s''}{\lambda c^2} - \frac{s - s'}{\lambda c^2} + \frac{s}{\lambda c^2}. \qquad (1A.8)$$

Substituting for (1A.8) back into (1A.7) gives an expression for the real rate of interest:

$$r = \frac{1}{(b + \lambda c^2 b)}\left((1 + c^2\lambda)d' + c\lambda\left(\frac{1}{\lambda c^2}s''\right) + c\lambda s'\right)$$

$$r = \frac{1}{b}\left(d + \frac{s}{c}\right) - \frac{(s' - s'')}{bc(1 + \lambda c^2)} - \frac{1}{b}\left(d - d' + \frac{s - s'}{c}\right). \qquad (1A.9)$$

Substituting for the real rate of interest from (1A.9) into (1A.1) gives a solution for the output gap as:

$$y = -\frac{s}{c} + \frac{(s' - s'')}{c(1 + \lambda c^2)} + \left(d - d' + \frac{s - s'}{c}\right). \qquad (1A.10)$$

The solution for inflation is given by substituting (1A.10) into (1A.2):

$$\pi = \pi_L + \frac{s''}{\lambda c^2} - s + \frac{(s' - s'')}{(1 + \lambda c^2)} + (c(d - d') + s - s') + s$$

$$\pi = \pi_L + \frac{(1 + \lambda c^2)s}{\lambda c^2} - \frac{s' - s''}{\lambda c^2} - \frac{s - s'}{\lambda c^2} + \frac{(s' - s'')}{(1 + \lambda c^2)}$$
$$\quad + (c(d - d') + (s - s'))$$

$$\pi = \pi_L + \frac{s}{\lambda c^2} - \frac{(s' - s'')}{\lambda c^2(1 + \lambda c^2)} + c(d - d')$$
$$\quad - \frac{(s - s')(1 - \lambda c^2)}{\lambda c^2}. \qquad (1A.11)$$

The central bank derives its view on demand and supply shocks from its knowledge of the model parameters and the macroeconomic data. Let us assume that the knowledge of the model parameters is perfect, but the knowledge of the macro data is not. The central bank knows only the nominal interest rate (i) with certainty. Inverting the equations (1A.1) and (1A.2) and conditioning on the central bank's information set gives us the following equations for the central bank's understanding of supply and demand shocks:

$$d' = b(i - \pi^{e'}) + y' \tag{1A.12}$$

and

$$s' = \pi^{e'} - \pi' - cy'. \tag{1A.13}$$

Notes

1 The optimal policy horizon – defined by Batini and Nelson (2000) as 'the time at which inflation should be on target in the future, when the authorities aim at minimising their loss function, and a shock occurs today'– depends on many factors, one of which is the stickiness of nominal prices and wages. In general, it seems to be either long enough (one to two years) or uncertain enough, or both, to necessitate some monetary policy forecast of the transmission mechanism.

2 See, for example, Amato and Gerlach (2001), who formalise how parameter estimates can be allowed to vary to reflect that the economy is undergoing structural change.

3 From a sample of 93 central banks surveyed in 1998, 73 report that they publish some forward-looking analysis in standard bulletins and reports (Fry et al., 2000).

4 In practice, the search for a consistent and accurate monetary policy forecast usually involves multiple iterations of steps 1 to 4.

5 The optimal policy response can be formalised as a 'target' rule that links interest rates to the current and past values of all variables and the expected values of the driving processes (Svensson, 1999). How the policy response reflects assessments of the uncertainty and skew that are associated with the future can also be important (Goodhart, 1999).

6 There are many references on whether disaggregated models provide additional information about the transmission mechanism compared with an aggregate model. See, for example, Lee, Pesaran and Pierse (1990), Barker and Pesaran (1990), Quah (1994), J. Taylor (1985) and Zarnowitz (1992). On temporal aggregation bias – the bias caused by aggregrating sectors with different speeds of adjustment – see Christiano and Eichenbaum (1986). There is less research on the costs and benefits of disaggregating the model compared with making appropriate off-model adjustments to an aggregate model.

7 The countries in the sample were Germany, France, Italy, Spain, the Netherlands, Belgium and Austria. For some tests, Finland was also included.

8 Fisher and Salmon (1986) evaluate the importance of linearity in a macroeconometric model.

9 Mankiw and Romer (1991a).

10 Mankiw and Romer (1991b) and Andersen (1994).

11 The IS curve, a policy rule and a Phillips curve describe, respectively, real output, nominal interest rates and inflation as a function of the other two plus lagged values of all three endogenous variables and driving processes (exogenous variables, time-varying parameters and off-model adjustments to endogenous variables).

12 The simplifications, which can be drastic, help to substitute for all other endogenous variables. For example, the uncovered interest rate parity condition can be used to substitute for the exchange rate with current and future interest rate differentials.

13 The discussion assumes that conditioning on constant nominal interest rates and expectations of constant nominal rates will not seriously distort the information that the model gives us about the transmission mechanism. The risk is when current market expectations are very far from this constant rate. It may be more appropriate to use an instrument rule or an explicit loss function for the correct conditioning assumptions about policy. See Westaway in this volume (chapter 8), Svensson (2001, pp. 44–46) and Tarkka and Mayes (1999).

14 In open economies, shocks can feed quickly through the exchange rate onto inflation before they affect the output gap. In principle, a fundamental equilibrium exchange rate can be used here in an analogous manner to a measure of potential output, to classify demand versus supply shocks in real exchange rate space. Deviations of the velocity of money demand both from long-run velocity of demand and from the proportion of short-run, reversible capital flows constitute versions of the 'demand- versus supply-side' scheme that might be expected to work in other types of economies.

15 See, for example, Harvey and Jaeger (1993). Quah (1994) discusses the difficulties in measuring potential output with a single time series. There have been many attempts to bridge the gap between theory and data in potential output measurement. See, for example, Adams and Coe (1994), Kuttner (1994), Astley and Yates (1999) and Blanchard and Quah (1989). Typically, a structural equation for sticky nominal prices (or wages) and an equation for output adjustment are estimated and then a variety of identifying assumptions can be used to obtain a series for potential output from this model. For example, potential output (or its cousin, the non-accelerating inflation rate of unemployment (NAIRU)) can be given as the output value that would result when the inflation rate is constant. Most recently, efforts have integrated the output gap measurement with an understanding of what drives the mark-up of prices over costs (Galí and Gertler, 1999; Galí, 2000; Batini et al., 2000).

16 That the aggregate demand relationship (aggregate demand on real interest rates) has not been affected by policy changes suggests that the real interest rates are super-exogenous to the parameters in the aggregate demand curve. Econometric tests for the many notions of causality and exogeneity are relevant in identifying the role that policy plays in our models of the transmission mechanism (Ericsson, 1994; Banerjee, Hendry and Mizon, 1996).

17 The impulse responses from their Bayesian VARs are shown to be very different from those from a standard constant parameter (VARs), suggesting that there may be information gained from allowing parameters to vary.

18 For its analysis, the IMF uses a suite of models, one of which is MULTIMOD. See Isard (2000).

19 Other key behaviour relationships would measure the effect of private sector and public sector bank credits on investment, and the relationship between government revenue and nominal output (IMF, 1996, p. 72).

20 Woodford (1999b) has argued that the potential level of output growth was overestimated in the 1970s, at least in the USA, and this overestimation led policy-makers to support too high a level of inflation.

21 More generally, the long-run objectives of the central bank – its target for the output gap and the long-run rate of inflation – could be to some extent uncertain. In other words, the central bank may not be fully transparent about its objectives (by not publishing a fully specified inflation target, for example). The final objective for nearly all central banks is price stability, but the definition may not be precise; and the relations between the objective of price stability and other objectives (for example for output and employment), may not be precisely specified either. This uncertainty in objectives would add to the volatility of output and inflation. A final caveat is that these shocks could reflect uncertain movements in the underlying optimal rates of the inflation and potential output and, in this case, the volatility in inflation and output could be welfare enhancing. For example, uncertainty in the optimal rate of inflation could arise from price measurement bias (Clarida, Galí and Gertner, 1999; Boskin et al., 1998).

22 We are assuming that both the public and the central bank form rational expectations based on the information available to them and that the learning process about these shocks has converged. Since the transparency errors and the control errors are white noise disturbance terms, their variance is known. The demand shock, its transparency error and its control error must all be uncorrelated with each other, as must the supply shock, its transparency error and its control error.

23 When inflation is sticky, transparency errors in demand will be important for both output and inflation.

24 See Barro and Gordon (1983), Cukierman and Meltzer (1986), Cukierman (2000), Faust and Svensson (1998, 1999), Jensen (2001) and Geraats (2001). More stickiness in inflation (for example, Bean, 1998; Jensen, 2001), learning (for example, King, 1996; Faust and Svensson, 1998, 1999; Sargent, 1999) and uncertainty about parameters (for example, Sack, 1998; Srour, 1999) could also change the trade-offs of the model.

25 More generally, these transactions can be made in different currencies and across national borders; these two international dimensions can also be important in further disaggregating the monetary sector. Sectoral data on cross-border flows of capital can be unreliable, however (Patel, 2001).

26 For simplicity, they abstract from the overseas sector, government and the central bank.

27 This sector is dominated by pension funds and life assurance companies in the United Kingdom, which specialise in repackaging personal sector savings into funds for corporations (channelled either through direct loans or as equities).

28 See Friedman and Kuttner (1993) and subsequent comments, discussion and references, especially to the early literature by Brainard and Tobin.

29 For example, the transaction costs of securing a loan seem to fall with the amount of deposits held in the United States (Fama, 1985).

30 See Sims (1980) and Levtchenkova, Pagan and Robertson (1998), for example.

31 The authors also compare a third model that adds inertia by allowing the exchange rate level to be a weighted combination of that predicted by UIP and its lagged value.

32 See Wadhwani (1999b) for references.

33 The single equations estimated between exchange rate change and interest rates are in effect a reduced-form relation between the UIP equation and other parts of the transmission mechanism, including the policy reaction function. As consistent estimates of the reduced-form equations, they can pass the standard diagnostics for goodness of fit and serial correlation. A test of simultaneity bias would identify problems.

34 See Britton, Fisher and Whitley (1998), Jondeau, Bihan and Sédillot (1999) and Tarkka and Mayes (1999).

35 For the problems caused by targeting too short or too long a horizon, see Clarida, Galí and Gertner (1999), Woodford (2000b) and Bernanke and Woodford (1997).

36 Recent forecast errors can be decomposed by comparing recent out-turns for key endogenous variables against the predicted values derived from a forecast using the following three assumptions (Wallis and Whitley, 1995):
- the model with ex post values of exogenous variables but without adjustments;
- the model with ex post values of exogenous variables and with adjustments; and
- the model with ex ante values of exogenous variables and with adjustments.

The most recent implied residuals are relevant because structural breaks could have made the explanatory power of the model for earlier data less relevant for the forecast.

2 Are the effects of monetary policy in the euro area greater in recessions than in booms?

Gert Peersman and Frank Smets

2.1 Introduction

This paper investigates whether the effects of monetary policy on economic activity in the euro area depend on the state of the economy. At least two strands of the literature predict that monetary policy is more effective in a recession than during a boom.[1]

The first class of theories is based on credit market imperfections.[2] In these models, asymmetric information between borrowers and lenders gives rise to agency costs. These agency costs are reflected in an external finance premium, which typically depends on the net worth of the borrower. A borrower with higher net worth is able to post more collateral and can thereby reduce its cost of external financing.

As emphasised by Bernanke and Gertler (1989), the dependence of the external finance premium on the net worth of borrowers creates a 'financial accelerator' propagation mechanism. For example, when an economy is hit by a recession, the net worth of firms will typically fall. This decline leads to an increase in the cost of external financing, which in turn may aggravate the effects of the initial shock. During an expansion, firms can largely finance themselves with retained earnings. Moreover, because their balance sheets are strong, the external finance premium is likely to be relatively low. As a result, monetary policy changes have only a limited impact on this premium. In contrast, when cash flows are low during a recession, firms are more dependent on external finance, collateral values are depressed and the external finance premium will be much more sensitive to changes in the interest rate. Monetary policy is, therefore, likely to have much stronger effects on economic activity during recessions.

A second class of theories predicts that asymmetric monetary policy propagation is based on a convex short-run aggregate supply curve. Convexity implies that the slope of the supply curve is steeper at higher levels of capacity utilisation and inflation than at lower levels. As a result, shifts in aggregate demand driven by changes in monetary policy will have a stronger effect on output and a weaker effect on inflation in recessions. The reverse occurs during expansions.

Several classes of models give rise to a convex short-run aggregate supply curve.[3] The so-called capacity constraint model assumes that, as the economy expands, more firms find it difficult to increase their capacity to produce in the short run. As a result inflation becomes more sensitive to shifts in aggregate demand at higher rates of capacity utilisation. This finding is consistent with the early empirical work on the Phillips curve, including Phillips (1958), which assumed that the relationship was non-linear. A second class of models is based on the presence of menu costs. For example, Ball and Mankiw (1994) show that, as the level of inflation rises, and as firms adjust the timing and size of price changes, aggregate demand shocks will have less effect on output and more effect on the price level.

In this paper we do not attempt to distinguish between these various theories.[4] Instead, we want to document empirically whether monetary policy in the euro area indeed has different effects in recessions compared with booms. To do so, we employ a multivariate extension of Hamilton's (1989) two-state Markov Switching Model (MSM). This methodology allows us to determine endogenously whether the euro area economy is in a boom or a recession and to test whether the effects of policy are significantly different in the two states of the economy. The multivariate MSM methodology has previously been used by Garcia and Schaller (1995), Kakes (1998) and Dolado and Maria-Dolores (1999) to examine similar questions in the United States, a group of five countries (the United States, Germany, the United Kingdom, Belgium, and the Netherlands) and Spain, respectively. In this paper we apply the methodology to eight countries of the euro area: Germany, France, Italy, Spain, the Netherlands, Belgium, Austria and Finland.[5]

The novelty of the paper is that we take a euro-area-wide approach, proceeding step-wise. In the first step (section 2.2), we test whether there has indeed been a common cycle in these eight countries, which now form part of the European Monetary Union (EMU). In other words, were the business cycles in each of these economies sufficiently synchronised that the underlying state (boom or recession) was identical? In testing this presumption, we do allow for different mean growth rates in each of the economies. In the estimation, we use quarterly data on the growth of industrial production from 1978 to 1998. With the exception of Finland, we find that we cannot reject the hypothesis that there was a single business cycle in each of these countries. In the rest of the analysis, therefore, we exclude Finland. These results confirm the findings of Artis, Krolzig and Toro (1999), who also find support for a common European cycle using both univariate and multivariate MSMs.[6] This section is of independent interest because it suggests that, at least for a large part of the euro area, differences in cyclical situation are not likely to complicate monetary policy.

In section 2.3, we then extend the multivariate MSM to test whether monetary policy impulses have different effects on euro-area industrial activity in booms versus recessions. Rather than using domestic monetary policy impulses in each of the seven countries, we analyse the effects of an area-wide change in monetary policy. This is a useful exercise not only because it more closely resembles the current single monetary policy in the euro area, but also because during most of the sample domestic monetary policies in those seven countries were coordinated largely through participation in the exchange rate mechanism (ERM) and other fixed exchange rate mechanisms.[7] To avoid the simultaneity bias that may result from the fact that through the central banks' reaction function short-term interest rates depend on economic activity, we use an area-wide vector autoregression (based on Peersman and Smets, 2000a) to identify area-wide monetary policy shocks. The VAR is estimated over the same period as the MSM analysis (1978–98) and includes area-wide real GDP, consumer prices, the real effective exchange rate and a short-term, three-month interest rate as endogenous variables. Commodity prices, the US short-term interest rate and US real GDP are the exogenous variables. Using a standard Choleski identification scheme, we show that a monetary policy tightening leads to an immediate rise in the short-term interest rate and an appreciation of the exchange rate. Subsequently, this tightening of monetary conditions has a significant negative impact on output and prices.

We then use the contribution of these policy shocks to the euro-area interest rate as our measure of monetary policy impulses and estimate the effects of policy tightening in the two states of the economy (section 2.3.2). Like Garcia and Schaller (1995), Kakes (2000) and Dolado and Maria-Dolores (1999), we find that monetary policy has considerably larger effects on activity when the economy is in a recession in the euro area. These results are robust to using the change in the average euro-area short-term interest rate as a measure of monetary policy.

In section 2.4, we examine whether these asymmetries in the effects of monetary policy are similar across countries. We find that the asymmetries are most pronounced in Germany, France, Spain, Italy and Belgium. We also find that the effects of the monetary policy shock are much larger in Germany than in the other countries. To some extent, this finding may be due to the large weight of the German economy in our estimates of the common monetary policy shock.

Finally, in section 2.5, we ask whether monetary policy shocks also affect the probability of switching from a boom to a recession, and vice versa. We find only weak evidence that a tightening of monetary policy reduces the probability of staying in a boom and no evidence that it increases the probability of going from a recession to a boom. We conclude with some final remarks in section 2.6.

2.2 Is there a common cycle in the euro area?

To test whether monetary policy in the euro area has different effects in booms versus recessions, determining the likely timing of switches in the state of the euro-area business cycle is necessary. Hamilton's (1989) MSM approach provides a natural framework in this context because it allows an endogenous determination of the most likely switching dates between the two regimes. One option is to estimate Hamilton's MSM model on synthetic euro-area output growth data and to test whether there are indeed two regimes – one with a low or negative growth rate and one with a high growth rate.

Two problems exist with this euro-area-wide approach. First, the sample of quarterly observations is relatively small owing to data availability. As a result, the limited degrees of freedom make it quite difficult to distinguish empirically between the two regimes.[8] Secondly, by using the synthetic euro-area data, one implicitly assumes that the state of the economy is identical in each of the countries participating in EMU. If this is not the case, the results may be biased against finding two different regimes. A second option is to estimate the MSM model jointly for each of the countries participating in EMU. In joint estimation, the estimates are likely to be more precise. In addition, it allows us to test whether the countries do share the same business cycle.[9]

In this paper, therefore, we follow the second approach. For each country i, out of n countries, we estimate the following equation:

$$\Delta y_{i,t} - \mu_{i,s_t} = \phi_1(\Delta y_{i,t-1} - \mu_{i,s_{t-1}}) + \phi_2(\Delta y_{i,t-2} - \mu_{i,s_{t-2}}) + \varepsilon_{i,t}, \tag{2.1}$$

where

$$\begin{bmatrix} \varepsilon_{1,t} \\ \vdots \\ \varepsilon_{n,t} \end{bmatrix} \sim \text{i.i.d.} N \left(\begin{bmatrix} 0 \\ \vdots \\ 0 \end{bmatrix}, \begin{bmatrix} \sigma_{11} & \cdots & \sigma_{1n} \\ \vdots & \ddots & \vdots \\ \sigma_{1n} & \cdots & \sigma_{nn} \end{bmatrix} \right) = N(0, \Omega). \tag{2.2}$$

$\Delta y_{i,t}$ is the quarterly growth rate of industrial production in country i. μ_{i,s_i} is the mean growth rate conditional on country i being in state s_t. In this model, we assume that the state of the economy is identical in each of the n countries. Following Hamilton (1989), we assume that the autoregressive parameters (ϕ_1, ϕ_2) are independent of the state and the country. s_t is assumed to follow a two-state Markov chain with the following transition probability matrix:[10]

$$P = \begin{bmatrix} p_{00} & p_{01} \\ p_{10} & p_{11} \end{bmatrix}, \tag{2.3}$$

where

$$p_{ij} = \Pr[s_t = j \mid s_{t-1} = i], \quad \text{with} \sum_{j=0}^{1} p_{ij} = 1 \text{ for all } I. \qquad (2.4)$$

We assume that these transition probabilities are constant over time and take the following logistic form:

$$p_{00} = \Pr[s_t = 0 \mid s_{t-1} = 0] = \frac{\exp(\theta_0)}{1 + \exp(\theta_0)} \qquad (2.5)$$

$$p_{11} = \Pr[s_t = 1 \mid s_{t-1} = 1] = \frac{\exp(\theta_1)}{1 + \exp(\theta_1)}. \qquad (2.6)$$

For $\boldsymbol{Y}_t = [\Delta y_{1,t} \cdots \Delta y_{n,t}]'$, the vector of observations on output growth, this model implies that the conditional density takes the form:

$$f(\boldsymbol{Y}_t \mid \boldsymbol{Y}_{t-1}, \ldots, \boldsymbol{Y}_1, s_t)$$
$$= (2\pi)^{-1} |\Omega|^{-\frac{1}{2}} \exp\left[-\tfrac{1}{2}(\boldsymbol{Y}_t - \boldsymbol{h}_{t,s_t})' \Omega^{-1}(\boldsymbol{Y}_t - \boldsymbol{h}_{t,s_t})\right], \qquad (2.7)$$

where

$$\boldsymbol{h}_{t,s_t} = \begin{bmatrix} \mu_{1,s_t} - \phi_1 \mu_{1,s_{t-1}} - \phi_2 \mu_{1,s_{t-2}} + \phi_1 \Delta y_{1,t-1} + \phi_2 \Delta y_{1,t-2} \\ \vdots \\ \mu_{n,s_t} - \phi_1 \mu_{n,s_{t-1}} - \phi_2 \mu_{n,s_{t-2}} + \phi_1 \Delta y_{n,t-1} + \phi_2 \Delta y_{n,t-2} \end{bmatrix}.$$
$$(2.8)$$

With these assumptions, we also obtain a sequence of joint conditional probabilities $\Pr(s_t = i, \ldots, s_{t-r} = j \mid \Phi_t)$, which are the probabilities that the series is in state i or j at times t, $t-1$, until $t-r$ respectively, conditional upon the information available at time t. By summing these joint probabilities, we can obtain the filtered probabilities, which are the probabilities of being in state 0 or 1 at time t, given the information available at time t:

$$\Pr(s_t = j \mid \Phi_t) = \sum_{i=0}^{1} \ldots \sum_{k=0}^{1} \Pr(s_t = j, s_{t-1} = i, \ldots, s_{t-r} = k \mid \Phi_t)$$
$$i, j, \ldots, k = 0, 1. \quad (2.9)$$

These probabilities provide information about the regime in which the series is most likely to have been at every point in the sample.

We estimate the model given by equations (2.1) to (2.9) using quarter-to-quarter growth rates of de-seasonalised industrial production in eight of the 11 euro-area countries: Germany, France, Italy, Spain, Austria, Belgium, the Netherlands and Finland (coded DE, FR, IT, ES, AT, BE, NL and FI, respectively). Figure 2.1 shows (detrended) industrial production for each of these countries.

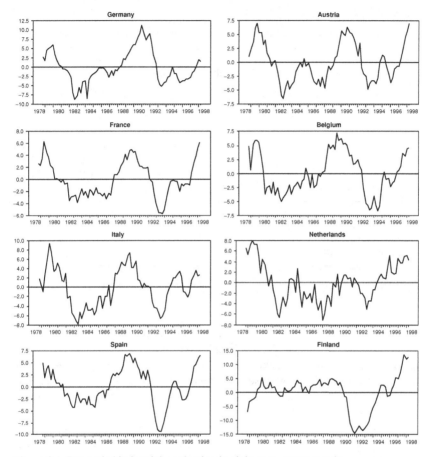

Figure 2.1 Detrended industrial production in eight euro-area countries.

To test whether these eight countries share the same business cycle, we estimate the joint model for seven of the eight countries and the eighth country separately. A comparison of the sum of the log likelihoods with the log likelihood of the eight-country model can then be used to assess whether that country has the same business cycle as the other seven. In table 2.1, we report the log likelihoods as well as the corresponding Schwarz and Akaike statistics. Based on a visual inspection of figure 2.1, we started with Finland as the country that was most likely not to share the same business cycle as the other countries. Column 1 of table 2.1 shows that the sum of the log likelihood of the Finnish model and the common model for the other seven countries is higher than the log likelihood of the common model for the eight countries (bottom panel). These data indicate that we can reject the hypothesis that Finland shares the

Table 2.1 *Tests for a common business cycle in the euro area*

Country	7 + 1 countries			6 + 1 countries		
	Log lik	Schwarz	Akaike	Log lik	Schwarz	Akaike
DE				−622.83	−718.75	−666.83
FR				−625.71	−721.63	−669.71
IT				−627.87	−723.79	−671.87
ES				−623.62	−719.54	−667.62
AT				−632.43	−728.35	−676.43
BE				−619.55	−715.47	−663.55
NL				−617.31	−713.23	−661.31
FI	−699.36	−814.90	−752.36			

	Log lik	Schwarz	Akaike
DE,FR,IT,ES,AT,BE,NL,FI	−702.09	−824.17	−758.09
DE,FR,IT,ES,AT,BE,NL	−613.32	−713.60	−659.32

Note: The constant term involving 2π has been omitted from all calculations.

same business cycle as the other countries. Column 2 repeats the exercise for the other individual countries. The log likelihood of the individual country models and the common model for the other six countries are compared with a common model for the remaining seven countries. For these seven countries, we cannot reject the hypothesis that they share the business cycle.[11] In the rest of the analysis, we proceed with these seven countries.

The first column of table 2.2 shows the results of the estimation of our common model. Several features are noteworthy. In each of the seven countries, the mean growth rate in the first state (μ_0) is negative, ranging from −0.50% in Germany to −0.03% in the Netherlands. This state, therefore, also corresponds to a euro-area recession. Only in Germany, France and Belgium is the growth rate in a recession significantly different from zero. The probability of staying in a recession is relatively high at 0.85, which implies that the mean duration of a recession is about six to seven quarters. In each of the seven countries, the mean growth rate in the second state (μ_1) is significantly positive, ranging from 0.66% in the Netherlands to 1.50% in Austria. This state, therefore, also corresponds to a euro-area expansion. The average duration of an expansion is longer than that of a recession at about 10 quarters.

Figures 2.2 and 2.3 plot smoothed probabilities of being in a recession, together with, respectively, the detrended output level and output growth. The shaded area is the smoothed probability of being in a recession. The main

Table 2.2 *The cyclical effects of monetary policy*

Country		Common model	Common model + MP (s_{t-j})	Common model + MP (s_t)	Common model + $\Delta i(s_{t-j})$
Germany	μ_0	−0.50 (0.24)	−1.00 (0.16)	−0.97 (0.17)	−1.92 (0.26)
	μ_1	1.03 (0.17)	1.15 (0.12)	1.16 (0.12)	1.01 (0.12)
France	μ_0	−0.35 (0.14)	−0.58 (0.14)	−0.55 (0.14)	−0.97 (0.23)
	μ_1	0.87 (0.13)	0.86 (0.10)	0.86 (0.11)	0.68 (0.10)
Italy	μ_0	−0.28 (0.30)	−0.25 (0.29)	−0.22 (0.30)	−0.90 (0.41)
	μ_1	1.00 (0.24)	0.84 (0.21)	0.85 (0.22)	0.80 (0.20)
Spain	μ_0	−0.28 (0.22)	−0.34 (0.21)	−0.31 (0.22)	−0.99 (0.31)
	μ_1	0.98 (0.17)	0.86 (0.15)	0.87 (0.16)	0.81 (0.14)
Austria	μ_0	−0.24 (0.19)	−0.53 (0.16)	−0.50 (0.16)	−0.71 (0.28)
	μ_1	1.50 (0.15)	1.47 (0.11)	1.48 (0.11)	1.13 (0.15)
Belgium	μ_0	−0.44 (0.22)	−0.57 (0.23)	−0.54 (0.23)	−1.22 (0.32)
	μ_1	1.02 (0.18)	0.93 (0.16)	0.93 (0.17)	0.82 (0.15)
Netherlands	μ_0	−0.03 (0.32)	−0.42 (0.26)	−0.38 (0.27)	−0.63 (0.38)
	μ_1	0.66 (0.23)	0.80 (0.19)	0.81 (0.19)	0.61 (0.18)
Common coefficients	ϕ_1	−0.24 (0.04)	−0.28 (0.04)	−0.28 (0.04)	−0.26 (0.04)
	ϕ_2	−0.07 (0.04)	−0.08 (0.04)	−0.08 (0.04)	−0.08 (0.04)
	p_{00}	0.85 (0.07)	0.78 (0.08)	0.78 (0.08)	0.62 (0.12)
	p_{11}	0.90 (0.05)	0.89 (0.04)	0.88 (0.05)	0.89 (0.04)
	β_0		−0.89 (0.14)	−0.75 (0.14)	−0.73 (0.34)
	β_1		−0.52 (0.15)	−0.66 (0.16)	−0.20 (0.19)
	$\beta_1 - \beta_0$		0.37 (0.03)	0.08 (0.04)	0.52 (0.12)

Note: Standard errors in parentheses.

recessionary periods are from 1980 to 1982 and from 1990 to 1993. Somewhat more surprisingly, the probability of being in a recession is also relatively high in 1986 and in the second half of 1995.

2.3   The asymmetric effects of area-wide monetary policy shocks

In this section, we test whether monetary policy in the euro area has different effects on output when the economy is in a recession or an expansion. As our measure of the monetary policy stance in the euro area, we take a weighted average of the three-month interest rate in each of the 11 countries participating

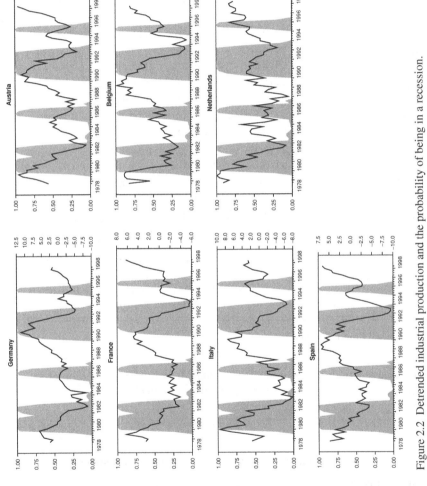

Figure 2.2 Detrended industrial production and the probability of being in a recession.

Note: the solid line is detrended industrial production (right axis); shaded areas denote the probability of being in a recession (left axis).

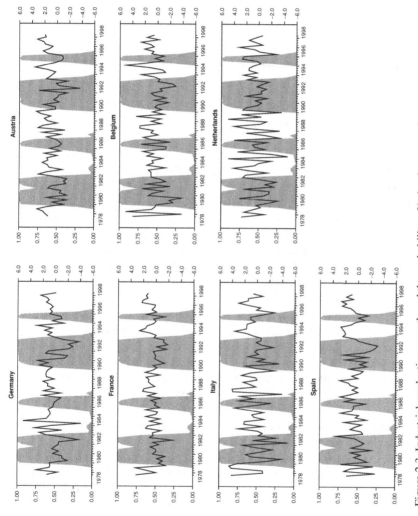

Figure 2.3 Industrial production growth and the probability of being in a recession.

Note: the solid line is industrial production growth (right axis); shaded areas denote the probability of being in a recession (left axis).

in EMU. To avoid the simultaneity bias we use monetary policy innovations derived from an identified VAR.[12] Section 2.3.1 presents the VAR results. In section 2.3.2, we then extend the multivariate MSM model of section 2.2 to include the effects of these monetary policy shocks.

2.3.1   A monetary policy VAR for the euro area

To derive the euro-area-wide monetary policy shocks, we follow Peersman and Smets (2000a). They estimate the following block-recursive VAR model over the period 1978 to 1998:

$$\begin{bmatrix} X_t \\ Y_t \end{bmatrix} = \begin{bmatrix} A(L) & 0 \\ B(L) & C(L) \end{bmatrix} \begin{bmatrix} X_{t-1} \\ Y_{t-1} \end{bmatrix} + \begin{bmatrix} a & 0 \\ b & c \end{bmatrix} \begin{bmatrix} \varepsilon_{X,t} \\ \varepsilon_{Y,t} \end{bmatrix}, \qquad (2.10)$$

where X_t is a vector of exogenous variables comprising a world commodity price index, the US short-term interest rate and US real GDP; Y_t is a vector of endogenous euro-area data including real GDP, consumer prices, the nominal three-month short-term interest rate and a real effective exchange rate. The monetary policy shocks are identified through a recursive Choleski decomposition with the variables ordered as above.[13] The identifying assumptions are that monetary policy shocks do not have a contemporaneous impact on output and prices. A monetary policy shock does have an immediate impact on the exchange rate, but the central bank does not respond to changes in the exchange rate within the quarter.

Figure 2.4 shows the results of the VAR analysis. This graph summarises the effect of a one-standard deviation monetary policy shock on real GDP, consumer prices, the real effective exchange rate and the short-term interest rate together with a 90% confidence band. The graph clearly indicates that a typical monetary policy tightening in the euro area gives rise to a temporary increase of the nominal interest rate and a temporary appreciation of the real exchange rate. This tightening of monetary conditions leads to a significant, temporary fall in output after about two quarters. Prices respond more sluggishly and fall significantly below zero after about two years.

In the next section, we use the historical contribution of the monetary policy shocks to the euro-area interest rate, as depicted in figure 2.5, as our benchmark measure of monetary policy impulses in the extended MSM model.[14] The advantage of using the historical contribution to the interest rate rather than the monetary policy shocks themselves is that fewer lags need to be used in the MSM, because the historical contribution is itself a moving average of the monetary policy shocks. Figure 2.5 plots the historical contribution of the monetary policy shocks together with the short-term interest rate and shows 1982, 1987, 1990 and 1992–3 as periods of relatively tight monetary policy; in 1984 and 1991, policy is estimated to be relatively loose.

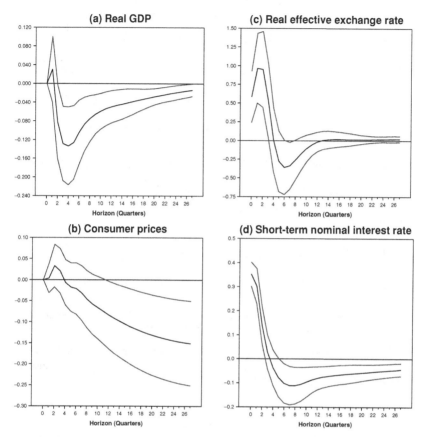

Figure 2.4 Impulse responses to a monetary policy shock in the euro area: effect on real GDP, consumer prices, the short-term interest rate and the real effective exchange rate.

Note: The upper and lower lines are 90% confidence interval bands.

2.3.2 Monetary policy shocks in the multivariate MSM model

To test whether there are asymmetric effects of monetary policy on output growth depending on the state of the business cycle when the monetary policy stance changes, we extend the basic model of section 2.2 as follows:

$$\Delta y_{i,t} - \mu_{i,s_t} = \phi_1(\Delta y_{i,t-1} - \mu_{i,s_{t-1}}) + \phi_2(\Delta y_{i,t-2} - \mu_{i,s_{t-2}})$$
$$+ \beta_{s_{t-1}} MP_{t-1} + \varepsilon_{i,t}, \tag{2.11}$$

where β_{s_t} is the coefficient on the monetary policy indicator (MP_t) in a recession $(s_t = 0)$ or an expansion $(s_t = 1)$. In this specification, we assume that the

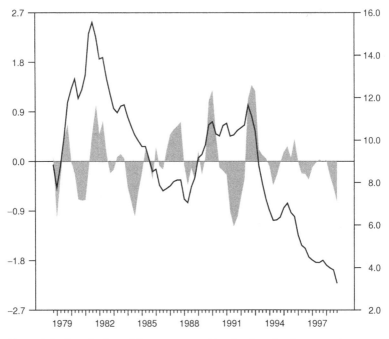

Figure 2.5 Contribution of the monetary policy shock to the short-term interest rate.
Note: the solid line is the short-term interest rate (right axis); shaded areas denote the contribution of the monetary policy shocks to the short-term interest rate (left axis).

β-coefficients are identical across countries. The other variables are the same as equation (2.1).

The results are reported in the second column of table 2.2. A tightening of monetary policy clearly has a significant negative impact in both states of the euro-area economy. As expected, however, the effects on economic activity are significantly larger in a recession compared with those in an expansion. Figure 2.6(a) plots the impulse response function of output to a one-standard deviation monetary policy shock in a recession (solid line) and in an expansion (dashed line). As in the VAR, the maximum impact is after three to four quarters, but whereas the maximum impact on output is more than 50 basis points in a recession, the impact in an expansion is only about 30 basis points.

To test the robustness of our results, we re-estimate the model assuming that the effects of a monetary policy action on output growth depend on the current state of the economy. In this case, the following model is estimated:

$$\Delta y_{i,t} - \mu_{i,s_t} = \phi_1(\Delta y_{i,t-1} - \mu_{i,s_{t-1}}) + \phi_2(\Delta y_{i,t-2} - \mu_{i,s_{t-2}})$$
$$+ \beta_{s_t} MP_{t-1} + \varepsilon_{i,t}. \tag{2.12}$$

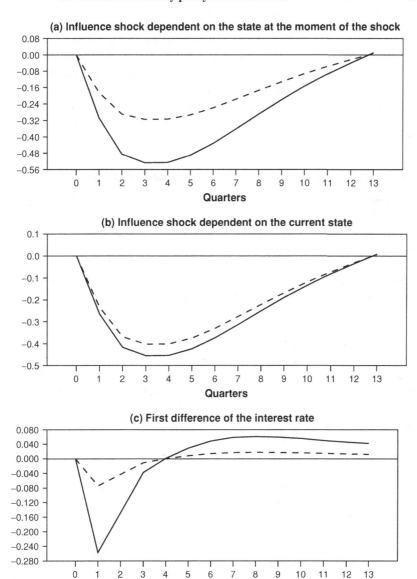

Figure 2.6 Impulse responses to a monetary policy shock.
Note: the solid line is the effect on production in a recession; the dashed line is the effect in a boom.

The third column of table 2.2 reports these results. In this case, the difference between the monetary policy effects in a recession and an expansion are smaller, though still significant. Figure 2.6(b) also reflects this difference. Finally, the fourth column of table 2.2 reports the results when we use the first difference of the interest rate as our monetary policy indicator. Again, we find a significantly larger effect of monetary policy in a recession compared with an expansion. Figure 2.6(c) plots the impulse response functions to a monetary policy shock in both regimes.

2.4   Are the monetary policy effects different across countries?

In section 2.3, we assumed that the effects of the euro-area-wide monetary policy shocks were different across states of the economy, but identical across countries. To test whether this is true we allow the β-coefficients in equation (2.11) to vary across countries. Table 2.3 reports the results of this exercise. The upper and middle panels report the estimates of β_1 and β_2 for each of the countries as well as the differences across countries. The lower panel reports the estimates of the difference between β_1 and β_2.

Several results are noteworthy. First, in all cases, the effect of monetary policy on output growth is negative. In a recession, the effect varies from -0.60 in the Netherlands to -1.44 in Germany and (with the exception of the Netherlands) is always significant. This compares with an average effect of -0.89 in the restricted model of section 2.3. The effect on output during downturns is significantly larger in Germany than in the other countries. In an expansion, the effect ranges from -0.21 in France to -0.76 in Austria, compared with -0.52 in the restricted model of section 2.3.

Second, with the exception of the Netherlands, the effect of policy is always greater in downturns than in booms. The difference is high and significant in Germany, France, Spain and Belgium and high, but less significant, in Italy. Little evidence of asymmetries exists in Austria and the Netherlands. In the latter case, this may be due to the fact that the Dutch business cycle was not completely in line with the euro-area one. Overall, there appears to be little evidence of significant differences in asymmetries across countries.

These results are confirmed in the impulse response analysis presented in figure 2.7.

2.5   Does monetary policy change the likelihood of a recession?

In this final section, we follow Garcia and Schaller (1995) and Dolado and Maria-Dolores (1999) in testing whether changes in monetary policy also affect the transition probabilities of going from one state to the other. In the MSM models of sections 2.2 and 2.3, these probabilities were assumed to be constant.

Table 2.3 *The cyclical effects of monetary policy in the individual countries*

Country	β_1	NL	AT	BE	DE	ES	FR
NL	−0.60						
	0.37						
AT	−0.89	−0.28					
	0.22	0.19					
BE	−0.72	−0.12	0.16				
	0.33	0.24	0.14				
DE	−1.44	−0.84	−0.55	−0.71			
	0.23	0.19	0.10	0.13			
ES	−0.99	−0.39	−0.10	−0.27	0.44		
	0.32	0.23	0.14	0.14	0.12		
FR	−0.65	−0.04	0.23	0.07	0.79	0.34	
	0.20	0.16	0.93	0.11	0.06	0.08	
IT	−0.88	−0.28	0.00	−0.15	0.55	0.11	−0.23
	0.43	0.28	0.21	0.24	0.20	0.19	0.16

	β_2	NL	AT	BE	DE	ES	FR
NL	−0.74						
	0.43						
AT	−0.76	−0.01					
	0.25	0.24					
BE	−0.28	0.46	0.47				
	0.36	0.30	0.18				
DE	−0.65	0.08	0.10	−0.37			
	0.25	0.22	0.13	0.16			
ES	−0.44	0.30	0.31	−0.15	0.21		
	0.34	0.28	0.18	0.17	0.15		
FR	−0.21	0.53	0.54	0.07	0.44	0.23	
	0.22	0.20	0.11	0.14	0.08	0.10	
IT	−0.24	0.50	0.52	0.04	0.41	0.20	−0.02
	0.47	0.34	0.26	0.31	0.25	0.24	0.20

Table 2.3 (*cont.*)

Country	$\beta_1 - \beta_2$	NL	AT	BE	DE	ES	FR
NL	−0.14						
	0.35						
AT	0.12	0.27					
	0.11	*0.45*					
BE	0.43	0.58	0.31				
	0.24	*0.58*	*0.33*				
DE	0.78	0.92	0.65	0.34			
	0.11	*0.44*	*0.24*	*0.30*			
ES	0.55	0.69	0.42	0.11	−0.23		
	0.23	*0.54*	*0.32*	*0.32*	*0.27*		
FR	0.43	0.58	0.31	−0.00	−0.34	−0.11	
	0.09	*0.38*	*0.20*	*0.25*	*0.15*	*0.19*	
IT	0.64	0.78	0.51	0.20	−0.14	0.09	0.20
	0.41	*0.66*	*0.48*	*0.56*	*0.46*	*0.44*	*0.37*

Note: Standard errors in italics.

To do so, we modify the logit functions (2.5) and (2.6) determining the transition probabilities as follows:

$$p_{00} = \Pr[s_t = 0 \mid s_{t-1} = 0] = \frac{\exp(\theta_{00} + \theta_{01}MP_t)}{1 + \exp(\theta_{00} + \theta_{01}MP_t)} \qquad (2.13)$$

$$p_{11} = \Pr[s_t = 1 \mid s_{t-1} = 1] = \frac{\exp(\theta_{10} + \theta_{11}MP_t)}{1 + \exp(\theta_{10} + \theta_{11}MP_t)}. \qquad (2.14)$$

To isolate the effect of the shocks on the transition probabilities from the linear effect examined above, we constrain the β-coefficients to be equal to zero as in equation (2.1). Based on equations (2.13) and (2.14), we would expect θ_{01} to be positive because a monetary policy tightening is likely to increase the probability of staying in a recession. In contrast, θ_{11} is expected to be negative because a monetary policy tightening is expected to reduce the probability of staying in an expansion.

Table 2.4 reports the results of using both the monetary policy shock and the first difference of the interest rate as our measure of changes in the monetary policy stance. These results show that θ_{01} is insignificant, suggesting that monetary policy shocks have no effect on the probability of staying in a recession. We do find that θ_{11} is negative, but it is significantly different from zero only at the 10% confidence level.

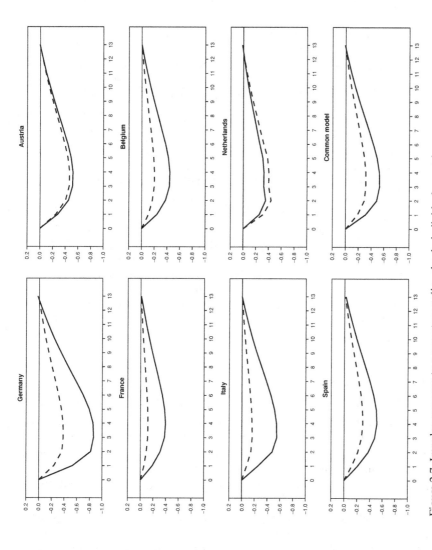

Figure 2.7 Impulse response to a monetary policy shock: individual countries.
Note: the solid line is the effect on production in a recession; the dashed line is the effect in a boom.

Table 2.4 *The effects of monetary policy on state switches*

Country		MP shock	ΔI
Germany	μ_0	−0.53 (0.22)	−0.75 (0.23)
	μ_1	1.05 (0.17)	1.04 (0.15)
France	μ_0	−0.36 (0.14)	−0.38 (0.15)
	μ_1	0.87 (0.12)	0.77 (0.12)
Italy	μ_0	−0.39 (0.27)	−0.30 (0.31)
	μ_1	1.07 (0.23)	0.89 (0.22)
Spain	μ_0	−0.28 (0.22)	−0.37 (0.23)
	μ_1	0.97 (0.17)	0.91 (0.16)
Austria	μ_0	−0.31 (0.17)	−0.40 (0.18)
	μ_1	1.54 (0.15)	1.43 (0.13)
Belgium	μ_0	−0.49 (0.21)	−0.49 (0.23)
	μ_1	1.05 (0.18)	0.91 (0.17)
Netherlands	μ_0	−0.04 (0.26)	−0.19 (0.29)
	μ_1	0.66 (0.23)	0.69 (0.21)
Common coefficients	ϕ_1	−0.24 (0.04)	−0.24 (0.04)
	ϕ_2	−0.07 (0.04)	−0.06 (0.04)
	θ_{00}	1.72 (0.57)	2.56 (1.00)
	θ_{01}	−0.75 (0.66)	1.86 (1.28)
	θ_{10}	2.10 (0.61)	2.66 (0.71)
	θ_{11}	−1.81 (1.06)	−1.60 (0.99)

Note: Standard errors in parentheses.

2.6   Conclusions

In this paper, we have investigated whether monetary policy impulses have asymmetric effects on the growth rate of industrial production in seven countries of the euro area. In particular, we have analysed whether these effects are stronger in recessions than in expansions. Such asymmetric effects could arise in models with a convex short-run aggregate supply curve (for example, owing to capacity constraints) or in models in which the financial accelerator propagation mechanism is more potent when the economy is in a recession.

One cannot reject the hypothesis that these seven countries share the same business cycle. This result suggests that, in a large part of the euro area, cyclical differences have not been an important factor in the past 20 years. Next, we found strong evidence that area-wide monetary policy impulses, measured as the contribution of monetary policy shocks to the short-term interest rate in a simple VAR for the euro-area economy, have significantly larger effects on output growth in recessions than in booms. Impulse response functions show that, on average, the maximum impact of a standardised monetary policy shock on output is about 20 basis points larger in a recession than in a boom. These differences are most pronounced in Germany, France, Spain, Italy and Belgium, while they are not significant in Austria and the Netherlands. Finally, we also analysed whether monetary policy shocks affect the probability of going from one state to another. We do not find strong evidence that this occurs.

The results of this paper confirm that it may be useful to investigate which factors give rise to these asymmetries in future research. In Peersman and Smets (2000b), we attempt a first step in that direction by analysing asymmetries across industries in the euro area. Differences in asymmetries in the impact of monetary policy across industries can then be related to industry-specific factors such as financial and economic structure, which may yield important insights into which factors drive those asymmetries.

Acknowledgements

Gert Peersman worked on this paper before he joined the Bank of England, while in the European Central Bank's Graduate Research Programme. We thank Gabriel Perez-Quiros for many useful suggestions during the development of this paper and for help with the GAUSS programs. We also would like to thank Peter Sinclair and Lavan Mahadeva for constructive comments.

Notes

1 See, for example, Kakes (2000). In the empirical work below a recession is a period of negative or below-average growth whereas a boom is a period of higher and positive growth.

2 An example is the financial accelerator model developed in Bernanke and Gertler (1989).

3 One could think of many other reasons why the elasticity of aggregate supply rises as output and employment rise. For example, the elasticity will rise if the quality of the marginal hire falls as the stock of unemployed falls.

4 In Peersman and Smets (2000b) we perform a more disaggregated industry analysis, which allows us potentially to distinguish the various hypotheses. One could also try to distinguish between both sets of theories by analysing the effect on manufacturing prices. The financial accelerator theories say that a given interest rate change has more impact on aggregate nominal demand when output is low than when it is high. The second set of theories predict that, when output is low, a given change in aggregate nominal demand has more impact on output and less on prices.

5 Owing to data limitations, we did not consider Portugal, Ireland, Luxembourg and Greece – the remaining countries participating in EMU.

6 Artis, Krolzig and Toro (1999) include the United Kingdom and Portugal in their analysis, but not Finland.

7 This is definitely the case for Germany, France, Austria, Belgium and the Netherlands. It is less clear-cut for Italy, and Spain went through various periods of floating exchange rate regimes during the sample. Even in this case, however, a large component of monetary policy innovations is likely to be common with the other countries.

8 One reason for using industrial production indices rather than GDP figures is that the former show a stronger cyclical pattern, making it easier to identify the state of the business cycle.

9 See Hamilton and Perez-Quiros (1996) for an application of such a joint MSM model to different leading indicators.

10 In accordance with the usual typology of the business cycle in booms and recessions, we assume that there are only two states. Owing to limited degrees of freedom we cannot test whether more than two states would be appropriate.

11 A border case is the Netherlands, where the Schwartz criterion of the six plus one model is marginally below the joint business cycle model.

12 More correctly, we will use the historical contribution to the interest rate of the monetary policy shocks as our benchmark measure. See section 2.3.1 below.

13 These identifying assumptions are similar to the ones used by Eichenbaum and Evans (1995) for the United States.

14 The historical contribution of the monetary policy shock to the short-term interest rate consists of the cumulative effects of current and past monetary policy shocks on the interest rate.

3 Supply shocks and the 'natural rate of interest': an exploration

Jagjit S. Chadha and Charles Nolan

3.1 Introduction

We consider a small, open economy inhabited by an optimising corporate sector and a large number of optimising individuals who each period must formulate, amongst other things, dynamic programmes for investment and consumption following stochastic shifts in total factor productivity. We then ask three questions: What would the marginal productivity of capital, or real interest rate, look like over the course of the cycle in such an economy? How closely does the observed real interest rate in a small, open economy (the United Kingdom) resemble this hypothetical rate? And can we describe 'inflation and output determination as depending on the relation between a 'natural rate of interest' determined primarily by real factors and the central bank's rule for interest rates' (Woodford, 2000a, p. 2)?

We are accustomed to the supply side of an economy, as measured by the long-run average rate of productivity growth, being the most natural explanation for long-run real outcomes in growth and welfare (Griliches, 1996). But, as economists have recognised that the productivity cycle might be closely related to the propagation or impulses of the business cycle, the cyclical behaviour of productivity has increasingly attracted their attention (Cooley, 1995). Beginning with the seminal papers of Long and Plosser (1983) and Kydland and Prescott (1982), an important strand of macroeconomic research has attempted to construct small, theoretically coherent models based on optimising agents that capture key cyclical patterns in the actual data. In this paper, we follow the analyses of Backus, Kehoe and Kydland (1994) and Chadha, Janssen and Nolan (2000) and extend the real business cycle model to the case of the open economy. We then analyse the marginal productivity of capital in this economy in response to both the standard measure of productivity growth, the Solow residual, and a measure that attempts to correct for capacity utilisation.

To carry out this experiment we must develop two distinct models of a small, open economy that nevertheless share many characteristics. Both are inhabited by a corporate sector and a large number of individuals (really cohorts) who face finite lives. Both model economies face an exogenous steady-state interest rate determined in a perfectly integrated world capital market, and both economies have access to this world capital market when determining their portfolio allocation decisions.[1] In both economies the factors of production receive their marginal product, and there are otherwise no barriers to price flexibility. However, these economies differ in what makes them grow stochastically through time. In both models the driving process is stochastic variation in a productivity shift term, but in one it is the standard Solow residual whereas in the other the residual is employed in modified form with a correction for the cyclical variation in capital utilisation (see, for example, Burnside, Eichenbaum and Rebelo, 1995; Basu and Fernald, 2000).

There are a number of reasons to distrust the standard Solow residual as a measure of total factor productivity (TFP; see King and Rebelo, 1999). We shall concentrate on the two we think most pertinent. First, the standard measure of the Solow residual implies an implausibly large probability of technological regress and, concomitantly, an unrealistically high volatility of productivity growth relative to output.[2] Second, cyclical variations in factor inputs, through either labour hoarding or capital utilisation, can lead to mismeasurement of the Solow residual. Barro (1999) summarises many of the possible reasons, in particular where failure to allow for improvements in labour or capital quality tend to lead to an overestimate of growth due to technological change. In a series of very influential papers, Basu (see, for example, Basu, 1996, and, Basu and Fernald, 2000) argues that the main reason for the strong procyclicality of TFP is measurement error resulting from variable capital and labour utilisation. He further finds that variable utilisation is not merely a bias, but is itself an important propagation mechanism for an economy's primitive driving forces.

King and Rebelo (1999) build on this insight and argue that variable capacity utilisation tends to result in a high-substitution economy amplifying the 'vanishing' productivity shock, in which aggregate hours are very responsive to changes in the real wage or interest rates and the supply of capital responds strongly to changes in aggregate hours. One purpose of this paper is to examine the amplification properties of a standard Solow residual purged of the effects of variable capacity utilisation. Figures 3.1 and 3.2 illustrate the impact of this purge on the resulting distribution of shocks, which becomes significantly negatively skewed.

The simulation of these two models, a standard real business cycle (RBC) and a high-substitution RBC economy, allows us to obtain a marginal productivity of capital. We find that the marginal productivity of capital is significantly procyclical, thereby confirming Vickers' (2000, pp. 11–12) conjecture. We interpret,

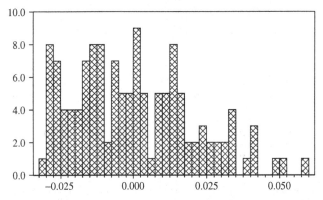

Figure 3.1 Histogram of standard Solow residual.

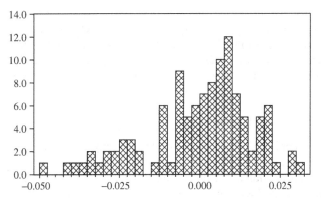

Figure 3.2 Histogram of corrected Solow residual.

in our model, the artificial marginal productivity capital as the 'natural rate of interest', which is consistent with constant inflation in the medium run. In some sense we also follow Blinder's (1998, p. 34) suggestion to compute the 'neutral' rate in response to durable shocks. Our aim in this paper, then, is essentially twofold. First, we wish to investigate whether our measure of the corrected productivity shock may still be a plausible candidate for a principal source of the UK business cycle.[3] Second, looking at the difference between the hypothetical marginal productivity of capital and the observed real rate in the UK economy, we ask, in the manner of Wicksell, to what extent the divergence can explain inflation and output outcomes.

The paper is structured as follows. Section 3.2 outlines a number of facts relating to the business cycle in the United Kingdom and in particular to the real

Table 3.1 *Observed data: summary UK facts*

Variable	σ	y_{t-4}	y_{t-3}	y_{t-2}	y_{t-1}	y_t	y_{t+1}	y_{t+2}	y_{t+3}	y_{t+4}
y	1.59									
c	1.52	0.491	0.598	0.706	0.785	0.805	0.749	0.624	0.459	0.284
i	3.76	0.430	0.563	0.671	0.736	0.744	0.690	0.585	0.453	0.315
w	0.91	0.310	0.220	0.182	0.177	0.163	0.108	0.013	−0.093	−0.179
ca	3.83	−0.385	−0.469	−0.532	−0.565	−0.561	−0.513	−0.414	−0.272	−0.113
n	1.67	0.520	0.646	0.769	0.840	0.817	0.691	0.491	0.270	0.075
k	0.10	0.180	0.119	0.063	0.017	−0.014	−0.034	−0.044	−0.056	−0.075
r	1.69	−0.076	0.043	0.156	0.244	0.300	0.320	0.310	0.274	0.210

Notes: The presented moments refer to the bandpass-filtered data with 12 quarters' weights; see Baxter and King (1999) for further details. The full sample for all data is 1963:1 to 1998:4.

interest rate. Section 3.3 develops a more or less canonical dynamic stochastic general equilibrium model driven by supply shocks measured in one of two ways: either as total factor productivity or as total factor productivity corrected for changes in capacity utilisation. Section 3.4 presents the calibration techniques used to assess the fit of this model. Section 3.5 provides the main results. Section 3.6 offers some conclusions on the 'natural rate of interest' hypothesis.

3.2   The real rate of interest: some observations

This section outlines some basic facts about the UK economy. When assessing the models presented, we will try to map the UK economy along two main dimensions: (a) the covariation of the main economic indicators with the economic cycle, measured by the business cycle fluctuation in output per head, and (b) the relative volatility of each series. Table 3.1 presents the observed data on the business cycle component of the UK economy obtained with the bandpass filter recommended by Baxter and King (1999).[4] Investment (i) and the current account (ca) are the most volatile series. Output (y), consumption (c) and real rates (r) display lower, similar levels of volatility. Observed real wages (w) show little cyclical variation and, as suggested by King and Rebelo (1999), the capital stock (k) displays little important variation at the business cycle frequency. Consumption, investment, real wages and hours supplied (n) are procyclical while the current account is countercyclical. Output shows positive leads for consumption, investment and wages, while there are negative leads for the current account. The current account and, to some extent, real wages negatively lead output, while consumption, investment, real rates and labour supply positively lead output.

The behaviour of observed real rates needs further explanation. Figure 3.3 explores the cyclicality of real interest rates from a somewhat longer perspective.

Table 3.2 *Real rates and the business cycle*

	Filtering procedure		
	B–K	C–F	H–P
Annual postwar Corr. (y,r)	0.47	0.48	0.46
s.d. (y)	1.41	1.43	1.10
s.d. (r)	1.82	1.85	1.90

Notes: y = GDP per head; r = real interest rate; s.d. = standard deviation in percentage terms; and Corr. = correlation coefficient. Results refer to an annual UK study over the period 1871–1997 and to three different filtering procedures: Baxter–King (B–K), Christiano–Fitzgerald (C–F) and Hodrick–Prescott (H–P). *Source:* Chadha et al. (2000).

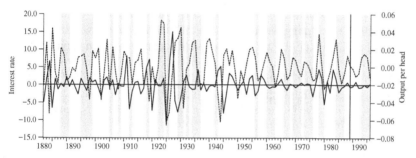

Figure 3.3 Real interest rates and the business cycle, 1871–1998 (deviation from trend).

We plot the cyclical component of the real interest rate (dashed line) against both the cyclical component of output per head (solid line) and the phases of expansion (light) and contraction (dark), and find fairly clear evidence that real interest rates have become procyclical in the postwar period and their volatility has fallen to that of output per head. Table 3.2 quantifies this finding. We find for an annual data set from 1947 that, irrespective of the filter employed, real rates are significantly positively associated with the business cycle and of a similar level of volatility. This finding stands at some variance to the somewhat puzzling and yet standard result in the US literature (see, for example, King and Watson, 1996), which reports countercyclical real rates.[5]

In the following section we build two versions of a canonical real business cycle model with each of two productivity measures driving an artificial general equilibrium economy. In addition to studying the ability of these two models to explain the key observed moments of real rates, we will examine their ability to explain the main business cycle moments found in expenditures and factors.

3.3   An open economy model

In this section we develop our small, open economy real business cycle (RBC) model. We employ two versions. The first model is driven by exogenous changes in technological capabilities, whereas the second is driven by the same chages purged of variable capacity utilisation. The incorporation of variable capacity utilisation in the first model requires some important changes to the equations describing optimal corporate behaviour and factor productivities. For ease of exposition, we detail the derivation of the first model only, and then indicate which equations change in the case of the preference shock model.

We model the UK economy as a small, open economy in the sense that it faces an exogenous real interest rate determined in fully integrated world capital markets. This characterisation means that, unless the interest rate exactly equals the discount factor, the agent (in our model, the cohort) will be accumulating (if $r > \delta$) or decumulating (if $r < \delta$) net foreign assets such that we strain the small country assumption.[6] We address this issue by adopting the approach of Yaari (1965), assuming that agents in our model face finite lives. In particular we follow Cardia (1991) by adopting the discrete time (open economy) version of Blanchard (1985). The first version of our model is taken from Chadha, Janssen and Nolan (2000). In the exposition below, a number of issues are treated somewhat lightly, particularly issues pertaining to the aggregation over cohorts; we refer the interested reader to Chadha, Janssen and Nolan (2000) for further details.

3.3.1   The representative agent

Equation (3.1) represents the expected lifetime utility of a representative agent.

$$V_0 = E_0 \sum_{t=0}^{\infty} \left(\frac{1}{1+\delta} \right)^t \left(\frac{1}{1+\lambda} \right)^t u(C_t, L_t). \qquad (3.1)$$

The agent gains utility from consumption of a single non-durable good, C_t, and leisure, L_t. Each period, she faces a time-independent probability of death, λ, which lies in the open unit interval. Let δ denote the subjective discount rate. We make the usual assumptions concerning the differentiability of the utility function, which we also assume is concave and increasing in both its arguments. Her maximisation is subject to a sequence of per-period budget constraints,

$$C_t + B_{t+1} = (1+r)(1+\lambda)B_t + \Pi_t + W_t N_t, \qquad (3.2)$$

plus a transversality condition, which we spell out below. That is, total consumption, C_t, plus purchases of net foreign assets, B_{t+1}, is equal to net income, in turn composed of net income from foreign assets, $(1+r)(1+\lambda)B_t$, income from shares in the representative firm, Π_t, and labour income, $W_t N_t$, which is in turn equal to the product of the per-period wage rate and the amount of time spent working. If an interior optimum exists, then the following two equations, amongst others, will characterise that optimum:

$$u'_c(C_t, L_t) = \left(\frac{1+r}{1+\delta}\right) E_t u'_c(C_{t+1}, L_{t+1}) \tag{3.3}$$

$$\frac{u'_l(C_t, L_t)}{u'_c(C_t, L_t)} = W_t. \tag{3.4}$$

Equation (3.3) demonstrates that, at the individual (cohort) level, the probability of death entails no tilting of consumption, other than what would normally occur in models with infinitely lived consumers and a discrepancy between market interest rates and the subjective discount factor. Frenkel and Razin (1992) suggest an intuitive interpretation of this result. Consider a net creditor who wishes to secure, in expectation, that his advance returns principal plus the risk-free interest rate. To do this he needs to take account of the fact that the borrower may not survive to repay the loan. Assuming a version of the law of large numbers such that the proportion of the population that does survive is given by $(1 + \lambda)^{-1}$, then his expected return is given by the product of the proportion of the cohort that survives and the amount repaid, $(1 + r)(1 + \lambda)B_{t+1}$. Equation (3.4) is also familiar, and governs the optimal supply of labour. Equation (3.3) also makes clear the problem in proxying the dynamics of a small, open economy using an infinitely lived representative agent set-up. The situation changes radically with respect to aggregate consumption when we integrate over all currently alive cohorts. First we note that the size of the cohort born each period is given by

$$\left(\frac{\lambda}{1+\lambda}\right)\left(\frac{1}{1+\lambda}\right)^t.$$

As a result of this, the size of the cohort decreases monotonically with time, and the sum of all currently alive cohorts is equal to unity, that is[7]

$$\frac{\lambda}{1+\lambda} \sum_{j=-\infty}^{t} \left(\frac{1}{1+\lambda}\right)^{(t-j)} = 1. \tag{3.5}$$

To obtain an expression for aggregate consumption we first need to calculate the agent's present-value budget constraint. Iterating on equation (3.2) in the usual way we get that

$$\sum_{s=t}^{\infty} E_t\left[\left(\frac{1}{1+r}\right)^{s-t}\left(\frac{1}{1+\lambda}\right)^{s-t} C_s\right]$$

$$= (1+r)(1+\lambda)B_t + \sum_{s=t}^{\infty} E_t\left[\left(\frac{1}{1+r}\right)^{s-t}\left(\frac{1}{1+\lambda}\right)^{s-t}\right][\Pi_s + W_s N_s].$$

$$\tag{3.6}$$

Again equation (3.6) is a familiar expression, except that both it and the transversality condition now reflect the probability of death:

$$E_t\left(\frac{1}{1+r}\right)^T \left(\frac{1}{1+\lambda}\right)^T B_{t+T+1} \to 0 \text{ as } T \to \infty. \tag{3.7}$$

Assuming log utility (as we do throughout this paper), we see that a simple stochastic difference equation governs consumption dynamics at the individual level, $E_s C_{s+1} = [(1 + r)/(1 + \delta)]C_s$. Using this expression in equation (3.6) successively to substitute for future consumption, we get that

$$C_t = \frac{(1+\lambda)(1+\delta) - 1}{(1+\lambda)(1+\delta)} \cdot \langle (1+\lambda)(1+\delta)B_t$$

$$+ E_t \sum_{s=t}^{\infty} \left[\left(\frac{1}{1+r}\right)^{s-t} \left(\frac{1}{1+\lambda}\right)^{s-t}\right][\Pi_s + W_s N_s]\rangle. \tag{3.8}$$

Ultimately (the details are contained in Chadha, Janssen and Nolan, 2001), we can use equation (3.8) to derive an expression for aggregate consumption dynamics. This is given in equation (3.9):

$$E_t C_{t+1} = \left(\frac{1+r}{1+\delta}\right)C_t - \lambda(1+r)\beta B_{t+1}, \tag{3.9}$$

where $\beta \equiv [(1 + \lambda)(1 + \delta) - 1]/[(1 + \lambda)(1 + \delta)]$. Here we see that any wedge between the subjective discount factor and the market interest rate need not imply a rising or falling level of net foreign assets. Equations (3.2) and (3.4), in aggregated form, along with equation (3.9), are the three key equations from the representative agent portion of the model.

3.3.2   The representative firm

We now turn to the problem facing the representative firm. First, we note that output is characterised by a Cobb–Douglas production function:

$$Y_t = A_t K_t^\alpha ((1+\gamma)^t N_t)^{1-\alpha}, \tag{3.10}$$

where A_t is the Solow residual, consisting of a trend and a stochastic component. We denote the log of the stochastic component by a_t, and we assume that $a_t = \rho a_{t-1} + \epsilon_t$, with $\epsilon \sim (0, \sigma_\epsilon^2)$ is independently and identically distributed (i.i.d.), $(1 + \gamma)$ is a labour-augmenting growth factor, and the common trend among the real magnitudes in our model. K_t is the capital stock and N_t is the labour input. Firms maximise total profits (suitably discounted so that aggregate utility is maximised) subject to a capital evolution equation, which says that the evolution of the capital stock is subject to a constant rate of depreciation, ψ, and a cost of adjustment $\phi(.)$ where ϕ is strictly concave, increasing in investment, I_t, and decreasing in the (predetermined) capital stock. That is,

$$K_{t+1} = (1 - \psi)K_t + \phi\left(\frac{I_t}{K_t}\right)K_t. \tag{3.11}$$

Let μ_t denote the marginal utility of aggregate consumption (the marginal utility of consumption is equal across cohorts, so aggregation is straightforward) and Λ_t denote an undetermined multiplier. The optimality conditions for a profit-maximising firm (which maximises aggregate utility at the same time, hence the presence of μ_t in these optimality conditions) are given by equation (3.11) as well as equations (3.12) and (3.13):

$$\Lambda_t \phi'(I_t/K_t) = \mu_t \tag{3.12}$$

$$\Lambda_t = E_t\left\{\alpha\left(\frac{1}{1+\delta}\right)\mu_{t+1}A_{t+1}K_t^{\alpha-1}N_{t+1}^{1-\alpha}\right\}$$

$$+ E_t\Lambda_{t+1}\left[\phi\left(\frac{I_{t+1}}{K_{t+1}}\right) - \phi'\left(\frac{I_{t+1}}{K_{t+1}}\right)\frac{I_{t+1}}{K_{t+1}} + (1 - \psi)\right]. \tag{3.13}$$

The preceding two equations are essentially a q model of investment. Roughly speaking, they indicate that investment will be positive when, other things being constant, the marginal utility of consumption is low, adjustment costs are low and the benefits of a higher capital stock (now and in the future) are high. The Cobb–Douglas production function (equation (3.10)) also provides expressions for the marginal product of labour and capital, and these are given, respectively, by equations (3.14) and (3.15):

$$W_t = (1 - \alpha)A_t K_t^{\alpha}[(1 + \gamma)^t N_t]^{-\alpha}(1 + \gamma)^t \tag{3.14}$$

$$Z_t = \alpha A_t K_t^{\alpha-1}[(1 + \gamma)^t N_t]^{1-\alpha}. \tag{3.15}$$

Two additional equations (or constraints) complete the description of our model economy. First there is a time constraint on the representative agent such that the total time available in any period for leisure and labour is normalised to unity.

$$N_t + L_t = 1. \tag{3.16}$$

The economy also faces a resource constraint that also determines the evolution of net foreign assets. This is given in equation (3.17):

$$B_{t+1} - B_t = rB_t + Y_t - C_t - I_t. \tag{3.17}$$

Equations (3.16) and (3.17) complete the description of the economy. The next stage involves making our equations stationary, that is, dividing through by our growth factor. So, for example, we use the following change of variables for variables observed at date t: $C_t \equiv C_t/(1+\gamma)^t$ and $K_{t+1} \equiv (1+\gamma)K_{t+1}/(1+\gamma)^{t+1}$. We then linearise our model equations. These transformed equations are collected in the next section.

3.3.3   The linearised model

In the equations that follow, time-subscripted lower-case letters refer to percentage deviations from steady state of our model equations in stationary format, and lower-case letters with no subscripts refer to steady-state values, i.e. $c_t \equiv dC_t/c$ where $C_t \equiv C_t/(1+\gamma)^t$ and c is the steady-state value of consumption:

$$(1+\gamma)E_t c_{t+1} = \left(\frac{1+r}{1+\delta}\right)c_t - \lambda(1+r)(1+\gamma)\beta(b/c)b_{t+1} \qquad (3.18)$$

$$y_t = (c/y)c_t + (i/y)i_t - (1+r)(b/y)b_t + (1+\gamma)(b/y)b_{t+1} \qquad (3.19)$$

$$c_t - l_t = w_t \qquad (3.20)$$

$$nn_t + ll_t = 0 \qquad (3.21)$$

$$(1+\gamma)k_{t+1} = (1-\psi)k_t + (i/k)i_t \qquad (3.22)$$

$$-(1+\gamma)\lambda_t = \frac{(i/k)}{(1+\delta)\zeta}E_t(i_{t+1} - k_{t+1}) + \frac{r+\psi}{1+\delta}E_t(c_{t+1} - z_{t+1})$$

$$- \left(\frac{1-\psi}{1+\delta}\right)E_t\lambda_{t+1} \qquad (3.23)$$

$$y_t = \alpha k_t + (1-\alpha)n_t + a_t \qquad (3.24)$$

$$w_t = \alpha(k_t - n_t) + a_t \qquad (3.25)$$

$$z_t = (\alpha - 1)(k_t - n_t) + a_t \qquad (3.26)$$

$$i_t = -\zeta(c_t + \lambda_t) + k_t, \qquad (3.27)$$

where $\zeta \equiv (\phi'(.))/(\frac{i}{k} \cdot \phi''(.))$ is the slope of the investment demand function. We have 10 endogenous variables, two of which, b_{t+1} and k_{t+1}, are predetermined, such that $E_t b_{t+1} = b_{t+1}$ and $E_t k_{t+1} = k_{t+1}$. The model has two stable roots, which can be associated with the two predetermined variables, and it otherwise meets the Blanchard–Kahn criteria for a unique bounded rational expectations solution.

3.3.4   The model with variable capacity utilisation

The above model can be relatively easily adapted to incorporate the effects of variable capacity utilisation. Here we follow the approach of King and Rebelo (1999). We do not incorporate an analogous effect into the labour market; hence the equations characterising aggregate consumption and asset accumulation, and labour supply given the real wage (where the real wage *is* affected by variable capacity utilisation), do not change. See King and Rebelo (1999) for more discussion of this point. Let v_t denote the extent of capacity utilisation.[8] We rewrite the Cobb–Douglas production function in this case as

$$Y_t = A_t v_t K_t^\alpha ((1+\gamma)^t N_t)^{1-\alpha}, \tag{3.28}$$

where, as before, A_t is the Solow residual and the log of the stochastic component is denoted a_t, and where $a_t = \rho a_{t-1} + \epsilon_t$, with $\epsilon \sim (0, \sigma_\epsilon^2)$ is i.i.d. Although the driving process is formally identical to the case analysed above, the stochastic process, under variable utilisation, is not as volatile and is less persistent. All variables have the same description as before, so K_t is the capital stock and N_t is the labour input. As before, firms maximise total profits; however, now we assume that there are no adjustment costs and that the depreciation rate is an increasing function of the level of capacity utilisation: $\psi(v_t)$. That is,

$$K_{t+1} = (1 + \psi(v_t))K_t + I_t. \tag{3.29}$$

In addition to the choices it faced in the previous problem, the firm now has to choose the level of capacity utilisation. In other words v_t is a choice variable. The optimality conditions are given by equations (3.30) to (3.32):

$$\Lambda_t = \mu_t \tag{3.30}$$

$$\Lambda_t = E_t\left\{\alpha\left(\frac{1}{1+\delta}\right)u_{t+1}A_{t+1}K_t^{\alpha-1}[(1+\gamma)^{t+1}N_{t+1}]^{1+\alpha}\right\}$$
$$+ E_t\Lambda_{t+1}[(1 - \psi(v_t))] \tag{3.31}$$
$$\psi'(v_t)K_t = \alpha A_t(v_t K_t)^{\alpha-1}K_t[(1+\gamma)^t N_t]^{1-\alpha}, \tag{3.32}$$

where in the final expression we have used the fact that $\Lambda_t = \mu_t$. The first two expressions are familiar, and reflect optimal investment behaviour in the absence of adjustment costs. This final expression is the efficiency condition characterising the optimal level of capacity utilisation. It indicates that increased capacity utilisation results in increased benefits in the form of higher output and hence higher profits in our set-up. It also raises costs, however, in the form of increased replacement investment. That is, increased utilisation results in a higher period depreciation rate. In addition to these changes, the expressions describing factor productivities also change:

$$W_t = (1-\alpha)A_t(v_t K_t)^\alpha[(1+\gamma)^t N_t]^{-\alpha}(1+\gamma)^t \tag{3.33}$$

$$Z_t = \alpha A_t(v_t K_t)^{\alpha-1}[(1+\gamma)^t N_t]^{1-\alpha}v_t. \tag{3.34}$$

Therefore, equations (3.3), (3.9), (3.16), (3.17) and (3.28) to (3.34) describe our economy in the presence of variable capacity utilisation. As before, we study a linear approximation to these equations in stationary form.

3.3.5   The linearised equations

As above, lower-case letters refer to percentage deviations from steady state. Equations (3.18) to (3.21) remain the same. However, we now replace equations (3.22) to (3.27) with equations (3.35) to (3.40), and we have an additional equation approximating optimal capacity utilisation (3.41):

$$(1 + \gamma)k_{t+1} = (1 - \psi(v))k_t + (i/k)i_t - \psi'(v)vv_t \tag{3.35}$$

$$-c_t = \lambda_t \tag{3.36}$$

$$((1 - \psi(v))E_t\lambda_{t+1} - (r + \psi(v))E_t(c_{t+1} - z_{t+1})$$
$$+ vv_{t+1} = (1 + \gamma)\lambda_t \tag{3.37}$$

$$y_t = \alpha k_t + (1 - \alpha)n_t + \alpha v_t + a_t \tag{3.38}$$

$$w_t = \alpha(k_t - n_t) + \alpha v_t + a_t \tag{3.39}$$

$$z_t = (\alpha - 1)(k_t - n_t) + \alpha v_t + a_t \tag{3.40}$$

$$v_t = \frac{1}{1 + \sigma - \alpha}a_t + \frac{(\alpha - 1)}{1 + \sigma - \alpha}(k_t - n_t), \tag{3.41}$$

where $\sigma \equiv (v \cdot \psi''(.))/(\psi'(.))$.

This version of our model also has two stable roots that are associated with the two predetermined variables. Both our models may be specified as a singular linear difference model under rational expectations (RE). In both cases a unique bounded RE solution is verified. The solution specifies the vector of non-predetermined endogenous variables as a function of predetermined variables and on the exogenous driving processes. The predetermined variables are expressed as functions of their state in the previous time period and of the previous period's driving processes. This recursive solution allows us to simulate easily the behaviour of our model economies under what we hope are realistic driving processes, and then compare the generated moments with those observed during the UK business cycle.[9]

3.4   The steady state of the model

We discuss only briefly the calibration of our models, and more details can be found in Chadha, Janssen and Nolan (2000).[10] For our 'free' variables we adopt standard parameter values. Table 3.3 lists these fundamental parameters, and we explain the derivation of the other steady values. The annual probability of death, λ, is taken to be 1/67. For quarterly data this translates into 0.373%. The quarterly real return on capital, r, in the United Kingdom is taken to be 1.25%. The share of capital, α, in the production function is taken to be 38.0%. We assume, in line with King and Rebelo (1999), that the quarterly rate of capital depreciation, ψ, is 2.5%. Per capita income growth, γ, in the UK is

Table 3.3 *Fundamental parameters: quarterly percentages*

λ	r	α	ψ	γ	δ
0.373	1.250	38.00	2.50	0.50	0.75

Notes: The presented moments refer to the bandpass-filtered data with 12 quarters' weights; see Baxter and King (1999) for further details. The full sample for all data is 1963:1 to 1998:4.

0.5%. And the quarterly rate of time preference is assumed to be around the level implied by market real interest rates, 0.75%. We explain the remaining parameters, β, b, c, y, i, l, N, L and θ in turn. In the steady state we have that

$$z = r + \psi = \alpha \left(\frac{K}{N} \right)^{\alpha - 1}, \tag{3.42}$$

where we have used the steady-state analogues of equations (3.11), (3.13) and (3.14). We solve for K/N and find 41.9. From equation (3.24) we note that $Y/N = K/N^{\alpha} = 4.135$ and thus $K/Y = 10.133$. From equation (3.22) we see $i/k = \gamma + \psi$ and $i/y = (\gamma + \psi)k/y$, which are calculated to be 10.130 and 0.304, respectively. Now note:

$$w_t = (1 - \alpha) \left(\frac{K}{N} \right)^{\alpha}, \tag{3.43}$$

which is equal to 0.513. We shall assume that we spend one-fifth of our time working and so $N/L = 0.250$ and y, k and i equal 0.827, 8.379 and 0.251, respectively. We now solve for b and c simultaneously using equation (3.18) and the current account identity:

$$y - c - i = (\gamma - r)b, \tag{3.44}$$

from which we calculate that b equals -0.501 and c equals 0.571. Finally, θ is given by the intratemporal efficiency condition given by equation (3.20) and is found to be 0.535.

3.5 Results

The main results are presented in tables 3.4–3.6, as direct analogues of table 3.1 on the observed data. The results in table 3.4, from the model driven by productivity shocks, are familiar from many studies in the RBC literature (for example, see the simulation results reported in King and Rebelo, 1999), although recall that here we are working in an overlapping generations framework. The model

Table 3.4 *Model output: total factor productivity*

Variable	σ	y_{t-4}	y_{t-3}	y_{t-2}	y_{t-1}	y_t	y_{t+1}	y_{t+2}	y_{t+3}	y_{t+4}
y	1.59									
c	0.45	0.120	0.336	0.592	0.824	0.960	0.940	0.801	0.605	0.416
i	7.28	−0.152	0.072	0.354	0.632	0.829	0.877	0.798	0.651	0.499
w	0.78	0.237	0.445	0.679	0.882	0.990	0.944	0.791	0.589	0.396
ca	6.40	0.271	0.051	−0.237	−0.529	−0.747	−0.819	−0.765	−0.637	−0.50
n	0.82	0.478	0.652	0.827	0.955	0.990	0.896	0.720	0.515	0.327
k	0.99	0.879	0.889	0.837	0.719	0.552	0.355	0.174	0.025	−0.092
r	1.33	−0.178	0.045	0.329	0.610	0.812	0.865	0.793	0.650	0.501

Notes: The presented moments refer to the bandpass-filtered data with 12 quarters' weights; see Baxter and King (1999) for further details. The full sample for all data is 1963:1 to 1998:4.

basically ranks variables, in terms of their standard deviations, in a manner consistent with the data (although notably it exaggerates the smoothness of consumption). In terms of the contemporaneous correlations with output per head, all of our results are consistent with the data, although the degree of these correlations is high, again a familiar result. We note, in particular, that the productivity-driven model captures both the fact that the current account is a relatively volatile countercyclical variable and that the real rate is procyclical but relatively smooth. The striking aspect of this result is the extent to which the artificial data capture the dynamic, as well as contemporaneous, correlations of the observed data, positive leads for consumption, investment, real interest rates, hours worked, real wages and the capital stock and negative leads for the current account. In each of the two models we consistently find that the marginal productivity of capital is procyclical. That is, the productivity shock, in either case, raises the marginal productivity of capital and leads to consumption growing, while the real rate is above the rate of time preference. Figure 3.4 shows the difference between the business cycle component of the simulated real rate series and observed real rates in the UK.

Tables 3.5 and 3.6 reflect the model of the high-substitution economy driven by the correct TFP shock with persistence set at 0.99 and 0.70, respectively. Overall, the fit seems less impressive. There are a number of striking issues. First, output appears about twice as volatile as the observed data, but more worrying is the variability in the generated investment and current account data, some 14 to 15 times more volatile than output compared with less than twice as volatile in observed data. The model also generates counterfactually signed contemporaneous correlations between the current account and output, but the current account is found to have consistent negative leads for output. The main failures of the high-substitution economy, when confronted with the data, are in the volatility of the main expenditure series; consumption is far too smooth and too small a fraction of output, while investment, the current

Table 3.5 *Model output: capacity utilisation stripped TFP shock,* $\rho = 0.99$

Variable	σ	y_{t-4}	y_{t-3}	y_{t-2}	y_{t-1}	y_t	y_{t+1}	y_{t+2}	y_{t+3}	y_{t+4}
y	4.430									
c	0.642	−0.211	0.053	0.396	0.732	0.958	0.975	0.789	0.463	0.101
i	69.840	−0.566	−0.725	−0.697	−0.438	−0.010	0.419	0.706	0.771	0.629
w	1.610	−0.122	0.187	0.540	0.841	0.994	0.931	0.686	0.339	−0.006
ca	70.170	0.561	0.738	0.729	0.486	0.065	−0.368	−0.670	−0.755	−0.632
n	2.830	−0.037	0.302	0.654	0.915	0.998	0.864	0.571	0.216	−0.103
k	4.360	0.017	0.366	0.711	0.946	0.989	0.818	0.502	0.143	−0.161
r	0.660	−0.565	−0.662	−0.569	−0.264	0.178	0.579	0.809	0.805	0.603

Table 3.6 *Model output: capacity utilisation stripped TFP shock,* $\rho = 0.70$

Variable	σ	y_{t-4}	y_{t-3}	y_{t-2}	y_{t-1}	y_t	y_{t+1}	y_{t+2}	y_{t+3}	y_{t+4}
y	5.67									
c	0.04	0.352	0.547	0.720	0.807	0.751	0.536	0.212	−0.139	−0.432
i	82.83	−0.579	−0.725	−0.678	−0.404	0.031	0.452	0.723	0.770	0.616
w	1.34	−0.076	0.254	0.609	0.888	0.999	0.895	0.621	0.271	−0.057
ca	82.84	0.574	0.723	0.720	0.465	0.038	−0.391	−0.681	−0.752	−0.620
n	4.33	−0.070	0.259	0.613	0.890	1.000	0.892	0.617	0.265	−0.064
k	5.14	0.033	0.385	0.726	0.953	0.985	0.804	0.484	0.126	−0.172
r	1.08	−0.509	−0.456	−0.231	0.143	0.561	0.851	0.927	0.775	0.469

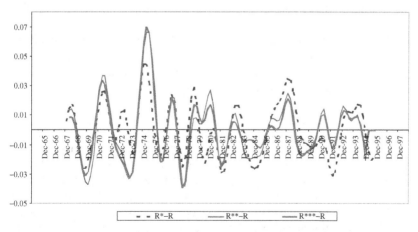

Figure 3.4 Wicksell gap for TFP and corrected TFP.

Note: R refers to observed real interest rates; R^* to the standard TFP model; R^{**} to the high-substitution economy with a highly persistent shock; and R^{***} to the high-substitution economy with a less persistent shock.

Table 3.7 *Model output: capacity utilisation stripped (by Kalman filter) TFP shock, $\rho = 0.99$*

Variable	σ	y_{t-4}	y_{t-3}	y_{t-2}	y_{t-1}	y_t	y_{t+1}	y_{t+2}	y_{t+3}	y_{t+4}
y	3.98									
c	0.57	0.223	0.415	0.633	0.839	0.975	0.981	0.859	0.650	0.415
i	49.74	−0.516	−0.568	−0.515	−0.305	0.030	0.370	0.597	0.657	0.589
w	1.45	0.286	0.496	0.718	0.904	0.997	0.956	0.801	0.583	0.357
ca	49.88	0.537	0.605	0.568	0.370	0.040	−0.305	−0.544	−0.691	−0.567
n	2.54	0.339	0.562	0.783	0.946	0.999	0.916	0.7351	0.512	0.299
k	3.88	0.380	0.604	0.819	0.965	0.993	0.885	0.687	0.460	0.250
r	0.48	−0.416	−0.418	−0.318	−0.076	0.263	0.575	0.752	0.756	0.637

Note: We measure capacity utilisation in the final model using the Kalman filter to proxy for cyclical movements in capacity utilisation.

account and the capital stock are too highly volatile. This is the result of the high-substitution economy amplifying what are in fact less volatile supply shocks, which we discover when we strip out the effects of capacity utilisation.[11] The high-substitution economy produces more elastic output responses (see equation 3.38) from which, in the case of non-separable utility, little is imparted to consumption and results in highly volatile investment and, in this model's complete market, current account balances. In future work we will modify this effect by lowering the elasticity of intertemporal substitution to below 1. Table 3.7 presents the results of the high-substitution economy shocked with TFP stripped of capacity utilisation by Kalman filter, rather than proxy. This changes little.

The results presented in this section would suggest that a model driven by productivity innovations, corrected for capacity utilisation, seems a reasonable approximation to the covariation of aggregate data with business cycle fluctuations and the dynamics of the business cycle.

3.5.1 Wicksellian flavours

There has been much interest recently in the Wicksellian interpretation of monetary policy (see Woodford, 2000a) as an interest rate feedback rule. The suggestion has been made that the evolution of the real sector of an economy sets the correct target for monetary authorities wishing to stabilise nominal and real variables. It is assumed that any deviation from this 'natural rate' of interest will affect inflation and growth outcomes.[12] We therefore ask to what extent the difference between the dynamic equilibrium real rate of interest in our purely real economy and the observed real rate in the UK ($R^* - R$) is related to developments in nominal income. Figure 3.5 plots this difference, which we call the Wicksell gap, for one of our four sets of calibrations: the TFP model. The coincident pattern is striking.

Table 3.8 *Wicksell gap and inflation and output outcomes*

X		R^*-R	$R^{**}-R$	$R^{***}-R$	$X \to R^*-R$	$R^*-R \to X$
Nominal income	Full	0.366	0.340	0.344	0.82 (0.59)	3.33 (0.00)
	Pre-1980	0.531	0.589	0.564	1.13 (0.36)	2.83 (0.04)
	Post-1980	0.028	−0.061	−0.108	1.28 (0.29)	2.46 (0.06)
Inflation	Full	0.180	0.420	0.442	0.68 (0.70)	3.21 (0.00)
	Pre-1980	0.475	0.635	0.652	2.77 (0.04)	1.20 (0.33)
	Post-1980	−0.366	0.058	0.005	1.39 (0.25)	5.49 (0.00)
Output growth	Full	0.292	−0.210	−0.244	1.17 (0.33)	0.76 (0.64)
	Pre-1980	−0.075	−0.298	−0.376	0.59 (0.67)	1.17 (0.34)
	Post-1980	0.532	−0.142	−0.118	2.28 (0.07)	4.45 (0.00)

Notes: We present simple correlations of the difference between the calibrated real rate and the standard model $(R - R^*)$ and the two versions of the high-substitution economy $(R - R^{**}$ and $R - R^{***})$. The final two columns present the Granger causality tests for the null of the variable in column 1 (X) not causing the $R - R^*$ and $R - R^*$ not causing X, respectively. Note that we employ eight lags for the full sample tests and four lags for the subsamples. The results of Granger causality tests for the two versions of the high-substitution economy are available on request.

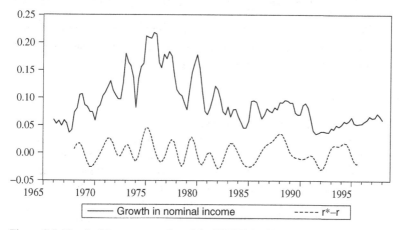

Figure 3.5 Nominal income growth and the UK Wicksell gap, 1965–98.

Table 3.8 gives the correlations of the Wicksell gap and nominal income, inflation and output growth for the whole sample and for samples before and after the second oil-price shock. We find that each of the macroeconomic variables is closely matched by developments in the Wicksell gap. We find evidence to suggest that, in the first half of our sample, the Wicksell gap was inflationary, whereas later it seemed more closely related to output growth. The flattening of the short-run Phillips curve is an issue we leave to future research. We do find, however, that the Wicksell gap seems to be exogenous to macroeconomic developments: in not one case does either output or inflation Granger cause the Wicksell gap.

3.6 Concluding remarks

This paper has examined the hypothesis that in a model driven by supply shocks, defined in one of two ways, the marginal product of capital will be procyclical. We have found evidence to support this hypothesis. Both the economy with low substitutability and the economy with high substitutability produce relatively stable real rates, but the low-substitution economy tends to experience significantly greater procyclicality of real rates. This excessive cyclicality in generated data is often a poor diagnostic test of real business cycle models, but in this case it leads to a Wicksell gap that seems well placed to explain macroeconomic outcomes. We might therefore be tempted to suggest that, however we define supply shocks, it would appear that a monetary authority concerned with nominal income volatility would seek to adopt an aggressively procyclical attitude to the setting of a short-run interest rate.

In future work we will extend these results to incorporate a policy rule and a fully specified nominal sector so that, *inter alia*, alternative policy rules can be properly evaluated.[13] But we suggest that the basic insight will remain that a monetary authority concerned about stabilising inflation and output over the course of the business cycle should not fail to account for the impulses to inflation and output generated by the more primitive process of economic growth itself. That care must be taken in measuring the process of economic growth (see Crafts, 2000) does not alter the strength of this message.

Acknowledgements

We are grateful for helpful conversations, constructive criticisms and comments from participants in seminars at which versions of this paper were presented, including the Bank of England, University of Cambridge, University of Leicester and Warwick Business School. In particular we are grateful for the comments of Philip Arestis, Laurence Ball, Sean Holly, Lavan Mahadeva, Anton Muscatelli and Peter Sinclair. Any views expressed, or errors that remain, are solely the responsibility of the authors. We are grateful for research assistance from Wesley Fogel. Part of this research has been funded by Leverhulme Grant no. F/09567/A.

Notes

1 The assumption of an exogenous long-run real rate does not affect the dynamic equilibrium path of adjustment of the domestic rate, in so far as the real rate will return to that set by the rest of the world eventually. The question we ask is how that adjustment might vary over the cycle.

2 Burnside et al. (1995) estimate that the quarterly probability of technological regress falls from 37% in US manufacturing to some 10% when variable capacity utilisation is accounted for. We do not find such a stark fall in the probability on economy-wide

data in the UK, where the probability of regress falls from 39% to 23%. See figures 3.1 and 3.2 for UK data from 1965 to 1998.

3 Chadha, Janssen and Nolan (2000) find that the standard Solow residual captures the main moments of the UK business cycle very well. Basu (1996) finds that the corrected Solow residual cannot produce enough volatility in the business cycle.

4 A wider range of series' moments results are available on request, as are the results of different filtering procedures. The programs we used for implementing the filter are also available, as is a full data annex, but note that all data are sourced from the Office of National Statistics. All expenditure series are measured in per capita terms.

5 See Chadha and Dimsdale (1999) for a discussion of possible reasons for the postwar procyclicality of real rates. They also suggested that acyclicality resulted from high inflation volatility, thereby injecting noise into the real rate cycle and its measured association with the business cycle.

6 We are not implying, of course, that the underlying optimisation is ill posed since the budget set remains compact, and in fact bounded. The point is simply that, for reasonable parameter values, $r \neq \delta$ can imply large steady-state net asset holdings. In our discussion of the steady-state properties of our model, we discuss this point further and compare our steady state net asset position with that of a more conventional representative agent model.

7 We outline in more detail in an appendix to Chadha, Janssen and Nolan (2001) the construction of our discrete approximation to the continuous exponential density.

8 We measure v_t from the Quarterly European Commission Business Consumer Surveys, Directorate General for Economic and Financial Affairs, July 2000, p. 4, table 2.

9 Full solution results, including Markov decision rules, are available on request.

10 A spreadsheet calculating all our parameter values and steady-state values (including extensive sensitivity calculations) is available on request. There are also some quantitatively minor differences in the steady-state of our two models. We do not discuss these differences further.

11 Note that the standard devation of the TFP shock is 2.07%, compared with 1.62% in the case of stripped capacity utilisation.

12 See Fischer (1972) for an earlier exposition along these lines.

13 Naturally, because the real-world data contain monetary policy shocks, we would like to incorporate an explicit derivation for our explanation of inflation and output outcomes within this framwork.

4 Some econometric issues in measuring the monetary transmission mechanism, with an application to developing countries

Derick Boyd and Ron Smith

4.1 Introduction

Formal models are an essential input to the policy-making process. Most central banks, like other organisations, have a suite of different models designed for different purposes and to answer different questions. The papers in Den Butter and Morgan (2000) examine the use of empirical models in policy-making. Constructing these models involves blending economic theory, local knowledge and econometric methods. A longstanding issue of dispute has been the right way to blend these three ingredients, with different approaches giving each a different weight. In most countries a large amount of 'tender loving care' will have been bestowed on the individual equations of the policy model in order to obtain sensible results and to get the model to work. Typically this involves adding a range of country-specific variables, which makes it difficult to compare results across models and means that what should be the same equation applied to different countries can look very different. This variability can prompt the suspicion that the results are the product of data mining and may not be robust. Such criticism has been directed at models such as Project Link that combine highly heterogeneous country models. When standard specifications are estimated for a large number of different countries, they tend to produce a high degree of parameter heterogeneity. This is illustrated by Pesaran, Shin and R.P. Smith (1999), who estimate an error correction consumption function for OECD countries, and Baltagi and Griffin (1997), who estimate a gasoline demand function for OECD countries.

In this paper we want to review the econometric issues involved in estimating models of the transmission process and to examine the heterogeneity issue as it applies to four equations that play a major role in the transmission mechanism for monetary policy: a purchasing power parity condition, a trade balance equation, an IS curve and a Phillips curve. We estimate these four equations for 57 developing countries using annual data over the period 1966–96. One motivation for this exercise is that in related work[1] the objective is to estimate models of the transmission mechanism for a number of countries and examine whether the measured differences in the mechanism can be explained by differences in financial structure. An important issue in such an exercise is whether the measured differences represent real differences or merely specification errors. In this paper we examine the possible sources of specification error for a fairly noisy sample of data. Using developing countries also has the advantage that we can get a fairly large number of cases, so the properties of averages should be better. Section 4.2 discusses the statistical framework, briefly sets out the model of the transmission mechanism we have in mind and examines some of the issues. Section 4.3 presents average estimates of the four equations we examine and looks at the properties of the system. Section 4.4 presents evidence on the degree of heterogeneity within the sample. Section 4.5 examines some econometric explanations for the heterogeneity. Section 4.6 concludes the paper.

4.2 The structure of the transmission mechanism

4.2.1 Statistical structure

Suppose we have a set of $I(1)$ domestic variables, x_{it}, an $m \times 1$ vector, and a set of $I(1)$ exogenous world variables, x_t^*, an $m^* \times 1$ vector, for countries $i = 1, 2, \ldots, N$ and time periods $t = 1, 2, \ldots, T$. Define z_{it} as $(x_{it}', x_t'^*, t)'$, a $k \times 1$ vector, where $k = m + m^* + 1$. An important practical issue is the size of the model, the dimensions chosen for k, m and m^*. A large number of possible variables could potentially be included, but, given the sample sizes typically available, systems with a large number of variables have poor statistical properties, so there is a difficult trade-off. Traditional simultaneous equations models solved this problem by imposing a large number of overidentifying restrictions. Because of their size, however, their reduced forms could not be estimated and so the restrictions could not be tested. Forecast performance is often used as a way to judge the quality of the model. But the best model for forecasting may not be the best model for policy-making. The extreme example would be that, even if a univariate model proved to be best for forecasting inflation, it would be of no use for deciding how to set interest rates, since interest rates would have no influence on the forecast.

Assume that there are r long-run cointegrating equilibrium relationships, with trends restricted to lie within the cointegration space, and define the $r \times 1$ set of $I(0)$ variables:

$$\varsigma_{it} = \beta_i' z_{it} = \beta_{0i}' x_{it} + \beta_{1i}' x_t^* + \beta_{2t}' t.$$

The framework is a standard dynamic simultaneous equations system. In such systems, determining the appropriate lag length is an important empirical issue, but here assume a second-order process for expositional simplicity. Then the 'structural' form of the system is a cointegrating vector autoregressive distributed lag (VARDL) model:

$$A_{0i} \Delta x_{it} = a_i + b_i \varsigma_{i,t-1} + B_{0i} \Delta x_t^* + A_{1i} \Delta x_{i,t-1} + B_{1i} \Delta x_{t-1}^* + \varepsilon_{it},$$

where ε_{it} is the $m \times 1$ vector of unobserved structural disturbance, with $E(\varepsilon_{it} \varepsilon_{it}') = \Sigma_i$. This expression abstracts from expectations, and one can suppose that these have been solved out in terms of the observables. Treating expectations explicitly would bring out the fact that the 'structural' coefficients in the equation above are mixtures of behavioural and expectational parameters, thus potentially subject to the Lucas critique. Treating expectations explicitly might also provide cross-equation restrictions that aid identification. The structural form can also be written in a 'final form' that expresses the endogenous variables as an infinite distributed lag of the exogenous variables and an infinite moving average of the structural errors. This and other representations are given in Pesaran and Smith (1998). In structural VARs where there are no exogenous variables, the moving average representation of this structural form is used as the basis of identification, as surveyed in Levtchenkova et al. (1998).

The reduced form is the augmented vector error correction model (VECM):

$$\Delta x_{it} = A_{0i}^{-1} a_i + A_{0i}^{-1} b_i \varsigma_{i,t-1} + A_{0i}^{-1} B_{0i} \Delta x_t^* + A_{0i}^{-1} A_{1i} \Delta x_{i,t-1}$$
$$+ A_{0i}^{-1} B_{1i} \Delta x_{t-1}^* + A_{0i}^{-1} \varepsilon_{it}$$

or

$$\Delta x_{it} = \gamma_i + \alpha_i \varsigma_{i,t-1} + \Phi_{0i} \Delta x_t^* + \Gamma_{1i} \Delta x_{i,t-1} + \Phi_{1i} \Delta x_{t-1}^* + u_{it},$$

where u_{it} is the vector of reduced form disturbances, with $E(u_{it} u_{it}') = \Omega_i = A_{0i}^{-1} \Sigma_i A_{0i}'^{-1}$. The reduced form can be consistently estimated by ordinary least squares (OLS) on each equation. However, it has m^2 fewer parameters than the structural form, which gives rise to the short-run identification problem discussed below. Since $\alpha_i = A_{0i}^{-1} b_i$, it is clear that the 'adjustment coefficients' in the standard VECMs are not the 'structural' responses to disequilibria b_i but depend also on the simultaneous interactions between the endogenous variables. Thus feedback to disequilibria in the reduced form is likely to be substantially more complicated than in the structural form.

Estimation of the reduced form gives us consistent estimates of γ_i, α_i, Φ_{0i}, Γ_{1i}, Φ_{1i} and Ω_i. We can also estimate $\Pi_i = \alpha_i \beta_i'$. For pure forecasting purposes this is all that is required. For interpretation and policy-making, however, we require estimates of the structural coefficients, and to obtain these we need extra a priori just-identifying restrictions. To a large extent, just-identifying restrictions must be a matter of taste, since they cannot be tested. Ideally, the just-identifying restrictions would be agreed features of the world that seem plausible to all economists on the basis of theoretical or institutional considerations. In fact, economists are prone to disagree about what they regard as plausible. This matters because, starting from the same reduced form, different identification conditions can lead to different structural estimates and policy recommendations.

In getting to the estimates of the structural parameters, two separate identification issues are involved. The first is the identification of the long-run equilibrium parameters β_i. As it stands, any transformation of the form $\alpha_i PP^{-1}\beta_i'$ can give an observationally equivalent cointegrating vector $P^{-1}\beta_i'$. To identify β_i we need r^2 just-identifying restrictions, r of which are provided by normalisation restrictions (choosing the dependent variable in the equation). Obtaining these identification restrictions is less of a problem, since there tends to be more agreement about the arbitrage, parity and solvency conditions that would arise from imposing a theoretically coherent long-run solution on the model. What is more controversial is the identification of the short-run dynamic parameters, A_{0i}. This requires m^2 extra restrictions, m of which will be provided by normalisation. These restrictions should be on A_{0i}, B_{0i} and Σ_i. Restrictions on the dynamic adjustment parameters, A_{1i}, B_{1i}, are much less likely to be credible (Sims, 1980), since any past variable that is used in forming expectations will implicitly appear in the relevant structural equation.

Unless Σ_i is restricted, the relation $\Omega_i = A_{0i}^{-1}\Sigma_i A_{0i}'^{-1}$ does not yield any restrictions on A_{0i}. The classic recursive structure assumed Σ_i diagonal and that, after suitable ordering, there was a causal chain that made A_{0i} triangular (zeros above the diagonal). Together with normalisation, these assumptions provided the m^2 restrictions. The recursive just-identifying assumptions are also the basis for the calculation of orthogonalised impulse response functions, which require an a priori causal ordering to be specified. This approach has been developed through structural VARs, which identify the model by other assumptions about the characteristics of unobserved shocks, not merely that they are orthogonal. It is not obvious that statements such as 'Demand and supply shocks are uncorrelated' or 'Demand shocks are transitory and supply shocks are permanent' should be regarded as more plausible than statements such as 'Current world output does not appear in the domestic money demand function', which previously provided the basis for identification. Central bankers need to be able to distinguish supply shocks from demand shocks, because the policy responses to the two types of shock are different. However, what we know about such shocks does not suggest that they have any particular statistical structure. Shocks caused by oil price movements, for instance, have both demand and supply effects, making them correlated. The interwar depression was almost certainly a demand shock, but it had very long-lasting effects. Natural disasters, such as hurricanes, are clearly supply shocks; but in industrialised countries they generally have transitory economic effects.

Short-run identification has been regarded as more difficult than long-run identification. The difficulty has been exaggerated, however, by the closed economy focus of US work with small models. For the rest of the world, it is natural to treat foreign variables as exogenous, and this can provide additional restrictions to identify A_{0i}. For most of the world the important shocks are observable and in effect exogenous: oil price fluctuations; terms of trade shocks; weather-related shocks, such as droughts; foreign financial crises; changes in world real interest rates; unusual events such as wars or German reunification; and so on. These can be proxied by foreign variables or exogenous domestic variables such as the weather or dummy variables. For small open economies, explicit quantification of the shocks and their impact on the economy seems a more effective route than speculating about the stochastic properties of unobservable demand and supply shocks.

In economic terms it is natural to consider short-run and long-run identification conditions separately, because the theory is rather different. The short-run theory relates to the behavioural rules of the agents, the standard equations of macroeconomics: IS curve, LM curve, Phillips curve and Taylor rule, for instance. The long-run theory relates to market-clearing and arbitrage conditions such as real interest rate and purchasing power parity. The standard equations used in any open economy macroeconomics textbook implicitly impose a large number of restrictions, both short run and long run. These standard equations provide not only just-identifying restrictions that enable the structural form to be estimated but also overidentifying restrictions, which can be tested. This is the framework that we shall use. An alternative framework is suggested by Wickens and Motto (2000). They achieve identification with the assumptions that the variables can be classified as endogenous or exogenous, that the system is complete (that is, that there are the same number of endogenous variables as cointegrating vectors) and that the cointegrating vectors are identified.

4.2.2 Economic structure

The system we have in mind is the set of standard equations, which tend to turn up in models of small open economies. Their theoretical genealogy and interpretation can be quite varied and they probably should not be treated as either structural or reduced-form equations. Let lower-case letters denote logarithms, superscript stars denote foreign variables, tildes denote 'natural' or target values for the variables, and superscript 'e' denote expected values for that period. The data are largely taken from the International Monetary Fund's (IMF) International Financial Statistics and are described in appendix 2 to this paper. Let y_t be the logarithm of real GDP in year t, p_t the logarithm of the domestic price level, p_t^* the logarithm of the foreign price, s_t the logarithm of the nominal exchange rate (domestic units per dollar, so an increase indicates a depreciation), $e_t = s_t - p_t + p_t^*$, the logarithm of the real exchange rate, m_t the logarithm of real money supply, R_t the nominal interest rate, g_t some measure of fiscal policy and b_t a measure of the balance of trade. We measure b_t by the logarithm of the export–import ratio, for reasons discussed in Boyd, Caporale and Smith (2000), but it could also be measured as the ratio of the balance of trade to GDP.

The equations are an LM equation

$$m_t = \beta_0 - \beta_1 R_t + \beta_2 y_t, \tag{4.1}$$

a Taylor-type rule (which could be extended to allow for possible exchange rate targeting or expected inflation targeting)

$$R_t = \Delta p_t + \gamma_0 + \gamma_1(y_t - \tilde{y}_t) + \gamma_2(\Delta p_t - \widetilde{\Delta p_t}), \tag{4.2}$$

an IS equation

$$y_t = \alpha_0 - \alpha_1 R_t + \alpha_2 g_t + \alpha_3 y_t^* + \alpha_4 e_t, \tag{4.3}$$

a purchasing power parity (PPP) adjustment equation

$$\Delta e_t = \eta(\tilde{e} - e_{t-1}), \tag{4.4}$$

a trade balance equation

$$b_t = \theta_0 - \theta_1(y_t - \tilde{y}_t) + \theta_2 e_t + \theta_3 y_t^*, \tag{4.5}$$

and a Phillips curve

$$\Delta p_t - \Delta p_t^e = \delta_0 + \delta_1(y_t - \tilde{y}_t). \tag{4.6}$$

For the developing economies that we are examining, we had difficulty finding good measures of money and interest rates, so our focus will be on estimating simplified versions of the last four equations. Omission of interest rates will involve a specification error to the extent that the interest rate should appear in the IS curve and may appear in the exchange rate equation, through an interest parity condition. Converting these general specifications into forms that can be estimated requires choosing measures for the unobservables $\tilde{y}_t$ and Δp_t^e, specifying dynamics and adopting some identifying restrictions. The Lucas critique might also lead us to be sceptical about the stability of the estimated parameters, particularly for the exchange rate equation because many of these countries had fixed exchange rates in the early part of the period. The econometric issues are discussed further in section 4.5. Although we are not concerned here with the theoretical status of these equations, it should be emphasised that the interpretation of the parameters depends on the theoretical derivation. For instance, a trade balance equation such as (4.5) can be derived from standard export and import demand equations, from the solution to an intertemporal optimisation model, or in other ways. Prasad (1999), for example, uses a similar empirical relationship within a quite different theoretical and methodological framework. Although the estimated equations would be identical, the interpretation of the parameters would differ, depending on whether they came from a trade model or an intertemporal optimisation model.

4.3   Average estimates

Suppose data are available for years $t = 1, 2, \ldots, T$ and countries $i = 1, 2, \ldots,$ N, where $T = 31$ and $N = 57$. Equations are estimated for each country, and the parameters of interest are the average value of the coefficients and the degree of dispersion across countries. One advantage of working with averages across countries (or pooled estimates) is that the danger of spurious regression through lack of cointegration is substantially reduced. Suppose the price differential is $I(1)$ and that changes in the price level are completely reflected in the spot exchange rate, so that $\beta_i = 1$ in

$$s_{it} = \alpha + \beta_i (p_t^* - p_{it}) + u_{it}.$$

However, if u_{it} is an $I(1)$ error, which may be plausible given the factors influencing foreign exchange markets, the real exchange rate will be non-stationary. In that case, one cannot get consistent estimates of β_i from a single time-series regression. This is because the noise – the covariance of the non-stationary regressor with the non-stationary error – swamps the signal, the value of β, even as the sample size goes to infinity. However using cross-sections (Pesaran and Smith, 1995) or pooled (Phillips and Moon, 1999; Kao, 1999) or averaged estimates across countries attenuates the noise and allows the estimation of a long-run effect. The usual estimates of the standard errors of the pooled estimates will, however, be wrong, so inference using them may be misleading.

Suppose a typical equation is

$$y_{it} = \alpha_i + \beta_i x_{it} + u_{it},$$

where the estimate of a coefficient for a particular country is $\widehat{\beta}_i$, the mean is

$$\overline{\beta} = \sum_{i=1}^{N} \widehat{\beta}_i / N,$$

with variance

$$s(\widehat{\beta}_i)^2 = \sum_{i=1}^{N}(\widehat{\beta}_i - \overline{\beta})^2/(N - 1),$$

and the variance of the estimate of the mean $\overline{\beta}$ is

$$s(\overline{\beta})^2 = s(\widehat{\beta}_i)^2/N.$$

We shall use both the unweighted mean, $\overline{\beta}$, sometimes called the mean group estimator, and the Swamy (1970) random coefficient model estimate of the mean, denoted $\widetilde{\beta}$ with standard error of the mean $s(\widetilde{\beta})$. This estimates $\widehat{\beta}_i$ for each of the countries and then constructs a variance-weighted average of $\widehat{\beta}_i$. The estimator is described in appendix 1. For comparison, we also sometimes present results for the pooled fixed-effect estimator, which imposes equality of slopes but lets the intercepts differ across countries. This is obtained by OLS on

$$y_{it} = \alpha_i + \beta x_{it} + u_{it},$$

giving $\widehat{\beta}^{FE}$. In dynamic models with a lagged dependent variable, the fixed-effect estimator is likely to show the heterogeneity bias discussed in Pesaran and Smith (1995), which biases the coefficient of the lagged dependent variable upwards, in the direction opposite to the traditional lagged dependent variable initial condition bias. The estimated standard errors of the fixed-effect estimator are also likely to be wrong. The fixed-effect estimator can also be interpreted as a weighted average of the OLS estimates, with different weights from the Swamy estimator. It can also allow for time effects, a completely flexible trend common to all groups,

$$y_{it} = \alpha_t + \beta x_{it} + u_{it},$$

which can be obtained by using OLS on

$$y_{it} - \overline{y}_t = \beta(x_{it} - \overline{x}_t) + u_{it}.$$

When the slope parameters are not constrained to be the same, this estimator cannot be implemented, but similar effects can be achieved using deviation from year mean data or, as is done in some cases below, including averages of the variables, $\overline{y}_t$ and $\overline{x}_t$ as additional explanatory variables.

The Swamy estimates of the means of the coefficients (standard errors of the means in parentheses) for a general specification of the purchasing power parity adjustment equation are

$$\Delta s_t = 0.683 + 0.967\Delta p_t - 2.428\Delta p_t^* - 0.403 s_{t-1} - 0.269 p_{t-1}^*$$
$$\quad\quad (0.439)\quad (0.128)\quad\quad (0.418)\quad\quad\quad (0.042)\quad\quad\quad (0.077)$$

$$+ 0.361 p_{t-1} - 0.191\Delta p_{t-1} + 0.142\Delta s_{t-1} + 0.369\Delta p_{t-1}^*.$$
$$\quad (0.061)\quad\quad (0.101)\quad\quad\quad (0.056)\quad\quad\quad (0.339)$$

All the variables except Δp_{t-1}^* and Δp_{t-1} are significant. The two long-run PPP restrictions have a joint p value of 3.7%, so they would be accepted at the 1% though not at the 5% level. The coefficient of Δp_t is not significantly different from unity. The coefficient of Δp_t^* is significantly less than -1, but the measure used may not be a very good proxy for many of these countries. The coefficient of s_{t-1} indicates rather rapid adjustment to fundamentals. These results are quite close to those reported in Boyd and Smith (1999) for a smaller sample of developing countries.

Imposing the symmetry restriction by defining $d_t = p_t - p_t^*$, the Swamy estimates are

$$\Delta s_t = 0.623 + 0.981\Delta d_t - 0.219 s_{t-1} + 0.238 d_{t-1} + 0.191\Delta s_{t-1} - 0.245\Delta d_{t-1}.$$
$$\quad\quad (0.179)\quad (0.097)\quad\quad (0.032)\quad\quad (0.042)\quad\quad (0.046)\quad\quad (0.075)$$

Again this largely confirms purchasing power parity. The estimates of the same equation obtained using the pooled fixed-effect estimator are:

$$\Delta s_t = \alpha_i + 1.021\Delta d_t - 0.127 s_{t-1} + 0.130 d_{t-1} + 0.236\Delta s_{t-1} - 0.248\Delta d_{t-1}.$$
$$\quad\quad\quad (0.014)\quad\quad (0.012)\quad\quad (0.013)\quad\quad (0.024)\quad\quad (0.029)$$

The estimate of the long-run coefficient is very similar, but the measured speed of adjustment is much slower (because of the bias of the fixed-effect estimator) and the measured standard errors are much smaller. The Swamy estimates of the most restricted version, which we shall use in simulations and report for each country, are

$$\Delta s_t = 0.432 + 0.951\Delta d_t - 0.155 e_{t-1} + 0.155\Delta e_{t-1}.$$
$$\quad\quad (0.0121)\quad (0.075)\quad\quad (0.022)\quad\quad (0.031)$$

This is equivalent to a model in which the real exchange rate two years ago causes adjustment.

Whereas the specification for the PPP equation is very straightforward, the specification for the trade balance equation and the Phillips curve are not. The major difficulty is to provide an estimate of the natural rate of output. Demand shocks to output worsen the trade balance and increase inflation; supply shocks to output improve the trade balance and reduce inflation. Decomposing observed output into demand and supply components is not straightforward, particularly for developing countries suffering large demand (for example, policy induced) and supply (for example, terms of trade) shocks that cannot be described by any simple stochastic process and are unlikely to be orthogonal. Given the size and nature of these shocks, simple filters of output that try to extract a trend may not work as well as they do in industrial countries.

The Swamy estimates for the most plausible trade balance equation that we could obtain are

$$b_t = -0.344 + 1.200\Delta\bar{y}_t - 0.381\Delta y_{t-1} + 0.097e_t + 0.560b_{t-1},$$
$$\quad (0.236) \quad (0.416) \quad\quad (0.102) \quad\quad (0.023) \quad (0.031)$$

where $\bar{y}_t$ is the unweighted average of y_{it}, log GDP, for the 57 countries in the sample. This average is endogenous to some extent, but the effect is likely to be small. The fixed-effect estimates of the long-run coefficients were very similiar, though the speed of adjustment was substantially slower with the coefficient of b_{t-1} being 0.69 (0.018). A high domestic growth rate last period worsens the balance of payments; world growth and a depreciation of the real exchange rate, an increase in e_t, improve the balance of payments.

In the case of the Phillips curve, no plausible equation that gave positive excess demand effects on inflation could be found and a simple inflation persistence equation was estimated instead:

$$\Delta p_t = 0.063 + 0.602\Delta p_{t-1} - 0.067\Delta p_{t-2}.$$
$$\quad (0.008) \quad (0.039) \quad\quad (0.032)$$

The IS curve is a very simple trend-stationary model in which a real depreciation (increase in e_t) raises output:

$$\Delta y_t = 3.370 + 0.032e_{t-1} - 0.134y_{t-1} + 0.003t.$$
$$\quad (0.642) \quad (0.015) \quad\quad (0.023) \quad (0.001)$$

Lee, Pesaran and Smith (1997) discuss the issues in assuming a trend-stationary output process in the context of a Solow model of growth. Although this average relationship looks sensible, it will become clear in the next section that for many of these countries a linear trend is not a good description of the evolution of output over this period.

This small ad hoc system, which is intended only to be illustrative, is then

$$\Delta p_t = a_0 + a_1\Delta p_{t-1} + a_1\Delta p_{t-2} + \varepsilon_{1t} \tag{A}$$

$$\Delta s_t = b_0 + b_1(\Delta p_t - \Delta p_t^*) + b_2\Delta e_{t-1} + b_3 e_{t-1} + \varepsilon_{2t} \tag{B}$$

$$\Delta y_t = c_0 + c_1 e_{t-1} + c_2 y_{t-1} + c_3 t + \varepsilon_{3t} \tag{C}$$

$$b_t = d_0 + d_1 e_t + d_2\Delta\bar{y}_t + d_3\Delta y_{t-1} + d_4 b_{t-1} + \varepsilon_{4t}. \tag{D}$$

Were we to assume that the covariance matrix of the ε_{jt} is diagonal (though there is no reason to believe this in general), then the system is recursive and efficiently estimated by least squares, as has been done above. Even without the diagonal covariance matrix assumption, the system is overidentified and could be consistently estimated by two-stage least squares. In principle, it is relatively straightforward to test whether this small system encompasses the unrestricted VAR. In practice, given the limited degrees of freedom in the unrestricted VAR, the asymptotic tests may not be very reliable.

The average coefficients are all significant and of the right sign, though that is largely the product of specification search: variables that were insignificant or of the wrong sign were excluded. The estimated coefficients produce system responses that are not implausible. An inflationary shock in year 0 is largely, though not completely, reflected in the nominal exchange rate in that year, so the real exchange rate appreciates and continues appreciating until year 2, when it reaches a maximum, then slowly returns to base. Inflation fairly quickly returns to zero, though the price level is permanently higher. The real exchange rate appreciation causes the trade balance to deteriorate, again at its worst in year 2, then slowly return to base. The real appreciation also causes output to fall, with a slow return to trend because the root is quite close to unity.

4.4   Dispersion

The results given above represent an average of the coefficients estimated for each of the 57 countries. We now want to consider the degree of dispersion across countries. The parameter estimates for each country for the four equations are given in appendix 3 as tables 4A.1 to 4A.4. Each table provides the estimate of the parameter $\widehat{\beta}_i$ for a particular coefficient (for example, $a1$) and its standard error (for example, $se(a1)$) for all countries and some regional groupings. Each table also gives two measures of how far from the mean the country-specific estimate is. The first is the number of standard deviations from the mean (for example, $Z(a1)$) where

$$Z(\beta_i) = \frac{\widehat{\beta}_i - \overline{\beta}}{s(\widehat{\beta}_i)}$$

$$\overline{\beta} = \sum_{i=1}^{N} \widehat{\beta}_i / N$$

$$s(\widehat{\beta}_i)^2 = \sum_{i=1}^{N} (\widehat{\beta}_i - \overline{\beta})^2 / (N - 1),$$

and the second is the number of standard errors from the mean,

$$t(\beta_i) = \frac{\widehat{\beta}_i - \overline{\beta}}{se(\widehat{\beta}_i)}.$$

$Z(\beta_i)$ measures whether the estimate is an outlier in the distribution of all the $\widehat{\beta}_i$; $t(\beta_i)$ measures whether the estimate is significantly different from the mean, using the standard error of that particular country's estimate. Note that $t(\beta)$ is not a measure of whether the coefficient is significantly different from zero. Outliers are shown in bold if either they are more than one standard deviation from the mean (since the standard deviations are so large, this indicates an economically significant divergence) or the coefficient is two standard errors from the mean.

In the inflation persistence equation (table 4A.1), the coefficient on the first lag of inflation, $a1$, has a mean of 0.57, a standard deviation of 0.30 and a range from -0.07 to 1.42. Argentina, at 0.99, is more than one standard deviation from the mean and significantly different from the mean. The average is rather higher in Latin America and lower in Africa, and the dispersion within the three regional groups is rather lower than in the sample as a whole.

In the exchange rate equation (table 4A.2), the coefficient of current inflation, $b1$, has a mean of 1.00, a standard deviation of 0.61 and a range from -0.58 to 2.35. There are large differences between the regions in the average values. In Latin America and Africa the short-run impact of inflation on the exchange rate is greater than unity; in the Middle East and Asia it is rather small. The coefficient of the lagged real exchange rate, $b2$, measures the speed of adjustment and has a mean of 0.16, with adjustment being slower in Latin America.

In the output equation (table 4A.3), the coefficient of the trend, $c3$, is negative for 16 countries, though in six of these cases this is counterbalanced by a positive value of $c2$, the coefficient of the lagged dependent variable, indicating explosive behaviour.

In the balance of payments equation (table 4A.4), the exchange rate effect, $d1$, has the wrong sign in 14 of the 57 countries, but in each of the three regions the Marshall Lerner condition seems to hold on average. It is clear that, although the average results look plausible, there is massive and implausible variation in the coefficients across countries.

To determine how sensitive the dispersion is to specification, we will investigate alternative versions of the purchasing power parity equation in some detail. This is a natural choice because the average fits the theory so closely. First, we consider a simple levels equation, with $d_{it} = p_{it} - p_t^*$:

$$s_{it} = \alpha_i + \beta_i d_{it} + u_{it}.$$

The estimates (with standard errors) are $\bar{\beta} = 1.13\,(0.069)$, $\tilde{\beta} = 1.13\,(0.068)$, and $\widehat{\beta}^{\mathrm{FE}} = 1.02\,(0.003)$. The weighted and unweighted means are identical and both rather higher than the fixed-effect estimator. As is well known, on average there is very strong evidence for approximate purchasing power parity. However, the dispersion of estimates is very large: $s(\widehat{\beta}_i) = 0.5213$. The range for $\widehat{\beta}_i$ is from -0.40 to $+2.47$.

Second, we consider a first-difference regression

$$\Delta s_{it} = \alpha_i + \beta_i \Delta d_{it} + u_{it}.$$

The estimates are $\bar{\beta} = 0.832$ (0.058), $\tilde{\beta} = 0.839$ (0.066), and $\widehat{\beta}^{\mathrm{FE}} = 0.998$ (0.0028). Again, although supportive of PPP, the dispersion is only slightly smaller than the levels estimate: $s(\widehat{\beta}_i) = 0.439$ with a range from -0.512 to 1.368, with 10 estimates below 0.500. The tails in the distributions of the level and first-difference estimators are not being caused by the same countries and the correlation between the level and first-difference estimates is only 0.35. Whereas in levels the average estimates were greater than the fixed-effect estimator, in the first differences they are less than the fixed-effect estimator. In both cases the fixed-effect estimate is very close to unity.

Third, consider an error correction model that allows for both short-run and long-run responses

$$\Delta s_{it} = \alpha_i + \beta_i \Delta d_{it} + \lambda_i (s_{i,t-1} - \theta_i d_{i,t-1}) + u_{it}.$$

The estimates for the long-run parameter are $\bar{\theta} = 0.986$ (0.277), $\tilde{\theta} = 1.028$ (0.099) and $\widehat{\theta}^{\mathrm{FE}} = 0.984$ (0.015). The dispersion is much larger: $s(\widehat{\theta}_i) = 2.095$ with a range from -9.02 to 8.20. Although most estimates are clustered around unity, the large tails arise from cases where the estimated coefficient of the lagged dependent variable λ is close to zero (the small sample distribution of $\widehat{\theta}_i$ does not have any moments). The short-run coefficients and their dispersion are rather similar to the previous case, with $\bar{\beta} = 0.943$ and $s(\widehat{\beta}_i) = 0.598$; for the adjustment parameter, $\bar{\lambda} = -0.25$ and $s(\widehat{\lambda}_i) = 0.177$. Using the Johansen estimator to measure the long-run coefficient produced even larger dispersion.

When $\Delta s_{i,t-1}$ and $\Delta d_{i,t-1}$ are added, $\bar{\theta} = 1.11$ and the dispersion is slightly smaller at $s(\widehat{\theta}_i) = 1.22$, with a range from -2.21 to 7.93. To investigate whether using just those estimates with a significant long-run effect would reduce the problem, we calculated the F-statistic for the hypothesis that the coefficients of s_{t-1} and d_{t-1} were jointly zero. This is equivalent to the hypothesis that there is no cointegration. Then only those long-run coefficients that were significantly different from zero at some level of significance were included in the sample. Table 4.1 gives the values of the F-statistic used, the number of estimates

Table 4.1 *The effect of removing*
insignificant estimates

F	N	$\bar{\theta}$	$s(\widehat{\theta}_i)$	$\widehat{\theta}_{min}$	$\widehat{\theta}_{max}$
0.0	57	1.110	1.220	−2.21	7.93
1.0	46	1.001	0.587	−0.95	2.01
2.0	34	1.000	0.607	−0.95	2.01
3.0	19	1.030	0.629	−0.95	1.94
3.5	11	0.910	0.639	−0.95	1.39
4.0	9	1.103	0.170	0.84	1.39

remaining in the sample (N), the average long-run coefficient for those remaining ($\bar{\theta}$), the standard deviation ($s(\widehat{\theta}_i)$) and the range for those remaining (θ_{min}, θ_{max}). If the variables were $I(0)$, the 5% critical value would be 2.45; if they were $I(1)$, the critical value would be 3.34 (Pesaran, Shin and R. J. Smith, 1999).

As is well known from the literature, most countries do not show strong evidence for cointegration of the nominal rate and price differentials, and our results confirm that finding. What is interesting is that, until over 80% of the sample has been removed, the dispersion is not substantially reduced. Furthermore, over the range from $F = 1.0$ to $F = 3.5$, eliminating insignificant cases increases the dispersion rather than reduces it. Some of the outliers are quite significant; the low estimate of −0.95 is not deleted until the critical value of F is greater than 3.5.

The dispersion is very similar in the other equations. For instance, in the trade balance equation, the unweighted mean of the coefficients of the real exchange rate is 0.128 (rather larger than the weighted mean above), with standard deviation 0.222 and range −0.540 to 0.675. The coefficient of the lagged trade balance has a mean of 0.46 (slightly lower than the weighted estimate), a standard deviation of 0.24 and a range from −0.030 to 1.010.

Not only are the estimates widely dispersed, they do not seem to be structurally stable. Given the relatively small sample it is difficult to conduct a sophisticated structural stability analysis. If one takes the first-difference PPP equation (change in log spot on a constant and change in log price differential), the correlation between the estimates in the first and second half of the sample period is almost exactly zero. If one estimates inflation persistence, by a regression of inflation on a constant and lagged inflation, the correlation between the estimates in the first and second half of the sample period is 0.36. However, the fixed-effect estimates are rather stable between the first and second periods, which suggests that the instability is a country-specific rather than a generic problem. The only major change between periods when the fixed-effect estimator was estimated for both sub-periods was that the average growth measure in the trade balance equation went from being significantly positive over 1969–82 to insignificantly negative over 1983–96. Stable pooled estimates seem to be consistent with very unstable country estimates.

4.5 Explanations

Having established that the dispersion across countries is large, in this section we consider various explanations.

First, the dispersion reflects real differences between countries. Although the countries are different, their differences cannot be large enough to explain the implausible range of the estimates. Whatever economic theory one adopts, the prior plausibility of the extreme estimates must be very close to zero.

Secondly, the dispersion is the product of poor data. The data certainly have severe limitations, but a similar degree of dispersion has been found on much better data. For instance, after estimating gasoline demand functions for 18 OECD countries over the period 1960–90, Baltagi and Griffin (1997, p. 310) comment: 'These estimates reveal the wide variability of individual country estimates. . . . Such variation is particularly distressing when it is recognised that all 18 countries are OECD countries and should share considerable commonalities.' Later (p. 313) the authors comment that the range of the estimates suggests that the individual country estimates are highly unstable and unreliable.

Thirdly, the dispersion is the result of simultaneity bias. Again, the covariances would have to be economically implausible to give, for instance, negative effects of inflation on the exchange rate. The most serious simultaneity bias is likely to be endogenous policy, but the policy responses would have to be quite perverse to create such large effects. Simultaneity bias can be interpreted as the asymptotic difference between the OLS estimates and a consistent estimate of the paramenter of interest, obtained by instrumental variables for instance. This requires that the parameter of interest is identified. If this is not the case and the OLS estimates are measuring a mixture of structural parameters, our usual prior expectations for likely values of the parameters would not be relevant.

Fourthly, the dispersion is the result of spurious regression. The variables such as the nominal spot rate and the price differential are not cointegrated, the error is $I(1)$ and the coefficient estimate converges even asymptotically to a non-degenerate random variable, accounting for the dispersion. This may be the case, but it seems unlikely to be the main explanation because the dispersion in the estimate of the coefficients in the first-difference PPP regressions is almost as large as in the levels regression. The first-difference regression would be appropriate if the variables were $I(1)$ and not cointegrated or if they were $I(2)$ and cointegrated to $I(1)$. Also, deleting insignificant cases where there was less evidence for a long-run relation had little effect on the dispersion.

A fifth and more likely explanation is that country-specific idiosyncratic shocks and measurement errors associated with unobservables such as expected inflation and the natural rate of output act like omitted variables correlated with the regressors. This is closely related to lack of identification, discussed above, if the identifying shift variables are omitted. One could tell a different story for each country, which would involve such factors as the decline of staple industries, discovery of raw materials, large terms-of-trade shocks, wars, policy mistakes, stabilisation plans, etc. Suppose we wrap all these omitted variables up in a single variable w_{it}, which measures their impact on the dependent variable, and the model is

$$y_{it} = \beta_i' x_{it} + w_{it} + u_{it}$$

for sample $t = 1, 2, \ldots, T$, where u_{it} is uncorrelated with the included regressors x_{it}. However, the w_{it} are correlated, in this particular sample, with the regressors:

$$w_{it} = b_{iT}' x_{it} + v_{it},$$

giving sample estimates in the regression excluding w_{it} of

$$\widehat{\beta}_{iT} = \beta_i' + b_{iT}'.$$

The specification error in the estimate, b_{iT}', could be large and significant if the w_{it} have a big effect on y_{it} and are highly correlated with x_{it}. If the w_{it} are structural factors, operating in all time periods and countries, this would cause a systematic bias in the average estimate of β. If they are not structural, but just happen to be correlated in a particular sample, then $E(b_{iT}) = 0$, and these biases would cancel out when averaged across countries or longer time periods. Such correlated shocks will cause structural instability (because b_{iT} is not constant over time) and heterogeneity (because b_{iT} is not constant over countries). Both structural instability and heterogeneity seem characteristic of much economic data, including this set. In addition it seems that the b_{iT} tend to be associated with large shocks, given the range of the estimates.

One statistical solution may be robust estimators that reduce the effect of outliers. A very simple version involves using a second-stage regression, weighting the observations inversely to the square of the residuals from a first-stage regression. This technique does reduce the dispersion by about 15%, but still leaves a high degree of dispersion, perhaps because influential observations may not be associated with large residuals. A second statistical solution may be shrinkage estimators, using as the estimate for a country a weighted combination of the overall average and the country-specific estimate. This solution is similar to a Bayesian posterior estimate using the average as an empirical prior. In the case of the Swamy estimator, this technique reduces the dispersion by between 25% and 50% for the PPP equation. Although this change is quite substantial, the range also remains quite large, from −0.21 to 1.97 for the coefficient of current inflation in the PPP equation. This reflects the fact that the differences from the mean were often very significant, which leads to the shrinkage estimator giving greater weight to the country-specific estimate than might be ideal. Conventional standard errors are uninformative about this sort of specification error because a badly biased estimate can look very precisely estimated. The problem may be reduced by using explicitly Bayesian estimators, which put more weight on reasonable economic prior beliefs about the likely dispersion. Theorists tend to do this implicitly, by ignoring the data and calibrating their models a priori.

4.6   Conclusions

The evidence in this paper suggests that, in order to get sensible estimates of the transmission mechanism for a particular country, it is necessary to have reasonable measures for the unobservables, such as the natural rate and expected inflation, as well as reasonable proxies for the variety of idiosyncratic factors that may be important to particular countries and correlated with the standard regressors. This conclusion suggests that it is unlikely that we can write a clear protocol for estimating a useful policy model of the monetary transmission process. Each country is likely to be different, not merely in the values of parameters but in the variables that need to be included. Equations that work in American or British models may not work elsewhere. The dispersion of estimates in standard equations is very large. This is not a particularly novel observation, but it bears repetition. Mechanical application of standard equations can give very implausible estimates for many cases. Looking at a particular country, it is often fairly obvious what sort of idiosyncratic factors might be allowed for (for example, removal of capital controls, terms-of-trade shocks, particular policies, natural resource discoveries, etc.) and reasonable proxies might be constructed. It is noticeable that in cases where there do appear to be common structures across countries, for example the OECD estimates of Phillips curves in Turner and Seghezza (1999), a large amount of work has been done on the data, in particular on constructing measures of the unobservables, such as the natural rate of output, and on including country-specific dummies. These are examples of the country-specific 'tender loving care' discussed in the introduction that was so typical of traditional policy models. Such 'tender loving care' was often disparaged as data mining or specification searching to get the right answer, but in many cases it involved the careful quantification of local knowledge about the particular features of the economy concerned in the light of economic theory relevant to that particular economy. Of course, acquiring such local knowledge can be expensive. But, if this explanation is true, the solution to the dispersion is to supplement improved econometric methods and economic theory with better quantification of local knowledge.

Appendix 1: the Swamy random coefficient model estimator

Suppose y_i is a $T \times 1$ vector, X_i is a $T \times K$ matrix of regressors, $u_i \sim IN(0, \sigma^2 I)$, and the model is

$$y_i = X_i \beta_i + u_i.$$

It is assumed that the β_i are randomly distributed with $\beta_i = \beta + \eta_i$, $E(\eta_i) = 0$, and $E(\eta_i \eta_j') = \Gamma$, if $i = j$, $E(\eta_i \eta_j') = 0$, otherwise. Swamy (1970) suggests first estimating each equation by OLS giving estimates $\widehat{\beta}i = (X_i' X_i)^{-1} X_i y_i$; $\widehat{u}_i = y_i - X_i \widehat{\beta}_i$; $s^2 = \widehat{u}_i' \widehat{u}_i / (T - K)$, and $V(\widehat{\beta}_i) = s^2 (X_i' X_i)^{-1}$. Define the unweighted mean of the $\widehat{\beta}_i$ as $\overline{\beta} = \sum_i \widehat{\beta}_i / N$, then the variance–covariance matrix of the β_i can be estimated as

$$\widehat{\Gamma} = \sum_{i=1}^{N} (\widehat{\beta}_i - \overline{\beta})(\widehat{\beta}_i - \overline{\beta})' / (N - 1) - \sum_{i=1}^{N} V(\widehat{\beta}_i) / N.$$

If this estimator is not positive definite (which it usually is not), the last term is set to zero. The Swamy estimator of the mean is

$$\widetilde{\beta} = \sum_{i=1}^{N} W_i \widehat{\beta}_i$$

$$W_i = \left\{ \sum [\widehat{\Gamma} + V(\widehat{\beta}_i)]^{-1} \right\}^{-1} [\widehat{\Gamma} + V(\widehat{\beta}_i)]^{-1}$$

$$V(\widetilde{\beta}) = \left\{ \sum [\widehat{\Gamma} + V(\widehat{\beta}_i)]^{-1} \right\}^{-1}$$

The predictions of the individual coefficients can be improved by shrinking the OLS estimates towards the overall estimate:

$$\widetilde{\beta}_i = Q\widetilde{\beta} + (I - Q)\widehat{\beta}_i$$

$$Q = [\widehat{\Gamma}^{-1} + V(\widehat{\beta}_i)^{-1}]^{-1} \widehat{\Gamma}^{-1}.$$

The estimates used in this paper were produced by Limdep. The Swamy estimator is one of a class of empirical Bayes estimators, reviews of which can be found in Hsiao, Pesaran and Tahmiscioglu (1999).

Appendix 2: data

The data cover 1966–96 for the 57 countries listed in tables 4A.1–4A.4. We sought to create a balanced panel with the maximum number of countries, using data from the IMF and the International Bank for Reconstruction and Development.

The nominal exchange rate, S (line rf), was obtained from the International Financial Statistics CD, IFS_1298.cd (IMF, 1998). Two observations were missing: Congo Democratic Republic for 1996, and Rwanda for 1994. The former was interpolated with a value based on the previous incremental change, and the latter with an average value.

The consumer price index data, P (line 64), for most of the countries came from IFS_1298.cd (IMF, 1998), with the following exceptions:

Brazil consumer price data source for 1966–92 (lines 64a, 64b, 64c) was the IFS Yearbooks (IFSY) 1993 and spliced onto the 1993–96 data from (line 64) IFSY 1999 (IMF, 1993, 1999).

Algerian data (line 64) came from the IFSY 1993 and 1999.

Central African Republic 1966–80 CPI B (line 64a) was spliced onto CPI A, 1981–96 (line 64) (IFSY 1993, 1999).

Congo Democratic Republic consumer price data source was the World Development Indicators (WDI) 1998_CD (IBRD, 1998). The 1995 and 1996 values were estimated to fill in the series.

Mauritania 1966–85 CPI B (line 64a) was spliced onto CPI A, 1986–96 (line 64) (IFSY 1993, 1999).

Tunisia 1966–92 (line 64) was spliced onto 1981–96 (line 64) (IFSY 1993, 1999).

Zambia 1966–91 (line 64) was spliced onto 1992–96 (line 64) (IFSY 1993, 1999).

The foreign price index P^* is the Industrial Countries Price Index obtained from IFS_1298.cd.

In order to maximise the number of real GDP series this data set was put together from three sources: IFS_0398.cd, IFS_1298.cd and WDI 1998_CD. Four missing observations were estimated: Bolivia 1996, Gambia 1996 and Israel 1966 and 1967. We used trend regression to predict the Israeli values.

The exports and imports series were constructed from WDI 1998_CD. Countries 1–20 used line codes $XGSN\$$ and $MGSN\$$; countries 21–57 used $XGSNL$ and $MGSNL$.

The data are available from the authors in Excel format.

Appendix 3: tables of results

Table 4A.1 *Inflation persistence equation*

Country	a0	se(a0)	a1	se(a1)	a2	se(a2)	Z(a1)[a]	t(a1)[b]	Z(a2)[c]	t(a2)[d]
1 Argentina	0.46	0.18	0.99	0.18	-0.48	0.18	**1.4**	**2.4**	**-1.5**	**-2.1**
2 Bolivia	0.24	0.17	0.78	0.19	-0.25	0.19	0.7	1.1	-0.6	-0.8
3 Brazil	0.25	0.19	0.83	0.20	-0.07	0.20	0.8	1.3	0.1	0.2
4 Chile	0.10	0.05	1.42	0.15	-0.66	0.15	**2.8**	**5.6**	**-2.2**	**-3.7**
5 Colombia	0.07	0.03	0.39	0.18	0.29	0.17	-0.6	-1.0	**1.6**	**2.4**
6 Costa Rica	0.09	0.03	0.71	0.19	-0.31	0.19	0.5	0.7	-0.8	-1.1
7 Dominican Republic	0.07	0.03	0.58	0.20	-0.09	0.20	0.0	0.0	0.1	0.1
8 Ecuador	0.05	0.03	0.84	0.20	-0.06	0.19	0.9	1.3	0.1	0.1
9 El Salvador	0.04	0.02	0.73	0.20	-0.04	0.19	0.5	0.8	0.2	0.2
10 Guatemala	0.07	0.02	0.59	0.19	-0.23	0.19	0.0	0.1	0.3	0.3
11 Haiti	0.04	0.02	0.55	0.20	0.09	0.20	-0.1	-0.1	-0.5	-0.6
12 Honduras	0.04	0.02	0.78	0.20	-0.20	0.22	0.7	1.1	-0.4	-0.5
13 Mexico	0.08	0.04	0.89	0.20	-0.17	0.19	**1.0**	1.6	-0.3	-0.4
14 Paraguay	0.06	0.02	0.72	0.20	-0.12	0.19	0.5	0.8	-0.1	-0.1
15 Peru	0.26	0.14	1.13	0.17	-0.49	0.17	**1.9**	**3.2**	**-1.6**	**-2.2**
16 Uruguay	0.34	0.09	0.59	0.18	-0.35	0.18	0.0	0.1	-1.0	-1.4
17 Venezuela	0.02	0.03	0.70	0.21	0.33	0.22	0.4	0.6	**1.7**	**1.9**
18 Jamaica	0.11	0.04	0.56	0.20	-0.13	0.19	0.0	-0.1	-0.1	-0.1
19 Trinidad & Tobago	0.04	0.02	0.79	0.20	-0.18	0.19	0.7	1.1	-0.3	-0.4
20 Israel	0.10	0.06	1.10	0.19	-0.37	0.18	**1.8**	**2.8**	-1.1	-1.4
21 Saudi Arabia	0.01	0.01	1.13	0.18	-0.43	0.18	**1.9**	**3.1**	-1.3	-1.8
22 Egypt, Arab Rep.	0.04	0.01	0.22	0.17	0.51	0.16	**-1.2**	**-2.1**	**2.5**	**3.7**

Table 4A.1 (cont.)

Country	a0	se(a0)	a1	se(a1)	a2	se(a2)	$Z(a1)^a$	$t(a1)^b$	$Z(a2)^c$	$t(a2)^d$
23 Myanmar	0.04	0.02	0.69	0.20	0.03	0.20	0.4	0.6	0.6	0.7
24 India	0.08	0.02	0.35	0.18	-0.40	0.18	-0.7	-1.2	**-1.2**	-1.7
25 Indonesia	0.10	0.02	0.20	0.11	-0.08	0.09	**-1.2**	**-3.4**	0.1	0.3
26 Korea, Republic of	0.04	0.02	0.79	0.20	-0.23	0.20	0.7	1.1	-0.5	-0.6
27 Malaysia	0.03	0.01	0.66	0.18	-0.31	0.18	0.3	0.5	-0.8	-1.1
28 Nepal	0.10	0.02	0.01	0.19	-0.18	0.17	**-1.9**	**-3.0**	-0.3	-0.4
29 Pakistan	0.05	0.02	0.78	0.18	-0.32	0.18	0.7	1.2	-0.9	-1.2
30 Philippines	0.14	0.03	0.23	0.18	-0.35	0.18	**-1.1**	-1.9	**-1.0**	-1.4
31 Singapore	0.03	0.01	0.71	0.17	-0.50	0.17	0.5	0.8	**-1.6**	**-2.3**
32 Thailand	0.04	0.01	0.72	0.19	-0.34	0.19	0.5	0.8	-1.0	-1.3
33 Algeria	0.03	0.02	0.79	0.21	0.03	0.23	0.7	1.1	0.6	0.6
34 Cameroon	0.06	0.02	0.30	0.20	-0.02	0.20	-0.9	-1.4	0.3	0.4
35 Central African Rep.	0.04	0.02	0.41	0.20	-0.15	0.21	-0.6	-0.8	-0.2	-0.2
36 Congo, Republic of	0.07	0.02	0.23	0.20	-0.20	0.21	**-1.2**	-1.7	-0.4	-0.5
37 Congo, Dem. Rep.	0.31	0.26	0.52	0.20	0.14	0.20	-0.2	-0.3	1.0	1.2
38 Gabon	0.06	0.02	0.27	0.20	-0.12	0.20	**-1.0**	-1.5	-0.1	-0.1
39 Gambia, The	0.05	0.03	0.46	0.20	0.09	0.20	-0.4	-0.5	0.8	1.0
40 Ghana	0.15	0.07	0.23	0.19	0.33	0.18	**-1.2**	-1.8	**1.8**	**2.4**
41 Côte d'Ivoire	0.05	0.02	0.43	0.21	-0.03	0.21	-0.5	-0.7	0.3	0.3
42 Kenya	0.06	0.02	0.72	0.19	-0.23	0.19	0.5	0.8	-0.5	-0.6
43 Madagascar	0.07	0.03	0.65	0.21	-0.19	0.24	0.3	0.4	-0.3	-0.3
44 Mauritania	0.08	0.02	0.22	0.20	-0.15	0.19	**-1.2**	-1.8	-0.2	-0.2
45 Mauritius	0.06	0.02	0.50	0.20	-0.12	0.20	-0.2	-0.4	0.0	-0.1

46 Morocco	0.03	0.01	0.30	0.20	0.21	0.18	-0.9	-1.4	**1.3**	1.7
47 Niger	0.04	0.02	0.41	0.20	-0.03	0.20	-0.6	-0.8	0.3	0.4
48 Nigeria	0.13	0.04	0.65	0.20	-0.29	0.21	0.2	0.4	-0.7	-0.9
49 Rwanda	0.06	0.02	0.66	0.20	-0.28	0.22	0.3	0.4	-0.7	-0.8
50 Senegal	0.05	0.02	0.20	0.20	0.09	0.20	**-1.3**	-1.9	0.8	1.0
51 Sierra Leone	0.08	0.06	0.55	0.20	0.19	0.19	-0.1	-0.1	**1.2**	1.5
52 Swaziland	0.06	0.02	0.34	0.19	0.19	0.18	-0.8	-1.2	**1.2**	1.6
53 Togo	0.04	0.02	0.31	0.20	0.11	0.20	-0.9	-1.3	0.9	1.1
54 Tunisia	0.02	0.01	0.20	0.17	0.50	0.17	**-1.3**	-2.2	**2.4**	**3.6**
55 Burkina Faso	0.05	0.02	-0.07	0.19	0.24	0.19	**-2.2**	**-3.4**	**1.4**	1.8
56 Zambia	0.06	0.05	0.94	0.20	-0.12	0.20	**1.2**	1.8	-0.1	-0.1
57 Papua New Guinea	0.05	0.02	0.31	0.20	-0.07	0.22	-0.9	-1.3	0.1	0.1
Mean coefficient			**0.57**		-0.10					
s.d. of mean coefficient			**0.30**		0.25					
Latin America & Caribbean (countries 1–19)	Mean		0.77		-0.16					
	s.d.		0.23		0.25					
Middle East & Asia (countries 20–32)	Mean		0.59		-0.23					
	s.d.		0.35		0.26					
Africa & Papua New Guinea (countries 33–57)	Mean		0.42		0.01					
	s.d.		0.23		0.20					

Notes: **Bold** figures indicate coefficients are outliers. Values of 1.0 that are not bold were less than 1.0 before rounding.

[a] $(Z > 1) = 30\%$.
[b] $(t > 2) = 18\%$.
[c] $(Z > 1) = 30\%$.
[d] $(t > 2) = 14\%$.

Table 4A.2 *Purchasing power parity equation*

Country	b0	se(b0)	b1	se(b1)	b2	se(b2)	b3	se(b3)	Z(b1)[a]	t(b1)[b]	Z(b2)[c]	t(b2)[d]	Z(b3)[e]	t(b3)[f]
1 Argentina	−0.71	0.22	1.17	0.08	0.15	0.19	−0.66	0.19	0.3	**2.1**	0.0	0.0	**−2.4**	**−2.2**
2 Bolivia	0.04	0.10	1.04	0.02	−0.16	0.21	−0.05	0.11	0.1	1.9	**−1.3**	−1.6	0.9	1.5
3 Brazil	−3.76	2.55	1.00	0.02	0.42	0.18	−0.14	0.09	0.0	0.0	**1.1**	1.4	0.5	0.9
4 Chile	0.17	0.41	1.13	0.09	0.13	0.19	−0.04	0.07	0.2	1.4	−0.1	−0.2	**1.0**	**2.5**
5 Colombia	0.30	0.38	0.80	0.34	0.62	0.15	−0.05	0.07	−0.3	−0.6	**1.9**	**3.1**	1.0	**2.5**
6 Costa Rica	1.16	0.38	2.00	0.34	−0.57	0.24	−0.29	0.10	**1.6**	**3.0**	**−3.0**	**−3.1**	−0.4	−0.7
7 Dominican Republic	0.51	0.21	1.73	0.28	−0.06	0.19	−0.30	0.12	**1.2**	**2.6**	−0.9	−1.1	−0.4	−0.6
8 Ecuador	1.36	0.63	1.38	0.21	0.10	0.19	−0.23	0.11	0.6	1.8	−0.2	−0.3	0.0	−0.1
9 El Salvador	−0.03	0.33	1.10	0.41	−0.18	0.22	0.00	0.15	0.2	0.2	**−1.4**	−1.5	**1.2**	1.5
10 Guatemala	0.22	0.09	1.57	0.20	0.13	0.18	−0.23	0.09	0.9	**2.8**	−0.1	−0.2	−0.1	−0.1
11 Haiti	0.98	0.33	0.84	0.19	0.61	0.18	−0.55	0.19	−0.2	−0.8	**1.8**	**2.6**	**−1.8**	−1.7
12 Honduras	0.40	0.12	2.35	0.38	−0.29	0.18	−0.41	0.13	**2.2**	**3.6**	**−1.8**	**−2.4**	**−1.0**	−1.4
13 Mexico	0.63	0.13	1.58	0.14	0.08	0.16	−0.79	0.15	**1.0**	**4.3**	−0.3	−0.5	**−3.1**	**−3.7**
14 Paraguay	1.19	0.79	1.50	0.37	−0.29	0.20	−0.18	0.12	0.8	1.3	**−1.9**	**−2.3**	0.2	0.3
15 Peru	−0.05	0.11	0.95	0.04	0.03	0.23	−0.04	0.09	−0.1	−1.3	−0.5	−0.5	1.0	**2.1**
16 Uruguay	−0.09	0.08	1.16	0.20	0.48	0.19	−0.36	0.14	0.3	0.9	**1.3**	1.7	−0.8	**−1.0**
17 Venezuela	1.07	0.49	1.50	0.26	−0.06	0.24	−0.34	0.16	0.8	**2.0**	−0.9	−0.9	−0.6	−0.7
18 Jamaica	0.33	0.13	1.63	0.22	0.14	0.18	−0.23	0.08	**1.0**	**3.0**	−0.1	−0.1	−0.1	−0.1
19 Trinidad & Tobago	0.56	0.24	0.22	0.55	0.15	0.19	−0.36	0.15	**−1.3**	−1.4	0.0	0.0	−0.7	−0.9
20 Israel	0.29	0.08	1.15	0.04	0.12	0.15	−0.47	0.12	0.2	**3.7**	−0.2	−0.3	**−1.3**	**−2.0**
21 Saudi Arabia	0.01	0.02	0.06	0.13	0.20	0.11	−0.02	0.02	**−1.5**	**−7.0**	0.2	0.3	**1.1**	**10.0**
22 Egypt, Arab Rep.	0.14	0.06	0.83	0.53	0.45	0.18	−0.29	0.12	−0.3	−0.3	**1.2**	1.6	−0.4	−0.6
23 Myanmar	0.07	0.09	−0.01	0.19	0.13	0.17	−0.03	0.04	**−1.6**	**−5.3**	−0.1	−0.2	**1.1**	**5.2**
24 India	−0.16	0.12	0.16	0.26	0.01	0.18	0.08	0.05	**−1.4**	**−3.2**	−0.6	−0.9	**1.7**	**6.4**
25 Indonesia	0.46	0.34	−0.06	0.36	0.25	0.17	−0.05	0.05	**−1.7**	**−2.9**	0.4	0.5	0.9	**3.5**

26 Korea, Republic of	2.35	0.79	0.57	0.28	0.42	0.17	-0.35	0.12	-0.7	-1.5	**1.1**	1.5	-0.7	**-1.1**
27 Malaysia	-0.06	0.05	-0.58	0.48	0.05	0.19	0.06	0.07	**-2.6**	**-3.3**	-0.4	-0.5	**1.5**	**4.3**
28 Nepal	-0.21	0.13	0.13	0.25	0.03	0.14	0.09	0.04	**-1.4**	**-3.5**	-0.5	-0.9	**1.7**	**7.0**
29 Pakistan	0.15	0.20	0.10	0.72	0.12	0.20	-0.03	0.08	**-1.5**	-1.3	-0.2	-0.2	**1.0**	**2.4**
30 Philippines	0.84	0.39	0.87	0.28	0.18	0.21	-0.28	0.13	-0.2	-0.5	0.1	0.1	-0.3	-0.4
31 Singapore	0.00	0.04	-0.49	0.23	0.01	0.14	-0.07	0.07	**-2.4**	**-6.6**	-0.6	-1.1	0.8	**2.2**
32 Thailand	0.17	0.17	-0.10	0.20	0.04	0.13	-0.05	0.06	**-1.8**	**-5.5**	-0.5	-0.9	0.9	**3.0**
33 Algeria	0.81	0.49	2.01	0.55	0.05	0.21	-0.26	0.16	**1.7**	1.8	-0.4	-0.5	**-1.5**	-0.2
34 Cameroon	2.91	0.92	1.62	0.40	0.28	0.19	-0.50	0.16	**1.0**	1.5	0.5	0.7	0.4	-1.8
35 Central African Rep.	0.86	0.74	1.11	0.54	0.01	0.24	-0.15	0.13	0.2	0.2	-0.6	-0.6	0.4	0.5
36 Congo, Republic of	2.55	0.91	1.41	0.28	0.06	0.20	-0.45	0.16	0.7	1.4	-0.4	-0.5	**-1.2**	-1.4
37 Congo, Dem. Rep.	-2.10	1.36	1.11	0.05	0.67	0.25	-0.19	0.12	0.2	**2.1**	**2.1**	2.1	0.2	0.3
38 Gabon	1.95	0.90	1.11	0.38	0.26	0.22	-0.34	0.16	0.2	0.3	0.4	0.5	-0.6	-0.7
39 Gambia, The	0.46	0.24	1.33	0.22	0.02	0.19	-0.24	0.12	0.5	1.5	-0.6	-0.7	-0.1	-0.1
40 Ghana	1.08	0.42	0.45	0.30	0.48	0.17	-0.18	0.07	-0.9	-1.8	**1.3**	1.9	0.2	0.6
41 Côte d'Ivoire	2.30	0.91	0.97	0.49	0.29	0.20	-0.40	0.16	0.0	-0.1	0.6	0.7	-1.0	-1.1
42 Kenya	0.75	0.37	1.40	0.27	-0.12	0.19	-0.26	0.13	0.7	1.5	**-1.1**	-1.4	-0.2	-0.3
43 Madagascar	0.60	0.54	1.22	0.28	0.01	0.22	-0.09	0.08	0.4	0.8	-0.6	-0.7	0.7	1.7
44 Mauritania	0.34	0.42	1.04	0.49	0.29	0.22	-0.08	0.11	0.1	0.1	0.5	0.6	0.8	1.3
45 Mauritius	0.34	0.21	0.79	0.25	0.25	0.19	-0.13	0.08	-0.3	-0.8	0.4	0.5	0.5	1.2
46 Morocco	0.23	0.14	1.28	0.74	0.40	0.20	-0.12	0.08	0.5	0.4	**1.0**	1.2	0.6	1.4
47 Niger	0.86	0.58	1.09	0.33	0.25	0.23	-0.16	0.11	0.2	0.3	0.4	0.4	0.4	0.6
48 Nigeria	0.19	0.14	0.37	0.31	0.45	0.17	-0.08	0.10	**-1.0**	-2.0	**1.2**	1.8	0.8	1.4
49 Rwanda	0.68	0.43	0.97	0.16	0.30	0.20	-0.15	0.09	0.0	-0.1	0.6	0.7	0.4	0.8
50 Senegal	1.67	0.93	1.36	0.45	0.06	0.22	-0.29	0.16	0.6	0.8	-0.4	-0.4	-0.4	-0.4
51 Sierra Leone	2.72	0.88	1.05	0.11	0.26	0.20	-0.57	0.18	0.1	0.5	0.4	0.5	**-1.9**	-1.9

Table 4A.2 (cont.)

Country	b0	se(b0)	b1	se(b1)	b2	se(b2)	b3	se(b3)	Z(b1)[a]	t(b1)[b]	Z(b2)[c]	t(b2)[d]	Z(b3)[e]	t(b3)[f]
52 Swaziland	0.24	0.11	1.17	0.52	0.21	0.20	-0.30	0.16	0.3	0.3	0.2	0.3	-0.4	-0.5
53 Togo	1.18	0.71	1.35	0.37	0.07	0.21	-0.21	0.13	0.6	0.9	-0.4	-0.4	0.1	0.1
54 Tunisia	-0.07	0.08	1.77	1.04	-0.02	0.23	-0.12	0.11	**1.3**	0.7	-0.7	-0.8	0.5	0.9
55 Burkina Faso	0.84	0.76	1.19	0.47	-0.06	0.24	-0.15	0.14	0.3	0.4	-0.9	-0.9	0.4	0.6
56 Zambia	0.13	0.05	1.24	0.12	0.68	0.17	-0.37	0.11	0.4	**2.1**	**2.2**	**3.2**	-0.8	-1.4
57 Papua New Guinea	-0.04	0.02	1.09	0.39	0.40	0.20	-0.24	0.12	0.2	0.2	**1.0**	1.2	-0.1	-0.2
Mean coefficient			**1.00**		**0.16**		**-0.22**							
s.d. of mean coefficient			0.61		0.24		0.18							
Latin America & Caribbean (countries 1–19)	**Mean**		1.30		0.08		-0.28							
	s.d.		0.48		0.31		0.22							
Middle East & Asia (countries 20–32)	**Mean**		0.20		0.15		-0.11							
	s.d.		0.52		0.15		0.18							
Africa & Papua New Guinea (countries 33–57)	**Mean**		1.18		0.22		-0.24							
	s.d.		0.35		0.22		0.13							

Notes: **Bold** figures indicate coefficients are outliers. Values of 1.0 or 2.0 that are not bold were less than 1.0 or 2.0 before rounding.

[a] $Z(b1) = 33\%$. [b] $t(b1) = 32\%$. [c] $Z(b2) = 33\%$.
[d] $t(b2) = 33\%$. [e] $Z(b1) = 28\%$. [f] $t(b3) = 26\%$.

Table 4A.3 IS equation

Country	c0	se(c0)	c1	se(c1)	c2	se(c2)	c3	se(c3)	$Z(c1)^a$	$t(c1)^b$	$Z(c2)^c$	$t(c2)^d$	$Z(c3)^e$	$t(c3)^f$
1 Argentina	11.46	4.12	-0.05	0.03	-0.46	0.17	0.006	0.002	-0.56	**-2.49**	-1.24	-1.48	0.1	0.4
2 Bolivia	-0.65	1.12	0.16	0.03	0.03	0.05	-0.004	0.001	**1.18**	**4.92**	1.21	**5.01**	-1.1	**-6.6**
3 Brazil	2.11	1.10	0.04	0.03	-0.13	0.05	0.002	0.002	0.18	0.64	0.41	1.55	-0.4	-1.6
4 Chile	-7.52	4.83	0.17	0.08	0.23	0.16	-0.016	0.010	**1.30**	**2.08**	**2.26**	**2.86**	-2.5	**-2.1**
5 Colombia	4.44	2.63	0.02	0.02	-0.16	0.09	0.005	0.004	0.08	0.49	0.30	0.67	0.0	0.0
6 Costa Rica	9.34	2.78	-0.11	0.04	-0.34	0.10	0.015	0.005	**-1.01**	**-2.91**	-0.63	-1.22	**1.2**	**2.1**
7 Dominican Republic	4.29	1.63	0.01	0.03	-0.18	0.07	0.005	0.004	0.00	-0.02	0.19	0.57	0.0	-0.1
8 Ecuador	0.93	2.72	0.06	0.06	-0.04	0.09	-0.002	0.005	0.35	0.74	0.88	**2.00**	-0.9	-1.5
9 El Salvador	2.49	1.94	0.13	0.09	-0.12	0.08	0.005	0.003	0.93	1.26	0.50	1.19	0.0	-0.1
10 Guatemala	-0.42	1.65	0.12	0.04	0.02	0.07	-0.004	0.003	0.85	**2.58**	**1.16**	**3.36**	-1.1	**-3.4**
11 Haiti	3.46	2.24	-0.12	0.09	-0.14	0.09	-0.001	0.002	**-1.10**	-1.40	0.38	0.82	-0.7	**-3.9**
12 Honduras	6.37	3.27	0.02	0.04	-0.28	0.15	0.009	0.005	0.03	0.10	-0.34	-0.46	0.5	0.7
13 Mexico	2.74	1.89	-0.01	0.04	-0.11	0.07	0.002	0.003	-0.19	-0.59	0.55	1.47	-0.4	-1.1
14 Paraguay	0.44	3.16	0.01	0.05	-0.01	0.10	-0.001	0.006	-0.05	-0.14	**1.01**	1.93	-0.8	-1.0
15 Peru	7.10	3.16	0.04	0.04	-0.32	0.14	0.006	0.003	0.22	0.67	-0.50	-0.71	0.1	0.1
16 Uruguay	2.38	5.45	0.04	0.06	-0.10	0.24	0.002	0.005	0.21	0.43	0.56	0.46	-0.3	-0.6
17 Venezuela	1.90	2.50	0.14	0.04	-0.08	0.09	-0.004	0.003	**1.03**	3.07	0.68	1.54	-1.1	**-3.0**
18 Jamaica	2.75	2.04	0.09	0.04	-0.12	0.09	-0.002	0.002	0.59	1.78	0.49	1.14	-0.9	**-4.5**
19 Trinidad & Tobago	-1.78	1.58	0.26	0.08	0.06	0.06	-0.002	0.001	**2.05**	**3.10**	**1.38**	**4.34**	-0.9	**-6.4**
20 Israel	10.50	3.62	-0.01	0.15	-0.43	0.15	0.021	0.009	-0.24	-0.19	**-1.08**	-1.44	**1.9**	1.9
21 Saudi Arabia	3.30	3.45	0.03	0.10	-0.12	0.13	-0.001	0.006	0.12	0.15	0.46	0.70	-0.7	-1.1
22 Egypt, Arab Rep.	0.32	1.79	0.01	0.02	-0.01	0.08	-0.001	0.005	-0.06	-0.35	**1.03**	**2.66**	-0.7	-1.2
23 Myanmar	-1.49	2.68	-0.05	0.02	0.07	0.11	-0.004	0.004	-0.54	**-2.86**	**1.43**	**2.52**	-1.1	**-2.1**

Table 4A.3 (cont.)

Country	c0	se(c0)	c1	se(c1)	c2	se(c2)	c3	se(c3)	$Z(c1)^a$	$t(c1)^b$	$Z(c2)^c$	$t(c2)^d$	$Z(c3)^e$	$t(c3)^f$
24 India	9.08	4.39	0.10	0.07	-0.33	0.16	0.012	0.006	0.69	1.18	-0.57	-0.71	0.9	1.2
25 Indonesia	6.19	5.33	-0.01	0.03	-0.19	0.16	0.012	0.011	-0.22	-0.93	0.12	0.14	0.9	0.6
26 Korea, Republic of	7.07	4.10	0.12	0.05	-0.25	0.13	0.020	0.011	0.87	**2.16**	-0.19	-0.28	**1.7**	**1.3**
27 Malaysia	4.60	4.19	-0.02	0.08	-0.19	0.18	0.014	0.013	-0.32	-0.46	0.12	0.14	**1.0**	0.6
28 Nepal	5.21	3.06	0.09	0.08	-0.22	0.13	0.006	0.004	0.66	0.94	-0.03	-0.05	0.1	0.2
29 Pakistan	5.67	2.13	0.04	0.03	-0.22	0.08	0.011	0.005	0.21	0.85	-0.02	-0.04	0.7	1.2
30 Philippines	4.49	2.08	-0.10	0.06	-0.15	0.08	0.005	0.003	-0.95	**-2.04**	0.31	0.81	-0.1	-0.2
31 Singapore	6.97	2.37	-0.01	0.05	-0.30	0.10	0.022	0.003	-0.17	-0.40	-0.42	-0.81	**2.0**	**2.1**
32 Thailand	0.11	2.56	0.09	0.06	-0.01	0.09	0.001	0.007	0.62	1.22	**1.02**	**2.18**	-0.5	-0.6
33 Algeria	3.06	4.10	-0.02	0.07	-0.11	0.15	0.002	0.008	-0.30	-0.52	0.51	0.66	-0.3	-0.4
34 Cameroon	-0.27	1.84	0.10	0.07	-0.01	0.06	-0.003	0.003	0.67	1.19	**1.05**	**3.27**	**-1.0**	**-2.5**
35 Central African Rep.	8.82	4.13	0.03	0.04	-0.34	0.15	0.002	0.003	0.16	0.44	-0.63	-0.81	-0.3	-1.1
36 Congo, Republic of	0.38	2.20	-0.13	0.10	0.02	0.09	-0.003	0.005	**-1.21**	-1.41	**1.17**	**2.46**	**-1.0**	-1.7
37 Congo, Dem. Rep.	1.20	0.92	0.01	0.02	-0.08	0.08	-0.005	0.001	0.00	-0.02	0.69	1.83	**-1.2**	**-6.9**
38 Gabon	4.77	2.99	0.01	0.11	-0.17	0.10	0.001	0.004	-0.04	-0.04	0.22	0.44	-0.5	-1.1
39 Gambia, The	14.31	3.74	-0.19	0.10	-0.69	0.18	0.027	0.007	**-1.73**	**-2.20**	**-2.36**	**-2.59**	**2.6**	**2.9**
40 Ghana	9.62	3.19	0.05	0.01	-0.35	0.12	0.006	0.002	0.27	**2.41**	-0.69	-1.19	0.1	0.5
41 Côte d'Ivoire	3.49	2.15	0.05	0.05	-0.13	0.07	0.001	0.002	0.27	0.69	0.43	1.19	-0.6	**-2.2**
42 Kenya	5.20	3.06	-0.02	0.08	-0.21	0.12	0.008	0.006	-0.31	-0.45	0.05	0.08	0.3	0.4
43 Madagascar	18.11	4.79	0.07	0.03	-0.64	0.17	0.002	0.002	0.47	**1.95**	**-2.13**	**-2.55**	-0.4	**-2.3**
44 Mauritania	5.72	3.38	0.01	0.07	-0.25	0.14	0.013	0.008	-0.07	-0.13	-0.16	-0.22	0.9	1.0
45 Mauritius	3.52	3.67	0.10	0.09	-0.16	0.15	0.007	0.009	0.68	0.95	0.28	0.36	0.2	0.2
46 Morocco	9.21	4.11	-0.01	0.05	-0.37	0.16	0.015	0.007	-0.19	-0.43	-0.75	-0.92	**1.1**	**1.3**
47 Niger	11.04	4.16	-0.08	0.07	-0.39	0.15	0.005	0.002	-0.78	-1.43	-0.88	-1.16	-0.1	-0.2
48 Nigeria	6.20	2.01	0.05	0.02	-0.25	0.08	0.004	0.003	0.29	**1.76**	-0.16	-0.40	-0.2	-0.6

49 Rwanda	14.13	4.23	−0.64	0.21	−0.44	0.14	0.002	0.004	**−5.41**	**−3.12**	**−1.12**	−1.58	−0.4	−0.8
50 Senegal	25.13	5.69	−0.01	0.04	−0.91	0.21	0.022	0.005	−0.22	−0.65	**−3.50**	**−3.40**	**2.0**	**3.3**
51 Sierra Leone	5.27	2.61	−0.03	0.05	−0.21	0.11	−0.001	0.001	−0.37	−0.84	0.01	0.02	−0.7	**−4.1**
52 Swaziland	6.91	2.19	0.11	0.06	−0.35	0.11	0.015	0.006	0.83	1.59	−0.68	−1.21	**1.2**	1.6
53 Togo	10.21	4.68	−0.02	0.08	−0.38	0.17	0.007	0.005	−0.33	−0.50	−0.84	−0.99	0.2	0.3
54 Tunisia	4.57	2.15	−0.06	0.05	−0.21	0.10	0.011	0.005	−0.66	−1.51	0.02	0.05	0.7	1.0
55 Burkina Faso	13.36	4.65	−0.02	0.04	−0.50	0.17	0.019	0.007	−0.25	−0.80	**−1.44**	−1.64	**1.6**	**2.1**
56 Zambia	10.69	3.90	0.03	0.03	−0.42	0.15	0.002	0.002	0.13	0.58	**−1.04**	−1.34	−0.4	**−2.1**
57 Papua New Guinea	2.46	2.33	0.18	0.08	−0.11	0.11	0.002	0.003	**1.36**	**2.01**	0.52	0.94	−0.4	−1.1
Mean coefficient			**0.01**		**−0.22**		**0.01**							
s.d. of mean coefficient			**0.12**		**0.20**		**0.01**							
Latin America & Caribbean (countries 1–19)	Mean		**0.05**		**−0.12**		**0.00**							
	s.d.		**0.10**		**0.16**		**0.01**							
Middle East & Asia (countries 20–32)	Mean		**0.02**		**−0.18**		**0.01**							
	s.d.		**0.07**		**0.14**		**0.01**							
Africa & Papua New Guinea (countries 33–57)	Mean		**−0.02**		**−0.31**		**0.01**							
	s.d.		**0.35**		**0.22**		**0.01**							

Notes: **Bold** figures indicate coefficients are outliers. Values of 1.0 or 2.0 that are not bold were less than 1.0 or 2.0 before rounding.

[a] $(Z > 1) = 16\%$.   [b] $(t > 2) = 25\%$.   [c] $(Z > 1) = 26\%$.   [c] $(Z > 1) = 25\%$.   [d] $(t > 2) = 23\%$.   [e] $(Z > 1) = 25\%$.   [f] $(t > 2) = 33\%$.

Table 4A.4 Trade balance equation

Country	d0	se(d0)	d1	se(d1)	d2	se(d2)	d3	se(d3)	d4	se(d4)	Z(d1)[a]	t(d1)[b]	Z(d2)[c]	t(d2)[d]	Z(d3)[e]	t(d3)[f]	Z(d4)[g]	t(d4)[h]
1 Argentina	0.37	0.13	0.33	0.11	1.99	2.81	−1.74	0.93	0.26	0.16	0.9	1.8	0.0	0.0	−1.1	−1.2	−0.8	−1.3
2 Bolivia	0.36	0.22	−0.56	0.20	2.21	3.23	−1.87	1.46	0.13	0.22	−3.1	−3.4	0.0	0.0	−1.2	−0.9	−1.3	−1.5
3 Brazil	13.16	5.06	0.48	0.19	0.17	3.10	−0.81	0.82	0.56	0.12	1.5	1.9	−0.5	−0.6	−0.2	−0.3	0.4	0.9
4 Chile	−1.16	0.41	0.20	0.07	3.90	2.19	−1.16	0.35	0.26	0.16	0.3	1.1	0.5	0.8	−0.6	−1.7	−0.8	−1.2
5 Colombia	−1.15	0.84	0.19	0.14	4.36	2.67	−2.78	2.09	0.62	0.16	0.3	0.5	0.6	0.9	−2.1	−1.1	0.7	1.0
6 Costa Rica	−1.13	0.35	0.24	0.07	1.50	1.49	−1.06	0.47	0.19	0.15	0.5	1.5	−0.2	−0.4	−0.5	−1.0	−1.1	−1.8
7 Dominican Republic	−0.37	0.18	0.11	0.07	−1.93	1.40	0.45	0.54	0.05	0.20	−0.1	−0.3	−1.1	−2.9	1.0	1.9	−1.7	−2.0
8 Ecuador	−0.24	0.73	0.05	0.12	−1.52	3.17	0.01	0.79	0.47	0.22	−0.4	−0.7	−1.0	−1.1	0.6	0.8	0.1	0.1
9 El Salvador	−0.94	0.41	0.39	0.19	0.01	2.76	0.03	0.89	0.51	0.21	1.1	1.4	−0.6	−0.7	0.6	0.7	0.2	0.3
10 Guatemala	0.03	0.16	−0.23	0.12	2.33	2.70	−0.43	1.18	0.21	0.23	−1.6	−3.1	0.1	0.1	0.1	0.1	−1.0	−1.1
11 Haiti	0.13	0.48	−0.12	0.26	0.09	2.21	0.87	0.70	0.95	0.10	−1.1	−0.9	−0.5	−0.9	1.4	2.1	2.1	5.0
12 Honduras	−0.15	0.10	−0.01	0.07	1.30	1.24	−0.14	0.51	0.22	0.21	−0.6	−2.0	−0.2	−0.6	0.4	0.9	−1.0	−1.1
13 Mexico	−0.50	0.23	0.67	0.20	−4.44	2.02	0.22	0.92	0.41	0.14	2.4	2.7	−1.8	−3.2	0.8	0.9	−0.2	−0.3
14 Paraguay	−1.08	0.90	0.13	0.13	4.07	2.25	−2.10	0.93	0.19	0.20	0.0	0.0	0.6	0.9	−1.5	−1.6	−1.1	−1.3
15 Peru	0.17	0.13	0.17	0.08	0.44	2.07	−1.43	0.50	0.53	0.14	0.2	0.5	−0.4	−0.8	−0.8	−1.7	0.3	0.5
16 Uruguay	0.06	0.04	0.36	0.09	−1.00	1.00	−0.47	0.40	0.43	0.12	1.0	2.5	−0.8	−3.0	0.1	0.3	−0.1	−0.3
17 Venezuela	−0.19	0.67	0.09	0.18	2.98	4.09	−2.81	1.37	0.24	0.19	−0.2	−0.2	0.3	0.2	−2.2	−1.6	−0.9	−1.2
18 Jamaica	−0.23	0.16	0.08	0.07	0.74	1.38	−0.89	0.46	0.46	0.18	−0.2	−0.7	−0.4	−0.9	−0.3	−0.7	0.0	0.0
19 Trinidad & Tobago	0.31	0.50	−0.28	0.38	4.24	2.80	−0.96	0.79	0.69	0.20	−1.8	−1.1	0.6	0.8	−0.4	−0.5	1.0	1.2
20 Israel	−0.12	0.34	0.11	0.35	−0.53	3.19	0.01	0.35	0.72	0.30	−0.1	−0.1	−0.7	−0.8	0.6	1.7	1.1	0.9
21 Saudi Arabia	−0.55	0.18	0.28	0.14	8.86	3.04	0.47	0.49	0.80	0.09	0.7	1.1	1.9	2.2	1.0	2.2	1.4	3.7
22 Egypt, Arab Rep.	−0.75	0.30	0.20	0.19	10.37	4.66	−1.62	1.73	0.62	0.13	0.3	0.4	2.3	1.8	−1.0	−0.6	0.7	1.2
23 Myanmar	−0.42	0.20	0.21	0.08	−2.09	2.85	−0.36	0.97	0.16	0.23	0.4	1.0	−1.1	−1.5	0.2	0.2	−1.2	−1.3
24 India	−0.67	0.35	0.13	0.10	4.60	2.53	1.26	0.88	0.58	0.17	0.0	0.0	0.7	1.0	1.8	2.1	0.5	0.7

#	Country																		
25	Indonesia	0.20	0.61	−0.01	0.08	3.21	2.33	−2.63	1.43	0.72	0.17	−0.7	−1.9	0.3	0.5	−2.0	−1.4	1.1	1.5
26	Korea, Republic of	−3.57	1.11	0.55	0.17	0.05	1.41	−0.89	0.57	0.69	0.08	1.9	2.5	−0.5	−1.4	−0.3	−0.5	1.0	2.8
27	Malaysia	0.25	0.13	−0.15	0.12	1.55	1.41	−1.83	0.62	0.43	0.15	−1.2	−2.4	−0.1	−0.4	−1.2	−2.0	−0.1	−0.2
28	Nepal	−0.45	0.33	0.04	0.09	1.39	2.11	−0.04	0.89	0.47	0.17	−0.4	−1.0	−0.2	−0.3	0.5	0.6	0.0	0.1
29	Pakistan	−1.28	0.45	0.37	0.12	4.08	2.64	−3.76	1.26	0.35	0.16	1.1	2.0	0.6	0.8	−3.1	−2.5	−0.4	−0.7
30	Philippines	−1.65	0.52	0.41	0.16	5.72	1.49	−0.92	0.54	0.33	0.14	1.3	1.8	1.0	2.5	−0.3	−0.6	−0.5	−0.9
31	Singapore	0.07	0.04	−0.06	0.05	−0.69	0.46	−0.14	0.19	0.88	0.09	−0.9	−3.9	−0.8	−6.0	0.4	2.4	1.8	4.7
32	Thailand	−1.63	0.55	0.49	0.17	2.78	1.38	−1.64	0.73	0.59	0.14	1.6	2.1	0.2	0.5	−1.0	−1.5	0.6	1.0
33	Algeria	−0.09	0.40	0.07	0.11	−4.56	3.07	−0.38	0.74	0.09	0.25	−0.3	−0.6	−1.8	−2.2	0.2	0.3	−1.5	−1.4
34	Cameroon	−0.50	0.79	0.09	0.13	−0.20	1.75	−1.05	0.39	0.52	0.17	−0.2	−0.3	−0.6	−1.3	−0.4	−1.2	0.2	0.4
35	Central African Rep.	−1.84	0.58	0.26	0.09	4.74	1.90	−0.48	0.61	0.40	0.18	0.6	1.3	0.7	1.4	0.1	0.2	−0.2	−0.3
36	Congo, Republic of	0.20	1.80	−0.02	0.31	−4.70	4.03	−0.20	0.60	0.45	0.20	−0.7	−0.5	−1.9	−1.7	0.4	0.6	0.0	0.0
37	Congo, Dem. Rep.	0.14	0.62	0.01	0.06	−1.44	2.91	−0.54	0.74	0.38	0.21	−0.5	−2.1	−1.0	−1.2	0.0	0.1	−0.3	−0.4
38	Gabon	0.39	1.13	−0.05	0.20	−0.09	2.84	−0.44	0.35	0.65	0.18	−0.8	−0.9	−0.6	−0.8	0.1	0.4	0.8	1.1
39	Gambia, The	−1.43	0.56	0.51	0.24	3.92	2.56	1.25	0.50	−0.00	0.20	1.7	1.6	0.5	0.7	1.8	3.7	−2.0	−2.4
40	Ghana	0.13	0.23	−0.10	0.06	6.48	3.11	−0.46	0.70	0.23	0.23	−1.0	−4.1	1.2	1.4	0.1	0.2	−0.9	−1.0
41	Côte d'Ivoire	−2.07	0.61	0.38	0.11	0.75	1.83	−0.57	0.50	0.45	0.14	1.1	2.3	−0.4	−0.7	0.0	0.0	0.0	−0.1
42	Kenya	−0.62	0.63	0.10	0.21	1.96	2.37	−0.08	1.08	0.38	0.22	−0.2	−0.2	0.0	0.0	0.5	0.7	−0.3	−0.3
43	Madagascar	−0.03	0.87	−0.05	0.12	2.79	3.11	−0.41	0.46	0.09	0.22	−0.8	−1.5	0.2	0.2	0.2	0.2	−1.5	−1.7
44	Mauritania	−1.91	0.68	0.44	0.16	1.33	1.99	−0.34	0.47	0.69	0.11	1.4	2.0	−0.2	−0.4	0.2	0.5	1.0	2.2
45	Mauritius	−0.33	0.52	0.02	0.17	0.98	2.02	0.55	0.59	0.49	0.19	−0.5	−0.6	−0.3	−0.5	1.1	2.4	0.2	0.2
46	Morocco	−0.80	0.40	0.20	0.15	5.46	2.61	−0.23	0.29	0.56	0.15	0.3	0.5	0.9	1.3	0.3	0.6	0.4	0.7
47	Niger	−0.36	0.51	0.05	0.09	−2.08	1.72	0.98	1.07	0.45	0.14	−0.4	−1.0	−1.1	−2.4	1.5	5.4	0.0	−0.1
48	Nigeria	−0.33	0.24	0.20	0.13	8.69	4.16	−1.20	0.39	0.33	0.21	0.3	0.5	1.8	1.6	−0.6	−0.6	−0.5	−0.6
49	Rwanda	0.15	1.66	−0.20	0.38	10.79	4.84	0.09	0.39	0.57	0.16	−1.5	−0.9	2.4	1.8	0.6	1.7	0.5	0.7
50	Senegal	−0.94	0.50	0.13	0.08	1.52	1.31	−0.28	0.39	0.37	0.22	0.0	0.0	−0.1	−0.4	0.3	0.8	−0.4	−0.4
51	Sierra Leone	0.77	1.02	−0.15	0.21	−2.53	2.23	0.09	0.74	1.01	0.17	−1.2	−1.3	−1.3	−2.1	0.6	0.9	2.3	3.3

Table 4A.4 (cont.)

Country	d0	se(d0)	d1	se(d1)	d2	se(d2)	d3	se(d3)	d4	se(d4)	Z(d1)[a]	t(d1)[b]	Z(d2)[c]	t(d2)[d]	Z(d3)[e]	t(d3)[f]	Z(d4)[g]	t(d4)[h]
52 Swaziland	−0.23	0.19	0.09	0.17	1.84	2.40	0.52	0.58	0.76	0.13	−0.2	−0.2	−0.1	−0.1	1.1	1.9	1.3	2.3
53 Togo	−1.98	1.23	0.24	0.21	7.85	3.46	−1.15	0.72	0.27	0.18	0.5	0.5	1.6	1.7	−0.6	−0.8	−0.8	−1.1
54 Tunisia	−0.13	0.08	0.08	0.12	3.75	2.29	−0.32	0.67	0.44	0.12	−0.2	−0.4	0.5	0.7	0.3	0.4	−0.1	−0.2
55 Burkina Faso	−0.52	2.94	0.08	0.47	−2.97	7.08	−0.62	2.77	0.79	0.15	−0.2	−0.1	−1.4	−0.7	0.0	0.0	1.4	2.2
56 Zambia	−0.46	0.16	0.11	0.13	10.69	3.19	0.06	1.06	0.05	0.19	−0.1	−0.1	2.4	2.7	0.6	0.6	−1.7	−2.2
57 Papua New Guinea	−0.07	0.11	0.10	0.35	1.34	3.03	1.22	0.84	0.86	0.12	−0.1	−0.1	−0.2	−0.2	1.7	2.1	1.7	3.5
Mean coefficient			0.13		2.05		−0.58		0.46									
s.d. of mean coefficient			0.22		3.65		1.03		0.24									
Latin America & Caribbean (countries 1–19)	Mean		0.12		1.13		−0.90		0.39									
	s.d.		0.29		2.35		1.04		0.23									
Middle East & Asia (countries 20–32)	Mean		0.20		3.02		−0.93		0.56									
	s.d.		0.22		3.71		1.36		0.21									
Africa & Papua New Guinea (countries 33–57)	Mean		0.10		2.25		0.16		0.45									
	s.d.		0.17		4.34		0.65		0.26									

Notes: **Bold** figures indicate coefficients are outliers. Values of 1.0 or 2.0 that are not bold were less than 1.0 or 2.0 before rounding.

[a] $(Z > 1) = 33\%$. [b] $(t > 2) = 33\%$. [c] $(Z > 1) = 25\%$. [d] $(t > 2) = 18\%$.

[e] $(Z > 1) = 30\%$. [f] $(t > 2) = 18\%$. [g] $(Z > 1) = 33\%$. [h] $(t > 2) = 21\%$.

Acknowledgements

We are grateful for comments made at the Bank of England Centre for Central Banking Studies Conference on the Transmission Mechanism of Monetary Policy, June 2000, and the Macroeconomic Modelling Seminar, Warwick University, July 2000. Ron Smith is grateful for support under ESRC grant L138251003.

Note

1 The Birkbeck ESRC project of Driffill, Smith and Sola on Imperfect Financial Markets, Business Cycles and Growth.

5 Central bank goals, institutional change and monetary policy: evidence from the United States and the United Kingdom

V. Anton Muscatelli and Carmine Trecroci

5.1 Introduction

A considerable empirical literature has emerged on the estimation of policy re-action functions and the identification of the underlying preferences of monetary authorities (see Groeneveld, Koedijk and Kool, 1996; Muscatelli and Tirelli, 1996; Clarida and Gertler, 1997; Clarida, Galí and Gertner, 1998; Favero and Rovelli, 1999; and Muscatelli, Tirelli and Trecroci, 1999). Some of these contributions examine whether recent changes in institutional structure, such as the shift to inflation targeting, have had an impact on the conduct of monetary policy.[1] The evidence is mixed. For instance, Muscatelli, Tirelli and Trecroci (1999) show that there is only slight evidence that the introduction of inflation targeting affected forward-looking policy reaction functions in the United Kingdom, New Zealand, Sweden and Canada. In contrast they find some evidence of policy instability in Japan and the United States in the 1980s and 1990s, even in the absence of institutional change.

Of course one would also expect significant shifts in monetary policy that bring about a reduction in inflation expectations to affect the transmission mechanism of monetary policy. The standard New Keynesian model of aggregate demand and supply,[2] which has been used extensively for policy analysis (see Svensson, 1997; Rudebusch and Svensson, 1999; McCallum and Nelson, 1999a,b; and Rudebusch, 2000), suggests that forward-looking expectations are important on both the demand and the supply side. A typical formulation of a New Keynesian model is

$$y_t = E_t y_{t+1} - \alpha_1(i_t - E_t \pi_{t+1}) + \varepsilon_{1t} \tag{5.1}$$

$$\pi_t = \beta_1 E_t \pi_{t+1} + (1 - \beta_1)\pi_{t-1} + \beta_2 y_t + \varepsilon_{2t}, \tag{5.2}$$

where y is the output gap, i is the nominal interest rate, π is the inflation rate and E is the expectations operator. In empirical applications, lags of output could be added to equation (5.1) to capture costly adjustment of habit persistence, and a more complex lagged adjustment of inflation could be considered in equation (5.2). The presence of forward-looking expectations in these models means that any changes in monetary policy should lead to structural breaks in the aggregate supply relationship (5.2) or in the intertemporal aggregate demand equation (5.1). This is of course the standard Lucas (1976) critique. Hutchison and Walsh (1998) find that, in the case of New Zealand, the short-run output–inflation trade-off in a relationship like that in equation (5.2) increased in the 1990s after the monetary reform. For the United States, Rudebusch and Svensson (1999) find little evidence of structural breaks[3] in their (backward-looking) models of output and inflation estimated over a sample period 1961(Q1)–1996(Q4).

This paper makes two contributions. First, for the United States and the United Kingdom we check for any evidence that shifts in the transmission mechanism, as represented by the aggregate demand and supply relationships, have resulted from shifts in agents' expectations. We use a class of invariance tests developed by Engle and Hendry (1993) to test whether the Lucas critique has any force in this case. We find evidence of shifts in the output and inflation models in the past two decades. Second, because the invariance tests are not designed to examine the timing of shifts in the transmission mechanism, we use an alternative method to detect contemporaneous shifts in interest rate policy reactions and in the output and inflation equations. We estimate a Bayesian vector autoregression (VAR) of the monetary transmission mechanism for the United States and the United Kingdom, using a simple trivariate specification with the interest rate, output gap and inflation rate. In contrast to standard full-sample VAR estimates, we find the policy rules that emerge from our Bayesian VAR estimates to be more plausible and interpretable in terms of policy reactions. Our results show that policy in the United Kingdom and the United States has evolved since the late 1980s. We also detect some minor shifts in the way in which output and inflation have responded to policy, which may indicate expectations effects. Evidence, therefore, does exist that the Lucas critique is important in understanding the transmission mechanism. And, although it may have been less important in the relatively benign macroeconomic environment of the 1990s, it may become more significant in the future. The Lucas critique may be especially relevant at a time when the spectre of oil shocks has returned.

The rest of this paper is structured as follows. In section 5.2 we report our invariance tests of conditional models for the aggregate demand and supply relationships. In section 5.3 we present our Bayesian VAR results. Section 5.4 concludes the paper.

5.2   Invariance tests

For our purposes, we wished to test whether forward-looking expectations enter into equations (5.1) and (5.2), the output and inflation relationships.[4] The approach followed here entails estimating backward-looking conditional models for output and inflation and testing whether variations in the moments of the regressors in each model influence the parameters of the backward-looking conditional model.[5] Thus, we first estimate the output and inflation equations as backward-looking models, using autoregressive distributed-lag formulations:[6]

$$y_t = c_1 + \sum_{i=1}^{n} \alpha_{yi} y_{t-i} + \sum_{i=0}^{n} \alpha_{ri} \bar{r}_{t-i} + \varepsilon_{1t} \qquad (5.3)$$

$$\pi_t = c_2 + \sum_{i=1}^{n} \beta_{\pi i} \pi_{t-i} + \sum_{i=0}^{n} \beta_{yi} y_{t-i} + \varepsilon_{2t}, \qquad (5.4)$$

where c_i are constants and $\bar{r}$ is a measure of the real interest rate, calculated using the current inflation rate, $\bar{r}_t = (i - \pi)_t$. If forward-looking expectations of the interest rate and inflation are important in determining current output and inflation, then these equations will not be invariant to changes in policy regime because they will be convolutions of the 'deep' parameters of the forward-looking models and the forecasting equations. The impact of forward-looking expectations can be tested by checking if shifts in the first and second moments of the real interest rate or output affect the regressions in equations (5.3) and (5.4) (see appendix 1). To obtain measures of these moments, we fit marginal models for output and the real interest rate using simple autoregressive models.[7]

Table 5.1 shows the most parsimonious version of estimated equations (5.3) and (5.4). Our conditional models generally follow the specifications reported in Rudebusch and Svensson (1999) for the United States and in Hall et al. (1999) for the United Kingdom. Definitions of variables used can be found in the data appendix (appendix 2). In computing the output gap, we follow two alternative approaches. The first is to follow these earlier contributions in using the Bureau of Economic Analysis (BEA) estimate (y^{bea}, for the United States) and the OECD estimate (y^{oecd}, for the United Kingdom), of potential output, and computing the output gap as the deviation of actual from potential output as a percentage of potential output. The second approach is to fit a univariate structural time-series (STS) model (see Harvey, 1989) for output. This decomposes output into stochastic trend, cycle and irregular components, and we define potential output as the stochastic trend element. A convenient decomposition can be obtained by applying the Kalman filter on the trend component and using the one step ahead predictions of the state vector. The output gap measure obtained is labelled y^{kal}. The difference between the two output gap series in the case of the two countries is shown in figures 5.1 and 5.2. As can be readily seen, the

Table 5.1 *Backward-looking conditional models of output and inflation*

(a) United States

$$y_t^{bea} = 0.031 + 1.187y_{t-1}^{bea} - 0.279y_{t-2}^{bea} - 0.010\bar{r}_{t-1}$$
$$\quad\quad (2.44) \quad\quad (15.87) \quad\quad (-3.81) \quad\quad (-2.68)$$
$$R^2 = .90 \quad \sigma = 0.0997$$

$$y_t^{kal} = 0.021 + 0.512y_{t-1}^{kal} - 0.290y_{t-2}^{kal} - 0.007\bar{r}_{t-1}$$
$$\quad\quad (1.467) \quad (6.81) \quad\quad (-3.88) \quad\quad (-1.56)$$
$$R^2 = .59 \quad \sigma = 0.1187$$

$$\pi_t = 0.119 + 0.619\pi_{t-1} + 0.024\pi_{t-2} + 0.188\pi_{t-3} + 0.132\pi_{t-4} + 1.20y_{t-1}^{bea}$$
$$\quad\quad (0.82) \quad\quad (7.98) \quad\quad (0.266) \quad\quad (2.09) \quad\quad (1.706) \quad\quad (4.46)$$
$$R^2 = .85 \quad \sigma = 0.972$$

$$\pi_t = 0.117 + 0.711\pi_{t-1} + 0.027\pi_{t-2} + 0.228\pi_{t-3} + 1.06y_{t-1}^{kal}$$
$$\quad\quad (0.74) \quad\quad (9.32) \quad\quad (0.094) \quad\quad (2.91) \quad\quad (2.24)$$
$$R^2 = .84 \quad \sigma = 1.012$$

Sample: 1958(Q4) to 2000(Q1).

(b) United Kingdom

$$y_t^{oecd} = 0.001 + 1.711y_{t-1}^{oecd} - 0.766y_{t-2}^{oecd} + 0.023\bar{r}_{t-2} - 0.893q_{t-4}$$
$$\quad\quad (-) \quad\quad (24.95) \quad\quad (-11.713) \quad\quad (1.74) \quad\quad (-1.90)$$
$$R^2 = .98 \quad \sigma = 0.325$$

$$y_t^{kal} = 0.038 + 0.454y_{t-1}^{kal} + 0.497y_{t-2}^{kal} + 0.199y_{t-3}^{kal} - 0.278y_{t-4}^{kal} + 0.077\bar{r}_{t-2}$$
$$\quad\quad (0.246) \quad (4.47) \quad\quad (4.55) \quad\quad (1.88) \quad\quad (-2.91) \quad\quad (2.33)$$
$$\quad\quad - 2.195q_{t-4}$$
$$\quad\quad (-1.96)$$
$$R^2 = .88 \quad \sigma = 0.881$$

$$\pi_t = 0.255 + 1.081\pi_{t-1} - 0.165\pi_{t-2} - 0.132\pi_{t-3} + 0.513y_{t-2}^{oecd} - 0.381y_{t-3}^{oecd}$$
$$\quad\quad (1.60) \quad\quad (11.28) \quad\quad (-1.27) \quad\quad (-1.65) \quad\quad (3.14) \quad\quad (-2.35)$$
$$\quad\quad + 0.091pim_{t-1} - 0.146ulc_{t-1} + 0.255ulc_{t-2}$$
$$\quad\quad (4.40) \quad\quad (-3.30) \quad\quad (5.56)$$
$$R^2 = .97 \quad \sigma = 0.777$$

Sample: 1977(Q1) to 1994(Q4).

BEA and OECD measures lead to measures of the output gap that are much smoother, but that show a greater variance over the sample period.

The real interest rate effect $\bar{r}$ is measured as an average effect:[8] the deviation of the four-quarter average nominal interest rate, i, from the four-quarter inflation rate in the relevant price index, that is, $\bar{r}_t = (1/4)\sum_{i=0}^{3} i_t - (1/4)\sum_{i=0}^{3} \pi_t$.

In the case of the United Kingdom we also add some additional regressors to the models as specified in equations (5.3) and (5.4), following Hall et al.

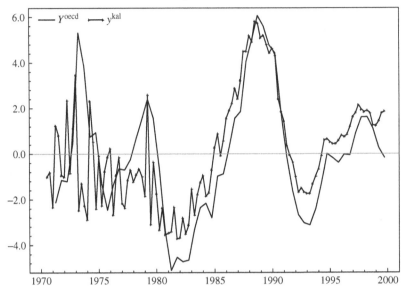

Figure 5.1 Output gaps: UK.

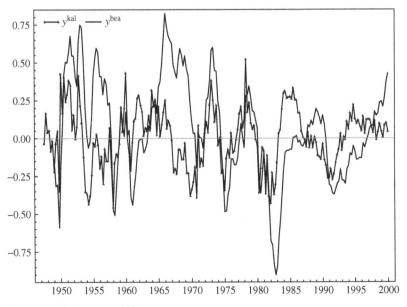

Figure 5.2 Output gaps: USA.

(1999).[9] In the case of the aggregate demand equation, we add a measure of the real effective exchange rate, q. In the case of the inflation equation, we add as regressors a series for the domestic currency value of import prices, *pim*, and a series on nominal unit labour costs, *ulc*. The former reflects the fact that the United Kingdom has a more open economy.

The results obtained for the United States are very similar to those reported in Rudebusch and Svensson (1999), which is not surprising since the sample we used is quite similar. The use of y^{kal} instead of y^{bea} does not yield very different results, although the fit using y^{bea} is slightly better; this is unsurprising given that it is a smoother series and has a higher sample variance than y^{kal}. The United Kingdom results are similar to those of the United States, except that the real interest variable has the wrong sign (but is insignificant if the y^{oecd} definition of the output gap is used). The additional regressors all have the right signs, and again the fit is generally better if the y^{oecd} measure is used. Next we conduct invariance tests using the y^{oecd} and y^{bea} measures of the output gap.

The marginal models fitted for the real interest rate and output are reported in table 5.2. It should be noted that these regression models are not designed to have a structural interpretation as outlined in appendix 1. They merely allow us to construct some series for the conditional mean of the interest rate and output, which can be used in the invariance tests. In order to obtain measures of the second moments of these variables, we fit fourth-order ARCH models for the fitted residuals ($\hat{\eta}_{t}^{2}$) from the regressions in table 5.2. In table 5.2 we also report the estimates of single-equation, forward-looking policy reaction functions[10] as a potential alternative to a naïve autoregressive model for the real interest rate. In practice, however, the best results from the invariance tests are obtained using the simple autoregressive model. As stressed in Engle and Hendry (1993), the marginal models can include dummy variables to capture important policy shifts. For the interest rate models we find that a dummy used to capture the 1992 Exchange Rate Mechanism (ERM) crisis improves the fit of the UK model, and a dummy used to capture the change in the Federal Reserve's operations in 1979–82 improves the fit of the US model.

Our invariance tests are reported in table 5.3. They are computed for two different sample periods for each country: the full sample available to us (1959(Q4)–1999(Q4) for the United States, and 1978(Q1)–1999(Q4) for the United Kingdom); and a shorter sample from 1984 through 1999. The latter period is usually seen as one of greater monetary stability, after the disinflation following the second oil shock.

The invariance tests show some evidence in favour of the Lucas critique for both the full sample and the post-1983 subsample. In the case of the United States, the null of invariance is rejected in both the output and inflation equations for the full sample period. If we focus only on the post-1983 period, however, we find evidence of the failure of invariance only in the case of the inflation

Table 5.2 *Marginal models of the interest rate, output and inflation*

(a) United States

Simple autoregressive model for interest rate:

$$r_t = 0.130 + 1.478r_{t-1} - 0.532r_{t-2} + 0.383D79/82$$
$$ (2.73) \quad (22.12) \quad\;\; (-8.19) \quad\quad (2.944)$$
$$R^2 = .97 \quad \sigma = 0.392$$

Forward-looking interest rate reaction function (1958(Q4)–1999(Q1)):

$$i_t = 0.091 + 1.062i_{t-1} - 0.150i_{t-2} + 0.124\pi^e_{t+4} + 1.21y^{kal}_t$$
$$ (0.49) \quad (13.75) \quad\;\; (-1.98) \quad\;\; (3.493) \quad\;\; (2.66)$$
$$R^2 = .92 \quad \sigma = 0.949$$

Forward-looking interest rate reaction function (1983(Q1)–1999(Q1)):

$$i_t = 0.062 + 1.264i_{t-1} - 0.390i_{t-2} + 0.910\pi^e_{t+4} + 0.277y^{kal}_t$$
$$ (0.33) \quad (12.19) \quad\;\; (-3.99) \quad\;\; (2.317) \quad\;\; (3.45)$$
$$R^2 = .96 \quad \sigma = 0.443$$

Simple autoregressive model for output gap:

$$y^{bea}_t = 0.003 + 1.195y^{bea}_{t-1} - 0.072y^{bea}_{t-2} - 0.224y^{bea}_{t-3}$$
$$\phantom{y^{bea}_t = } (0.40) \quad (10.09) \quad\;\; (-0.38) \quad\;\; (-2.01)$$
$$R^2 = .94 \quad \sigma = 0.055$$

Sample: 1958(Q4) to 2000(Q1), unless otherwise stated.
Note: D79/82 is a dummy variable used to capture the impact on federal funds rates of the Federal Reserve's change in operating procedures between 1979 and 1982.

(b) United Kingdom

Simple autoregressive models for real interest rate:

$$r_t = 0.420 + 1.160r_{t-1} - 0.234r_{t-2} - 0.178r_{t-3} + 0.167r_{t-4}$$
$$ (2.65) \quad (11.24) \quad\;\; (-1.57) \quad\;\; (-1.22) \quad\;\; (1.92)$$
$$R^2 = .91 \quad \sigma = 0.893$$

Simple autoregressive models for real interest rate (1983(Q1)–1999(Q4)):

$$r_t = 0.51 + 1.27r_{t-1} - 0.36r_{t-2} - 0.52D92/93$$
$$ (2.24) \quad (11.26) \quad\;\; (-3.17) \quad\;\; (-2.43)$$
$$R^2 = .90 \quad \sigma = 0.45$$

Forward-looking interest rate reaction function (1977(Q1)–1999(Q1)):

$$i_t = 0.773 + 0.825i_{t-1} + 0.163\pi^e_{t+4} + 0.148y^{kal}_t$$
$$ (1.91) \quad (17.45) \quad\;\; (3.83) \quad\;\; (3.03)$$
$$R^2 = .88 \quad \sigma = 1.12$$

Forward-looking interest rate reaction function (1983(Q1)–1999(Q1)):

$$i_t = 0.99 + 0.629i_{t-1} + 0.57\pi^e_{t+1} + 0.220y^{kal}_t$$
$$ (2.53) \quad (7.61) \quad\;\; (3.9) \quad\;\; (3.99)$$
$$R^2 = .91 \quad \sigma = 0.891$$

Simple autoregressive model for output gap:

$$y^{bea}_t = -0.011 + 1.80y^{oecd}_{t-1} - 1.034y^{bea}_{t-2} + 0.389y^{bea}_{t-3} - 0.2y^{oecd}_{t-4}$$
$$\phantom{y^{bea}_t = } (-0.034) \quad (17.15) \quad\;\; (-4.79) \quad\;\; (-1.80) \quad\;\; (-1.90)$$
$$R^2 = .98 \quad \sigma = 0.326$$

Sample: 1977(Q1) to 1999(Q4), unless otherwise stated.
Note: D92/93 is a dummy variable used to capture the impact on UK interest rates of the exit from the ERM, which allowed interest rates to fall rapidly between 1992(Q4) and 1993(Q4).

Table 5.3 *Invariance/superexogeneity tests*

Variable	USA: 1959(Q4)–1999(Q4)	USA: 1984(Q1)–1999(Q4)	UK: 1978(Q1)–1999(Q4)	UK: 1984(Q1)–1999(Q4)
Output equation				
$\hat{\eta}_r$	1.87*	0.56	1.50	2.60**
$\hat{x}_r^2$	−1.62*	0.11	0.07	−0.58
$\hat{\sigma}_{rr}^2$	0.57	−1.12	1.71*	−0.75
$(\hat{\eta}_r \hat{\sigma}_{rr}^2)$	−0.84	−0.14	−1.37	−2.40**
$(\hat{x}_r^2 \hat{\sigma}_{rr}^2)$	−0.09	−0.83	−1.24	0.27
Inflation equation				
$\hat{\eta}_r$	−5.18**	−3.19**	2.20**	−3.24**
$\hat{x}_r^2$	−0.38	−0.70	2.27**	0.37
$\hat{\sigma}_{rr}^2$	−1.54	−0.24	−0.69	0.49
$(\hat{\eta}_r \hat{\sigma}_{rr}^2)$	−0.03	0.16	−0.83	−0.66
$(\hat{x}_r^2 \hat{\sigma}_{rr}^2)$	−1.79*	−0.32	1.86*	0.68
$\hat{\eta}_y$	−1.54	1.10	0.34	0.7
$\hat{x}_y^2$	−0.46	−0.84	0.89	−0.63
$\hat{\sigma}_{yy}^2$	−0.55	0.48	−0.96	0.29
$(\hat{\eta}_y \hat{\sigma}_{yy}^2)$	2.02**	−1.15	−0.19	−0.06
$(\hat{x}_y^2 \hat{\sigma}_{yy}^2)$	0.07	0.53	0.36	2.01**

Note: Numbers reported in table are t-values for addition of variable to conditional models for output and inflation. The notation for the variables follows the description of the tests in appendix 1. *test statistic significant at the 10% level; **test statistic significant at the 5% level.

equation. In the case of the United Kingdom the results are very similar, but stronger. There is evidence of non-invariance in both the full sample and the post-1983 sample, in both the output and inflation equations.

Of course one has to be cautious in concluding from invariance/super-exogeneity tests alone that Lucas critique type effects are present. One could argue that the empirical size of these tests will depend critically on the correct specification of the marginal models.[11] It should also be noted that, even when the null hypothesis of invariance is rejected, we cannot date the shift in policy regime using these tests.

As stated in the introduction, we have strong evidence from previous studies (for example, Muscatelli, Tirelli and Trecroci 1999) that some policy regime shifts have occurred over the past two decades, even in the United States. We now turn to an alternative method of checking for shifts in the transmission mechanism that correspond to interest rate policy regime shifts; that is, ascertaining whether shifts in the transmission mechanism are attributable to the Lucas critique.

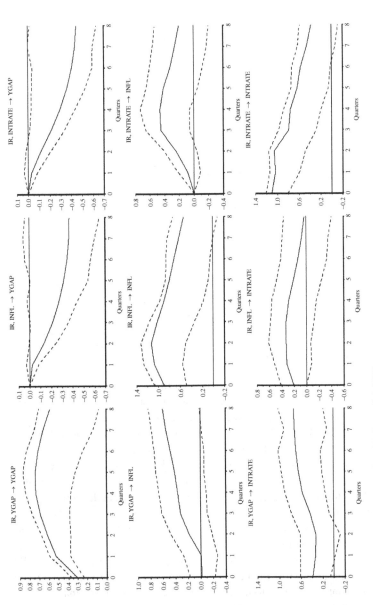

Figure 5.3 Standard trivariate VAR model: UK.

Notes: YGAP = output gap; INFL = quarter-on-quarter inflation rate; INTRATE = nominal policy interest rate. The upper and lower lines are 95% confidence interval bands.

5.3 The monetary transmission mechanism: Bayesian VAR estimates

5.3.1 Standard VAR analysis

Before turning to our Bayesian VAR estimates, we estimate a standard traditional VAR of the transmission mechanism as a benchmark. Figures 5.3 and 5.4 show the impulse responses and 95% confidence bands for the UK and USA (respectively) from a trivariate VAR that includes the nominal policy interest rate, the quarter-on-quarter inflation rate and the output gap (using the y^{oecd} and y^{bea} definitions).[12] Four lags of the variables are included. For reasons of space we show impulse responses only for up to eight quarters in figures 5.3 and 5.4. Although some of the impulse responses seem not to converge towards zero (especially for the United Kingdom), in fact the VAR is stationary, and convergence generally occurs for all the impulse responses after 8 to 16 quarters. The impulse responses have been derived using a Cholesky factorisation with a causal order as follows: the output gap, inflation and the interest rate. The VAR estimates[13] have been conducted for nearly the same sample as our invariance tests, namely 1961(Q3)–2000(Q1) for the United States and 1977(Q4)–1999(Q4) for the United Kingdom.

The United States results are, not surprisingly, very similar to those reported in Rudebusch and Svensson (1999) for an equivalent trivariate VAR for the United States during a similar sample period. The impulse responses in figure 5.4 show a positive response of the Federal Funds Rate to shocks to the output gap and the inflation rate. There is a slight price-puzzle effect following an interest rate shock, but generally the other impulse responses are as one would have expected: an output gap shock leading to a significant inflation response after three quarters and an inflation shock leading to a fall in output, significant after eight quarters; interest rate shocks lead to output falls after two to three quarters.

In the case of the United Kingdom the price puzzle is also present, but the impulse response is insignificant (except in quarters 3 and 4). The only other feature of note is that the response of the interest rate to an inflation rate shock is insignificant, reflecting the inclusion of the 1970s data in our full sample.

These impulse responses reveal the typical weaknesses of VAR analysis. One problem with unrestricted VARs is that they are overfitted, which explains why some of the responses are insignificant. Another problem is the interpretation of the implicit policy rule of the monetary authorities. As noted by Rudebusch (1998), the implicit policy rule that emerges from a just-identified VAR model is implausible, suggesting a response of the funds rate to a unit shock in the inflation rate of less than one. But the problem with the policy rule is also that it covers periods during which the Federal Reserve's behaviour changed dramatically. The same applies to the United Kingdom where, as we have already noted, the response of the interest rate to an inflation shock has the right

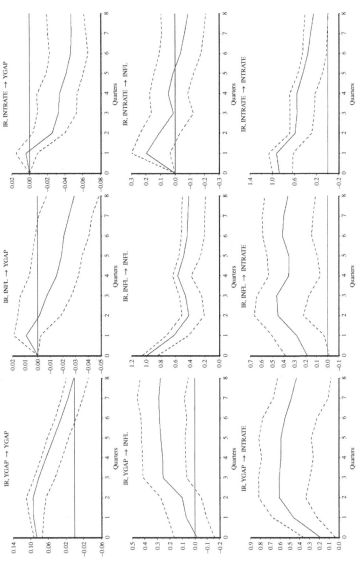

Figure 5.4 Standard trivariate VAR model: USA.

Notes: YGAP = output gap; INFL = quarter-on-quarter inflation rate; INTRATE = nominal policy interest rate. The upper and lower lines are 95% confidence interval bands.

sign but is insignificant, reflecting the very different nature of monetary policy in the early part of the sample.

Despite their limitations, VARs can be useful as descriptors of the dynamic correlations of jointly endogenous variables. In our case, we are particularly interested not only in examining policy responses, but also in examining whether any changes in policy regime elicited a change in transmission mechanism responses.

The alternative to VARs has been to estimate single-equation interest rate reaction functions (as in Clarida, Galí and Gertner, 1998; and Muscatelli, Tirelli and Trecroci, 1999). These single-equation interest rate reaction functions can be estimated using rolling or recursive estimation. However, single-equation approaches typically ignore the fact that we are dealing with jointly endogenous variables. It is therefore important to check that the results obtained from single-equation models are not due to the arbitrary imposition of a theoretical structure on the reaction function. VARs remain useful in this context because they impose the minimum amount of theoretical structure. However, we have to allow explicitly for changes or evolution in monetary policy regimes. In order to do this, we have to allow for some time variation in the parameters of the VAR.

Before turning to our models we should mention that there are some caveats to interpreting shifts in the response of interest rates to the output gap and inflation as shifts in policy preferences. These caveats apply to both single-equation reaction functions and VARs. Setting interest rates usually involves a complex decision-making process, in which a policy committee or council bases its decisions on a host of different macroeconomic indicators and models (see Bank of England, 1999b; Vickers, 1999). Where interest rates are set by committee, each member of the decision-making body might rely on a different subset of indicators and a different preferred 'model' of the transmission mechanism. Estimated interest rate reaction functions clearly cannot, and do not set out to, model every aspect of this complex decision-making process. Instead they focus on simple policy rules governing interest rate responses to expected inflation and the output gap (and to short-term inertia). If the estimated reaction functions are found to be stable, this stability can be seen as indicating that the actual information set used by the policy authorities displays a stable relationship with the final policy objectives (output and inflation) of the estimated rule *and* that the policy authorities' preferences did not change over the estimation sample. On the other hand, instability in a reaction function indicates either a shift in policy preferences *or* a shift in the relationship between the final objectives of policy and the wider information set (including the many indicators) used by the policy committee.

Some observers see VAR reaction functions as particularly prone to problems of interpretation (see Rudebusch, 1998). Part of the reason for this drawback is that most monetary policy VARs include many indicator and intermediate objective variables. Because our approach focuses only on a trivariate VAR, it has more in common with those contributions that estimate single-equation reaction functions (Clarida, Galí and Gertner, 1998; Muscatelli, Tirelli and Trecroci, 1999; Nelson, 2000a). However, we are able to consider not only potential shifts in interest rate policy, but also the consequences of these policy shifts for the transmission mechanism.

5.3.2 Bayesian VAR analysis

The estimation of VAR models with time-varying coefficients was pioneered by Doan, Litterman, and Sims (1984). We will now employ this Bayesian approach to VAR estimation, which allows the parameters of the VAR to evolve as more observations are added.[14] This technique has intuitive appeal for modelling a situation in which monetary policy changes have occurred, because policy regime changes are likely to be followed by a gradual evolution of responses. This is even the case where shifts in policy regime seem sudden. In the United Kingdom, after exit from the ERM and the implementation of inflation targets, it arguably took some time before the new system of inflation targeting became fully functional. In 1997, after the Bank of England acquired independence, it took time for the new Monetary Policy Committee to learn how to react optimally to new information. Even in the case of the United States, where the underlying institutional structure has not changed, the 1990s was a period in which the authorities had to learn gradually about the changing nature of the underlying macroeconomic relationships. For instance, in the mid-1990s the Federal Reserve (the Fed) tightened monetary policy at a time when it was uncertain about the 'productivity miracle' and the inflationary consequences of a tightening labour market. Similarly, if the monetary authorities' policy stance changes over time, we would expect private sector expectations to evolve gradually as they learn about the effects of changes in policy response. The fact that the Bayesian VAR takes this into account makes it a particularly attractive approach.

The estimation procedure can be outlined as follows. We begin with the definition of a standard VAR(p):

$$X_t = c + \sum_{j=1}^{p} A_j X_{t-j} + \varepsilon_t, \tag{5.5}$$

where X_t is an $n \times 1$ vector of endogenous variables, A_js are the $n \times n$ matrices of parameter coefficients and ε_t is an $n \times 1$ vector of disturbances for which

$$E\{\varepsilon_t\} = 0$$
$$E\{\varepsilon_t \varepsilon_t'\} = \Sigma \tag{5.6}$$
$$E\{\varepsilon_t \varepsilon_s'\} = 0, \quad \forall t \neq s.$$

In our case, $X'_t = (y, \pi, i)_t$ and $n = 3$. Following Lütkepohl (1991) and Hamilton (1994), we can write the model in the following way:[15]

$$X = AZ + U,$$
$$X = (X_{p+1} \quad X_{p+2} \quad \ldots \quad X_T);$$
$$A = (c \quad A_1 \quad \ldots \quad A_p); Z = (Z_p \quad Z_{p+1} \quad \ldots \quad Z_{T-1}) \qquad (5.7)$$

$$Z_t = \begin{pmatrix} 1 \\ X_{t-1} \\ X_{t-2} \\ \vdots \\ X_{t-p} \end{pmatrix}; U = (\varepsilon_{p+1} \quad \varepsilon_{p+2} \quad \ldots \quad \varepsilon_T),$$

where now we have only $T^* = T - p$ observations available in each equation. Assuming that the model is stationary, the VAR has the following finite MA representation:

$$X_t = \sum_{j=0}^{\infty} B_j \varepsilon_{t-j}, \qquad (5.8)$$

where the B_js are the $n \times n$ MA parameter matrices. Given the information set Ω, if the residual variance–covariance matrix Σ is diagonal, the impulse response function will be defined as

$$IR_X(h, \delta, \Omega_{t-1}) = E\{X_{t+h}|\varepsilon_t = \delta, \Omega_{t-1}\} - E\{X_{t+h}|\Omega_{t-1}\}, \qquad (5.9)$$

that is, the difference between the expected value of X_t at horizon h, given that a shock δ hits the system in time t, and the expected value of X_t in the absence of shocks. The MA parameters φ can then be intepreted as responses of X_{t+h} to a shock in t on variable j:

$$\varphi_{j,h} = B_h e_j, \qquad (5.10)$$

where e_j is a vector of zeros with one as the jth element. If, on the other hand, Σ is not diagonal, contemporaneous interactions amongst the variables prevent any interpretation of the VAR residuals as fundamental disturbances, and the system is not identified. The method of identification employed here orthogonalises the shocks according to a Choleski decomposition of the residual variance–covariance matrix: $PP' = \Sigma$, where P is a lower triangular matrix. This way, the orthogonalised responses are recovered as

$$\varphi_{j,h}^O = B_h P e_j. \qquad (5.11)$$

This defines the standard VAR model.

Next we consider the possibility of time-varying parameters. If we assume the VAR coefficients are time dependent, j from equation (5.5) can be written as

$$x_{t,j} = Z' \begin{pmatrix} c_j \\ \beta_{j1}^1 \\ \vdots \\ \beta_{jn}^1 \\ \vdots \\ \beta_{j1}^p \\ \vdots \\ \beta_{jn}^p \end{pmatrix} + \varepsilon_{t,j} = Z'\beta_t + \varepsilon_{t,j}, \tag{5.12}$$

where the βs represent the elements of the VAR parameter matrices. A state–space representation of such a model would have equation (5.12) as the measurement equation. The Doan et al. (1984) procedure assumes that the VAR coefficients follow an AR(1) process, and the transition equation of the system is therefore

$$\beta_t = c + T\beta_{t-1} + \upsilon_t. \tag{5.13}$$

Doan et al. suggest using a Bayesian prior distribution for the initial value of the coefficient vector, $\beta \sim N(\bar{\beta}, P_{1|0})$, and then allowing the parameters to be updated according to some law of motion. In fact, we assume that the VAR parameters behave as follows:[16]

$$\beta_t = (1 - \pi_1)\bar{\beta} + \pi_1 I_{np+1}\beta_{t-1} + \upsilon_t. \tag{5.14}$$

In equation (5.14), the parameter vector follows an autoregressive process, in which the weighting parameter π_1 determines the importance of the steady-state value for the coefficient vector $\bar{\beta}$. The disturbance term is uncorrelated with the disturbances in the original VAR: $Cov[\varepsilon_t, \upsilon_t] = 0$. The expected value $\bar{\beta}$ consists of a vector with a one as the element corresponding to the own variable $x_{t-1,j}$ at lag 1 for each equation, and zeros elsewhere. This prior distribution holds that changes in the endogenous variable modelled are so difficult to forecast that the coefficient on its lagged value is likely to be near unity, while all other coefficients are assumed to be near zero. This prior distribution is independent across coefficients, so that the mean square error of the state vector is a diagonal matrix.

The matrix $P_{1|0}$ is given by

$$P_{1|0} = \begin{pmatrix} g\hat{\tau}_1^2 & 0' \\ 0 & (B \otimes C) \end{pmatrix}, \tag{5.15}$$

where

$$
B = \begin{pmatrix}
\gamma^2 & 0 & 0 & \cdots & 0 \\
0 & \gamma^2/2 & 0 & \cdots & 0 \\
0 & 0 & \gamma^2/3 & \cdots & 0 \\
\vdots & \vdots & \vdots & & \vdots \\
0 & 0 & 0 & \cdots & \gamma^2/p
\end{pmatrix},
$$

$$
C = \begin{pmatrix}
1 & 0 & 0 & \cdots & 0 \\
0 & \omega^2\hat{\tau}_1^2/\hat{\tau}_2^2 & 0 & \cdots & 0 \\
0 & 0 & \omega^2\hat{\tau}_1^2/\hat{\tau}_3^2 & \cdots & 0 \\
\vdots & \vdots & \vdots & & \vdots \\
0 & 0 & 0 & \cdots & \omega^2\hat{\tau}_1^2/\hat{\tau}_n^2
\end{pmatrix}
$$

Also, Q, the variance of υ_t, is equal to

$$
Q = \pi_2 P_{1|0}. \tag{5.16}
$$

Doan, Litterman and Sims (1984) suggest the use of predefined values for the parameters in equations (5.15) and (5.16). The following assumptions are made:

$$
\omega^2 = \frac{1}{74}, \qquad g = 360, \qquad \pi_1 = 0.999 \quad \text{and} \quad \pi_2 = 10^{-7}.
$$

Note that this assumes that the coefficient vector $\boldsymbol{\beta}$ converges only very slowly towards the mean. Finally, if γ defines the analyst's confidence that the first-order autoregressive coefficient $\phi_{ii,1}^{(1)}$ relating y_{it} to $y_{i,t-1}$ attached to each series, $i = 1, \ldots, n$ is near unity, Doan et al. recommend $\gamma^2 = 0.07$.

This general time-varying formulation turns the estimation problem into one of forecasting in each period the optimal state vector based on information available up to the previous period. Using the normality and independence assumptions about the disturbances, the computation of the state vector is obtained simply by applying the Kalman filter (Harvey, 1989; Hamilton, 1994). Doing so allows us to obtain filtered estimates of the VAR parameters and the residual variance–covariance matrix for each observation in the sample. Orthogonalised impulse responses are finally computed according to the standard Choleski decomposition, producing a set of different impulse responses (5.10) for each period of our sample.

Let us first examine the impulse responses for the United Kingdom. Figures 5.5 and 5.6 show the impulse responses[17] of the interest rate at the first-, second-, third-, fifth- and eighth-quarter horizon following unit shocks to the inflation rate and the output gap, respectively, over the sample period 1988–99.

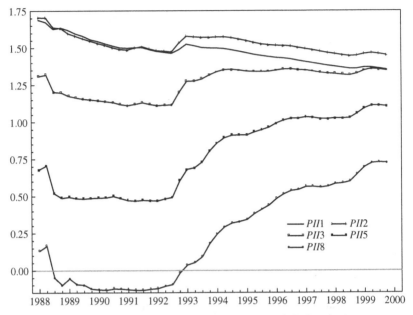

Figure 5.5 UK Bayesian VAR: effect on interest rate of an inflation shock.
Note: *PIIx* denotes the impulse response of the interest rate (*I*) following an inflation shock (*PI*)
after *x* periods.

Note that, in figure 5.5, *PIIx* denotes the impulse response function for the interest rate (*I*) following an inflation shock (*PI*) after *x* periods. In figure 5.6,
YIx denotes the impulse response of the interest rate (*I*) following a shock to
the output gap (*Y*) after *x* periods. Four points can be noted.

First, from figure 5.5 we can clearly see that the interest rate response to
the inflation rate is much greater than unity, at least for the first three quarters
following an inflation shock. This confirms that the some of the usual critique
of VAR policy rules (Rudebusch, 1998; Rudebusch and Svensson, 1999) is
directly attributable to the use of constant coefficient VARs.

The second point to note, from both figures 5.5 and 5.6, is that the implicit
policy rule seemed to change in the early 1990s. In this our analysis confirms evidence from some earlier contributions (Muscatelli, Tirelli and Trecroci, 1999;
Nelson, 2000a). There is a sharp shift in 1992. From figure 5.5 it is apparent that
the interest rate response to an inflation shock becomes more sustained, even
after the third quarter, suggesting a more concerted and persistent response of
monetary policy to the inflation shock. Figure 5.6 shows that the response to
the output gap has also changed: prior to 1992 there was a perverse response to
the output gap, whereas a more consistent response over time is apparent later
in the 1990s.

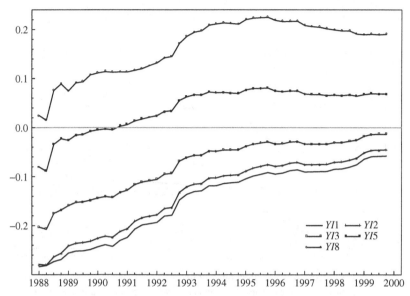

Figure 5.6 UK Bayesian VAR: effect on interest rate of an output gap shock.
Note: *YIx* denotes the impulse response of the interest rate (*I*) following a shock to the output gap (*Y*) after *x* periods.

Thirdly, Bank of England independence does seem to have had some effect on policy responses, with the interest rate responding more decisively to inflation shock from late 1998. However, it is probably too early to say whether this change represented a shift in the policy rule, or whether it was due to the need to tighten policy more dramatically after the 1997 election, following the failure of the Conservative administration to tighten policy sufficiently early in 1997.

Fourthly, the evolution of the policy rule after 1992 explains the fact that the invariance tests pick up shifts in the output and inflation equations. It appears that the shift in policy stance has affected the transmission mechanism (the response of output and inflation to interest rates). This is shown in figures 5.7 and 5.8.[18] The response of inflation to shocks in the output gap (*YPIx* in figure 5.7) seems to have changed only little post-1992. Most of the evolution (essentially a more inflationary response to an output shock after eight quarters) seemed to take place during the ERM membership phase (1990–92). The UK result seems to contradict the Hutchinson–Walsh (1998) result for New Zealand, namely that the acquisition of credibility should increase the output–inflation trade-off.[19] Figure 5.8 shows that there has also been a marked decrease in the responsiveness of output to the interest rate in the United Kingdom (*IYx*) after 1992. This result has implications for the degree of policy activism to be used. This result can be interpreted in three ways. The first is that in the early part of the

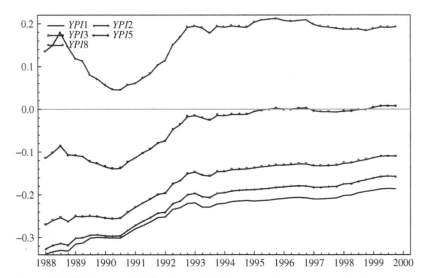

Figure 5.7 UK Bayesian VAR: effect on inflation rate of an output gap shock.

Note: *YPIx* denotes the impulse response of the inflation rate (*PI*) following a shock to the output gap (*Y*) after *x* periods.

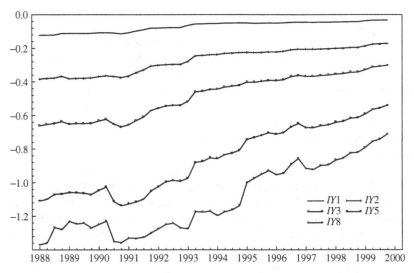

Figure 5.8 UK Bayesian VAR: effect on output gap of an interest rate shock.

Note: *IYx* denotes the impulse response of the output gap (*Y*) following a shock to the interest rate (*I*) after *x* periods.

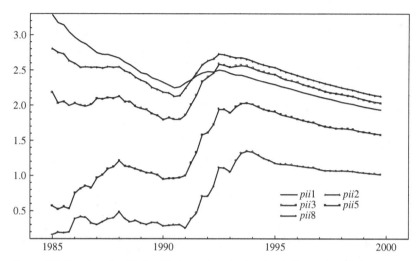

Figure 5.9 US Bayesian VAR: effect on interest rate of an inflation shock.
Note: piix denotes the impulse response of the interest rate (*i*) following an inflation shock (*pi*)
after *x* periods.

1988–98 period nominal interest rate shifts had a more dramatic impact on real
interest rates as inflationary expectations adjusted downward. Once inflation
expectations adjusted downward in the mid-1990s, nominal interest rate shocks
had a smaller impact on real interest rates, and hence on aggregate demand. The
second possibility is that a non-linear relationship exists between interest rates
and aggregate demand, so that the responsiveness of the output gap is different
at different interest rate levels. The third interpretation is that the UK economy
became less sensitive to interest rate increases in the late 1990s as the problems
with mortgage indebtedness of the early 1990s were gradually reduced.

Turning next to the United States, we see from figures 5.9 and 5.10 that,
despite the absence of formal institutional change, the Fed's reaction to inflation
and output gap shocks in the 1980s and 1990s evolved markedly. The change,
however, has not been monotonic, as was the case in the United Kingdom.
In figure 5.9, we see that the interest rate response to inflation (*piix*) increased
sharply between 1991 and 1994, but fell back sharply afterward. This pattern fits
with general commentaries on Fed policy, which suggest that in 1994–95 the Fed
reconsidered its policy stance in the light of evidence on productivity growth.
Again, in contrast to the points made in Rudebusch (1998) and Rudebusch and
Svensson (1999), the impulse responses show a greater-than-unit response of
the Federal Funds Rate to a unit shock in the inflation rate, so that real interest
rates are raised by the Fed following a shock. The pattern of impulse responses
is similar to that for the United Kingdom in terms of timing (the peak is reached

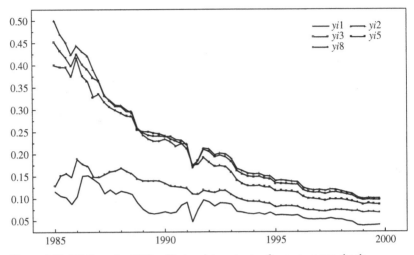

Figure 5.10 US Bayesian VAR: effect on interest rate of an output gap shock.

Note: yix denotes the impulse response of the interest rate (*i*) following a shock to the output gap (*y*) after *x* periods.

two quarters after the shock), but the US responses are larger. In figure 5.10 we see that, in contrast, the response of the Fed to the output gap (*yix*) tended to decrease from 1992 onwards, especially over the medium horizon (*x* = 3,5).[20] The final observations from our sample are of particular interest because, using the BEA potential output data, the output gap shows a major surge in 1999–2000. This is because the implicit assumption is that the rate of growth in potential output has not increased, that is there has been no 'productivity miracle'. The interpretation that emerges from the VAR is then that monetary policy became less countercyclical in the late 1990s. Using our alternative series for the output gap, based on a Kalman filter procedure (see figure 5.2), would yield slightly different results for the late 1990s, because this technique interprets the recent increase in output growth as partly due to an increase in potential output.

Have recent changes in policy responses affected the nature of the transmission mechanism in the United States? Figures 5.11 and 5.12 show the response of output and inflation to an interest rate shock and an output gap shock, respectively.[21] Figure 5.11 shows that, as opposed to the case in the United Kingdom, there is very little evidence of the United States experiencing a shift in the response of output to interest rate shocks, despite the presence of apparent policy shifts. This finding is consistent with the evidence from the application of invariance tests to our estimated aggregate demand equation (see table 5.3). The absence of expectations effects in the output equation might be attributable to the absence of formal institutional change in the United States, which means that the transmission mechanism has remained more stable. Figure 5.12 shows

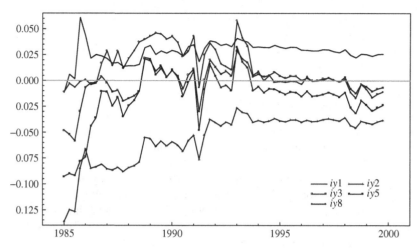

Figure 5.11 US Bayesian VAR: effect on output gap of an interest rate shock.
Note: *iyx* denotes the impulse response of the output gap (*y*) following a shock to the interest rate (*i*) after *x* periods.

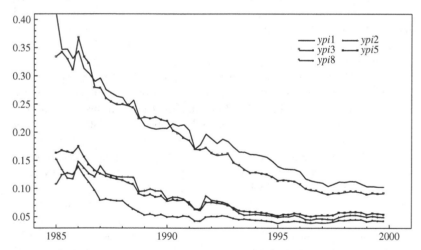

Figure 5.12 US Bayesian VAR: effect on inflation rate of an output gap shock.
Note: *ypix* denotes the impulse response of the inflation rate (*pi*) following a shock to the output gap (*y*) after *x* periods.

again that, in contrast to the United Kingdom situation, the short-run output–inflation correlation has shifted. An output gap shock resulted less readily in an inflationary surge in the 1990s. This result is in line with the results of Hutchison and Walsh (1998) for New Zealand, but whether it reflects an expectations effect or the impact of more rapid productivity remains an open issue. It might also explain why the Fed's interest rate response to the output gap declined over the same period. Although the impulse responses in figure 5.12 seem to change, it is hard to ascribe the shifts to an expectations effect, because they do not match variations in the implicit VAR interest rate policy response to inflation.

5.4 Conclusions

In this paper we have examined how interest rate policy responses to both output and inflation shocks in the United Kingdom and the United States have evolved during the past two decades, and how the transmission mechanism has been affected by apparent shifts in the policy rules followed by the Fed and the UK monetary authorities. Tests for invariance/superexogeneity seem to show some evidence in support of the Lucas critique, confirming the importance of forward-looking expectations in aggregate demand and supply. The evidence relates both to full sample estimates, which cover known policy shifts (the switch to much tighter inflation control beginning in the 1980s), and post-1983 findings reflecting formal institutional change limited to the United Kingdom. In the UK analysis, there is evidence that the Lucas critique has some weight in both the output and inflation equations, and its role might be linked to the presence of formal institutional change (the adoption of inflation targeting and the granting of instrument independence to the Bank of England). However, even for the United States we find evidence of expectations effects in the post-1983 sample estimates.

Our Bayesian VAR analysis shows a much richer picture. It confirms the finding that interest rate policy rules shifted in both the United States and the United Kingdom in the 1990s. In the United Kingdom this was linked to institutional change, and in particular to the adoption of inflation targets, but also, in a minor way, to the granting of independence to the central bank in 1997. US policy changes have been less systematic, with a more activist policy pursued until the mid-1990s, and a less responsive interest rate policy since 1995. This trajectory is probably attributable to the Fed's changing attitude toward the US 'productivity miracle'. The shift in policy rule seems to coincide, at least in the United Kingdom, with shifts in the transmission mechanism, lending some weight to the notion that the Lucas critique may need to be taken into account in setting interest rates if policy-makers significantly change their policy stance. Although independent central banks may be more immune to problems of credibility, it would appear that forward-looking expectations are still an important dimension of monetary policy design.[22] This fact has important implications for the vast theoretical literature that has emerged on the optimal design of feedback rules for monetary policy (see Haldane and Batini, 1998; Rudebusch and Svensson, 1999; Rudebusch, 2000; and Onatski and Stock, 2000). This literature has far too often ignored forward-looking expectations in the specification of underlying structural models.

Appendix 1: invariance/superexogeneity tests

The following tests are developed fully in Engle and Hendry (1993). This appendix briefly summarises the approach taken to the statistical tests of the Lucas critique in section 5.2.

Consider the following joint distribution of the variables x_t and y_t, which are assumed to be conditional normal, with conditional means

$$E(x_t|\Omega_t) = \mu_t^x$$
$$E(y_t|\Omega_t) = \mu_t^y \qquad (5A.1)$$

and covariance matrix

$$\Sigma_t = \begin{bmatrix} \sigma^{yy} & \sigma^{yx} \\ \sigma^{xy} & \sigma^{xx} \end{bmatrix}, \qquad (5A.2)$$

where the means and covariances need not be constant but may depend on the information set, Ω. This information set contains past values of the two variables and also current and past values of other valid conditioning variables, z_t.

Consider a model that relates the two conditional means of x_t and y_t:

$$\mu_t^y = \beta\mu_t^x + z_t'\gamma. \qquad (5A.3)$$

Given the expectation of y_t conditional on x_t, and its conditional variance, we can write the following conditional model for y_t:

$$y_t = \beta x_t + z_t'\gamma + (\delta_t - \beta)(x_t - \mu_t^x) + \omega_t, \qquad (5A.4)$$

where $\delta_t = (\sigma_t^{yx}/\sigma_t^{xx})$, $\omega_t = \sigma_t^{yy} - ((\sigma_t^{yx})^2/\sigma_t^{xx})$.

The efficient estimation of (5A.4) requires: (i) the weak exogeneity of x_t, which is satisfied if $\delta_t = \beta$; (ii) constancy of the regression coefficients, which requires the constancy of δ_t; and (iii) invariance, which requires the parameter β to be invariant to changes in the process generating x_t. Weak exogeneity and invariance imply that the variable x_t is superexogenous for the parameters of interest in our model.

To test for superexogeneity, Engle and Hendry examine the impact of changes in the moments of x_t on β. Allowing β to be a function of the moments of x_t and using a linear expansion for $\beta(.)$ yields:

$$\beta = \beta_0 + \beta_1\mu_t^x + \beta_2\sigma_t^{xx} + \beta_3(\sigma_t^{xx}/\mu_t^x) \qquad (5A.5)$$

(where higher-order terms of the expansion can be considered). The test regression then becomes

$$y_t = \beta_0 x_t + z_t'\gamma + (\delta_t - \beta_0)(x_t - \mu_t^x) + \beta_1(\mu_t^x)^2 + \beta_2\mu_t^x\sigma_t^{xx}$$
$$+ \beta_3\sigma_t^{xx} + \varepsilon_t. \qquad (5A.6)$$

Table 5A.1 *Data sources*

Time series	United Kingdom	United States
Price index	CPIX up to 1987(Q1) (OECD), RPIX thereafter (ONS)	GDP chain-weighted price index (BEA)
Output	GDP	GDP
Output gaps	Interpolated OECD estimates	Bureau of Economic Analysis estimates
Short-term interest rate	London Clearing Banks Overnight Rate (IFS)	Federal Funds Rate (IFS)
Real exchange rate	Real effective exchange rate, index 1995 = 100 (OECD)	
Unit labour cost	Unit Labour Cost, in Manufacturing Industries, Sterling Pounds, index, 1995 = 100 (OECD)	
Import prices	Import Price Index, 1995 = 100 (IFS)	

Table 5A.2 *Definition of variables*

Symbols adopted	Variable definition
y^{bea}	Output gap, BEA series. Gap between actual and potential, as a percentage of potential output
y^{kal}	Output gap, Kalman-filtered series. Gap between actual and potential, as a percentage of potential output
y^{oecd}	Output gap, OECD series. Gap between actual and potential, as a percentage of potential output
π	Quarterly inflation in percentage points at an annual rate
i	Short-term interest rate, in percentage points at an annual rate
$\bar{r}$	Real-interest rate, difference between four-quarter average i and π
q	Real effective exchange rate, in logs
pim	First difference in the (log of) Import Price Index
ulc	First difference in the (log of) Unit Labour Cost Index

To implement this test regression, one has to fit marginal models for the variable(s) x_t and use the residuals for this model to obtain a measure of $(x_t - \mu_t^x)$, and the fitted values to obtain a measure of μ_t^x; and one can model the variance σ_t^{xx} through, say, an ARCH model fitted to the residuals of the marginal model for x_t.

Appendix 2: data

Data sources and definitions are provided in tables 5A.1 and 5A.2. Data were obtained from IMF International Financial Statistics (IFS), OECD Main Economic Indicators, the United Kingdom Office of National Statistics (ONS) and the US Bureau of Economic Analysis (BEA). Where available, seasonally adjusted series were employed.

Acknowledgements

We are extremely grateful to our colleague Ulrich Woitek for providing us with the basic GAUSS code used to perform the Bayesian VAR estimates in section 5.3. We are grateful for helpful comments from participants at the Bank of England Centre of Central Banking Studies Conference on the transmission mechanism held at the CCBS in June 2000, and at the Royal Economic Society Conference 2000, held in St. Andrews. In particular, we should mention (without implicating them) Larry Ball, Jon Faust, Lavan Mahadeva and especially Ed Nelson, who acted as discussant on the paper.

Notes

1 In addition to making contributions that estimate policy reaction functions, a number of authors have used a variety of methods to test whether the introduction of inflation targeting had an impact on inflation expectations (see Freeman and Willis, 1995; King, 1995) or on a range of monetary policy indicators (see Almeida and Goodhart, 1996).

2 See, *inter alia*, Goodfriend and King (1997), Walsh (1998), Clarida, Galí and Gertner (1999), McCallum and Nelson (1999a,b), Rotemberg and Woodford (1999).

3 They use Andrews (1993)-type stability tests.

4 A full account of the relevant concepts of weak exogeneity, constancy, invariance and superexogeneity is provided elsewhere in the literature and will not be repeated here (see Favero and Hendry, 1990; Engle and Hendry, 1993).

5 More details of the test procedure used here are provided in appendix 1.

6 In the case of the United Kingdom some additional regressors are added to take account of the greater openness compared with the United States economy.

7 As an alternative, one could fit marginal models for the interest rate that have a structural interpretation. We experimented with the use of estimated policy reaction functions such as those estimated in Muscatelli, Tirelli and Trecroci (1999). The results obtained, however, were not very different from those that used an autoregressive model for the interest rate.

8 This provided a better fit than the use of a distributed lag of individual interest rates.

9 However, we do not follow Hall et al. in adding terms for foreign demand, fiscal policy and real money balances in the aggregate demand equation. In any case, our models are not strictly comparable because our dependent variable is the output gap rather than growth in real output.

10 These have the same structure as the forward-looking policy reaction functions reported in Muscatelli, Tirelli and Trecroci (1999) and Clarida, Galí and Gertner (1998).

11 These tests can also suffer from the problem of low power.

12 For the United Kingdom we decided not to include additional variables such as the real exchange rate. Although such variables might be helpful in describing the transmission mechanism in an open economy, restricting our attention to the output gap and inflation allows us more readily to interpret the policy rules that emerge from the VAR. Including the real exchange rate would also raise issues regarding the appropriate ordering of the variables in the Cholesky factorisation, given that the United Kingdom has experienced different exchange rate regimes over the sample period.

13 All estimates in this paper are produced using GAUSS routines.

14 For a recent application of Bayesian VAR analysis to the US economy during the Great Depression, see Ritschl and Woitek (2000).

15 Henceforth we assume that p is known and fixed.

16 The description here closely follows the notation used in Hamilton (1994), ch. 13.

17 We do not report confidence bands, because for each period and each impulse response we would need to report a confidence interval, making the graph difficult to read. However, having checked the impulse responses and confidence intervals (constructed using bootstrap methods) for critical periods discussed in the text, when the policy regimes were subject to change, we can confirm that the impulse responses discussed are significantly different from zero at the 95% confidence interval. Detailed results are available on request from the authors.

18 The response of inflation to an interest rate shock still shows a minor price puzzle (one that tends to be statistically insignificant), and is not shown here. It appears from the VAR impulse responses that the main channel of transmission from interest rates to inflation is through the output gap.

19 See also Lucas (1973) on the slope of the short-run aggregate supply relationship.

20 This is partly in line with the findings of Favero and Rovelli (1999), although their single-equation policy reaction function estimates seem to suggest that the output gap did not matter to the Fed throughout their sample period (1983–98).

21 Once again the impulse responses of inflation to the interest rate show a slight price puzzle, which disappears after three quarters, and eventually a negative response of inflation to an interest rate increase. But there is little evidence of a change in the transmission lag or in the size of interest rate shocks to inflation.

22 It is perhaps also worthwhile reminding ourselves that time-inconsistency does not only arise in static models where there is a conflict between the objectives of policy-makers and the monetary authorities. It is also present in models where the authorities target the natural rate of unemployment (so no Barro–Gordon type time-inconsistency problem exists), but forward-looking variables enter into the structural model.

6 The transmission mechanism of monetary policy near zero interest rates: the Japanese experience, 1998–2000

Kazuo Ueda

The Bank of Japan (BOJ) has gone through a unique experience in the past few years. When I joined the Bank's newly formed policy board in April 1998, the overnight call market rate, the key policy instrument of the BOJ, was already below 0.5%. The economy was in the midst of the most serious recession in the postwar period, although it took us a little while to realise this. We guided the call rate down to virtually zero in the first quarter of 1999 and followed up by promising to keep it there until deflationary concerns had been dispelled. Finally, in August 2000, we brought the rate up to 25 basis points after having kept the zero rate for one and a half years.

In this short paper, I would like to discuss some of the key aspects of the evolution of our thinking on monetary policy over the period 1998–2000. In so doing, I would like to focus specifically on the characteristics of the 1997–98 Japanese recession, the transmission process of monetary policy in the neighbourhood of a zero rate and the background thinking behind the rate hike in August 2000.

6.1 The nature of the 1997–98 recession

It is appropriate to begin with a brief discussion of the nature of the recession that started in 1997(Q4), which is what the BOJ was trying to respond to in 1998–2000. Clearly, the most important characteristic of the recession was the credit crunch caused by the slow and inappropriate handling of the bad loan problem. In addition, the Asian economic crisis, a premature tightening of fiscal policy in 1997 and the Russian crisis in 1998 added to the severity of the recession.

More specifically, the onset of the Asian economic crisis and the absence of fundamental measures to address the bad loan problem finally resulted in the failure of three medium- to large-sized financial institutions in the fall of 1997.

Table 6.1 *Movements in components of GDP in terms of contribution to GDP changes, 1997–98*

Quarter	GDP	Consumption	Investment (fixed)	Government spending
1997(Q3)	0.9	0.9	0.1	0.3
(Q4)	−0.6	−0.5	−0.1	−0.3
1998(Q1)	−1.2	0.2	−0.5	−0.3
(Q2)	−0.2	0.1	−0.5	0.0
(Q3)	−1.2	0.0	−0.7	−0.3
(Q4)	−0.5	−0.1	−0.9	0.9

There was a small default in the call market in the case of the failure of Sanyo Securities, the first of the three that went under. The default generated a panic in the money and financial markets, became a trigger for the failure of the other two institutions and led to sharp increases in risk premiums and the demand for liquidity across the financial system.

Japanese banks, already suffering from bad loans, were now facing difficulty in raising funds. Naturally, they started calling in their loans to non-financial companies, especially small firms. Business fixed investment started to decline immediately with the onset of the recession. As can be seen in table 6.1, the decline in fixed investment is the major story about the recession on the aggregate demand side.

Strains in the financial system eased somewhat in the first half of 1998, but resurfaced with increasing awareness of the problem of the Long-Term Credit Bank of Japan and later with the Russian economic crisis. Even large companies were feeling the pressure of the credit crunch. Many said in our interviews that 'all but the main bank are saying that they will not be able to roll over the loans at the year's end'. It followed that businesses had to cut back on their investment.

Such was the background for our policy-making during the period 1997–2000.

6.2   The monetary policy response to the credit crunch

Central banks around the world have responded to credit crunches in different ways. The justifications for response have not been unique, but have largely been based on worries about systemic risks or about the risk of generating a serious deflation in the future.

In any case, a variety of instruments has been used by central banks to mitigate credit crunches. The typical instrument has been injection of liquidity

Figure 6.1 The monetary base in Japan, 1995–2000.

into the system, usually supported by a lowering of short-term interest rates.[1] Depending on the circumstances, more unorthodox interventions have also been applied. During the collapse of the commercial paper (CP) market in the early 1970s, the US Federal Reserve Board (FRB) announced that it would lend automatically to banks that had in turn extended loans to companies having difficulty rolling over their CPs. The Fed even announced that it would lend directly to non-financial corporations if necessary, although apparently this was never done.

In the fall of 1998 the Fed injected large amounts of reserves into the financial system and lowered the Federal Funds Rate three times consecutively. The Fed also reportedly participated in a meeting to discuss a bailout package for Long-Term Capital Management.

During 1997–98, the BOJ also injected huge reserves into the financial system (figure 6.1) and in September 1998 the Bank cut the call rate from around 0.43% to 0.25%.[2] Several other attempts were made to ease the credit crunch. The BOJ supplied liquidity to the CP and corporate bond markets by essentially lending short-term funds to banks against these instruments.

In addition, the BOJ carried out a version of 'twist operations' to flatten the yield curve in the money market, in response to the steepening of the curve during the credit crunch at horizons of a few months. These operations also served to lower the Japan premium on dollar interest rates by letting Japanese banks acquire funds in the yen money market and then swap them into dollars.

All these measures were attempts to address the credit crunch nature of the recession or to redress the impaired ability of the private financial system to carry out financial intermediation.

6.3   The adoption of the zero interest rate policy

BOJ monetary policy, together with the recapitalisation of credit guarantee associations and private banks, eased the strains in the financial system somewhat. But the financial instability did not disappear. Toward the end of 1998 and early in 1999 the long-term interest rate increased and the yen appreciated, both sharply, and to levels probably unjustified by the strength of the economy at the time. To be sure, the real side of the economy was stabilising temporarily, thanks to the return of the fiscal stimulus, but uncertainties remained about the second half of the year and beyond. The rate of inflation was around zero. We worried that a dip in real economic activity from that point on might lead to a vicious circle, with anticipated or actual price declines feeding upon, and aggravating, the weakening of real economic activity.

Such considerations led the BOJ to ease monetary policy in an unprecedented way, that is, to lower the overnight call rate to zero. The decision was made in February 1999. Eventually, the overnight rate was set at 0.01% for lenders and 0.02% or above for borrowers. We followed up in April 1999 by declaring that the 'zero rate will be maintained until deflationary concerns are dispelled'. The combination of the zero rate and the central bank's commitment to maintain it until a certain set of conditions was met has sometimes been called the zero interest rate policy (ZIRP) outside the BOJ. I shall use this terminology in this paper.

The ZIRP produced significant impacts on money and financial markets and then on the rest of the economy. The yield curve flattened considerably all the way out to 10 years. Rates on instruments with maturities of less than a year were virtually zero during most of 1999. (The 10-year Japanese government bond rate had been between 1.6% and 2.0% for the previous one and a half years.) Stock prices rose sharply in 1999. Yield differences between corporate and government bonds narrowed substantially. Thus, the ZIRP forced investors to take risks, resulting in declines in risk premiums in many places. One of the few exceptions has been the bank loan market, where the growth rate of loans is still negative; this testifies to the seriousness of the bad loan problem we have been facing.

Over time, the ZIRP, rising exports, fiscal stimuli and investment in information technology related areas have produced a slow recovery from the most serious recession of the postwar period. Incidentally, I think that the time pattern of the current recovery can be seen more clearly in movements in the index of production and the index of total industry activity than in the GDP statistics, which suffer from numerous problems (figure 6.2).

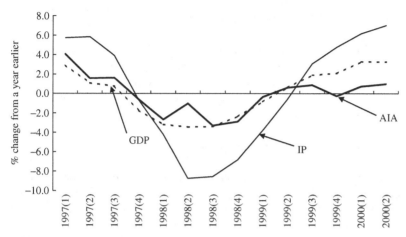

Figure 6.2 Measures of real economic activity, 1997(Q1)–2000(Q2).

6.4 The transmission channels of the ZIRP

In retrospect, it is clear that the ZIRP exerted a much larger effect on the economy than many had expected at the time of its introduction. What were the reasons for this?

The ZIRP involved a lowering of the overnight rate by about 25 basis points, which produced the usual chain of impacts. But the effects of the policy seem to have been larger than justified by the small change in the short rate. The commitment component of the policy must have played a large role. There have been essentially three mechanisms through which the central bank's commitment has exerted strong effects on the economy. They all concern the policy's effects on the term structure of interest rates. Simply put, even a small rate cut may exert a large impact on the economy if it is expected to stay for a long period of time.

First, the commitment minimised policy uncertainties, especially in the early days of the ZIRP. In March 1999 money market traders feared that the zero rate and accompanying liquidity injections by the BOJ would be only a temporary policy measure designed to get financial institutions through the fiscal year end, 31 March. Such a perception limited the effect of the zero rate on longer-term interest rates. Hence, in April the BOJ announced its commitment to maintain the zero rate until deflationary concerns had been dispelled. As a result, interest rates across the yield curve declined.[3]

Second, the commitment mitigated financial institutions' liquidity concerns. With the ZIRP, differences in funding costs among banks in the money market virtually disappeared. To see why, it is important to observe that the zero rate on average meant zero for all financial institutions, given that there were no negative rates.[4] And the zero rate was expected by market participants to stay in place for at least a few months because of the commitment element of the ZIRP. Any serious liquidity problem driving up the interest rate would be counteracted by the BOJ. Hence, the ZIRP became a powerful tool for dealing with the liquidity concerns prevailing in the economy at the time. Some of the pick-up in consumption and investment in 1999 was, I think, due to the easing of liquidity constraints faced by households and firms. This feature of the ZIRP goes a long way toward explaining why a mere 25 basis point cut in the overnight rate produced such a large impact on the economy – a reaction consistent with the credit crunch aspect of the recession.

Third, there was a more technical aspect of the ZIRP. In a sense the ZIRP was an attempt to produce larger stimulative effects on the economy than the zero rate would produce alone. It can be argued that, even with no explicit commitment from a central bank, rational market participants would expect the zero rate to be maintained for as long as it was appropriate to do so, but no longer. In order to counter the limiting effects of those expectations, the central bank had to commit to maintaining the zero rate into the future even if it would become appropriate, according to some criteria, to raise the interest rate again.

This point is made briefly by Woodford (1999a) and by Reifschneider and Williams (1999), who carried out simulations using the FRB/US model in which the performances of two policy rules are compared. One rule dictates simply that the Federal Funds Rate is equal to the Taylor rule rate when the latter is positive and it is zero when the Taylor rule rate is negative. The other policy rule is similar except that it contains a commitment that, once the Federal Funds Rate hits zero, the zero rate will be maintained until the Taylor rule rate exceeds a certain positive number. Their simulations show that the second rule delivers better economic performance in terms of output and inflation stability. Intuitively, the second rule borrows a relaxation of monetary policy from future periods for use in the present, and by so doing compensates for the central bank's inability to lower the rate below zero when it is desirable to do so.

The ZIRP in this sense approximates other methods that go beyond the zero rate proposed by academic economists. For example, the proposal that the BOJ buy large amounts of Japanese government bonds (JGBs) is an attempt to affect the long-term interest rate. Unless the BOJ can move the risk premium on long-term bonds systematically, the BOJ should be able to achieve the same result by making commitments regarding future short rates. The Krugman proposal to reflate the economy can be implemented simply by announcing that the zero rate will be maintained for a sufficient period of time.[5]

What then did the statement 'the zero rate will be maintained until deflationary concerns are dispelled' mean exactly? I must confess that there was some ambiguity in our commitment. We certainly had the first and second mechanisms described above in mind from early on. We knew of the third argument. But we rejected the adoption of the extreme Krugman-type proposal if it meant pursuit of a high inflation target such as 4% or 5%. Benchmarking our policy against the Taylor rule did not seem easy, given the wide ranges of the interest rate coming out of the rule. I will come back to this point later.

Our stance became a more informal one. Many of the board members made remarks to the effect that 'the zero rate will be kept until the risk of the inflation rate declining to a large negative number becomes small enough'. This was further paraphrased to 'inflation will fall significantly when aggregate demand declines sharply. Hence, we will wait until we are confident that domestic private demand is on a sustained recovery path.' But such a stance left room for a fairly wide range of interpretation, as we shall see below.

6.5   The end of the ZIRP

By the second quarter of 2000 it became apparent that, with high probability, the economy was going to grow in fiscal 2000 at a much higher rate than the government forecast of 1%. Naturally, there was much discussion among the board members – as can be seen in the published minutes of monetary policy meetings – about the appropriate timing for ending the ZIRP. There remained, however, the question of how much growth would be enough. Below I highlight some of the key arguments for and against the rate hike and illustrate the difficulties we faced.

6.5.1   Arguments against the rate hike

In a sense it was straightforward to argue against the rate hike. Although the economy had started to recover, it had been in a long and serious slump. With the exception of the wholesale price index (WPI), prices were still falling. Hence, there was no need to rush to increase interest rates.

More formally, we may calculate the Taylor rule rate.[6] The rate turns out to be negative under many sets of assumptions. For example, Hayakawa and Maeda (2000) present estimates of the output gap under several assumptions. The most standard estimate, based on a production function with a linear trend for the productivity term, results in a figure of 8% to 9% for 2000. One needs to know the neutral level of the gap in terms of its effect on the rate of inflation. The rate of Consumer Price Index (CPI) inflation was around zero toward the end of 1996 when the gap was between 4% and 5%. This implies that the gap is larger, on the deflationary side, by about 4% over the neutral level. With a coefficient of 50% on the gap in the Taylor rule formula, the gap term already contributes -2% to the interest rate. The inflation term also contributes negatively, but the size of the contribution depends on the target rate of inflation and the price index used. The growth rate of potential output consistent with the gap estimate is below 2%. Thus, there is no chance for the Taylor rule rate to become positive under such assumptions.

To be sure, the above calculation is rough at best. But it does indicate the possibility that the optimal level of the policy rate was still negative in August 2000. Moreover, given the Reifschneider–Williams scenario discussed above, we needed to wait until the rate exceeded a certain positive number rather than zero.

6.5.2   Arguments for the rate hike

One can point out a number of problems with the type of calculation presented above. Perhaps the most serious one is the following. Standard inferences result in estimates of a very large output gap, which should then be putting great negative pressure on prices. In fact, this was exactly the line of logic that guided us to the adoption of the ZIRP. To our surprise, prices did not decrease much in 1999. Standard Phillips curve type calculations would have suggested a decline in the CPI or WPI by about 2% in 1999. Actually, as of December 1999, the core CPI had declined by only 0.1%, and the WPI by 0.5%, over a year earlier. Admittedly, there was a rise in oil prices and, on top of this, the lagged effect of the depreciation of the yen in 1998. These factors alone, however, did not seem to explain the forecast error. Either there was a serious overestimate of the output gap or something was missing from the price equation.

It is not difficult to find reasons for possible upward biases in output gap estimates. A significant portion of investment in structures during the late 1980s and early 1990s may have been just wasted, which was one facet of the bad loan problem. Instead of using the actual capital stock through a production function, we could regress actual output on a non-linear time trend and, say, various measures of demand pressure in the goods market, for example the 'supply and demand conditions for products' diffusion index in our Tankan (Short-Term Economic Survey of Enterprises) to estimate potential output and the gap. This method results in a much smaller output gap estimate. Depending on what is assumed about other parameters in the Taylor rule formula, it is not impossible to come up with a Taylor rule rate that was already positive in August 2000.

We could go a little further here. Uncertainties about output gap size have important implications for the Taylor rule. Orphanides et al. (1999) report interesting simulation results. They suggest policy attenuation, that is, a decrease in the response of the interest rate to the gap in the response of large measurement errors with respect to the output gap. Moreover, when measurement errors are very large, it is better to respond to the difference between the growth rates of actual and potential output rather than to the output gap. In other words, the interest rate is seen to respond to the change in the output gap rather than its level. They call this the growth rate rule.[7]

Most of the board members believed in the summer of 2000 that, assuming no major negative shocks, the economy would grow in fiscal year 2000 at a higher rate than some of the highest reasonable estimates of the growth rate of potential output. If that occurred, the growth rate rule, assuming that its usefulness carried over in the context of the zero bound on the interest rate, would seem to have given us a positive interest rate under a wide range of assumptions.[8]

I hasten to add that these did not exactly correspond to how the proponents of the rate increase presented their arguments. I also realise that these may constitute less than compelling justifications for the rate hike decision, but they do illustrate the difficulty of using the Taylor rule type benchmark in the face of large measurement errors in output gap. Even with measurement errors, the rule seems to get the *change* in the optimal level of the interest rate roughly right. Assuming that one's previous decision was correct, the central bank can use the rule to decide on policy changes. But, in order to end the zero rate, the BOJ needed to know the optimal *level* of the interest rate, which turned out to be very difficult.[9]

6.6   Some final comments

Let me summarise the major messages of the paper. The ZIRP was a unique experiment in the history of the BOJ, not just because it set the level of the overnight rate at zero but because it involved some commitment regarding the future course of monetary policy. The effects of the policy on the economy were significant as a result of this commitment influencing the expectations of market participants. The commitment was a useful way to address the liquidity crunch associated with the recession. It also helped to contain expectations of premature rate hikes, especially at the early stages of the ZIRP. Given that the ZIRP was lifted in August 2000, it is probably fair to say that we did not complete the Reifschneider–Williams type experiment.

It was easy to make a case against the rate hike proposal in August. As I hope I have demonstrated, however, the analytical foundation of such an argument is less tight than one might think. And it was not impossible to support the rate hike with analytical arguments. The indeterminacy here results from our inadequate understanding of the supply side of the economy. I would add that other central banks around the world have been facing similar difficulties.[10] We have also not yet developed effective tools to deal with mismeasurements and uncertainties in our policy-making. Certainly, more research is needed in this area.

6.7   Acknowledgements

Earlier versions of this paper were given at the conference on the Transmission Mechanism of Monetary Policy held at the Bank of England, June 2000, and the Japan Project Meeting of the NBER held at the Swedish Embassy in Tokyo, September 2000.

Notes

1 Goodfriend (2000) points out the signalling role of a rate cut during a liquidity crunch. He argues that, because the accommodation of increased demand for liquidity usually takes place automatically, it is desirable to have an accompanying rate cut to demonstrate the central bank's commitment to maintaining financial stability.

2 Incidentally, this was a period of extreme volatility in the demand for money. It is almost possible to detect a negative correlation between monetary aggregates and the pace of real economic activity. Hence, use of a money supply rule, such as the McCallum rule for the monetary base, would very likely have aggravated the economic instability of the period.

3 Tinsley (1999) discusses what a central bank can do to generate stimulative effects when short rates are near zero. He suggests that the central bank writes put options on short-term securities in order to minimise the expectation that short rates will be raised in the near future. In a sense the BOJ achieved the same end using a less formal approach.

4 Actually, there were some foreign banks that enjoyed negative funding rates. They entered into yen–dollar swap arrangements with Japanese banks on favourable terms and thus took advantage of the existence of the large Japan premium.

5 Similarly, the ZIRP in this sense seems to overlap at least partially with proposals to generate a weaker yen.

6 I am not suggesting that the Taylor rule is the benchmark we use. I am using the rule simply to illustrate an analytical approach to the determination to the optimal rate.

7 In a later paper, Orphanides (2000) develops this into what he calls the natural growth targeting rule.

8 See also note 9.

9 Even if the zero rate had been a correct decision a quarter ago, it may have been so because the Taylor rule rate was negative. An upward movement in the Taylor rule rate from there is no reason to end the zero rate, because the Taylor rule rate may still be negative. This line of thinking suggests that one needs a special check to see whether the result of Orphanides et al. (1999) holds true at the zero bound.

10 See, for example, Meyer (2000) and Wadhwani (2000) for discussions of the relationship between uncertainties about the supply side of the economy and monetary policy.

7 What does the UK's monetary policy and inflation experience tell us about the transmission mechanism?

Edward Nelson

7.1 Introduction

The United Kingdom's monetary policy and inflation history over the past 45 years provides a rich source of information about the effects of monetary actions. It is a reflection of the wealth of this experience that several of the key catchphrases used in macroeconomic policy analysis were originally coined to describe regularities in UK policy-making or UK data: 'stop–go', 'the Phillips curve' and 'stagflation' are prominent examples.

Monetary policy in the United Kingdom has undergone several regime changes over this period: from a fixed exchange rate with foreign exchange controls until 1972; to free-floating with no domestic nominal anchor until 1976,[1] followed by a loose system of monetary targeting until the mid-1980s; then a renewed emphasis on exchange rate management (so-called 'shadowing' of the Deutsche Mark), which culminated in a fixed exchange rate regime – membership of the Exchange Rate Mechanism (ERM) – from 1990 to 1992.[2] Since 1992, of course, the UK monetary policy regime has been one of inflation targeting – with interest rate decisions made by the Treasury up to May 1997, and by the Monetary Policy Committee of the Bank of England thereafter.

For the period as a whole, the swings of inflation and economic growth have also been drastic. Inflation was continually in double digits from 1974 to 1977, and returned there in the early 1980s and early 1990s. Economic growth, already lower in the United Kingdom than in all of its major trading partners in the 1960s, underwent a slowdown after 1973, with a partial recovery beginning in the 1980s. There were recessions in 1972, 1974–5, 1979–81 and 1990–2. On the other hand, the disinflation associated with the early 1990s recession has been followed by a long period of low and stable inflation and reasonably stable real GDP growth.

In this paper, I discuss some key aspects regarding the transmission mechanism of monetary policy raised by the UK experience. My analysis of the

UK monetary policy record uses the tools of monetary policy rules and dynamic stochastic general equilibrium (DSGE) models.[3] I first discuss, in section 7.2, aggregate supply relationships (the Phillips curve and potential output). In section 7.3 I discuss the specification of aggregate demand in the UK. Section 7.4 concludes.

7.2   Aggregate supply: the Phillips curve and potential output

I turn first to aggregate supply, that is, the interrelationship of inflation, output and potential output. Following the work of Friedman (1966, 1968) and Phelps (1967), most macroeconomic models adopt an expectations-augmented Phillips curve. These can be regarded as variants or extensions of the equation:[4]

$$\pi_t = \alpha(y_t - y_t^*) + E_t \pi_{t+1} + u_t, \tag{7.1}$$

where π_t is inflation, y_t is the log of real GDP, y_t^* is the log of potential real GDP and $E_t \pi_{t+1}$ is inflation expected next period; u_t is a disturbance term. Generalisations of equation (7.1) could allow for lags of the output gap or inflation to appear in the equation, for the inclusion of additional variables (for example the exchange rate, as in Ball, 1999b), or for separate modelling of wage and price formation (for example, Erceg, Henderson and Levin, 1999). For the present discussion, however, equation (7.1) suffices. In the remainder of this section, I discuss three issues connected with the use of equation (7.1): its value in the analysis of the Great Inflation of the 1970s; and two aspects of the specification of the Phillips curve.

7.2.1   Why did the Great Inflation of the 1970s happen?

The first aspect of the Phillips curve that I discuss pertains to the specification of the relationship, and even more fundamentally to its use as an *explanation of policy history*. The monograph by Sargent (1999) formalises and builds upon a familiar explanation for the 'Great Inflation' in the United States (say, 1965 to 1982). This explanation attributes policy mistakes to a particular misspecification by policy-makers of the monetary transmission mechanism. In Sargent's account, policy-makers estimated empirical Phillips curves on early postwar data but, instead of using the correct specification (7.1), they estimated equations of the form

$$\pi_t = \alpha(y_t - y_t^*) + b\pi_{t-1} + u_t, \tag{7.2}$$

or dynamic generalisations of this equation that allowed for multiple lags of inflation or the gap. Sargent argues that policy-makers treated the estimated value of the lagged inflation coefficient, b, as though it was a structural parameter – that is, it would remain constant in the face of changes in monetary policy regime. In so doing, they modelled inflation as though it evolved mechanically in a backward-looking manner as a function of lagged inflation and the output gap, regardless of policy regime. In reality, however, $b\pi_{t-1}$ was serving as a proxy for the expected inflation term in equation (7.1). The b coefficient would therefore be a function of the time-series process for inflation, and would typically change with monetary policy regime.

Empirical estimates of equation (7.2) on data for the 1950s and early 1960s for the United States[5] typically delivered a value of b that was above 0 and below 1.0.[6] Thus, the steady state of equation (7.2) is $y - y^* = [(1 - b)/\alpha)]\pi$, which appears to imply that output can be raised permanently above its potential value by appropriate choice of steady-state inflation rate. It took, according to Sargent's story, a period in which policy-makers attempted to keep output above potential for them to realise that there was no such trade-off. A policy aiming to keep y_t above y_t^* by a constant amount produced a sequence of lasting increases in the inflation rate, not the once-and-for-all rise in the steady-state inflation rate suggested by equation (7.2). Moreover, the period of sharply rising inflation changed the time-series behaviour of inflation to a unit root ($I(1)$) process, tending to raise the estimated value of b in equation (7.2) – in regressions on updated sample periods – closer to 1.0. Since their own estimates of the Phillips curve parameters now indicated no gains from steady high inflation, policy-makers disinflated.[7]

Taylor (1997, p. 278) endorses the position that 'the idea that there was a long-run [downward-sloping] Phillips curve' was a major factor in generating the Great Inflation in the United States. He notes that the acceptance of a long-run trade-off between inflation and unemployment was enshrined in official US government documents such as the 1969 *Economic Report of the President*.

The United Kingdom, however, is a different matter. Since the Phillips curve was originally derived from UK data, and a breakdown of the Phillips curve occurred in the 1960s and early 1970s in the United Kingdom (around the same time as in the United States), it is tempting to conclude that Sargent's hypothesis serves as a good explanation of the UK's own 'Great Inflation'. The details of UK policy formation in the 1960s and 1970s, and the state of UK macroeconomic thinking at the time, however, argue against this interpretation.

Although, in the United States, the government's economic advisers subscribed to the Phillips curve trade-off idea, the corresponding advisers in the United Kingdom rejected it. A prominent example is Nicholas Kaldor, who was a full-time special adviser to the Chancellor of the Exchequer from 1964 to 1968 and again from 1974 to 1976.[8] Far from accepting the Phillips curve trade-off, Kaldor was a deep sceptic, speaking negatively about the 'uncritical acceptance of the econometric studies of Professor Phillips' (Kaldor, 1971, p. 499). He even described the Phillips curve as a 'crazy idea' (Kaldor, 1972, p. 377). Lesson

(1998) notes that Kaldor rejected the trade-off interpretation of the Phillips curve as early as February 1959. More generally, Kaldor's colleagues both in the Treasury and in UK academia subscribed predominantly to a non-output-gap-based – and, indeed, non-monetary – model of inflation.[9] According to this view, demand management, including monetary policy, could affect real variables such as output, and excesses of output above potential would result in inflation. But there was great scepticism that holding output below potential exerted much significant dampening effect on inflation – at least if output gaps as great as those in the interwar period were not contemplated.[10] As discussed below, this view tended to shape the formation of anti-inflationary policy in the United Kingdom well into the mid-1970s. It certainly was not an environment conducive to acceptance of the Phillips curve either as a model of inflation or as a guide to macroeconomic policy choices.

Quite apart from policy-makers' views, the details of the timing of events in the UK also seems inconsistent with the Sargent hypothesis. Estimates of the conventional downward-sloping Phillips curve exhibited instability starting in the mid-1960s, and the implied trade-off became more unfavourable. Indeed, the term 'stagflation' was coined by the Conservative Party spokesman on economic affairs, Iain Macleod, in November 1965.[11] The presence of stagflation was an issue in the 1966 general election campaign, with the Leader of the Opposition, Edward Heath, using the slogan '9–5–1' to describe the prevailing conditions of 9% wage inflation, 5% price inflation, and 1% economic growth (Butler, 1989, p. 25). Stagflation can be regarded as a symptom of the breakdown of the original, non-vertical Phillips curve. According to the Sargent hypothesis, the advent of stagflation in the mid-1960s should have triggered a movement to disinflationary policies; but such policies were not introduced decisively until the late 1970s.

Figure 7.1 plots recursive estimates on UK data of a backward-looking Phillips curve such as equation (7.2) for sample periods beginning in 1956(Q2).[12] The lagged inflation coefficient, b, became sharply higher in 1959–62 and again from 1969, and shifted to the vicinity of unity in 1973, where it has remained. The breakdown of this downward-sloping Phillips curve should, according to Sargent's hypothesis, have motivated UK policy-makers to adopt tighter monetary policies and to reduce inflation, culminating in an abandonment of expansionary monetary policies once the estimated value of b had hit unity. Yet in the United Kingdom, inflation continued to rise until 1975, and in 1980 stood at close to its 1975 peak; a sustained shift to single-digit inflation did not emerge until 1982.

In Sargent's scenario, the failure of unemployment to decline permanently in the face of rising inflation convinces policy-makers that the Phillips curve has vertical long-run properties. Although this did happen eventually in the UK, it did not occur in the decade from 1965 to 1975, which saw almost constantly increasing inflation and higher unemployment than previously. Rather,

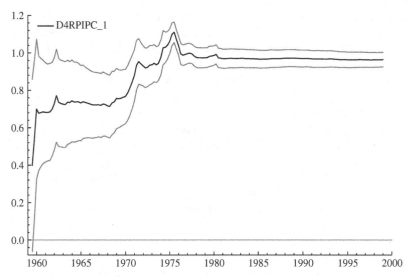

Figure 7.1 Recursive least squares estimates of b in equation (7.2), UK data.
Note: The upper and lower lines are 95% confidence interval bands.

policy-makers were, as noted above, *already* sceptical about the value of any demand- or output-gap-oriented model of inflation. For many, the onset of simultaneously high inflation and low growth seemed only to confirm the pre-existing position that inflation was largely an institutional, cost-push phenomenon independent of the output gap, the stance of monetary policy or the state of aggregate demand.[13] This reaction was shared by a sizeable fraction of the financial press. For example, an editorial in *The Banker* magazine of March 1971 argued,

[T]he Paish/Phillips relationship between unemployment and wage levels worked in the '50s and early '60s. Today it manifestly does not. Or at least the place where unemployment starts to limit wage claims is not at a politically acceptable 2 or $2\frac{1}{2}$ per cent but at 5, 6, or even 10 per cent. Since this type of analysis essentially relating inflation to aggregate demand is no longer helpful it seems silly to be crucified by it. It does not follow that if limiting demand fails to reduce inflation, expanding it will not increase it. But since the Government already tacitly accepts that the large part of the cure to inflation is institutional ... this is a risk that it has no option but to take. (1971, p. 237)

With a climate of opinion such as this, it is perhaps not surprising that the reaction of UK policy-makers to rising inflation in the 1960s and 1970s was a combination of lax monetary policy, or even aggressive monetary expansion, and the employment of various non-monetary devices to hold down inflation. These devices typically took the form of measures designed to affect the prices of particular products, or attempts to intervene in the labour market through controls or agreements on wages. A six-month wage and price freeze was imposed in July 1966, more than five years before one was introduced in the United States, and was followed by legislative incomes policy until 1968. Edward Heath, as Leader of the Opposition in the 1970 election campaign, argued that reductions in payroll taxes and restraint in price increases by government-owned corporations would 'at a stroke, reduce the rise in prices, increase productivity and reduce unemployment' (quoted in Campbell, 1993, pp. 281–2). Direct price and wage controls were reintroduced in November 1972 and maintained until 1974, when they were followed by a voluntary wages policy until 1979 (supported by legislation in 1975–76).[14] Initiatives announced in budgetary statements in 1974 attempted to reduce the retail price index through subsidies on food prices and through cuts in indirect taxation.[15]

The emphasis on incomes policy and on influencing specific prices to control inflation was largely at the expense of measures to control aggregate demand. Although tightenings in monetary and fiscal policy did accompany incomes policies in 1966–8 and 1976, the opposite was true on other occasions. For example, monetary policy was already very loose when the wage and price controls of 1972–4 were introduced, and the controls were accompanied by an aggressive fiscal expansion.[16]

From late 1973, policy-makers did react to the growing criticism of the rapid money growth they had permitted. However, in large part because of the close relationship between mortgage interest rates and short-term market interest rates, there remained an unwillingness to accept the political unpopularity resulting from the rise in nominal interest rates associated with monetary tightening.[17] Consequently, the government gave an instruction to the Bank of England that the growth rate of broad money (the Sterling M3 aggregate) was to be reduced – but not by a policy that involved increasing interest rates (Goodhart, 1997). The Bank of England responded by introducing a direct quantitative control on £M3, the 'Corset', which imposed heavy marginal reserve requirements if increases in banks' deposits exceeded a limit. Although this device did accomplish a reduction in observed £M3 growth, it did so largely by encouraging the growth of deposit substitutes, distorting £M3 as a monetary indicator and weakening its relationship with future inflation. For the remainder of the 1970s, monetary policy often looked tight as measured by £M3 growth, but loose as measured by interest rates or monetary base growth. Indeed, it is significant that, not long after adopting £M3 targeting in 1976, UK policy-makers unilaterally adopted a target for the sterling–dollar exchange rate for the first 10 months of 1977, a policy that explains why nominal interest rates were cut all the way to 5% (less than half the rate of inflation) in 1977.[18] Thus, even monetary targeting, like incomes policy, became a way of appearing to deal with inflation while avoiding genuine restrictions on aggregate demand.[19]

Figure 7.2 displays the actual values of the end-of-quarter nominal Treasury bill rate in the UK (R) against the value that, at each point in time, is suggested

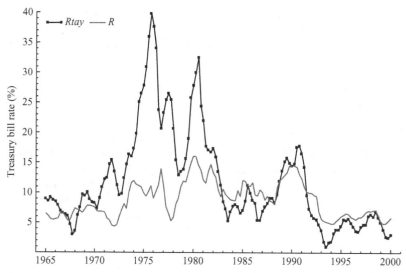

Figure 7.2 Actual nominal interest rate in the United Kingdom and the value implied by a Taylor rule.

by a Taylor (1993) rule. The specific form of the Taylor rule used is

$$Rtay_t = r^{ss} + 4\pi^* + 1.5(100^*[P_t - P_{t-4}])/P_{t-4} - 4\pi^*)$$
$$+ 0.5(100^* y_{t-1}), \tag{7.3}$$

where P_t is the quarterly average of the retail price index (RPI) and y_{t-1} is detrended log output (with the trend measured by a linear trend that breaks in 1973(Q4) and 1981(Q2). The right-hand-side variables in rule (7.3) are lagged to allow for delays in data collection,[20] and multiplied by 100 to be in units comparable to the nominal interest rate. The assumed inflation target is $4\pi^* = 2.5\%$, which corresponds to the actual UK inflation target since 1992, and the steady-state real interest rate (r^{ss}) is set at 2%, the number used by Taylor (1993) and close to the average value of the UK ex post real interest rate since 1965.

As figure 7.2 shows, the actual nominal rate was below the Taylor rule's prescription throughout the period 1969–81. (In recent years the two series have been much closer to each other.)[21] This finding supports the notion that in the 1970s there was a persistent unwillingness to rely on monetary policy to control inflation.

With the breakdown in 1978–9 of the last UK attempt at incomes policy and the change in government in May 1979, there was a shift to a monetary policy more consistent with controlling inflation. Lord Cockfield, the government's minister in the House of Lords responsible for economic matters, summarised the situation:

It was the failure of incomes policies, as well as of other devices, which brought home not only to the Government but to most people that there was no alternative to a strict monetary policy... as the means of controlling inflation. (House of Lords speech, 15 November 1979, *Hansard*, col. 1414)

A tightening of monetary policy (as measured by monetary base growth or interest rates)[22] followed, and inflation declined sharply after 1980. Although there was a serious renewed breakout of inflation in 1988–90, policy-makers' acceptance of the role of monetary policy in controlling inflation remained. The Treasury in the 1990/91 *Financial Statement and Budget Report* stated, 'Inflation is a monetary problem and so monetary policy has to be in the fore-front of the battle to conquer it' (HM Treasury, 1990, p. 11). Consistent with this, the United Kingdom has had a formal inflation target since October 1992, and this target was assigned to the Bank of England when it received inde-pendence in 1997. The Monetary Policy Committee, which makes interest rate decisions in the United Kingdom, stated in its publication *The Transmission Mechanism of Monetary Policy* that '[m]onetary growth persistently in excess of that warranted by growth in the real economy will inevitably be the reflection of an interest rate policy that is inconsistent with stable inflation. So control of inflation ultimately implies control of the monetary growth rate' (Bank of England, 1999a, p. 169).

The evidence suggests, I argue, that until the late 1970s policy-makers pre-dominantly did not believe that restraint in aggregate demand was very effective in controlling inflation; and they regarded the inflation that they did observe as emerging from institutional sources rather than from mismanagement of aggre-gate demand. This was not a model of inflation that would emerge from Phillips curve analysis. Policy-makers did believe that monetary policy could affect real variables, even in the long run, and so followed demand management policies quite similar to those that might emerge from subscribing to a Phillips curve. In terms of an acceptance by UK policy-makers of the importance of monetary policy actions for inflation, and of the long-run neutrality of output and unem-ployment with respect to monetary policy, 1976 was probably the watershed year. But it was not until later in the 1970s that policy-makers were prepared to accept the movements in interest rates and exchange rates, and the initial cost in the form of a recession, that would result from a policy that brought inflation down.

So Phillips curve analysis did not, I argue, play a substantial role in either generating or ending high inflation in the United Kingdom. Rather, the key analytical flaw in UK policy-making in the 1960s and 1970s was neglect of the links between monetary policy and inflation. Such links conveniently bring me to the next topic: the relationship between Phillips curves and the proposition that inflation is a monetary phenomenon.

7.2.2   Is the Phillips curve consistent with inflation being a monetary phenomenon?

A second aspect of the Phillips curve that is important in a discussion of the monetary transmission mechanism is a particular specification issue. As noted above, empirical Phillips curves (for example, Gordon, 1997; Brayton, Roberts and Williams, 1999; Driver, Greenslade and Pierse, 2000) typically have more lags and/or leads of the output gap and inflation than appear in equation (7.2). Beginning with Phillips (1958), they usually also have included other forcing variables beside the output gap term. Examples include dummy variables for periods of statutory price control; the prices of volatile elements of the price index such as food and energy; and the exchange rate or import prices to represent open economy influences.

I do not question the inclusion of these extra terms in empirical Phillips curves – and, indeed, largely abstract from them from now on by concentrating on closed economy Phillips curves.[23] What I do question is the less common practice of including money growth (or other measures of monetary stance) in estimated empirical Phillips curves. The Phillips curve studies mentioned above do not follow this practice, but Perry (1978) and Hendry (2000), for example, do. These papers aim to 'test' monetary theories of inflation against other theories by estimating a regression, with inflation as the dependent variable, that includes both money growth and the output gap as explanatory variables. The implication would appear to be that the validity of 'monetary explanations' of inflation rests on the statistical significance (with positive signs) of money growth terms when used as additional regressors in estimates of equation (7.2).

These sorts of tests are, I believe, wide of the mark. I contend that the theoretical proposition that inflation is a monetary phenomenon rests on the specification of *aggregate demand* in an economic model. Essentially, the statement amounts to a claim that influences on the growth rate of nominal aggregate demand do not tend to be persistent if they are not associated with similar movements in the growth rate of the nominal quantity of money. It follows that sustained movements in inflation are largely accompanied by movements in the growth rate of the nominal quantity of money per unit of output. None of these statements requires a specification of the aggregate supply segment of the model. The Phillips curve does not even have to be vertical for these statements to hold; they could be just as true if equation (7.2) were structural, for example. The statements certainly do not require terms in money growth to appear in the Phillips curve equation.[24]

I agree with Lionel Robbins (1960) that no reputable quantity theorist has argued that money affects prices other than via its effect on aggregate expenditure.[25] In a sticky-price world, changes in nominal aggregate demand tend to be manifested also in changes in the real volume of spending relative to the potential output of the economy – that is, in the output gap. In this sequence, the output gap is the route through which movements in monetary growth are transmitted to the inflation rate. Thus, the output gap and monetary growth are not 'alternative explanations' of inflation. Meyer and Varvares (1981, p. 24) made this point earlier: 'We do not view the Phillips Curve and monetarist re-duced form as mutually exclusive [models], but rather as structural vs. reduced form approaches to explaining inflation.'

I would not therefore expect money growth to have a non-zero coefficient in a correctly specified Phillips curve. What, then, are we to make of regression results (such as those in Hendry, 2000) in which both the output gap and money growth enter significantly? There seem to me to be two key elements underlying such results.

First, the estimated significance of money growth may reflect changing de-grees of nominal rigidity in the economy. If prices were perfectly flexible – so that output equalled potential each period – the output gap would be zero every period, and so would not (could not!) help at all in predicting inflation. Money growth and inflation, on the other hand, would continue to fluctuate together. Money growth would explain many (or all) of the movements in inflation, and the output gap would not explain any. If, on the other hand, the degree of excess demand were the only determinant of inflation, and if the degree of nominal rigidity in the economy were constant (for example, if a fixed fraction of firms changed their price every period), the output gap would have a perfect relation-ship with inflation, and money growth would provide no extra information.

In practice, economies may behave between these two extremes, with the degree of price stickiness varying over time. For example, if the extent to which firms are prepared to change prices is state contingent, the degree of nominal rigidity in the economy will change each period (Dotsey, King and Wolman, 1999). In these circumstances, the economy may behave like a hybrid of one in which only money growth matters for inflation and one in which only the output gap matters for inflation. Money growth may therefore provide auxiliary information about inflation not present in the output gap.

Money growth may also enter estimated inflation equations alongside the output gap if the empirical measure of the output gap is a poor approximation of the true output gap series. In particular, the behaviour of potential output may in practice be very different from the behaviour implied by most empiri-cal procedures for measuring potential. Let me turn now to this measurement problem.

7.2.3   Measurement of potential output

In a recent paper, Galí and Gertler (1999) estimate versions of the Phillips curve equation (7.1) on US data.[26] Following standard practice, they initially estimate it by measuring the output gap, $y^t - y_t^*$, by a measure of detrended log output. They find that the estimated coefficient α is wrongly signed, a result that has often been interpreted as a rejection of forward-looking Phillips curves such as equation (7.1). But Galí and Gertler note that the economic theory that generates equation (7.1) implies that the output gap is proportional to log real marginal cost. When Galí and Gertler use the latter as the forcing process for inflation, they find that the resulting model describes the data well.[27] Thus, the inflation equation fits well with marginal cost but poorly with detrended output.

These results have two alternative interpretations. One is that detrended output has a close relationship with the output gap, but marginal cost does not. This result might suggest the need for a richer model of marginal cost determination that is given in standard dynamic stochastic general equilibrium (DSGE) models.[28] The alternative interpretation, on which I focus, is that detrended output is not a good proxy for the output gap.

This second interpretation has considerable theoretical appeal. Standard output gap measures are based on the assumption that potential output evolves according to a deterministic trend (such as a linear or quadratic trend, or a linear trend with breaks). High-frequency movements in potential output are not generally permitted. On the other hand, the economic theory that underlies DSGE modelling suggests instead that potential output fluctuates over the business cycle in response to all real shocks (such as technology, preference, fiscal and terms of trade shocks). Standard measures of the output gap would, therefore, appear to be invalid unless the response of potential output to real shocks is very flat, in which case detrended output provides a good approximation of the output gap.

Such behaviour seems unlikely, however, in light of the results from many dynamic general equilibrium models that suggest that potential output fluctuates considerably. Some evidence on the quantitative importance of this point is provided in Neiss and Nelson (2000). In that paper we carry out stochastic simulations of a sticky-price DSGE model subject to a monetary policy rule estimated on UK data. Owing to the complete specification of the real side of our model, we are able to keep track of the behaviour of both actual output (the realised value of output under sticky prices) and potential output (the output level that *would* prevail *if* prices were flexible). Consequently, we are able to measure the output gap in the model directly, instead of using a measure based on detrended output. Our results suggest that detrended output is an extremely poor proxy for the output gap: in the baseline simulations the correlation between the two series is -0.68! Price stickiness does cause output to diverge from potential, especially in the presence of monetary shocks. But the response of actual output and potential output to real shocks is qualitatively similar, and these real shocks account for a large fraction of cyclical behaviour, implying that detrended output is more closely related to detrended potential output than it is to the output gap.[29]

A high priority in the future modelling of inflation behaviour, therefore, is to improve measures of potential output, so as to incorporate more of the response to real shocks that is suggested by economic theory. Incorporating these factors seems if anything more important for the UK than in the USA, since the greater openness of the UK economy probably increases the variety and importance of real shocks for cyclical behaviour. Improved measures of potential would lead to more reliable estimates of the Phillips curve and, therefore, increase our understanding of the relationship between monetary policy actions and inflation.

7.3   The IS relationship in the United Kingdom: an empirical puzzle

I turn now to the aggregate demand side of the economy. For the transmission mechanism, the most pertinent aspect of aggregate demand behaviour is how changes in monetary policy – open market operations and changes in the authority's interest rate instrument – manifest themselves in changes in private spending decisions. I use the simple aggregate demand specification of Rudebusch and Svensson (1999, 2000) as a reference point. This specification is a single-equation empirical model of the relationship between real interest rates and aggregate demand, according to which (detrended) log output (y_t)[30] depends on lags of itself, and on the previous year's average of a real interest rate measure.[31] Rudebusch and Svensson (2000), for example, present the following IS equation, estimated over US data for 1961(Q1)–1996(Q4):

$$y_t = 1.161\,y_{t-1} - 0.259\,y_{t-2} - 0.088\big(\big[\Sigma_{j=0}^{3}\,R_{t-1-j}\big] - \Delta_4 p_{t-1}\big),$$
$$\quad\quad (0.079) \quad\quad (0.077) \quad\quad (0.032)$$
$$\text{SEE} = 0.0082 \quad\quad\quad\quad\quad\quad\quad\quad\quad\quad\quad\quad (7.4)$$

Rudebusch and Svensson (1999, 2000) use equation (7.4) as the aggregate demand segment of a model that they use to conduct comparisons of alternative monetary policy rules.

Equation (7.4) has become one of the standard compact models of aggregate demand behaviour in the US economy (Estrella and Fuhrer, 2000). It does not appear easy, however, to obtain an analogous model of aggregate demand from UK data. Estimation of the Rudebusch–Svensson specification on UK data for the sample period 1958(Q1)–2000(Q2) produces:[32]

$$y_t = -0.0002 + 0.854\,y_{t-1} + 0.032\,y_{t-2} + 0.015\big(\big[\tfrac{1}{4}\Sigma_{j=0}^{3}\,R_{t-j-1}\big] - \Delta_4 p_{t-1}\big)$$
$$\quad (0.0008) \quad (0.078) \quad\quad (0.077) \quad\quad (0.019)$$
$$R^2 = .79,\ \text{SEE} = 0.0101,$$

so that the real interest rate term is insignificant and incorrectly signed. The results become even more at variance with those of Rudebusch and Svensson if the sample period is restricted to the last 20 years, 1980(Q1)–2000(Q2):

$$y_t = -0.0035 + 1.317y_{t-1} - 0.395y_{t-2} + 0.082\left(\left[\frac{1}{4}\Sigma^3_{j=0} R_{t-j-1}\right] - \Delta_4 p_{t-1}\right)$$
$$\quad\quad (0.0014) \quad (0.101) \quad\quad (0.099) \quad\quad (0.031)$$

$R^2 = .95$, SEE $= 0.0061$.

In this case, the interest rate term is not only incorrectly signed, but *significantly* positive. The positive sign on the interest rate persists in a more general dynamic specification: a regression of y_t on four lags of itself and of the interest rate term. When this specification is estimated, it delivers a long-run coefficient sum on the real interest rate of 0.73 (standard error 0.43). Muscatelli and Trecroci (2000) also report a positive sign on the real rate in estimated backward-looking IS equations estimated on UK data.

So there is a puzzle: why do UK estimates of the Rudebusch–Svensson specification deliver a positive sign on the real interest rate? I refer to this as the *IS puzzle* as I go through a few candidate explanations.

One explanation for the IS puzzle is that the UK specification is delivering inconsistent parameter estimates owing to the omission of real exchange rate terms. In Nelson (2000b), however, I find that including the real exchange rate in the equation has very little effect on the estimated real interest rate terms; they continue to have positive coefficients.

A second possibility is that the results are due to the exclusion of foreign output. In their estimated IS equation for Australia, Beechey et al. (2000) find that the level of foreign output enters very significantly, and is a better proxy for open economy influences on the economy than the exchange rate. Conditional on this effect, they are also able to pick up a significant negative effect on output of the domestic real interest rate. For the United Kingdom, however, this approach does not resolve the IS puzzle. If y_t is regressed on lags 1–4 of itself and of the real rate, and lags 0–4 of detrended log US output,[33] the estimated long-run coefficients for 1980(Q1)–2000(Q2) are 0.50 (standard error 0.43) on foreign output and 0.47 (standard error 0.31) on the real rate.[34]

Another explanation for the IS puzzle is that the variations in the real rate measure ($[\frac{1}{4}\Sigma^3_{j=0} R_{t-j}] - \Delta_r p_t$) are dominated by the sharp fall in its mean from the 1980s to the 1990s. This fall – which was greater in the United Kingdom than in the United States – might reflect a decline in the steady-state value of the 'natural' real interest rate, or a higher 'risk premium' term in interest rates in the 1980s (perhaps owing to lack of credibility of monetary policy before inflation targeting). Either of these effects could mean that monetary policy was not as tight in the 1980s as the real rate measure suggests, and that it is therefore harder to determine reliably the effects of monetary policy on aggregate demand. This explanation, however, does not account for the results in Beechey et al. (2000) for Australia. Australia had a decline in the mean value of the real interest rate from the 1980s to the 1990s similar in magnitude to that in the United Kingdom, but Beechey et al. are able to pick up a significant negative coefficient on the real rate. In light of this, the UK results above remain anomalous.

Another possible explanation for the IS puzzle is that equations of the Rudebusch–Svensson type are not structural, owing to forward-looking behaviour in the economy. If the true structure of the economy is one in which the private sector's spending decisions are based on utility maximisation (as in a DSGE model), then the implied IS equation for the economy will include expected future output, not just the lags of output that appear in (7.4). In this environment, the coefficients in the Rudebusch–Svensson specification are reduced form, and not invariant to policy rule changes. This factor may partially explain why the Rudebusch–Svensson model does not produce robust results when estimated on different countries. But it is less likely to explain the IS puzzle found above in UK data. In Nelson (2000b), I generate data from a dynamic stochastic general equilibrium model with sticky prices, solved under monetary policy reaction functions estimated on historical US or UK data. When the Rudebusch–Svensson specification is estimated on the artificial data, the resulting regressions do produce a positive, near-unit coefficient sum on lagged output and a negative coefficient on the real interest rate, just as in Rudebusch and Svensson's estimates. Because these coefficients are reduced form, plausible changes in the monetary policy rule do change the sizes of the estimated coefficients. But the coefficient on the real interest rate remains negative. So, by itself, forward-looking behaviour may not account for the IS puzzle.

A related, but more generic, criticism of equations of the Rudebusch–Svensson type applies irrespective of whether the private sector is forward looking. The criticism is that these equations do not isolate the effects of monetary policy on aggregate demand because the endogenous component of monetary policy – the response of monetary policy to past and prospective shocks to aggregate demand and supply – makes the coefficients in the estimated equation a function of both the economic structure and the monetary policy rule that was in effect during the estimation period. To estimate the effects of monetary policy, one should instead, according to this argument, attempt to isolate the truly exogenous component of policy, for example through vector autoregression (VAR) or narrative techniques (as described in Christiano, Eichenbaum and Evans, 1999). In the present context, a limitation of this argument is that it does not tell us why real interest rate coefficients are negative and significant in IS equations based on US and Australian data, but not in those based on UK data. Presumably identification problems should be pervasive, and similar, for all three countries; yet an IS puzzle exists for only one. On the other hand, Leeper and Zha (2000) find that certain VAR identification schemes deliver 'reasonable' estimates of structural parameters for some subsamples of US data but not for other subsamples. This finding could indicate that the identification problem is indeed prevalent in all countries, and that the degree to which it affects estimates of IS parameters is sensitive to the specific sample period.

Several other possible explanations should be noted. First, it is possible that variations in the unobserved natural real rate of interest are large enough to generate a positive average relationship between actual real interest rates and output. Secondly, unmodelled financial restrictions, such as borrowing or liquidity constraints, could be distorting the estimates of the IS equation. And my estimated equation abstracts from fiscal policy, which could be important empirically for the behaviour of both real interest rates and aggregate demand.

In my opinion, the most promising single explanation for the IS puzzle is that other asset yields are relevant for aggregate demand. If these asset yields are correlated with the short-term real interest rate, then excluding them from the regression will deliver unreliable estimates of the real rate coefficient. Two pieces of evidence make this explanation the most plausible. First, Goodhart and Hofmann (2000) find that house prices are highly significant in an estimated IS equation for the United Kingdom, and that the real interest rate coefficient is negative once house prices are included in the specification.[35] Second, in Nelson (2000b), I find that real money base growth is highly significant when added to the Rudebusch–Svensson specification. This result is consistent with the arguments of Friedman and Schwartz (1963) and Meltzer (1999) that yields on many assets are relevant for aggregate demand, and that money growth can be a useful summary of the effects of these yields. The short-term real interest rate, by itself, may not be a sufficient statistic for all the asset prices relevant for aggregate demand in the United Kingdom.

7.4   Conclusions

In this paper, I have discussed several aspects of aggregate supply and demand determination that are relevant to the analysis of the transmission mechanism in the UK. To state my conclusions briefly: the evolution of beliefs about the Phillips curve probably did not play a major role in generating the policy mistakes that led to inflation in the United Kingdom in the 1960s and 1970s; rather, poor understanding of the role of monetary policy in controlling inflation was much more important. At the same time, there are few grounds for believing that monetary policy variables should appear directly in structural models of inflation. The most important modification to the latter should be improved, theory-based measures of potential output. Finally, on the aggregate demand side the relationship between real interest rates and aggregate demand seems more complicated in the United Kingdom than it is in the United States, and modelling the effects of other asset prices on demand appears essential.

Acknowledgements

I thank Christopher Allsopp, David Gruen, DeAnne Julius, Eric Leeper, Allan Meltzer, Peter Sinclair and Geoffrey Wood, as well as seminar participants at the Centre for Central Banking Studies, for extensive comments. The views expressed in this paper are mine alone and should not be interpreted as those of the Bank of England, the Centre for Central Banking Studies, the Monetary Policy Committee or the Centre for Economic Policy Research.

Notes

1 As discussed below, monetary targeting was introduced in the United Kingdom in 1976. From 1980, monetary targeting became part of the Medium Term Financial Strategy (MTFS), a monetary and fiscal policy programme announced by the Conservative government in its annual budget. Formally, monetary targets (or projections) continued to be part of the MTFS until 1996. By 1988, however, monetary targets had been so de-emphasised in monetary policy formation that Nigel Lawson (the Chancellor of the Exchequer) could say, 'As far as monetary policy is concerned, the two things perhaps to look at are the interest rate and the exchange rate' (testimony, 30 November 1988, in Treasury and Civil Service Committee, 1988, p. 36).

2 Foreign exchange controls continued in the United Kingdom for the first seven years of floating exchange rates, but were abolished in 1979. Thus, one difference between the pre-1972 and the 1990–92 fixed exchange rate regimes is that the absence of exchange controls in the ERM period gave little room for domestic monetary policy to differ, even in the short run, from that consistent with the exchange rate target.

3 For examples of applications of these tools to the United States, see, for example, Clarida, Galí and Gertler (1999), Dotsey, King and Wolman (1999), Ireland (2000), Kiley (1998), Leeper and Zha (2000) and the papers in Taylor (1999). Recent applications to the analysis of the United Kingdom include Dhar and Millard (2000), Neiss and Nelson (2000) and Nelson (2000a,b).

4 This particular formulation is known as the 'New Keynesian Phillips Curve'. See Roberts (1995) and Clarida, Galí and Gertler (1999).

5 And also the United Kingdom; see figure 7.1 below.

6 See, for example, the estimates in Solow (1969). Solow believed that in finding $b < 1.0$ on US data in estimates of a specification similar to equation (7.2), he had found evidence against Friedman's (1968) claim of a long-run vertical Phillips curve.

7 As Cogley and Sargent (2000, p. 2) put it, 'the observations of the 1970s taught Volcker and Greenspan the natural rate hypothesis, which they eventually acted upon to reduce inflation'.

8 James Callaghan, the Chancellor from 1964 to 1967, names Kaldor as one of his advisers in his memoirs (Callaghan, 1987, p. 198).

9 See the survey by Laidler and Parkin (1975), especially pp. 761 and 764.

10 Nelson and Nikolov (2001) provide an extensive documentation of this view among UK policy-makers in the 1960s and 1970s, including quotations from prime ministers, Chancellors of the Exchequer, and Treasury officials.

11 The *Oxford English Dictionary* traces the origin of the term 'stagflation' to a speech Macleod made in the House of Commons on 17 November 1965. In his biography of Harold Macmillan, Horne (1989) has a chapter entitled ' "Stagflation" – The English Disease: 1960–end of 1961' in which he claims that in 1960–1 'a new word was entering the jargon of Westminster economists – "stagflation" '. If accurate, this statement may mean that Macleod (a member of Macmillan's government) used the term stagflation in the years prior to his first employment of it in a parliamentary speech.

12 This equation differs in two ways from equation (7.2). First, π_t is measured by *annual* growth in the retail price index, $(P_t - P_{t-4})/P_{t-4}$. Secondly, the output gap (measured in the same way as in figure 7.2 below, as deviations of log GDP from a linear trend that breaks in 1973(Q4) and 1981(Q4) enters with a one-period lag rather than contemporaneously.

13 This position is distinct from Christiano and Gust's (2000) characterisation of policy-makers' opinion in the United States. There, they argue, policy-makers recognised the dependence of inflation on monetary policy, but felt obliged to accommodate cost-push shocks with increased monetary growth. Closer to the position described here is Hetzel's (1998) characterisation of Federal Reserve views on inflation in the 1970s.

14 Harold Wilson (1979, p. 115) reported that the Treasury repeatedly urged him to introduce statutory wage controls during his administrations.

15 A key rationale for these 1974 measures was that the Labour government had inherited from the Heath government a statutory incomes policy that indexed wages to consumer prices. The 1974 actions on the retail price index were an attempt to offset some of the effect of the first oil shock on prices, and so cushion the extent to which nominal wages would rise.

16 The shift to these policies by the Heath government in 1972 is known as its 'U-turn' (see Campbell, 1993, ch. 26). Although monetary policy was loose in its own right, the sharp increase in fiscal deficits during this period was also heavily accommodated by money creation.

17 An example of this unwillingness is Margaret Thatcher's promise, during the October 1974 election campaign, that a Conservative government would impose a 'non-negotiable' upper limit of 9.5% on mortgage interest rates (Butler, 1989, p. 31; Campbell, 2000, p. 272).

18 See Browning (1986, pp. 104–8) and Dell (1996, pp. 438–9) for discussions of this episode.

19 For discussions of the development of UK monetary policy in the 1970s, see Goodhart (1989), Minford (1993) and Bank of England (1984).

20 However, the rule plotted makes no allowance for differences between initial and revised data.

21 Two points should be noted. First, the actual rate is above the Taylor rule prescription in the mid-1980s, yet inflation rose after 1987. Interest rates alone do not account for the excessive growth in aggregate demand in the late 1980s. This is consistent with the presence of the 'IS puzzle' described in section 7.3 below. On the other hand,

monetary base growth does seem to have been excessive prior to the late 1980s' breakout of inflation (Stuart, 1996; McCallum, 2000c), so a measure of monetary policy stance that included base money growth may suggest that policy was, indeed, excessively easy. Second, the actual rate is above the Taylor rule prescription recently. This partly reflects the fact that the inflation series used in figure 7.2 is one using the RPI, not the RPIX measure targeted by the Bank of England. In addition, the steady-state real interest rate of 2% assumed in rule (7.3) may be too low.

22 Monetary policy did not tighten as measured by £M3 (the government's monetary target), which, as discussed above, was distorted as a measure of monetary conditions by the imposition and, in 1980, removal of the 'Corset'. Bean and Symons (1989) note that by 1982 nominal GDP growth had reached the range that the government had intended for it with the policies it announced in 1979–80, so actual policy was at least as tight as intended.

23 This is not to say that all the additional terms used in empirical Phillips curves can be justified theoretically. Allan Meltzer (1980), for example, noted the 'generous use of dummy variables and extra effects' in Robert Gordon's pioneering empirical work on inflation.

24 These statements also do not exclude the likelihood that the money stock is endogenous. Every UK monetary policy regime has been one that made the money stock endogenous. For example, the money stock is endogenous whenever the central bank uses an interest rate instrument. But, as the Monetary Policy Committee (Bank of England, 1999a) notes, alternative choices of interest rate paths by a central bank imply alternative paths for the money stock. The same is true of other monetary arrangements that also make the money stock endogenous, such as a fixed exchange rate regime. The endogeneity of the UK money stock under fixed exchange rates was emphasised by Williams, Goodhart and Gowland (1976) and Williamson and Wood (1976).

25 The specific statement by Robbins was that 'the immediate determinant of the price level and the general level of activity is the volume of expenditure that derives, not only from the money supply but also from trade credit and all sorts of money substitutes; and if any reputable quantity theorist since Hume has denied this, let him be forever disgraced' (1960, pp. 102–3). The views of Milton Friedman are consistent with this statement. Friedman (1979, p. 302), for example, writes, 'The only cure for inflation is to reduce the rate at which total spending is growing.'

26 Galí and Gertler allow the coefficient on expected future inflation in equation (7.1), which theory suggests should be just *below* unity, to be estimated freely.

27 Sbordone (1998) estimates equation (7.1) by a different technique and also finds empirical support for it.

28 For example, as Galí and Gertler observe, the labour market in standard models could be enriched by introducing rigidity in real or nominal wages. See also Erceg, Henderson and Levin (1999).

29 An even more striking example of the unreliability of detrended output as an output gap proxy appears in Rotemberg and Woodford (1999, p. 69). Their DSGE model features a standard deviation of detrended potential output of 13.7%, compared with only 2.1% for detrended actual output. The shock processes in Rotemberg and

Woodford's model, however, have much larger variances than are standard in other models, inflating their estimate of the variance of detrended potential output.

30 The series Rudebusch and Svensson use is an official output gap series but, in light of the discussion in section 7.2.3, it is best thought of as a measure of detrended log GDP.

31 The real interest rate measure used by Rudebusch and Svensson is a 'pseudo-real' interest rate, $R_t - 4^*\Delta p_t$, so called because it subtracts current realised inflation from the nominal rate instead of expected future inflation. Note that a four-quarter average of $4^*\Delta p_t$ is the annual inflation rate, $\Delta_4 p_t$, which is why the latter appears in equation (7.4) below.

32 This regression uses data from the IMF's International Financial Statistics on the quarterly average nominal Treasury bill rate to measure R, the four-quarter percentage change in the RPIX index (RPI before 1974) to measure $\Delta_4 p_t$, and the broken-trend measure of output used in figure 7.2 to measure y. The results are robust to alternative filtering procedures for the output series.

33 Measured by the residuals of a regression for 1955(Q1)–2000(Q2) of log US output on a broken linear trend (the breaks in slope and intercept occurring in 1973(Q4) and 1994(Q4).

34 If the lag length on the real rate is changed to eight, the estimated long-run coefficient is essentially unchanged at 0.49 (standard error 0.34). David Gruen has reported a similar but more significant coefficient sum on US output when the UK IS equation is estimated using levels of output (as opposed to detrended levels). In his results, the real interest rate coefficient sum is positive when the sample period is 1980–2000, and negative (but insignificant) when the sample is 1985–2000.

35 The Goodhart–Hofmann sample period begins in 1973, however, so it is not known whether their specification would deliver negative real rate coefficients if estimated on the 1958–2000 and 1980–2000 sample periods used above.

8 Modelling the transmission mechanism of monetary policy

Peter Westaway

The main question I wish to focus on in this chapter is: 'How should we think about the monetary transmission mechanism in a live policy-making environment?' I shall concentrate upon practical problems. There are essentially two sub-questions here. The first is 'How should we define monetary policy?' The second is 'How should we model the economy?' I shall offer a personal perspective on these two sub-questions, but one that is closely related to the Bank of England's current thinking about monetary policy transmission issues, represented by the book *Economic Models at the Bank of England* (1999b).

What do we mean, therefore, by monetary policy? This should be a phrase about which central bankers should be clear. Monetary policy in the UK context is what we can do to interest rates. Yet we know that monetary policy also concerns money. Inflation is a monetary phenomenon. Economists applying for positions at the Bank of England are often asked during their interview, 'Is inflation possible in a barter economy?' A correct answer to this question is closely correlated with our selection decision!

If inflation is a monetary phenomenon, what role is there for money? The policy process for setting interest rates is informed by the use of many models that appear to have little explicit role for money. Perhaps we should state that inflation is always and everywhere a *monetary policy* phenomenon. If we have an inflation target, it is tempting to say that inflation is an inflation target phenomenon. If we employed a money target, we might describe inflation as a money target phenomenon. So what precise role does money have in the models deployed to study transmission mechanisms?

There are two main possible interpretations of this question. The first – the conventional approach – gives money a passive role. Policy works by altering interest rates; the money supply is demand driven. A money demand function is driven primarily by interest rates, incomes and prices. The money supply contains no additional information, it would seem, over and above that contained in these three variables. It could, however, be that money does provide valuable contemporaneous information, both in aggregate and disaggregated into household sector money holdings, corporate sector money and public sector money, for example (see Chrystal and Mizen in chapter 9 in this volume). The money supply adjusts passively to the demand for it. This view, encapsulated in what Alan Meltzer has termed the 'workhorse model', can be summed up in this simple framework:

$$y_t = a_1(r_t - \Delta p_t) + a_2(e_t - p_t) \tag{8.1}$$

$$\Delta p_t = b_1 \Delta p_{t-1} + (1 - b_1)\Delta p_{t+1}^e + b_2 y_t \tag{8.2}$$

$$e_t = e_{t+1}^e + r_t \tag{8.3}$$

$$r_t = \Delta p_t + c_1(\Delta p_t - \Delta p_t^*) + c_2 y_t \tag{8.4}$$

$$m_t = p_t + y_t - d_1 r_t. \tag{8.5}$$

Equation (8.1) is a simple reduced-form IS curve in which aggregate demand depends on the real interest rate and the real exchange rate. Equation (8.2) describes a dynamic Phillips curve (combining backward- and forward-looking inflation expectations), in which there is no long-run output–inflation trade-off (output is defined here relative to some measure of potential). Equation (8.3) is an exchange rate equation assumed to be determined by the uncovered interest parity (UIP) condition. Equation (8.4) gives a policy rule that has become known as the 'Taylor form' (following Taylor, 1993). Finally, equation (8.5) defines a simple money demand function. Because money is a variable in the model, that could be consistent with inflation being a monetary phenomenon. What one sees quite readily, however, is that money does not actually go anywhere apart from that fifth equation – a vestigial stump on the end of the model. Now we can turn this simple workhorse model into one where inflation really is a monetary phenomenon – by introducing an explicit role for money in a policy rule (see equation 8.4a):

$$r_t = \Delta p_t + c_1(m_t - m_t^*) + c_2 y_t. \tag{8.4a}$$

Since inflation is a monetary policy phenomenon, if we want to define monetary policy in terms of some monetary target, then this would appear to do the trick. Instead of having an inflation target, we have a money supply target. In fact, we have slipped a derivative here since we are using the level of the money supply, not its growth rate over time, so that it is analogous to a price-level target. The key point remains that inflation is being driven by money.

There is, of course, an alternative approach in which money *does* have an independent role. One can introduce an explicit role for money into this model in several ways.

- The credit channel might matter. If one allows for a credit channel, the issue is of how capital market imperfections come to the fore. So lending restrictions both in and on commercial banking activity are likely to affect supply and demand.

- We can imagine a situation in which money balances have an additional effect. If consumers receive more money than they expected in their portfolio, this, in itself, would have some effect on expenditure. This phenomenon is typically endogenous, but this may motivate an explicit role for money over and above the effects of interest rates and income.
- The composition of wealth may be important. This gives rise to a consideration of the policy implications of the composition of assets, for example in the context of changes in government balance sheets either by means of intervention in the foreign exchange markets or by attempting to modify the slope of the yield curve. These methods introduce a role for money changes in the relative price of different assets (including money) as a reflection of underlying demands.

These examples are legitimate and commonly used ways of incorporating money into models. In fact, each is captured in a particular model that highlights some aspect of the role of money. Indeed, the Bank of England explicitly uses models that capture the effects of money in these different ways.

A host of other ways exist in which we can introduce money and make it matter. Equation (8.1), the IS curve, depends on the real rate of interest; equation (8.5), the LM, on the nominal rate. Had the interest rate adjustment equation (8.4) or (8.4a), been suppressed and had the authorities attempted to set the money supply m_t, aggregate demand would have increased with the rate of inflation – actual, expected or some blend of the two. But with nominal interest rate setting and the coefficient on inflation, as in equations (8.4) and (8.4a), set to unity, the rate of inflation ceases to affect aggregate nominal demand directly. In equation (8.4), with c_1 positive, aggregate demand is lowered if inflation exceeds its target rate Δp_t^* and is raised when below this rate.

The workhorse model makes the IS curve depend on the *short* real interest rate. This can be reconciled with intertemporal optimising microfoundations, as McCallum and Nelson (1999b) have shown, by inserting a term in the expected logarithm of the next period's consumption (or income) on the right-hand side of equation (8.1). The coefficient a is then the reciprocal of the coefficient of relative risk aversion (at least in simple cases). This approach interprets aggregate demand as consumption, which is clearly its largest component.

What about investment? If firms are averse to risk, they will seek to match the maturity structure of their obligations with the maturity structure of the assets that those obligations are issued to finance. Since most forms of capital are long lived, the long real rate of interest is likely relevant and not the short real rate. The only elements of capital that should respond directly to a short real rate of interest are inventories and working capital. Long real rates may be captured by an average of current and expected future short nominal rates, not of the inflation rate anticipated for each period. Since expected future nominal rates are unlikely to respond to current nominal rates, the sensitivity of y_t to r_t may be modest. Furthermore, lags in both investment and consumption will create phased responses and an even weaker immediate impact of r_t and y_t.

Turning to equation (8.2), it is not the level of real aggregate demand to which inflation reacts in the Phillips curve (via coefficient b_2) but the GDP output gate – the excess of output over the economy's normal productive capacity at that date. This situation raises the question of how potential output is treated.

One approach is to identify potential output with trend output, leading to a considerable simplification. Trend output is identified for two dates – separated by a considerable period – for which the rate of inflation is deemed stationary (and, $b_1 < 1$, inflation expectations appear fulfilled). The trend level of output for any date can then be ascertained by interpolation or extrapolation.

Yet this may well be an oversimplification. Trends in (potential) output may not be constant. Growth has been decelerating for several decades in Germany and Japan. In many economies, growth was lower from about 1973 until the early 1980s than either previously or later. In the later 1990s, the US trend growth may have increased.

More seriously, the course of potential output will depend on the evolution of capital – not just physical capital but knowledge and human capital as well, which are key drivers of labour productivity. Important implications exist for monetary policy because the data on capital reflect short-run influences on capital as well as movements in its deeper, potential value. To measure potential output, we may have to be able to identify the potential capital stock.

As for short-run movements, a tightening of monetary policy may temporarily lower the growth of all these components of capital. A relaxation may cause the opposite. A reduction in nominal interest rates may induce firms to advance investment plans, for example. The size of this effect will have been blunted, but not eliminated, if long interest rates showed little reaction to the path of short rates. On the other hand, an advance in investment plans may imply more mistakes. More is known about the potential profitability of investment if it is delayed, and waiting often brings fortune. When restrictive monetary policy leads to investment postponement, the investment decisions taken subsequently may turn out to be more profitable, and hence more productive. These market failures (real rigidities) involved in the investment decision are important because they play their part in determining the short-run effects of monetary policy actions on investment.

Greater variability in monetary policy – greater swings in nominal interest rates – may make for larger risk premia in the longer interest rates which are likely to be more relevant to investment decisions. A history of large monetary disturbances therefore may lower a country's long-run capital stocks and reduce the path of its potential output. Steadier monetary policy may mean higher long-run output. For all its virtues, the 'workhorse model' conceals numerous issues of this kind.

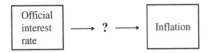

Figure 8.1 Interest rates to inflation.

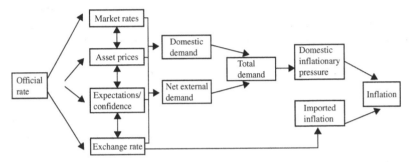

Figure 8.2 The transmission mechanism of monetary policy.
Source: Based on Bank of England (1999a).
Note: For simplicity of exposition, the chart does not show interactions between variables, but these can be important.

We now turn to the transmission mechanism itself. What is it that happens when a central bank changes its interest rates? Put simply, the transmission mechanism can be viewed as what happens between the two boxes in figure 8.1; that is, between the official interest rate change and its effect on inflation. Any central bank that targets inflation needs to have some idea what this mechanism is. Figure 8.2 shows a more detailed diagram of the transmission mechanism as published by the Monetary Policy Committee at the Bank of England in 1999 (Bank of England, 1999a).

Given that we have some models of the transmission mechanism that capture the stylised description in figure 8.2, how do we find out what interest rates do when their effects go through this model? What we need to do is simulate a model. Let us assume that we take the exogenous trajectory for the interest rate – whatever the level was in the base for the forecast – and simply shock that interest rate by some amount, say one percentage point for one year. This assumption seems straightforward. The problem is that typically, for many of the models that we use and certainly for the 'workhorse model' presented above, the solution to that problem is not particularly well defined. When the exchange rate is forward looking, it is not sufficient just to impose an exogenous change in interest rates. By assumption, the agents in the model need to know what will happen to the path of future interest rates. For some models, there are ways around this problem, particularly if we consider the fiscal theory of the price level. This

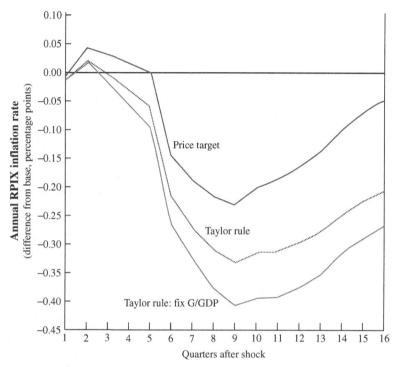

Figure 8.3 Effects on the inflation rate of an interest rate shock under different policy assumptions.

approach guides thinking about simulating models when we have an exogenous interest rate and when the model is essentially closed by the role of fiscal policy.

The alternative and more standard solution is to take some trajectory for interest rates based on an endogenous policy rule of the type defined above. We subject the model to a temporary change, but now we face a different problem. We generate a movement in interest rates not only from the exogenous shock but also from the endogenous response thereafter. But now the answer depends on the underlying endogenous policy rule. So, ultimately, the answer to the question 'What happens when we change interest rates?' is 'It depends!'

Figure 8.3 shows the results from a simulation taken from Bank of England (1999b) to illustrate this point. The figure shows the effects of a one-year shock to the short-term interest rate under the assumption of forward-looking rational exchange rate expectations. The only difference among the three lines is a differing underlying endogenous monetary policy rule. The top line shows the adoption of price-level targets, the middle line embodies a standard Taylor rule, and the third is a standard Taylor rule but with a different fiscal policy assumption. All three lines tell a fairly standard story about the effects of monetary policy: it takes about a year before the effects appear and the maximum effects are through in about two years. Although this is a conventional story about the workings of monetary policy, the actual details differ with the different policy assumptions. Therefore, there is not a simple answer to the question about what happens if we change interest rates. Unfortunately, there are no neat and simple interest rate ready-reckoners that we readily apply to a particular problem at hand.

So far, I have covered a structural macromodelling approach to the policy problem. An alternative vector autoregressive (VAR) modelling approach is much less restrictive in the structural assumptions of the model. No explicit structural parameters are estimated or assumed; several structural restrictions are imposed, however, in order to disentangle different types of shocks. This approach allows us to explain what happens if a shock to the interest rates occurs, over and above the effect from the underlying policy rule. This situation is exactly analogous to the simulation exercises just described. As such, it allows us to describe what happens if we shock a policy rule.

As central bankers, however, we are not particularly interested in *shocking* the monetary policy rule; we are interested in *designing* the monetary policy rule, or at least the systematic part of it. To what extent, then, is it interesting to examine this unsystematic part of monetary policy, which may represent only 5% of total interest rate movements? How *should* we think about the systematic part of monetary policy and deal with the familiar issue of estimating policy rules? To estimate a rule, we need to assume that the underlying policy rule over the estimation period has been stable. Can we really expect an estimated policy rule to track policy since there may have been regime changes? Certainly, evidence for the UK suggests that policy has been conducted under different regimes (Nelson, 2000a). More seriously, changes may have occurred in the inflation target itself. Is it plausible to think of an annual inflation target in the UK in 1975 of 2.5%? Probably not, but, to estimate a Taylor rule over such a long period, we would need to assume that the policy regime had been constant.

The actual policy rule in practice is likely to be much more complicated than the simple Taylor rule. When examining these simple characterisations of policy, therefore, it is not surprising that they do not track exactly. This finding is not due to an unsystematic policy rule; the rule is systematically more complicated and varies according to the shocks hitting the economy. Unfortunately, it also brings forth a problem that commonly arises in modelling the transmission mechanism. An ideal modelling strategy is one that is not completely dependent on knowing the 'true' model of monetary policy.

How do we know when we have a good model? One answer is that we have a good model for policy-making if we can forecast well with it. This seems to be a popular view, judging by popular debate about the Bank of England's or the Treasury's forecasting performance in the UK. Are these institutions especially good at forecasting? If they are, does their ability necessarily imply that they will adopt good policies?

In fact, recent developments in the applied econometrics literature have suggested that the forecasting criteria are neither necessary nor sufficient for effective policy making. David Hendry (see for example, Hendry and Doornik, 1997) and others have shown that really rather simple statistical models are often much better at simple short-term forecasting than the structural models normally used for policy.

Again this takes us back to the problem of the issues raised. Not only does a model need to forecast well, but it also needs to be able to capture the effects of monetary policy in a coherent and systematic way. It needs to be able to identify the different channels of the transmission mechanism pointed out above, and ideally should allow for possible changes in the policy rule. In a policy-making context, this suggests a policy modelling strategy that emphasises a structural rather than a reduced-form approach, and emphasises a theory-driven rather than a purely data-driven approach.

Of course, this is all too easy to say or write down, but when it gets to modelling, and to using empirical evidence to form policy then, as the saying goes, the devil is in the detail. In practice, we need somehow to develop a strategy that is part theoretical and part statistical. Clearly we have to be influenced by best practice theory. So we need models in which optimising agents, households and firms are assumed to operate in a well-specified framework. We need very specific models of nominal inertia. This type of adjustment cost is very important for a central bank because, without nominal inertia, central banks would not need to do very much at all. This adjustment is really the leverage derived when setting interest rates.

If we look at the type of empirical models in use in policy institutions 20 years ago, very little of this discussion would be familiar. In recent years, many models have attempted to introduce profit maximisation in the corporate sector. Certainly there are attempts to incorporate some forms of structural inertia and serious attempts to build stock-flow consistency into the models (McKibbin and Vines, 2001). Nevertheless, compared with many models in the theoretical literature, a big gap still exists between some empirical models used in policy institutions and the models in economics journals.

The key question that policy institutions have to confront is whether a bad theoretical model is better than a good ad hoc model. It is all very well to have an elegant representative agent theory of consumer behaviour but, if it comes up with implausible predictions, it may be better to have something slightly more ad hoc but more consistent with the data. Of course, this is not without risks, because what is consistent with the data is going to alter as soon as the policy rule is effected. Somehow, in practice, we have to get this balance.

A sub-question here relates to the importance of transparency criteria. These criteria are relevant because many policy institutions must not only answer questions about monetary policy but also be credible, so that policy-makers will utilise this model to set policy. We might imagine a situation in which the bank has a model that people can understand, but they do not believe the bank would use it because of its simplicity. On the other hand, the public may not understand how the bank makes use of a complex model but they trust that it is being used anyway. The issue of how to get a good balance between complexity and simplicity cuts across the debate.

In the practical model that economists have developed, the response has been to ensure that the model has enough theory to make clear what the central bank can and cannot do. This level of theory (say, the 'low-level theory') ensures that the objectives of monetary policy are as clearly defined as possible to make the choice between theory and practice. Three examples of theory that are important for a central bank's modelling strategy are as follows:

(1) Any model should embody long-run price-level neutrality. A central bank should generally not be using models that predict that changing the price level implies that we can change the real economy in the long run.

(2) Inflation neutrality, in its simplest form, mandates no inflation–output trade-off. This idea is attractive, but more controversial than the principle of long-run price neutrality. The real interest rate might be affected by the level of inflation (inflation non-neutrality) in the short run. Many economists have suggested that the vertical Phillips curve may not be the most sensible way to think about the issue. Furthermore, if inflation exerts no long-run real effects, why do central bankers worry about the need to hold it down?

(3) The minimum theoretical requirement for a model is that output should be determined by the supply side. This implies that there should be a well-defined natural level of potential and well-defined natural rate of unemployment. Views differ on this. Ball (1999a), for example, constructed a model in which demand shocks can actually change the supply side by changing the equilibrium unemployment for a protracted period.

For most central bankers, the first and third of these propositions are central whereas the merits of the second are open to challenge.

What are some other theoretical requirements? What about the Lucas critique? We want to build models that do not cease to be valid as soon as the policy regime changes. Indeed, policy change is a particular example of a regime shift. The Lucas critique can, in principle, apply to any type of structural change in the economy. The lesson that policy modellers have drawn from this is that one should incorporate an explicit role for expectations. So, rather than embody the policy rule in the parameters of the model, with the decision rule itself embodied, the decision rule would then respond to the policy rule if that changed.

This situation creates the additional problem of how to deal with expectations. There are a few ways to do this. Although rational expectations are the 'cleanest', way, they may not represent the correct assumption. Economists and central bankers increasingly consider learning models of expectations (Sargent, 1999). Clearly, in the real world, expectations are not immediately correct. Agents in the economy are unlikely immediately to perceive the true nature of a shock to the economy or to a policy change. The introduction of learning, however, means that the whole transmission mechanism of policy will slow down.

One final approach involves assuming that the enterprise of building new decision rules is just unrealistic. So, rather than trying to build in clever UIP rules for exchange rates or Euler conditions for behavioural relationships, one should instead rely on a purely data-driven 'non-rational' approach. Certainly, on the basis of empirical evidence, this strategy is hard to criticise. But of course we are then back into the theory versus data debate, which we discussed above.

This paper has dealt so far with what I would consider the big issues. Economists, however, have to face other issues at a practical level in using models of the transmission mechanism to inform their policy advice. Central bank policy-makers usually concern themselves with national aggregate inflation rates. These aggregate rates are likely to be constructed by aggregating the inflation rates of many different goods. The national output will constitute the sum of output produced in many sectors in different regions of the economy, which raises the dilemma of how much we want to disaggregate.

The easiest way to address the issue is to consider the components of aggregate demand. Typically, this is done by breaking them down into consumption, investment and government spending in the standard textbook manner. Considering GDP from the output side, however, should we attempt to explain the behaviour of different sectors, manufacturing services and other elements? Certainly in the UK, but also in many other countries that we analyse, these sectors can behave very differently, so it might be sensible to distinguish them behaviourally. On the other hand, if we are interested only in national aggregates (particularly the national inflation rate), then this complication may be unimportant.

In the same way, one can disaggregate output by region. In the UK, much debate concerns the asymmetric effects of monetary policy on different regions. This issue is very much alive currently in the European context. In setting monetary policy, is it appropriate for the European central banks to model the euro area as a single larger economy, or is it appropriate to continue treating the area as 11 separate economies? Economists providing monetary policy advice must inevitably face such questions.

It is misleading to suggest that there is a single 'right' modelling approach in thinking about monetary policy. Typically, a range of different modelling strategies is appropriate in different situations. Many other central banks and policy-related institutions are emphasising the usefulness of this eclectic approach to modelling.

Finally, this paper has provided several questions. First, how should the reader think about the role of money in the transmission mechanism? Is it appropriate to think simply about the interest rate channel, with money as a minor player, or should we allow money to play a more fundamental role? Second, how should we think about the systematic components of monetary policy? How optimistic can we be that one can characterise monetary policy in terms of a rule, whether it is complex or simple, and how much could we learn from this characterisation? A third and more general question concerns how one chooses between the two possibly conflicting ideals of theoretical rigour and data coherence. A related, though logically separate, question asks how complicated we want our models to be. Is small beautiful, or is small misleading?

9 Empirical evidence for credit effects in the transmission mechanism of the United Kingdom

K. Alec Chrystal and Paul Mizen

9.1 Introduction

This paper addresses the question of whether 'credit' contains information additional to that available in 'money'. There has been a long tradition of modelling monetary conditions in the economy by focusing on the demand for money (i.e. banks' liabilities), but monetary policy is implemented via changes in short-term interest rates. Changes to interest rates influence the demand for loans, and it is through the loan market that aggregate spending is affected, at least to some degree.[1] This issue has been addressed in theoretical terms in the 'credit channel' literature (See Bernanke and Gertler, 1995), and two variations on the credit channel story have been identified: a *balance sheet channel* and a *bank lending channel*. The first links the determinants of lending to observable characteristics of the financial health of the borrowing firms; the second suggests that some influences on lending flows originate within the banking system.

Banks typically have an ongoing relationship with the households and corporations to which they lend, and they use information about a company's financial position obtained through this banking relationship to determine the loan facility they will offer. Factors that are easily monitored, such as cash flow, financial wealth, previous loan payments history and outstanding debt, will affect the ability of a company to obtain loans, as will the value of collateral that a firm is able to offer. Although households typically do not construct balance sheets, their amount of credit will be conditional on measurable indicators of ability to repay, such as disposable income, liquid savings, previous loan history and outstanding debts.

Bank lending is the dominant type of external finance among smaller firms and households with limited access to securities markets. Small and medium-sized enterprises (SMEs) are typically more dependent on bank finance than large firms, because the latter can often borrow more easily and on better terms through debt issuance. Prudent banks will limit their exposure to any specific firm or household, so there will not generally be unlimited access to bank lending; hence the available supply of bank loans will be an important influence on real expenditure, in addition to any effect from market interest rates. The extent to which there is dependence on banks for finance, rather than on retained profits (internal sources) or securities markets (other external sources), can be studied empirically. For example, factors internal to the banking industry – such as capital losses in overseas lending or changes to the amount of regulatory capital required – influence the willingness of banks to lend. Shifts in these conditions of loan supply, via the bank lending channel, may lead directly to changes in aggregate spending.

This chapter asks what additional influence bank credit may have on the transmission mechanism over and above that of money. We build a model of the balance sheets and flows between sectors (based on Friedman and Kuttner, 1993) that embeds both of the credit channels mentioned above. We then estimate an empirical model of the demand for credit, money and expenditure by each of the sectors. This leads us to ask a further question: what role do non-bank institutions play in offering external credit to firms and households? There are a range of non-bank financial intermediaries such as pension funds, life assurance companies, factoring companies and loan guarantors, securities and derivatives dealers and leasing corporations that also take 'deposits' from the private sector. These financial intermediaries recycle the long-term savings of the household sector (through pension fund and insurance contributions, etc.) and move them toward the non-financial corporate sector by offering loans as well as by purchasing corporate securities. They may also operate as wholesalers of bank loans by bundling and securitisation, or they may secure loans on different collateral from that which banks require, such as invoices receivable.[2]

Sections 9.2 and 9.3 of this chapter build a framework within which financial flows can be analysed and explain the econometric methodology employed to model the systems by sector. Section 9.4 reports the findings for the private non-financial corporation (PNFC) and household (HH) sectors and the influence of lending by 'other financial corporations' (OFCs). We show that it is possible to model successfully the interaction of M4 lending to PNFCs, PNFCs' money holdings and investment spending. We also report estimates of the interactions of *unsecured* M4 lending to households and household money holdings and consumption spending. The conclusion we draw is that both bank and non-bank credit have an influence on real expenditure by firms and households.

9.2   A framework for modelling credit markets

To work through the effects of credit on real expenditures, we use an extended version of the Friedman and Kuttner (1993) model. We begin by analysing the balance sheets, sources and uses of funds and demands for assets and liabilities of three sectors of a stylised economy: private non-financial corporations, banks and households. This allows us to consider the lines of transmission from bank credit to real expenditures via the two other sectors. There are two fully specified alternatives to bank finance for investment/consumption arising from internally generated retained earnings/net saving and externally generated sources in the form of new issues of corporate bonds and commercial paper. A third source can be considered by introducing a fourth sector, comprising the non-bank financial intermediaries, which we refer to collectively as 'other financial corporations' (OFCs). We assume that they can offer loans to firms/households by acting as wholesalers of bank loans or by redirecting the household sector's long-term saving (pension funds) toward firms. For simplicity we assume no role for 'government', other than as the regulator of the banking system and the controller of the money stock, or for the overseas sector, but these other sectors could be added without altering the results. We will discuss each of the sectors that we include in turn.

9.2.1 Private non-financial corporations (PNFCs)

We assume that all individual firms, indexed 'f', are identical in financial structure and in the physical output they produce. The net worth of the firm to a shareholder is its share price multiplied by the (fixed) volume of shares, $S_t \overline{E} = E_{ft}$. Assuming no dividends, and that corporate equity is a perfect substitute for another asset, for example banking sector deposits, we have a parity condition for the share price, $S_{t+1}^e / S_t = r_{Dt}$.

The net worth of the firm is given by:

$$NW_{ft} = PE_{ft} + D_{ft} - L_{ft} - P_{ft} = S_t \overline{E}. \tag{9.1}$$

Firms cannot issue or buy back any of their equity, so the volume of shares $(\overline{E})$ is fixed, but the share price (S_t) can vary with market demand. PE_{ft} represents an individual firm's stock of physical capital and D_{ft} indicates its deposits. These are the only assets held in the absence of a government sector. The liabilities are represented by L_{ft} (loans), P_{ft} (commercial paper and corporate bonds) and E_{ft} (net worth of the firm, owed to the household sector as equity).

The use of funds imposes a financial constraint on the PNFCs by restricting current investment, I_{ft}, to equal the retained profits of the firm, RP_{ft}, and the flows arising from deposits, loans and commercial paper/corporate bonds:

$$I_{ft} = RP_{ft} - \Delta D_{ft} + \Delta L_{ft} + \Delta P_{ft}. \tag{9.2}$$

In aggregate, summing over all firms, this is written as:

$$\sum I_{ft} = \sum RP_{ft} - \sum \Delta D_{ft} + \sum \Delta L_{ft} + \sum \Delta P_{ft}. \tag{9.3}$$

The firm maximises utility over an infinite horizon, discounting with a rate of time preference (β) and a probability of bankruptcy (λ_t). The utility function is written as a function of the different components of net worth:

$$\sum_{s=t}^{\infty} (\beta \lambda_s)^{s-t} U(-L_{fs}, D_{fs}, -P_{fs}, PE_{fs}),$$ (9.4)

subject to (9.1) and a dynamic resource constraint:

$$PD_{t-1}\lambda_{t-1}[-(1 + r_{Lt-1})\theta_{Lt-1}L_{ft-1} - (1 + r_{Pt-1}\theta_{Pt-1})P_{ft-1}$$
$$+ (1 + r_{Dt-1}\theta_{Dt-1})D_{ft-1} + RP_{ft-1} - c_{Kt-1}PE_{ft-1}]$$
$$= PD_t\lambda_t(-L_{ft} - P_{ft} + D_{ft} + PE_{ft}),$$ (9.5)

where λ_t is the probability of bankruptcy on which an insurance rate has to be paid (hence it enters not only in the utility function but also in the resource constraint) and PD_t is the domestic price level. The variables r_D, r_L and r_P are the ex ante nominal rates of return on deposits, loans and commercial paper/corporate bonds, respectively, and θ_L and θ_P capture the non-price elements to borrowing and issuing that are central to a credit channel view (these will be defined later); c_{Kt} is the nominal cost of capital.

Retained profits are linked to physical capital via a strictly concave Cobb–Douglas production function for final output:

$$RP_{ft} = \sigma_t X_t (PE_{ft-1})^{\mu},$$ (9.6)

where σ_t is a profit share, X_t is the contribution of other factors of production, including technical progress and labour, and μ is the price elasticity of demand (or the mark-up). Firms not only care about aggregate net worth but also have preferences among the different types of loans/savings that compose wealth. The first-order condition for physical capital gives

$$U_{PEt} = \beta E_t U_{PEt+1} \frac{PD_t}{PD_{t+1}} \left(\frac{c_{Kt}}{1 + \sigma_t \mu X_t (PE_{ft})^{\mu-1}} \right)$$

$$= \beta E_t U_{PEt+1} \frac{PD_t}{PD_{t+1}} \left(\frac{c_{Kt}}{1 + \sigma_t \mu \left(\frac{Y_{ft}}{PE_{ft}} \right)} \right).$$ (9.7)

This implies that the amount of capital is positively related to output and negatively related to the real cost of capital. For the other components of the firm's net worth we have

$$U_{it} = (1 + r_{it})\theta_{it}\beta U_{it}(PD_t/PD_{t+1}) \quad \text{for} \quad i = L, D, P.$$ (9.8)

What happens next depends on the assumptions implied by the choice of the utility function. If two components of net worth are net substitutes in utility, then a rise in the rate of interest on one is likely, under fairly general assumptions, to lead to an increase in the net worth contribution of the other. The a priori signs on the demand functions of firms that follow this reasoning are based on the assumption that adding to deposits, paying off loans and reducing the outstanding stock of commercial paper are net substitute activities for each other. This assumption can be justified if the risks to the lender implicit in these funding activities are positively correlated. We also assume for simplicity that the sign of the partial derivative on the non-price cost per unit of an asset is the same as the interest rate on that asset. A more complete model would allow for intertemporal utility maximisation of firms, households, banks and non-bank financial corporations, and would solve for each sector's reaction functions after assuming specific functional forms.

The flow demand for assets and liabilities can be summarised as:

$$\Sigma \Delta D_{ft} = f_D(PE_{ft}, r_D, r_L, r_P, \theta_L, \theta_P) \tag{9.9a}$$

$$\Sigma \Delta L_{ft} = f_L(PE_{ft}, r_D, r_L, r_P, \theta_L, \theta_P) \tag{9.9b}$$

$$\Sigma \Delta P_{ft} = f_P(PE_{ft}, r_D, r_L, r_P, \theta_L, \theta_P). \tag{9.9c}$$

The variables r_D, r_L and r_P are the short-term rates of interest on deposits, loans and commercial paper/corporate bonds, respectively. The variables θ_L and θ_P capture the non-price elements to borrowing and issuing that are central to a credit channel view; these will be defined later. We can think of these as representing the charges and conditions that are imposed on borrowers in the form of fees or obligations to undertake certain services. The expected signs of the partial derivatives are

$$f_{D1} < 0, \ f_{D2} > 0, \ f_{D3} < 0, \ f_{D4} < 0, \ f_{D5} < 0, \ f_{D6} < 0$$
$$f_{L1} > 0, \ f_{L2} < 0, \ f_{L3} < 0, \ f_{L4} > 0, \ f_{L5} < 0, \ f_{L6} > 0$$
$$f_{P1} > 0, \ f_{P2} < 0, \ f_{P3} > 0, \ f_{P4} < 0, \ f_{P5} > 0, \ f_{P6} < 0.$$

9.2.2 Banks

Banks act as financial corporations that take deposits from and offer loans to the PNFC and household sectors subject to certain regulatory requirements. The banks are indexed 'b' and their balance sheets are represented individually by equation (9.10):

$$L_{bt} + R_{bt} = D_{bt} + CD_{bt} + K_{bt}. \tag{9.10}$$

We use R_b for reserves, CD_b for certificates of deposit and K_b for bank capital. The banks are required to ensure that individually they meet the regulations for capital and reserves such that $R_{bt} \geq \kappa_1 D_{bt} + \kappa_2 CD_{bt}$ and $K_{bt} \geq \kappa_3 L_{bt}$, for all t, where κ_1, κ_2 and κ_3 are set by the authorities and treated as constants.

We treat banks as financial firms that maximise a utility function similar in form to (9.4) subject to (9.10) and the equivalent dynamic constraint. The banks then choose to offer loans and accept deposits and certificates of deposit. We could think of them as financial firms with the following equations for loan provision and deposit taking:

$$\Sigma L_{bt} = b_L(r_D, r_L, r_P, \sigma^2, \theta_L, \Sigma R_{bt}, \Sigma K_{bt}), \tag{9.11a}$$

$$\Sigma D_{bt} = b_D(r_D, r_L, r_P, \sigma^2, \theta_L, \Sigma R_{bt}, \Sigma K_{bt}) \tag{9.11b}$$

and

$$\Sigma CD_{bt} = b_{CD}(r_D, r_L, r_P, \sigma^2, \theta_L, \Sigma R_{bt}, \Sigma K_{bt}), \tag{9.11c}$$

where σ^2 is the risk of default on the loans outstanding. Expected signs on the partial derivatives are

$$b_{L1} < 0, b_{L2} > 0, b_{L3} < 0, b_{L4} < 0, b_{L5} > 0, b_{L6} > 0, b_{L7} > 0.$$
$$b_{D1} < 0, b_{L2} > 0, b_{L3} > 0, b_{L4} < 0, b_{L5} > 0, b_{L6} > 0, b_{L7} > 0.$$
$$b_{CD1} > 0, b_{CD2} > 0, b_{CD3} < 0, b_{CD4} < 0, b_{CD5} > 0, b_{CD6}?, b_{CD7} > 0.$$

9.2.3   Households

Households, indexed 'h', are assumed to be the owners of the equity of the firms. They hold financial assets (NA_{ht}) in the form of deposits (D_{ht}), certificates of deposit (CD_{ht}) and corporate bonds/commercial paper (P_{ht}), and by subtracting their loans (L_{ht}) from the banking sector we determine their total net worth (NW_h). Individually, their balance sheets can be written as

$$NA_{ht} + D_{ht} + P_{ht} + CD_{ht} - L_{ht} = NW_{ht}. \tag{9.12}$$

The financial constraints on the households imply that the flows into financial variables must be equal to their net saving (NS_{ht}) plus any additional bank loans (ΔL_{ht}) (for simplicity we ignore capital gains and losses):

$$\Delta D_{ht} + \Delta P_{ht} + \Delta CD_{ht} = NS_{ht} + \Delta L_{ht}, \tag{9.13}$$

where net saving $NS_{ht} = \Delta NA_{ht} = (Y_{ht} - C_{ht})$. In aggregate

$$\Sigma \Delta D_{ht} + \Sigma \Delta P_{ht} + \Sigma \Delta CD_{ht} = \Sigma NS_{ht} + \Sigma \Delta L_{ht}. \tag{9.14}$$

We maximise utility as a function of the different components of net worth:

$$\sum_{s=t}^{\infty} (\beta \lambda_t)^{s-t} U(-L_{ht}, D_{ht}, -P_{ht}, CD_{ht}, NA_{ht}) \tag{9.15}$$

subject to (9.12) and a dynamic resource constraint:

$$PD_{t-1}\lambda_{t-1}[-(1 + r_{Lt-1})\theta_{Lt-1}L_{ht-1} - (1 + r_{Pt-1}\theta_{Pt-1})P_{ht-1}$$

$$+ (1 + r_{CDt-1}\theta_{CDt-1})CD_{ht-1} + (1 + r_{Dt-1}\theta_{Dt-1})D_{ht-1}$$

$$+ NA_{ht-1}] = PD_t\lambda_t(-L_{ft} - P_{ft} + D_{ft} + PE_{ft}), \qquad (9.16)$$

where variables are defined as before. The portfolio choice under standard assumptions about risk-averse behaviour yields demand functions for deposits, loans and commercial paper/corporate bonds:[3]

$$\Sigma\Delta D_{ht} = h_D(\Sigma NS_{ht}, r_D, r_L, r_P, \sigma^2, \theta_L, \theta_P, \Sigma Y_{ht}), \qquad (9.17a)$$

$$\Sigma\Delta L_{ht} = h_L(\Sigma NS_{ht}, r_D, r_L, r_P, \sigma^2, \theta_L, \theta_P, \Sigma Y_{ht}) \qquad (9.17b)$$

and

$$(\Sigma\Delta CD_{ht} + \Sigma\Delta P_{ht}) = h_{CD}(\Sigma NS_{ht}, r_D, r_L, r_P, \sigma^2, \theta_L, \theta_P, \Sigma Y_{ht})$$

$$\qquad (9.17c)$$

for all t. The signs of the partial derivatives are expected to be:

$$h_{D1} > 0, h_{D2} > 0, h_{D3} < 0, h_{D4} < 0, h_{D5} > 0, h_{D6} < 0, h_{D7} > 0,$$
$$h_{D8} > 0$$

$$h_{L1} > 0, h_{L2} < 0, h_{L3} > 0, h_{L4} < 0, h_{L5} > 0, h_{L6} < 0, h_{L7} > 0,$$
$$h_{L8} > 0$$

$$h_{CD1} > 0, h_{CD2} < 0, h_{CD3} > 0, h_{CD4} < 0, h_{CD5} < 0, h_{CD6} > 0,$$
$$h_{CD7} < 0, h_{CD8} > 0.$$

9.2.4 Financial market clearing

In order for the financial market to clear, the following conditions must hold:

$$\Sigma\Delta D_{bt} = \Sigma\Delta D_{ht} + \Sigma\Delta D_{ft}$$

$$\Sigma\Delta L_{bt} = \Sigma\Delta L_{ht} + \Sigma\Delta L_{ft}$$

$$\Sigma\Delta P_{ht} = \Sigma\Delta P_{ft}$$

$$\Sigma\Delta CD_{bt} = \Sigma\Delta CD_{ht}$$

$$\Sigma\Delta R_{bt} = \text{change in central bank balance sheet (exogenous)}.$$

Finally, we must define the conditions that determine the non-interest costs of borrowing or issuing, θ_L and θ_P. These variables enter the equation because loans are provided under conditions of informational asymmetry and providers resort to non-price means to screen applicants. Consider firms seeking to borrow. A typical basis for evaluating applicants is the financial health of the firm (RP_{ft}), the previous loan history and the current stock of loans outstanding (L_{ft}), the current loan rate (r_L) and default risk (σ^2). Hence a suitable definition for the non-price cost of a loan would be given by equation (9.18):

$$\theta_L = \theta_L(RP_{ft}, L_{ft}, r_L, \sigma^2). \tag{9.18}$$

The equation for θ_P would not depend on the same set of variables because market purchasers of bonds/paper do not have access to information about the firm (such as financial health and default risk) from ongoing relationships, as banks do. Hence, the charges depend only on the volume of bonds/paper in the market and the flow:

$$\theta_P = \theta_P(P_{ft}, \Delta P_{ft}). \tag{9.19}$$

9.2.5   Real expenditure

Last of all, we can explicitly define the real expenditure variables of the PNFC and household sectors. These are

$$\Sigma I_{ft} = I(\Sigma \Delta D_{ft} + \Sigma RP_f, r_D, r_L, \theta_L, \sigma^2) \tag{9.20}$$

$$\Sigma C_{ht} = C(\Sigma \Delta D_{ht} + \Sigma NS_{ht}, \Sigma NW_{ht}, r_D, r_L, \theta_L, \sigma^2). \tag{9.21}$$

Clearly, if 'credit matters' then it should influence equations (9.20) and (9.21) through r_L and θ_L. Our approach to modelling credit in section 9.4 involves the estimation of two systems of equations: for the PNFCs we estimate equations (9.9a), (9.9b) and (9.20), and for households we estimate equations (9.17a), (9.17b) and (9.21).

9.2.6   Other financial corporations

We have developed a system of equations with which to determine whether banks matter, that is, whether the loans that banks offer and the conditions attached to them have an influence on real expenditures. But why should banks be different from other loan providers such as pension funds, life assurance companies and other financial firms? Banks may have some 'special' features, but other financial firms may also offer credit in the form of loans even though they are not banks. We extend our original model by supposing that the typical OFC is a pension fund or life assurance company that is collecting contributions from the household sector and investing them in the commercial paper/corporate bonds issued by firms (we have ignored the government sectors; otherwise we might also add government bonds to the portfolio). We also suppose that OFCs borrow from banks and unbundle or rebundle these funds for the PNFCs. The balance sheet of the sector as a whole, indexing each OFC using 'o', gives the following:

$$(\Sigma L_o)_{ft} + \Sigma P_{ot} + \Sigma D_{ot} = (\Sigma L_{ot})_{bt} + \Sigma PF_{ot}, \qquad (9.22)$$

where the outer subscript refers to the destination/source loans, so that $(\Sigma L_o)_{ft}$ represents loans to PNFCs from the OFCs, and $(\Sigma L_o)_{bt}$ represents loans to OFCs from banks. ΣPF_{ot} refers to claims of the household sector on the pension fund. The aggregate flows between sources and uses of funds can be written as:

$$(\Sigma \Delta L_o)_{ft} + \Sigma \Delta P_{ot} + \Sigma \Delta D_{ot} = (\Sigma \Delta L_o)_{bt} + \Sigma NC_{ot}. \qquad (9.23)$$

Here ΣNC_{ot} represents the aggregated net contributions from the household sector to the OFCs. We can think of the OFCs operating as investors of the longer-term savings of the household sector and, therefore, we might expect their demand for assets to mimic that of the households (see equations (9.17a) – (9.17c)). With regard to loan behaviour, we might expect them to borrow from banks in much the same way as non-financial firms (see equation (9.9b)), and to rebundle loans and offer them to the PNFCs on the same basis as the banks (see equation (9.11a)). One difference between banks and non-banks may emerge through the non-price cost of borrowing: non-banks do not benefit from the close relationships that banks can foster as deposit takers, and non-banks accept different types of collateral and therefore monitor different measures of creditworthiness. OFCs may also be subject to different regulatory requirements that give them certain advantages or disadvantages relative to banks.

To make the model consistent, we must modify equation (9.9b) to allow firms to borrow from banks and non-banks. If we assume that the loan rate is arbitraged to a single rate, r_L, then the only difference will appear through $(\theta_L)_b$ offered by banks and $(\theta_L)_o$ offered by non-banks.

$$\Sigma \Delta L_{ft} = f_L(\Sigma I_{ft} - \Sigma \Delta D_{ft} - \Sigma RD_{ft}, r_D, r_L, r_P, (\theta_L)_{bt}, (\theta_L)_{ot}, \theta_P),$$
$$(9.9b')$$

where $\Sigma \Delta L_{ft} = \Sigma \Delta L_{bt} + \Sigma \Delta L_{ot}$ refers to *total* loans from bank and non-bank sources.

We must also modify equation (9.14) to include the net contributions to the OFCs by the household sector, noting that $\Sigma NC_{ot} = \Sigma NC_{ht}$ (by definition for a fully funded pension fund):

$$\Sigma NC_{ht} + \Sigma \Delta D_{ht} + \Sigma \Delta P_{ht} + \Sigma \Delta CD_{ht} = \Sigma NS_{ht} + \Sigma \Delta L_{ht}.$$
$$(9.14')$$

It is possible, but less likely, that the OFCs may offer loans to the household sector, in which case the loan equation for the household sector (9.17b) would be altered in exactly the same way as discussed above for the PNFCs.

9.3   Econometric methodology

The econometric methodology used in this chapter is described by Hendry and Mizon (1993), Hendry (1995) and Hoffman and Rasche (1996). We begin by modelling the PNFC and household sectors separately as two systems of three equations including real expenditure, money and credit. This involves estimates of equations (9.9a), (9.9b) and (9.20) for PNFCs and (9.17a), (9.17b) and (9.21) for households. We then go on to consider whether credit offered by OFCs influences the expenditure of these sectors.

9.3.1   A dynamic model for the PNFC and household sectors

The first step involves the estimation of an unconditional qth order VAR over a sample $t = 1, 2, \ldots, T$, where the model is estimated for sector i:

$$\Pi(L)z_{it} = \varepsilon_{it}, \tag{9.24}$$

where z_{it} is a vector of p variables, $\Pi(L) = I - \sum_{j=1}^{q} \Pi_j(L^j)$ is a qth-order lag polynomial and ε_{it} is a p-dimensional random vector of serially uncorrelated error terms. Equation (9.24) can be rewritten as a linear dynamic system as follows:

$$\Delta z_{it} = \Pi_i z_{it-1} + \sum_{j=1}^{q-1} \Gamma_{ij} \Delta z_{it-j} + \varepsilon_{it}, \tag{9.25}$$

where Γ_{ij} are matrices of short-term parameters and Π_i is a matrix of long-run coefficients.

The variables are all non-stationary with an order of integration equal to one. We test for the existence of rank-reducing cointegrating relationships among these variables using the maximum likelihood based approach of Johansen (1996), which entails examining the canonical correlations between Δz_{it} and z_{it-1}. Translating this into a problem in terms of eigenvalues, ranked from largest to smallest as $\lambda_1, \lambda_2, \ldots, \lambda_p$, a likelihood ratio $LR(r) = -T\log(1 - \lambda_r)$ where $H(r-1) = K - \frac{T}{2} \sum_{j=1}^{r-1} \log(1 - \lambda_j)$, $H(r) = K - \frac{T}{2} \sum_{j=1}^{r} \log(1 - \lambda_j)$ tests whether rank(Π_1) $\leq r$ by determining if λ_r is statistically different from zero (which it would be for a non-cointegrating combination). A trace test $Tr(r) = -T \sum_{j=1}^{r} \log(1 - \lambda_j)$ is a joint test of whether all λ_j for $j = r, r+1, \ldots, p$ are insignificantly different from zero. The distributions are non-standard but are given in Osterwald-Lenum (1992) and Johansen (1996). The reduction in the rank, r, allows us to write the long-run equilibrium relationships of the system given by the $p \times p$ dimensional matrix Π_i in the familiar form of the product of two $p \times r$ matrices α_i and β_i. The matrix β_i defines the cointegration space and the matrix α_i defines the error correction space.

The vector of variables z_{it} can be decomposed into endogenous variables v_{it} and exogenous variables x_{it} so that we can rewrite (9.25) as a partitioned conditional-marginal system:

$$\begin{pmatrix} \Delta v_{it} \\ \Delta x_{it} \end{pmatrix} = \sum_{j=1}^{q-1} \begin{pmatrix} \Gamma_{ijv} \\ \Gamma_{ijx} \end{pmatrix} \Delta z_{it-j} - \begin{pmatrix} \alpha_{iv} \\ \alpha_{ix} \end{pmatrix} \beta_i' z_{it-1} + \begin{pmatrix} \varepsilon_{ivt} \\ \varepsilon_{ixt} \end{pmatrix}. \quad (9.26)$$

Endogenous variables are defined by the conditional system (9.27), but exogenous variables are defined by a marginal process that excludes the long-run relationship: $\beta_i' z_{it-1}$. In effect, the part of the error correction space that determines the feedback of the long-run cointegrating relationships to the dynamics of the exogenous variables, x_t, is composed of zeros. A test of this weak exogeneity proposition can confirm the validity of the partition between endogenous variables, v_{it}, and exogenous variables, x_{it}. Only the endogenous variables, v_{it}, are conditionally dependent on the long-run cointegrating relationships $\alpha_i \beta_i' z_{it-1}$:

$$\Delta v_{it} = \omega_i \Delta x_{it} + \sum_{j=1}^{q-1} \Gamma_{ij} \Delta z_{it-j} - \alpha_i \beta_i' z_{it-1} + \varepsilon_{it}. \quad (9.27)$$

The conditional model is just identified, but to ensure that the model is exactly identified in a structural sense we must impose a minimum of further $s(s-1)$ restrictions, where $s = p - r$. We also introduce contemporaneous changes in exogenous variables on the right-hand side of the equation. Additional over-identifying restrictions may be imposed and tested based on economic considerations. Exact and overidentifying restrictions are imposed jointly by pre-multiplying by a contemporaneous coefficient matrix, A_i, and are tested by a likelihood ratio test.

$$A_i \Delta v_{it} = A_i \omega_i \Delta x_{it} + A_i \sum_{j=1}^{q-1} \Gamma_{ij} \Delta z_{it-j} - A_i \alpha_i \beta_i' z_{it-1} + A_i \varepsilon_{it}. \quad (9.28)$$

Once we have fully identified the system for the PNFC and household sectors, it can be determined whether there is evidence for a balance sheet channel and a bank lending channel for each sector.

9.3.2 Introducing the OFC sector

To deal with OFC lending to PNFCs and households, consider that there are now two sectors, so $i = 1, 2$. Assuming the same notation and lag length, we could write out the combined system as if the two models were stacked:

$$\begin{pmatrix} \Delta v_{1t} \\ \Delta v_{2t} \end{pmatrix} = \begin{pmatrix} \alpha_{11} & \alpha_{12} \\ \alpha_{21} & \alpha_{22} \end{pmatrix} \begin{pmatrix} \beta_1 z_{1t-1} \\ \beta_2 z_{2t-1} \end{pmatrix} + \sum_{j=1}^{q-1} G_j \begin{pmatrix} \Delta z_{1t-i} \\ \Delta z_{2t-i} \end{pmatrix} + \begin{pmatrix} \varepsilon_{1t} \\ \varepsilon_{2t} \end{pmatrix}, \quad (9.29)$$

where G_j are matrices of short-run coefficients. However, it is possible that there are interactions in the long-run relationships that imply that further long-run equilibria can be discovered. Taking $Z_{t-1} = (z_{1t-1}, z_{2t-1})$, where further cointegrating relations are represented as $\beta_3' Z_{t-1}$, we would write the model as:

$$
\begin{pmatrix} \Delta v_{1t} \\ \Delta v_{2t} \end{pmatrix} = \begin{pmatrix} \alpha_{11} & \alpha_{12} & \alpha_{13} \\ \alpha_{21} & \alpha_{22} & \alpha_{23} \end{pmatrix} \begin{pmatrix} \beta_1 z_{1t-1} \\ \beta_2 z_{2t-1} \\ \beta_3 Z_{t-1} \end{pmatrix}
$$

$$
+ \sum_{j=1}^{q-1} G_j \begin{pmatrix} \Delta z_{1t-j} \\ \Delta z_{2t-j} \end{pmatrix} + \begin{pmatrix} \varepsilon_{1t} \\ \varepsilon_{2t} \end{pmatrix}. \tag{9.30}
$$

The existence of further equilibria involving PNFC or household expenditure and lending by OFCs provides evidence for the importance of OFC credit as well as bank credit. Moreover, the financial linkages between OFCs and other sectors can be evaluated in weak exogeneity tests by setting restrictions to the error correction space. In effect we are testing the exogeneity of sector 1 (sector 2) to sector 2 (sector 1) by a test of the restriction $\alpha_{21} = 0$ ($\alpha_{12} = 0$). This implies that a departure from the long-run cointegrating relationship in sector 1 (sector 2) does not have an impact on the dynamic behaviour of sector 2 (sector 1).

In the next section, we will report results for two separate systems of equations representing PNFCs and households. We will then consider the OFC sector and the potential importance of OFC credit to PNFCs and households alongside that of bank credit.

9.4 Empirical results

9.4.1 Private non-financial corporations

We simultaneously estimate the equations (9.20), (9.9a) and (9.9b) using real gross domestic fixed capital formation (i_t),[4] real money holding (M4) of PNFCs (m_t) and real M4 lending to PNFCs (l_t) as endogenous variables. The explanatory variables used are: real GDP at market prices (y_t); a measure of the proportion of firms reporting more than adequate stocks of finished goods, taken from the CBI monthly survey (s_{ut}); PNFCs' real financial wealth (w_t); PNFCs' real retained earnings (π_t); the real user cost of capital (c_{kt}); the spread of the M4 deposit rate over three-month sterling LIBOR (r_{dt}), referred to as the 'deposit spread'; the spread of the interest rate on bank lending to companies over LIBOR (r_{lt}), referred to as the 'lending spread'; and the real value of mergers and acquisitions $(lrma_t)$. All except interest rates are converted to natural logarithms, and estimates apply to the sample period 1977(Q4)–1998(Q1).

Real GDP measures the general level of economic activity, and it is likely to influence the demand for investment goods and for bank borrowings. The CBI survey question on stocks can be thought of as a barometer of confidence about future demand prospects and reflects outcomes in the recent past relative

Table 9.1 *Long-run estimates for the PNFC sector*

$$i_t = y_t - s_{ut} - 2.813c_{kt}$$
$$m_t = 0.5i_t + 0.5w_t + 0.5s_{ut} + 11.204r_{dt} + 0.107lrma_t$$
$$l_t = 0.5i_t + w_t + 0.5s_{ut} - 0.5\pi_t + 4.432r_{dt} + 0.107lrma_t$$

to expectations. If firms consider themselves 'overstocked', they are likely to be relatively pessimistic about demand prospects and may be less willing to undertake further investment in fixed capital. They may also need to undertake distress borrowing. Total financial assets measure the liquidity of the sector, which will be related to money holdings and bank borrowing. Undistributed earnings are a measure of the supply of internal finance, which is an alternative to bank finance. The real user cost of capital is an indicator of the cost per period of raising capital in the financial markets. The deposit spread and the lending spread are, respectively, the return on retail deposits relative to wholesale money market rates and the cost of bank borrowing relative to money market rates.

The estimated long-run relationships for the PNFC sector are reported in table 9.1. The first equation shows that investment is proportional to real GDP in the long run and is negatively related to the survey measure of more than adequate stocks and to the cost of capital.[5] The first negative relationship captures the effects of excess capacity[6] and lack of business confidence about planned investment, while the second reflects the normal inverse relation between quantity demanded and price. The second and third equations explain long-run investment, money demand and demand for bank lending, but they both contain investment as an explanatory variable, and investment itself depends on other variables.

To obtain expressions for money and bank lending that do not rely on investment, we substitute out investment using the first equation to obtain:[7]

$$m_t = 0.5y_t - 0.5s_{ut} - 1.407c_{kt} + 0.5w_t + 11.204r_{dt} + 0.107lrma_t$$
$$l_t = 0.5y_t - 1.407c_{kt} + w_t - 0.5\pi_t + 4.432r_{dt} + 0.107lrma_t.$$

The first equation can be thought of as the PNFC long-run money demand function. The stock of PNFC M4 deposits varies positively with GDP, financial wealth, the bank deposit rate and mergers and acquisitions activity. It is negatively related to the cost of capital and the measure of firms reporting more than adequate stocks. The latter effect suggests that money is itself a 'buffer stock', such that money holding is reduced partly to finance unexpectedly high inventories of goods. The second equation shows the long-run determinants of the stock of bank lending to PNFCs. Lending varies in proportion to financial wealth and is also positively related to GDP, the deposit spread and mergers and acquisitions activity. It is negatively related to the cost of capital and to

Table 9.2 *Estimates of the dynamic structural model for PNFCs*

$$\Delta i_t = -0.1565(i - i^*)_{t-1} - 0.0923(l - l^*)_{t-1} + 0.0839(m - m^*)_{t-1} + 0.5430\Delta y_t - 0.4815\Delta c_{kt-1} - 0.7779\Delta r_{lt} - 0.9988\Delta r_{lt-1} + 0.2580$$
$$\qquad\quad (0.0266)\qquad\quad (0.0261)\qquad\qquad (0.0297)\qquad\qquad (0.2545)\quad\ (0.2175)\qquad (0.7154)\qquad (0.5666)\quad\ (0.1021)$$

$$\Delta l_t = 0.1631\Delta i_{t-1} + 0.4107\Delta l_{t-1} - 0.1246(l - l^*)_{t-1} + 0.0734(m - m^*)_{t-1} + 0.3466\Delta y_t - 0.2516\Delta y_{t-1} - 0.0418\Delta \pi_t + 0.0216\Delta \pi_{t-1}$$
$$\qquad\quad (0.0503)\qquad (0.0685)\qquad (0.0212)\qquad\qquad (0.0196)\qquad\qquad (0.1674)\qquad (0.1556)\qquad (0.0104)\qquad (0.0102)$$
$$\qquad + 0.1796\Delta s_{ut} - 0.7787\Delta r_{dt} - 1.307\Delta r_{dt-1} - 0.7539\Delta r_{lt} + 0.0072\Delta lrma_{t-1} - 0.3172$$
$$\qquad\quad (0.0453)\qquad (0.4218)\qquad\ (0.4323)\qquad\ (0.3730)\qquad (0.0017)\qquad\ (0.0598)$$

$$\Delta m_t = -0.1233\Delta i_{t-1} - 0.1863\Delta l_{t-1} + 0.2812\Delta m_{t-1} - 0.0350(l - l^*)_{t-1} - 0.0632(m - m^*)_{t-1} + 0.8271\Delta y_t + 0.1708\Delta w_t + 0.5427\Delta c_{kt}$$
$$\qquad\qquad (0.0928)\qquad (0.1084)\qquad (0.0881)\qquad\quad (0.0334)\qquad\qquad (0.0316)\qquad\qquad (0.2778)\quad\ (0.0837)\quad\ (0.2455)$$
$$\qquad + 0.5527\Delta c_{kt-1} + 3.1371\Delta r_{dt} + 1.4435\Delta r_{dt-1} - 1.0273\Delta r_{lt-1} + 0.0084\Delta lrma_t$$
$$\qquad\quad (0.2423)\qquad\quad (0.7383)\qquad\ (0.8026)\qquad\ (0.6413)\qquad\ (0.0031)$$

Notes: Standard errors are in parentheses. Data period: 1978(Q1) to 1998(Q1).
Portmanteau 9 lags = 100.32; AR 1-5 F(45,146) = 1.13 [0.28]; normality $\chi^2 (6) = 2.86$ [0.83].
Log likelihood = 961.76 T = 75; LR test of overidentifying restrictions: $\chi^2_{\chi} (46) = 46.02$ [0.47].

retained earnings. The latter finding indicates that bank lending to PNFCs falls as the preferred alternative – internal source of funds – expands.[8]

The estimated dynamic equations appear in table 9.2, and the actual and fitted values for each of these equations are shown in figure 9.1.[9,10] The coefficient on the deviation term in the investment equation indicates that investment adjusts by about 16% per quarter towards its long-run equilibrium. In the same equation, the coefficients on both $(l - l^*)$ and $(m - m^*)$ are significant at the 5% level.[11] The negative coefficient on the lending deviation term indicates that, when lending is above its long-run equilibrium, investment tends subsequently to fall, while the positive coefficient on the money deviation term indicates that excess money holding by firms is associated with higher investment. Lending adjusts by about 12% per quarter towards its long-run equilibrium, while money adjusts more slowly at 6% per quarter.

For PNFCs, the long-run level of lending is found to be heavily dependent on balance sheet items, such as real financial wealth and retained earnings, rather than on factors operating through the bank lending channel, such as the lending spread, which appears only in the short-run dynamics. A direct credit effect operates through 'excess' lending, which is associated with a decrease in investment, but the influence of the company balance sheet on banks' willingness to lend and firms' readiness to borrow supports both a supply-side 'balance sheet channel' and a demand-side interpretation.[12]

Lending adds significantly to our explanation of corporate spending, partly because the decision to invest and the decision to borrow are made simultaneously. The point is that 'excess' borrowing in one quarter helps to explain investment in the subsequent quarter. In addition to this direct evidence, the lending deviation term is significantly linked to money, and money in turn has significant explanatory power in the investment equation. Therefore we conclude that credit contains useful supplementary information to that found in the money data when explaining real corporate expenditure.

9.4.2 Households

The variables used in our model for the household sector are: real consumer expenditure by households (c_t), the stock of real M4 balances held by households (m_t) and the stock of real unsecured M4 lending to households by banks and building societies (l_t). These variables correspond to equations (9.21), (9.17a) and (9.17b). We include as explanatory variables: real net labour income (y_t); household real net total wealth (w_t), defined as housing wealth plus financial assets minus total debt; inflation (π_t), measured as the annual rate of change of the consumer expenditure deflator; a deposit spread, measured by the difference between the retail deposit rate and base rate (r_{dt}); and a credit spread of the credit card rate over base rate (r_{ct}). Two additional stationary variables used are an aggregate measure of consumer confidence ($conf_t$) and the percentage

Table 9.3 *Long-run estimated equations for the household sector*

$$c_t = -0.2m_t - 0.12l_t + 1.0y_t + 0.32w_t - 0.7\pi_t$$
$$m_t = 0.32l_t + 0.81y_t + 0.75r_{dt}$$
$$l_t = 0.85y_t + 0.77w_t - 1.5r_{ct} - 2.9\pi_t$$

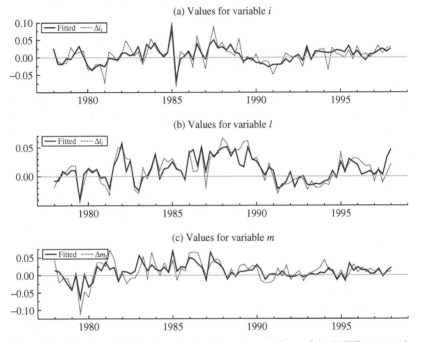

Figure 9.1 Actual and fitted values for the dynamic equations of the PNFC structural model.
Note: see table 9.2.

change in unemployment (Δu_t), measured by the claimant count. All data except the inflation rate, interest rate spreads and the change in the percentage unemployed are converted to natural logarithms. The sample period is 1978(Q1)–1998(Q4).

As with the PNFC model, we estimate three long-run relationships between the variables – one for each of the endogenous variables c_t, m_t and l_t in table 9.3. There are interactions among consumption, money and lending.[13] The levels of real money and credit appear in the equation for household real consumption. The inclusion of money in the consumption equation can be interpreted as indicating that liquid assets have a different impact on consumption in the long run than do other components of financial wealth. A higher stock of lending lowers consumption in the long run (for given wealth and labour income), because the debt has to be serviced.

Rewriting to ensure that only exogenous variables are on the right-hand side gives:

$$c_t = 0.69y_t + 0.18w_t - 0.17\pi_t - 0.15r_{dt} + 0.28r_{ct}$$
$$m_t = 1.08y_t + 0.25w_t + 0.75r_{dt} - 0.48r_{ct} - 0.9\pi_t$$
$$l_t = 0.85y_t + 0.77w_t - 1.5r_{ct} - 2.9\pi_t.$$

Lending to households is positively related to income and wealth, although it is less sensitive to labour income and more sensitive to net wealth than is money demand. As the credit spread rises, the stock of bank lending falls. The credit channel suggests that these effects could represent the influence of the balance sheet (that is, the importance of net wealth for credit provision) and bank lending channels (that is, the dependence of households on banks and of the stock of credit on the price of credit set by banks). But the results could also reflect demand factors – the negative effect of the credit spread is consistent with households undertaking less unsecured borrowing when credit rates rise relative to savings rates or rates on secured borrowing.

Real consumption has a plausible marginal propensity to consume out of real labour income of 0.69, and it is positively related to real net wealth. In theory, the sign of the impact of inflation on consumer expenditure is ambiguous; however, most previous studies have found that inflation reduces real consumption, as here. This could be because inflation increases uncertainty or because households expect a tightening of future monetary policy with rising inflation. A further reason could be that households attempt to restore the real value of their savings balances after erosion by inflation. The deposit spread has a negative effect on consumption, but surprisingly the credit spread has a positive effect. This latter effect comes from the fact that lending appears in this equation with a negative sign and the credit spread appears in the lending equation with a negative sign. Both of these effects are highly plausible – borrowing is reduced by a widening in the credit spread, and consumption is reduced (in the long run) if debt is higher (because interest on the debt has to be paid out of disposable income, so sustainable consumption will be lower). So the positive effect of the credit spread on consumption arises because, the higher the spread is, the lower the stock of debt in the long run. The money demand function is nearly homogeneous in labour income and has a smaller positive coefficient on net financial wealth. As deposit spreads increase, households add to their deposits.

The dynamic structural models are reported in table 9.4, and the actual and fitted values are shown in figure 9.2. Taking the equations in reverse order is helpful, given that deviations of money and consumption from their long-run

Table 9.4 Estimates of the dynamic structural model for households

$$\Delta c_t = -0.47840\Delta c_{t-1} + 1.0720\Delta m_t + 0.21298\Delta m_{t-1} - 0.42172\Delta l_t + 0.16647\Delta l_{t-1} - 0.19998(c-c^*)_{t-1} + 0.14894\Delta y_{t-1} - 0.21103\Delta r_{dt-1}$$
$$\quad\;\; (0.10039) \qquad\quad (0.17877) \qquad (0.13024) \qquad\quad (0.15033) \qquad (0.11404) \qquad\quad\; (0.04461) \qquad\qquad (0.078614) \qquad\quad (0.18126)$$

$$\qquad\;\; - 0.18266\Delta r_{ct-1} - 0.00922\Delta u_t + 0.00947\Delta u_{t-1} + 0.00058\,conf_t - 0.00032\,conf_{t-1} - 0.15265$$
$$\qquad\quad (0.06852) \qquad\quad (0.004937) \qquad\;\; (0.00499) \qquad\quad (0.00020) \qquad\qquad (0.00018) \qquad\qquad (0.026576)$$

$$\Delta m_t = -0.13773\Delta m_{t-1} + 0.19201\Delta l_t + 0.07308(c-c^*)_{t-1} - 0.13878(m-m^*)_{t-1} + 0.21249\Delta y_t + 0.03227\Delta y_{t-1} + 0.03701\Delta w_t$$
$$\qquad\quad\;\; (0.07729) \qquad\quad (0.04384) \qquad\quad (0.02143) \qquad\qquad (0.02248) \qquad\qquad\;\; (0.04118) \qquad\quad (0.04356) \qquad\quad (0.01504)$$

$$\qquad\; + 0.03879\Delta w_{t-1} - 0.35582\Delta r_{dt} + 0.11334\Delta r_{dt-1} - 0.19330\Delta r_{ct} - 0.31999\Delta\pi_t - 0.12454\Delta\pi_{t-1} - 0.009379\Delta u_{t-1}$$
$$\qquad\quad (0.01989) \qquad\quad (0.10317) \qquad\qquad (0.10146) \qquad\quad (0.04521) \qquad\quad (0.05263) \qquad\quad (0.06116) \qquad\qquad (0.001702)$$

$$\qquad\; - 0.000295\,conf_t + 0.045911$$
$$\qquad\quad (0.000007) \qquad\;\; (0.012100)$$

$$\Delta l_t = -0.45759\Delta c_{t-1} + 0.32978\Delta l_{t-1} + 0.31556\,(c-c^*)_{t-1} - 0.50685(m-m^*)_{t-1} - 0.17603(l-l^*)_{t-1} - 0.48094\Delta r_{dt-1} - 0.38030\Delta r_{ct}$$
$$\quad\;\; (0.09673) \qquad\quad (0.08441) \qquad\qquad (0.09312) \qquad\qquad (0.07401) \qquad\qquad\quad (0.03225) \qquad\qquad\;\; (0.17818) \qquad\quad (0.09175)$$

$$\qquad\; - 0.52959\Delta\pi_t - 0.32658\Delta\pi_{t-1} + 0.00691\Delta u_{t-1} + 0.00058\,conf_t - 0.00054\,conf_{t-1} - 1.5292$$
$$\qquad\quad (0.10147) \qquad\quad (0.12426) \qquad\qquad (0.00366) \qquad\quad (0.00019) \qquad\qquad (0.00019) \qquad\qquad (0.26598)$$

Notes: Standard errors are in parentheses. Data period: 1978(Q1) to 1998(Q4).
Portmanteau 9 lags $= 86.98$; AR 1-5 F(90,96) $= 1.02$ [0.46]; normality $\chi^2(6) = 3.86$ [0.72]LR.
Log likelihood $= 1107.8$ T $= 72$; LR test of overidentifying restrictions: $\chi^2(38) = 21.42$ (0.99).

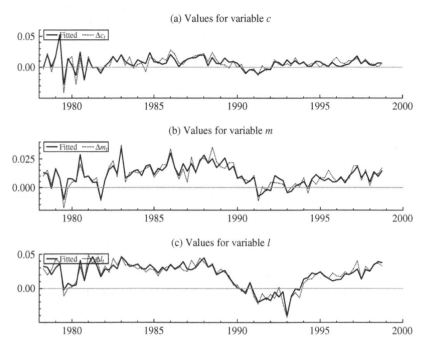

Figure 9.2   Actual and fitted values for the dynamic equations of the household structural model.
Note: see table 9.4.

fitted values influence the dynamics of lending, and the deviation of consumption from its long-run value affects the dynamics of money. The adjustment speed of lending toward its long-run value is 18% per quarter. Excess money and consumption have a very strong influence on lending, with estimated adjustment speeds per quarter of 31% and 50%, respectively. Excess money balances are associated with reduced lending, suggesting that excess money balances are used to pay off borrowing. Excess consumption leads to increases in lending, suggesting plausibly that a build-up of unsecured borrowing results from periods of abnormally high consumer spending. Past changes in lending have a positive influence on the contemporaneous change in lending, and increases in the cost of credit and the return on deposits (relative to base rate) reduce the growth rate of unsecured lending.

In the dynamic equation for money, the adjustment speed to excess money balances is 14%, consistent with the view that money is used as an inventory or buffer stock to 'mop up' shocks to financial resources coming from either unexpected income or unplanned spending. Contemporaneous adjustments to lending have a positive effect on current changes to money balances in these results, suggesting that, when households borrow to spend, they also run up money balances, reversing the effect in subsequent quarters.

Lastly, the consumption equation implies that 20% of the difference between actual consumption and its long-run fitted value is eliminated in each quarter. Consumption growth is negatively related to its own lagged value, which appears contrary to the idea of consumption smoothing, but this result may simply be an offset to the strong autocorrelation coming through money growth. There is a very strong positive relation between consumption growth and contemporaneous and lagged changes in money balances. Consumption is also negatively related to lending growth, but this is unwound the following quarter.

The key feature of these results is that the addition of lending does appear to add significant explanatory power. Although the lending deviation term does not appear in the consumption equation in this case, lending growth is significant in the consumption equation. Lending growth is also a significant determinant of money growth, which itself is a significant determinant of consumption growth. In addition to these dynamic effects, lending is significant in the long-run equation for consumption and there is evidence consistent with a balance sheet effect in the long-run equilibrium for credit. The combined impact of all these effects gives an indication that lending does influence the path of household consumption, but the effect may not be as influential as for PNFCs.

9.4.3   Credit from other financial corporations (OFCs)

We are interested in the impact of the OFC sector on the spending decisions of PNFCs and households. Our approach to this issue is to consider how disequilibria estimated separately for OFCs' money and lending might influence the system of equations for the two other sectors reported above. The OFC equilibria are:

$$l_t = 5.81 + 0.5m_t + y_t + 0.254w_t + 0.004r_{st}$$
$$m_t = 10.86 + 0.5l_t + 0.254w_t + 1.413\pi_t - 0.037r_{st} + 0.063(r_1 - dy)_t,$$

where the variables are: real M4 balances held by OFCs (m), real M4 lending to OFCs by banks and building societies (l), real gross domestic product (y), OFCs' real gross financial wealth (w), the real transfer earnings of the financial sector as a whole (including banks) from intermediation services (π),[14] a maturity spread measured by the difference between the long gilt rate and the three-month Treasury bill rate (r_s) and the spread of the long gilt rate over the Financial Times-30 dividend yield ($r_1 - dy$).

The argument we have proposed in the theoretical section is that OFCs may operate as quasi-banks by recycling 'deposits' into loans. The OFCs themselves borrow from banks and this fact may influence the PNFC sector as OFCs offer quasi-bank intermediation services and dealing facilities, and they purchase the capital equipment that they subsequently lease to PNFCs. We might expect that lending to OFCs would influence PNFC investment if OFCs' lending were a substitute for bank lending. Such substitutability would weaken the 'specialness' of banks and lessen the significance of the bank lending channel (especially if OFCs operate under different rules from banks) by widening the definition of credit through which the credit channel operates. OFC borrowing is shown to matter for real activity: increased OFC borrowing is associated with higher levels of real investment. This mechanism weakens the bank lending channel but would broaden the credit channel.

OFCs and households are likely to be linked through the long-term management of savings by institutional investors such as pension funds and life assurance companies, as well as through unit and investment trusts. These funds are liable to be 'locked in' for a considerable period of time, but the perceived wealth effects of these funds may influence the sustainable consumption that households believe they can maintain. The link between the wealth that is held and managed by OFCs and household wealth is very strong, and gross wealth has been shown to influence money and lending by OFCs. It is not immediately clear, however, that the levels of money or lending and hence disequilibria in these variables will affect the consumption of households, on whose behalf the wealth is invested.

Our method is to ask (a) how OFC lending affects other sectors' spending in the long run and (b) how short-run disequilibria in OFC lending might affect PNFCs and households. We ascertain whether these variables and those used to determine their equilibria 'explain' expenditure of PNFCs and households. This task involves a search for further long-run relationships between the variables explaining equilibrium money and credit held by the OFC sector and those used to augment the models of the other sectors. If there are new cointegrating relationships, then we must allow for their influence over the dynamic behaviour of the other two sectors.

In the case of the PNFCs, a new cointegrating relation is found, where an OFC lending variable, $l(ofc)_t$, influences firms' real investment in an otherwise similar long-run equation:

$$i_t = y_t - 0.494\,c_{kt} - s_{ut} + 0.054\,l(ofc)_t.$$

The discovery of the new relation is interesting because it shows that, even if OFCs expand and contract the asset and liability sides of their balance sheet proportionally, and have no direct spending component that feeds into aggregate demand, they still influence real investment by firms. In our model we replace the original investment equation with this new equilibrium.

Table 9.5 reports the results of disequilibria on the PNFC sector. There are two potential effects. The first comes through the new equilibrium investment

Table 9.5 *Financial linkages between sectors*

	PNFC response to disequilibria in:				
	PNFC investment	PNFC lending	PNFC money	OFC money	OFC lending
Coefficients	−0.2352	−0.041	0.0189	−0.0157	0.0111
Standard errors	(0.0345)	(0.032)	(0.0300)	(0.0469)	(0.0523)
	Household response to disequilibria in:				
	Household consumption	Household lending	Household money	OFC money	OFC lending
Coefficients	−0.2213	0*	0*	−0.0051	−0.051
Standard errors	(0.0583)	−	−	(0.0189)	(0.0255)

Note: *restricted to equal zero in structural model.

equation, where the results show that, compared with the original PNFC model, there is stronger feedback to the new investment disequilibrium. This implies that OFC lending does have an impact on whole-economy investment growth through loans to firms that undertake investment or through ODFs' own borrowing activity carried out to finance the purchase of capital equipment that they subsequently lease. The second effect operates through the direct influence of money and lending disquilibria on spending, but in this model there is no detectable influence on PNFC investment (see fourth and fifth terms, top panel).

The search for additional cointegrating relations among variables in the OFC and household models concluded that there were no new long-run relationships of the kind that we discovered between OFCs and the PNFC sector. This eliminates the possibility that OFC lending influences the long-run behaviour of households. The test of the significance of OFC disequilibria on household spending is reported in table 9.5 (see fourth and fifth terms, bottom panel). Only one feedback coefficient is significant, and it corresponds to the influence of disequilibrium in OFC money on consumption growth. Excess OFC money balances are associated with lower consumer expenditure growth, which may arise if OFCs hold more money than they desire at times when other assets are perceived as overvalued and consumer expenditures decline as the perceived wealth of households is revised.

The conclusion we draw is that OFC lending positively influences whole-economy investment. It may do so through the PNFC sector, supplementing bank lending as a complement or a substitute, or it may reflect investments undertaken by OFCs themselves as they purchase capital equipment for leasing. OFC lending has no detectable effect on households.

9.5   Conclusions

The objective of this chapter was to investigate the empirical evidence for credit effects in the transmission mechanism in the United Kingdom. We mentioned the two main channels by which credit can influence expenditure: the balance sheet channel and the bank lending channel. We sought to discover whether there was evidence consistent with these effects and to determine whether non-banks as well as banks influence PNFC and household spending.

Our results are clear-cut. There is support for the view that 'credit matters' and that balance sheet criteria are determinants of the level of equilibrium credit offered to firms. The feedback from credit disequilibria to investment implies that variations above or below the desired level of credit have real effects. There is also some evidence for a balance sheet effect on households, but the results are less supportive than for firms and there is no feedback from credit disequilibrium on spending.

The question of how important non-bank credit might be for expenditure is also answered. Extending the range of organisations offering credit facilities to include non-banks in the OFC sector reveals that non-bank credit also matters. OFC lending has a direct effect on total economy investment, and including OFC credit as a determinant of long-run equilibrium increases the strength of the feedback coefficient for PNFC real expenditure. There are no effects through the household sector, however.

In summary, the results are supportive of credit effects in the monetary transmission mechanism of the United Kingdom, and these effects extend beyond those of bank credit. The principal channel appears through lending to firms, which influences whole-economy investment, a major component of gross domestic product.

Acknowledgements

We are grateful to Lavan Mahadeva for helpful comments.

Notes

1 See Bank of England (1999a).
2 Note that the purpose of this chapter is to draw together the informational benefits derived from augmenting a model of investment/consumption with money and credit. We do not propose to explore the detailed questions thrown up by the credit channel literature, or to dwell on the methodological issues surrounding the identification of dynamic econometric systems. For these details the reader is directed to three Bank of England Working Papers that deal with these matters: Brigden and Mizen (1999) and Chrystal and Mizen (2001a, b).

3 Note that the market for certificates of deposit and commercial paper/corporate bonds is assumed to be arbitraged by the householders to ensure that the returns are identical. Since the two types of asset are perfectly substitutable, we record the demand for the composite.

4 The results reported here use whole-economy gross domestic fixed capital formation, but similar results can be obtained using business investment.

5 Note that all round-number coefficients are restricted. Some restrictions are necessary to achieve identification. The overidentifying restrictions are not rejected by the data. See Brigden and Mizen (1999) for further details.

6 It could be questioned whether a cyclical variable such as excess stocks should appear in the long-run relationships; however, this series is non-stationary in our sample. An explanation may be that the sample period is shorter than ideal, but the movement may also reflect big changes in inventory behaviour since the early 1980s.

7 These equations can be thought of as 'reduced forms' that relate endogenous variables to exogenous variables only.

8 Note that borrowing from securities markets is also available to firms. This alternative is excluded from the present study but could be included to provide a more complete picture.

9 Here we use the general notation x^* to denote the estimated long-run equilibrium of variable x. $(x - x^*)$ then denotes the disequilibrium in variable x (relative to the long run).

10 Full reports of the diagnostic tests and further discussions of the estimated specifications are available in Brigden and Mizen (1999).

11 Not all deviation terms appear in all equations. Some are excluded to satisfy the requirements of econometric identification, while others may be eliminated as insignificant. See Thomas (1997a) on this issue.

12 This is consistent with a credit channel, although we recognise that the limitations of using sectoral time-series data mean that the evidence may be consistent with alternative interpretations.

13 Again, some of these coefficients are restricted. Details can be found in Chrystal and Mizen (2001a).

14 The variable used is 'financial intermediation services indirectly measured (FISIM)', which measures interest payments to the financial sector that are considered a transfer from other sectors and not considered part of the economy's Gross Value Added (at basic prices). This used to be called 'adjustment for financial services'.

10 Uncovered interest parity with fundamentals: a Brazilian exchange rate forecast model

Marcelo Kfoury Muinhos, Paulo Springer de Freitas and Fabio Araujo

10.1 Introduction

Forecasting the nominal exchange rate path is one of the most challenging aspects of an inflation-targeting framework. According to Bank of Brazil estimates, the pass-through from nominal exchange rate movements to inflation is around 10% in each quarter.[1] Therefore, an accurate forecast of the nominal value of the currency is very important for the efficiency of an inflation-targeting regime. If the evaluation of the future exchange rate path can be made more precise, it may reduce the variance in output and inflation.

Uncovered interest parity (UIP), which relates the expected nominal depreciation to the nominal interest rate differential, has been a popular model for exchange rate forecasting. But UIP has been questioned as an adequate tool to forecast future exchange rates because many empirical tests have found a negative correlation between exchange rate changes and the interest differential,[2] in contradiction to what is predicted by UIP.[3] This situation has led us to consider what can be gained and lost with other models for forecasting the exchange rate.

A simple alternative is to assume that the exchange rate follows a random walk and is not cointegrated with any exogenous variable for which we have data. The expected future exchange rate therefore should be equal to the current value. This first approach, although simple and transparent, does not preclude the risk of occasional large forecast errors in the exchange rate and hence inflation. And although exchange rates appear to have random-walk-like properties, we cannot be sure that the econometric tests at our disposal are subtle enough to distinguish random walks from other processes with potentially very different forecasts over one- and two-year horizons.

Another simple alternative is to forecast a constant real exchange rate, according to purchasing power parity (PPP). To derive the nominal exchange rate path, we have to forecast the difference between domestic and foreign inflation. According to a survey by Mark Taylor (1995), PPP holds in the postwar period until the early 1970s, when the Bretton Woods system was abandoned. The high variability of the major currencies that followed led to the validity of PPP being seriously questioned. For high-frequency data, Meese and Rogoff (1983, 1988) made key findings in which tests overwhelmingly rejected PPP in favour of the random walk hypothesis up to the one-year horizon.[4]

Some recent tests of the cointegration between the nominal exchange rate and relative prices support the mean reversion property of the real exchange rate, a finding consistent with PPP.[5] This outcome is especially true when the authors use very long samples, covering several decades. Froot and Rogoff (1995) and Rogoff (1996) estimated that the convergence of PPP is very slow, with a half-life of three or four years, using linear models.[6]

The need to equalise the return of different nominal assets, avoiding arbitrage, yields the UIP relationship, which can be written as follows:

$$E_t e_{t+1} = e_t + i_t - (i_t^* + x_t), \tag{10.1}$$

where e_t is the nominal exchange rate at time t, defined as the units of domestic currency needed to buy one unit of foreign currency (in such a way that increases in 'e' mean a devaluation), i is the nominal interest rate of one-period maturity, x is the risk premium, the asterisk denotes foreign, and E_t is the expectations operator conditional on information at time t.

A simple test of UIP is based on the estimation of the following equation:

$$\Delta e_{t+k} = \alpha + \beta(i_t - i_t^*) + \upsilon_{t+k}. \tag{10.2}$$

Although UIP implies $\beta = 1$, researchers have almost invariably estimated values of β smaller than 1 that are sometimes negative. Allowing for a risk premium in equation (10.2) may imply that $\beta < 1$; however, it is unlikely to suggest that the true β is close to zero or negative (M. Taylor, 1995). Meese and Rogoff (1988) failed to reject the null hypothesis of no cointegration between the real exchange rate and the real interest rate for the dollar, yen and German mark for different periods. Meredith and Chinn (1998), however, found evidence for UIP using interest rate differentials embodied in bonds of longer maturity.

These models of the determinants of the exchange rate each has its own appeal. UIP is essentially a model of the exchange rate path, and PPP a model of the level. Rather than consider these determinant theories as strict substitutes, it seems natural and consistent to combine them in order to retain the information content of both.

In doing this, we are following quite closely the approach of Wadhwani (1999). He suggested that the main reason for the failure of a standard UIP approach is that it is too restrictive: 'the UIP straitjacket... requires variables like unemployment/growth to only affect exchange rate through interest rate.'[7] Instead he adapted UIP to allow for other influences, as follows:

$$\Delta e_{t+k} = \alpha + \beta(i_t - i_t^*) - \rho(q_t - \overline{q}, Z_t), \qquad (10.3)$$

where Z_t depends on other nominal assets such as bonds and stocks; and $q_t - \overline{q}$ is the estimated deviation of the real exchange rate, which depends on the difference in current account/GDP ratios, unemployment rates and the net foreign assets/GDP ratio, and on the relative ratios of wholesale and consumer price indexes.[8]

The object of this paper is to adapt the standard UIP relationship similarly for Brazil to incorporate longer-run determinants of the exchange rate explicitly. We compare the implications of this combined relationship with a random walk hypothesis in the context of a model of the Brazilian transmission mechanism. In our adaptation of the standard UIP model, we assume that, at some point in the future, the real exchange rate will converge to equilibrium, anchoring expectations in a forward-looking model. The equilibrium exchange rate is the one that achieves a sustainable balance of trade and is also determined within the model. The path between the current and future exchange rate follows the UIP hypothesis.

Section 10.2 presents the current specifications of the exchange rate forecast in the Brazilian inflation-targeting framework. Section 10.3 describes a model that is used to compare different strategies for forecasting the exchange rate. Section 10.4 shows the system solution, and section 10.5 presents and discusses the simulations. Finally, section 10.6 summarizes the results and presents the main conclusions.

10.2   The Central Bank of Brazil exchange rate forecast models

To forecast the nominal exchange rate path in our inflation-targeting structural models, we work with three alternatives. First, we model a random walk with monetary surprises (RWMS), which relates movements of the nominal exchange rate to movements in the interest differential adjusted by the risk premium. The second alternative is a UIP specification. The third procedure is a weighted average between the forecasts given by the UIP and the random walk hypothesis.

The first approach, the so-called RWMS, is in fact a UIP in first difference. It can be derived easily in the following way:

$$E_t e_{t+1} - e_t = i_t - i_t^* - x_t, \qquad (10.4)$$

where x_t is the risk premium. Taking the first difference in equation (10.4) and assuming that the difference in exchange rate expectations is a white noise process:

$$E_t e_{t+1} - E_{t-1} e_t = \eta_t,^9$$

will yield the RWMS model:

$$\Delta e_t = \Delta i_t^* + \Delta x_t - \Delta i_t + \eta_t = \Delta(i_t^* + x_t - i_t) + \eta_t. \qquad (10.5)$$

This model is unlike traditional UIP, in which exchange rate variations depend on the levels of interest rate differentials. In the RWMS approach, only changes in interest rate differentials cause movements in exchange rates. Despite the strong assumptions embodied in the RWMS model, it has two desirable features: there is no need to hypothesise about future exchange rates in this specification; and it combines the random walk hypothesis with the feature that exchange rates are sensitive to variations in the interest rate differential.

For simulation purposes, the foreign interest rate path is considered exogenous. The risk premium is modelled as either exogenously or endogenously determined according to the Brazilian macroeconomic fundamentals, such as fiscal variables or the behaviour of payments components. The latter model of the risk premium can be written as:

$$\Delta X_t = \gamma_1 \Delta X_{t-1} + \Delta PR_{t-3} + \sum_{j=0}^{J} \gamma_j \Delta z_{j,t-t_j}, \qquad (10.6)$$

where X is the risk premium, measured as the spread of a Brazilian sovereign bond over a US Treasury bond of equivalent duration; PR is the public sector borrowing requirement (PSBR) in its primary concept as a percentage of GDP; and each Δz_j is an exogenous variable that affects the change in the country risk with lag t_j ($j = 0, \ldots, J$). The PSBR is assumed to affect risk with a lag of three quarters.

The second approach is to forecast the nominal exchange rate path using UIP with 'model-consistent expectations'. Given an exogenously determined equilibrium nominal exchange rate at some period K ahead, and then using a model-consistent UIP, the expected nominal exchange rate path is calculated from period 0 to K. From $K + 1$ on, the future nominal exchange rate path follows PPP. According to this model, an increase in the domestic interest rate leads to a contemporaneous fall in the nominal exchange rate, which begins to devalue to offset the interest rate differential.

The third and final strategy for forecasting the exchange rate is a variation of the previous method, and is called UIP with 'adaptive expectations'. To allow for persistence in the exchange rate, the exchange rate path is a linear combination of the model-consistent UIP and the past value of the exchange rate.

10.3 UIP with fundamentals: the five-equation model

To work with our new proposal for UIP, we have to build a complete set of equations to characterise a small-scale inflation-targeting model. We present an aggregate demand equation, a Phillips equation, an interest rate rule (Taylor rule), the UIP and an equation for the balance of trade. The hypothesis in our UIP with fundamentals is that the expected real exchange rate makes the current account achieve its sustainable balance K periods ahead.

The IS equation is very simple. The output gap depends on itself with a lag, on the lagged real interest rate and on the real exchange rate:

$$h_{t+1} = a_{10} + a_{11}h_t + a_{12}(i_t - \pi_t) + a_{13}\theta_t + u_t, \tag{10.7}$$

where h is the log of the output gap, θ is the real exchange rate, i is the nominal interest rate, π is consumer inflation, and u is the error term.[10]

The Phillips curve complies with long-run nominal neutrality; in the long run, there is a vertical long-run Phillips curve. This restriction implies that the coefficients associated with the nominal variables should sum to 1. This equation is:

$$\pi_t = a_{21}\pi_{t-1} + a_{22}\pi_{t-2} + (1 - a_{21} - a_{22})(e_t - e_{t-1}) + a_{24}h_{t-1} + \varepsilon_t, \tag{10.8}$$

where ε is the cost-push disturbance and $(e_t - e_{t-1})$ is the nominal exchange rate variation.

The policy-maker sets interest rates following a simple rule, such as a Taylor rule as stated below:

$$i_t = a_{30} + a_{31}(\pi_{t-1} - \pi_{t-1}^*) + a_{32}h_{t-1}. \tag{10.9}$$

Exchange rate determination is based on UIP, as stated in equation (10.5). To estimate the exchange rate path, however, it is necessary to anchor the exchange rate at some point in the future. Our assumption is that, at period $t + K$, the nominal exchange rate will be consistent with a sustainable current account. For each period between t and $t + K$, the nominal exchange rate will evolve according to the interest rate differential corrected by the risk premium, as predicted by the UIP hypothesis. The following two equations, therefore, determine the path of the exchange rate:

$$E_t e_{t+n} = -\sum_{j=n}^{K-1} E_t(i_{t+j} - i_{t+j}^* - x_{t+j}) + E_t e_{t+K}, \quad \text{for } n < K \tag{10.10}$$

$$E_t e_{t+K} = \theta_{t+K} - p_{t+K}^f + p_{t+K}, \tag{10.11}$$

where θ is the expected real exchange rate that makes the balance of trade K periods ahead equal to its constant equilibrium value, x_t is an exogenous risk premium that follows an AR(1) process, and p_t^f and p_t are the foreign and domestic price levels in logs (respectively).

The fifth equation ensures that the balance of payments clear:

$$CA + BS = BC,$$

where CA is the capital account, BS is the balance of services and BC is the trade balance. Both CA and BS are treated as exogenous and BC is determined by:

$$BC = \sum_{j=1}^{7} \alpha_j . Q_j(y, \theta) . P_{j_j}, \qquad (10.12)$$

where the P_j are the price indices for agricultural exports, semi-industrialised exports, industrialised exports, capital goods; for durable consumption; for non-durable consumption goods; and for raw material imports. The Q_j are the quantitative indices for each good indexed by j. These depend on the output gap and the real exchange rate; αs are the weights to transform the indices in US\$ terms.

10.4   The system solution

Assuming that the balance of trade will return to its equilibrium K periods ahead, the economic system specified in equations (10.7) to (10.12) can be described by a quasi-linear system of equations. Taking expectations with respect to the information set available at time $t - 1$, the model can be written as follows:[11]

$$h_{t+1} = a_{10} + a_{11}h_t + a_{12}(i_t - \pi_t) + a_{13}\theta_t$$

$$\pi_t = a_{21}\pi_{t-1} + a_{22}\pi_{t-2} + (1 - a_{21} - a_{22})(e_t - e_{t-1}) + a_{24}h_{t-1}$$

$$i_t = a_{30} + a_{31}(\pi_{t-1} - \pi_{t-1}^*) + a_{32}h_{t-1}$$

$$qxb_t = exoqxb_t + a_{71}.y_t + a_{72}.qxb_{t-1} + a_{73}.qxb_{t-1}$$

$$qxs_t = exoqxs_t + a_{81}.\theta_t + a_{82}.y_t + a_{83}.qxs_{t-1}$$

$$qxm_t = exoqxm_t + a_{91}.qxm_{t-1} + a_{92}.qxm_{t-2} + a_{93}.\theta_t + a_{94}.y_{t-1}$$
$$\qquad + a_{95}.y_{t-2}$$

$$qkap_t = exoqkap_t + a_{101}.qkap_{t-1} + a_{102}.y_{t-2} + a_{103}.\theta_t$$

$$qmbc_t = exoqmbc_t + a_{111}.qmbc_{t-1} + a_{112}.y_t + a_{113}.\theta_t$$

$$qmnd_t = exoqmnd_t + a_{121}.qmnd_{t-1} + a_{122}.y_t + a_{123}.\theta_t$$

$$qint_t = exoqqint_t + a_{131}.qint_{t-1} + a_{132}.y_t + a_{133}.\theta_t$$

$$e_{t+n} = -\sum_{j=n}^{K-1}(i_{t+j} - i_{t+j}^* - x_{t+j}) + e_{t+K} \quad n < K$$

$$e_{t+K} = \theta_{t+K} - p_{t+K}^f + p_{t+K},$$

where *exoqmmm* denotes the exogenous component of volumes in the respective equation for the good indexed *mmm*. The variables are described in table 10A.1 in the appendix of this chapter.

The θ_{t+K} is the solution of the following non-linear equation:

$$BC = \sum_{j=1}^{7} \alpha_j.Q_j(y, \theta).P_j = BC_{eq}.$$

At the period $t + K$, the real exchange rate will be expected to be consistent with the balance of trade equilibrium, with exogenous paths for the balance of services and capital account. Using this hypothesis, we represent each variable in a different equation for the K periods, so the resulting system will have $[11(K + 1) - 1]$ linear equations,[12] as described in table 10A.1, and the non-linear equation that solves for θ.[13]

The system is solved for time t, generating expected paths for all endogenous variables from period t up to $t + K$. At time $t + 1$, the system takes the solution for t as given, and solves the equation again, yielding the solution for $t + 1$, which is used to generate the solution for $t + 2$, and so on.

In addition, we assumed that the system is steady state and the variables are defined as deviations from their equilibrium values. Hence, in the absence of shocks, the system will stay in a trivial equilibrium. To evaluate the dynamic properties of the system, we assumed shocks in some key variables; the resulting impulse responses are presented in the following section.[14]

10.5 Simulations

All the coefficients of the system are calibrated on the basis of previous estimations. The system is solved 150 periods ahead subject to demand, supply, interest rate and risk premium shocks. The purpose of the simulations is to compare the impulse responses using different hypotheses of the nominal exchange rate path, using the random walk with monetary surprises and the UIP with fundamentals. We ran the simulation for different horizons over which the balance of trade is expected to reach its equilibrium and found that the results were robust across these different hypotheses. The plausible horizon of three years ($K = 12$) was retained in all the subsequent simulations.

Figure 10.1 shows the impulse responses to a 1% shock in inflation. We consider it a supply shock.[15] One clear result is that there is no great difference between the two exchange rate models in terms of the output gap response to the inflation shock. The inflation and interest rate responses are also quite similar, especially in the very short run (the first four periods). After that, with the random walk hypothesis the inflation rate converges very rapidly.

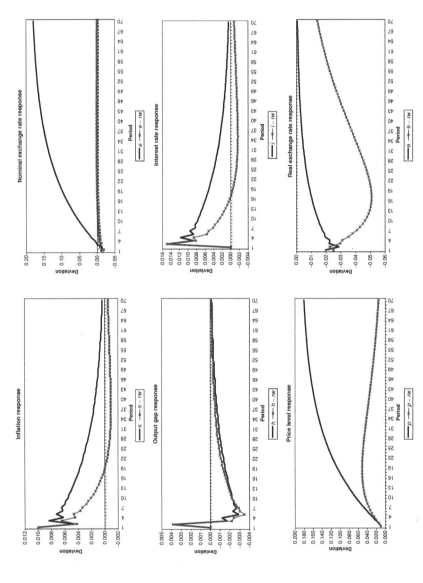

Figure 10.1 Impulse responses to an inflation shock.

The main difference concerns the exchange rate. The nominal exchange rate stays very close to its initial value for a very long time with RWMS, but it moves to the new equilibrium almost immediately in the UIP plus fundamentals model. This slow convergence of the real exchange rate under RWMS occurs because the only force that drives this model back to the equilibrium is the real exchange rate term in the IS curve. The appreciation of the real exchange rate reduces aggregate demand and then (to the extent that it affects GDP) lowers inflation through the output gap, correcting the imbalance in the real exchange rate by decreasing the price level, rather than through nominal exchange rate changes. On the other hand, forward-looking expectations with a PPP terminal condition return the exchange rate to equilibrium more rapidly in the UIP plus fundamentals model.

Figure 10.4 shows the impulse response to an interest rate shock. The interest rate and output gap responses are very similar: they both converge very quickly to the equilibrium. At first sight, the inflation responses look different, but they are similar in the short run when we observe the price-level responses. The real exchange rate with RWMS remains undervalued for a longer period when compared with the other hypothesis.

The impulse responses to an output gap shock (figure 10.2) yield, not surprisingly, similar profiles to the inflation shock, because both shocks feed into inflation quickly. The impulse responses to a risk shock (figure 10.3), however, seem very different both compared with the other shocks and between the two exchange rate models. The RWMS responses converge much faster to the equilibrium here, even those for the real exchange rate, and the amplitude of the responses is also smaller than with the UIP hypothesis. What this shows is that this exercise, of comparing the two exchange rate formulations in terms of their impulse responses, is shock dependent.

10.6   Conclusions and final remarks

Our UIP plus fundamentals model allows for balance of payments considerations to affect the equilibrium real exchange rate. The equilibrium exchange rate acts as a terminal condition for UIP with rational expectations. The impulse responses of the UIP with fundamentals model appear to be more realistic than those obtained from the RWMS model. For example, the response to a supply shock implies a much quicker return to equilibrium of the real exchange rate under the UIP with fundamentals model than under the RWMS model.

The simulation results change only slightly when the expected time horizon for the balance of trade sustainability is lengthened. Furthermore, all the impulse responses have the same expected shape and the real variables return to the steady-state value after a plausible lag.

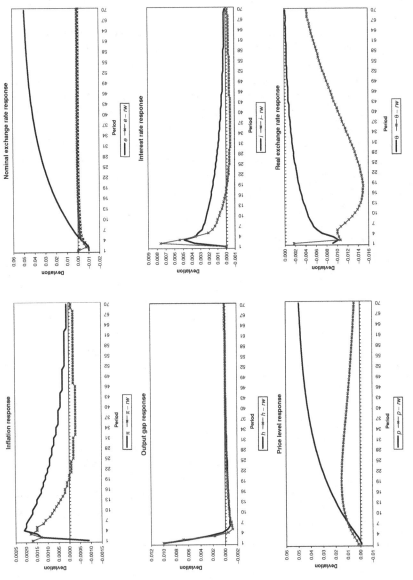

Figure 10.2 Impulse responses to an output gap shock.

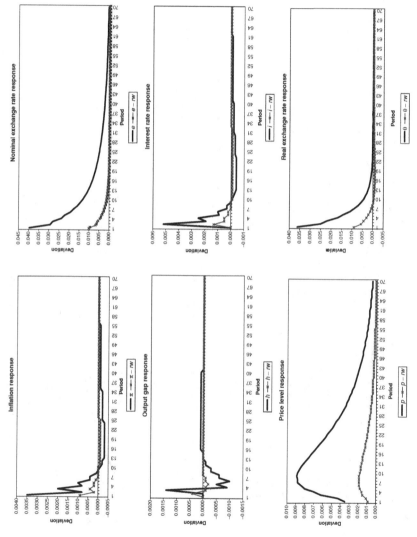

Figure 10.3 Impulse responses to a risk shock.

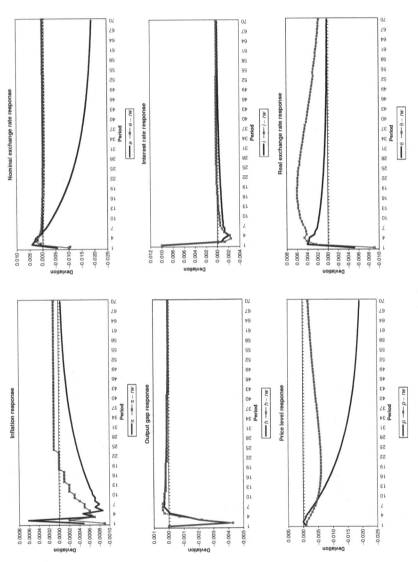

Figure 10.4 Impulse responses to an interest rate shock.

From the impulse response functions, we could see that there is a slower convergence after inflation shocks when compared with the other shocks. Interest rates and inflation take approximately 40 quarters to converge to a 0.2% deviation from equilibrium for both exchange rate models. That is because the interest rate has a direct impact on the output gap and the exchange rate but only an indirect effect on inflation in our model of the transmission mechanism. Shocks to the risk premium, which quickly feed through to the nominal exchange rate, are followed by the quickest convergence to equilibrium; it takes up to six periods for the interest rate, inflation and the output gap to converge to equilibrium.

We hope to work on several interesting extensions to the model developed in this paper in the future. The equilibrium condition might be reformulated as a constant current account to GDP ratio or as a steady net external debt to GDP ratio. Another possibility is to endogenise the equilibrium criterion to solve the real exchange rate with other system variables at the terminal date. A richer model of the transmission mechanism, including a forward-looking Phillips curve, more endogenous variables as risk premiums and other rules for the interest rate, could also be explored. Evaluating the exchange rate models on countries with a longer period of exchange rate floating and inflation targeting, such as Australia, Canada, the UK and New Zealand, might also prove interesting.

Appendix

We used the following procedure to solve a system with $10(K + 1) - 1$ linear and 1 non-linear (the balance of trade clearance) equations. The first step was to separate the linear from the non-linear parts of the model. The linear part can be written in matrix notation as the following system:

$$\mathbf{AX} = \mathbf{B} + \mathbf{E}, \qquad (10A.1)$$

where:

$\mathbf{A}$ is a $[11(K + 1) - 1]$ by $[11(K + 1) - 1]$ matrix with the coefficients of the endogenous variables of the model;

$\mathbf{X}$ is a $[11(K + 1) - 1]$ column vector of the endogenous variables ($\pi, h, i, e, qxb, qxm, qxs, qkap, qmbc, qmnd, qint$);

$\mathbf{B}$ is a $[11(K + 1) - 1]$ column vector summarizing the exogenous variables (each element of this vector is the product of the exogenous variables multiplied by their respective coefficients);

$\mathbf{E}$ is a $[11(K + 1) - 1]$ error term column vector.

Table 10A.1 below describes the variables pertaining to this linear system. Given the exogenous and predetermined variables, this system has a unique solution for each θ_{t+K}, so that $X = X(\theta_{t+k})$. Furthermore, according to equation (10.12),

Table 10A.1 *Description of the variables in the model*

Left-hand-side variables	Period	Right-hand-side variables — Exogenous and predetermined	Right-hand-side variables — Endogenous
π	T	$\pi_{t-1}, \pi_{t-2}, h_{t-1}, e_{t-1}, p^f_{t-1}, p^f_t$	E_t
	$t+1$	$\pi_{t-1}, h_t, p^f_t, p^f_{t+1}$	π_t, e_t, e_{t+1}
	$t+j, j = 2 \dots K$	p^f_{t+j-1}, p^f_{t+j}	$\pi_{t+j-2}, \pi_{t+j-1}, e_{t+j-1}, e_{t+j}$
h	$t+1$	h_t	i_t, p_t
	$t+j, j = 2 \dots K$	None	$i_{t+j-1}, \pi_{t+j-1}, h_{t+j-1}$
i	T	π^*_t, h_t, i_{t-1}	π_t
	$t+j, j = 1 \dots K$	π^*_{t+j}	$\pi_{t+j}, h_{t+j}, i_{t+j-1}$
e	$t+j, j = 0 \dots K-1$	$i^f_{t+j} \dots i^f_{t+K-1}, x_{t+j} \dots x_{t+K-1}$	$i_{t+j} \dots i_{t+K-1}, e_{t+K}$
	$t+K$	p_{t-1}, p^f_{t+K}	$\pi_t \dots \pi_{t+K}, \theta_{t+K}$
qxb	T	$pxb_{t-1}, wy_t, qxb_{t-1}, qxb_{t-2}$	Y_t
	$t+1$	$pxb_t, wy_{t+1}, qxb_{t-1}$	Y_{t+1}, qxb_t
	$t+j, j = 2 \dots K$	pxb_{t+j-1}, wy_{t+j}	$y_{t+j}, qxb_{t+j-2}, qxb_{t+j-1}$
qxs	T	$pxs_{t-1}, wy_t, qxs_{t-1}$	y_t, θ_t
	$t+j, j = 1 \dots K$	pxb_{t+j-1}, wy_{t+j}	$y_{t+j}, qxs_{t+j-1}, \theta_t$
qxm	T	$wy_t, wy_{t-1}, y_{t-1}, y_{t-2}, qxm_{t-1}, qxm_{t-2}, qxm_{t-3}$	θ_t
	$t+1$	$wy_{t+1}, wy_t, y_{t-1}, qxm_{t-1}, qxm_{t-2}$	y_t, qxm_t, θ_{t+1}
	$t+2$	$wy_{t+2}, wy_{t+1}, qxm_{t-1}$	$y_t, y_{t+1}, qxm_t, qxm_{t+1}, \theta_{t+2}$
	$t+j, j = 3 \dots K$	wy_{t+j}, wy_{t+j-1}	$y_{t+j-1}, y_{t+j}, qxm_{t+j-2}, qxm_{t+j-1}, \theta_{t+j}$
$qkap$	T	$pkap_t, tkap_t, qkap_{t-1}, y_{t-2}$	θ_t
	$t+1$	$pkp_{t+1}, tkp_{t+1}, y_{t-1}$	θ_{t+1}
	$t+j, j = 2 \dots K$	pkp_{t+j}, tkp_{t+j}	y_{t+j-2}, θ_{t+j}
$qmbc$	T	$pmbc_t, tmbc_{t-1}, qmbc_{t-1}$	y_t, θ_t
	$t+j, j = 2 \dots K$	$pmbc_{t+j}, tmbc_{t+j-1}$	$y_{t+j}, qmbc_{t+j-1}, \theta_{t+j}$
$qmnd$	T	$qmnd_{t-1}$	y_t, θ_t
	$t+j, j = 2 \dots K$	None	$y_{t+j}, qmnd_{t+j-1}, \theta_{t+j}$
$qint$	T	$pint_t, tint_{t-1}, qint_{t-1}$	y_t, θ_t
	$t+j, j = 2 \dots K$	$pint_{t+j}, tint_{t+j-1}$	$y_{t+j}, qint_{t+j-1}, \theta_{t+j}$

Endogenous variables
π – inflation
p – price index
h – output gap
i – interest rate
e – exchange rate
θ – real exchange rate
qxb – basic goods export volume
qxs – semi-manufactured goods export volume
qxm – manufactured goods export volume
$qkap$ – capital goods import volume
$qmbc$ – durable goods import volume
$qmnd$ – non-durable goods import volume
$qint$ – raw material import volume

Exogenous variables
π^* – inflation target
i^f - foreign interest rate
wy – world GDP
pxb – basic goods price
pxs – semi-manufactured goods quantum
$pkap, tkap$ – capital goods price and tax
$pmbc, tmbc$ – durable goods price and tax
$pint, tint$ – raw material price and tax

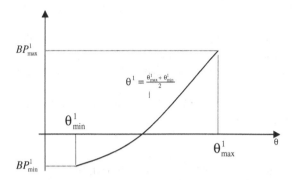

Figure 10A.1 Balance of payments as a function of θ.

the trade balance is a function of θ_{t+k} and X, and, therefore, the balance of payments will be a function of these variables as well. Hence, we can rewrite the balance of payments as in equation (10A.2) below, where we refer to θ_{t+k} as θ for simplicity.

$$BP = BP(X, \theta_{t+k}) = BP(X(\theta_{t+k}), \theta_{t+k}) = BP(\theta). \qquad (10A.2)$$

The next step, therefore, is to interact the linear part of the model (equation 10A.1) with the non-linear equation (equation 10A.2) to determine the real exchange rate that will clear the balance of payments by using the bipartition numerical method. This method chooses two values for $\theta(\theta_{min}^1$ and $\theta_{max}^1)$ in such a way that $BP_{min}^1 = BP(\theta_{min}^1) < 0$ and $BP_{max}^1 = BP(\theta_{max}^1) > 0$. Figure 10A.1 illustrates the method.

Step 1: In the nth iteration, for $n \geq 0$, set $\theta^{n+1} = (\theta_{max}^{n+1} + \theta_{min}^{n+1})/2$. Solve the linear part of the system to get the path for the output gap and recalculate the balance of payments, $BP^{n+2} = BP(\theta^{n+1})$. If $|BP^{n+2}| < \varepsilon$, where $\varepsilon > 0$ is a (small) predetermined value, we consider that the system has reached the final solution, with $\theta_{t+k} = \theta^{n+1}$ and $X = X(\theta^{n+1})$. Otherwise:

1a: if $BP^{n+2} < 0$, then $\theta_{min}^{n+2} = \theta^{n+1}$ and $\theta_{max}^{n+2} = \theta_{max}^{n+1}$.
1b: if $BP^{n+2} > 0$, then $\theta_{max}^{n+2} = \theta^{n+1}$ and $\theta_{min}^{n+2} = \theta_{min}^{n+1}$.

Step 2: Add 1 to n and return to step (1).

At time t, this procedure will yield a trajectory for each of the endogenous variables from t to $t + K$. At time $t + 1$, the system takes the solution for t as given and repeats the procedure, yielding trajectories for the endogenous variables from $t + 1$ to $t + K + 1$. At time $t + 2$, we take the solution for $t + 1$ as given and redo the algorithm. We repeat this exercise until we get the response functions for 70 periods.

Acknowledgements

We would like to thank Lavan Mahadeva for very useful comments on an earlier version of this paper. Ilan Goldfajn and Ken West also made useful comments in the seminar 'One Year of Inflation Targeting in Brazil' held in Rio de Janeiro in 2000. We also acknowledge the participants in the CCBS Academic Workshop, University of Brasilia, University of São Paulo, Brazilian Econometric Society seminars. Any remaining errors are ours.

Notes

1 The estimated coefficient a_{22} in equation (10.8) is approximately 0.10 and significant at conventional levels. In Muinhos (2001), many different specifications of the Phillips curve are estimated. In a shorter sample, which started in 1995, the pass-through coefficient was 0.10 (with a t-statistic of 3.25) when there was no forward-looking term for inflation and 0.09 (with a t-statistic of 3.0) with the forward-looking term. With a larger sample, starting in 1980, the pass-through was 0.11 and the t-statistic was 3.77.

2 The exchange rate is defined here as the domestic price of foreign currency and the interest rate differential as domestic minus foreign.

3 See Wadhwani (1999) and M. Taylor (1995).

4 MacDonald (1999, p. 681) summarises the results of Meese and Rogoff (1983):

M + R took the simple flexi-price monetary model (which relates an exchange rate to relative short-term interest rates), the Dornbusch–Frankel model (which essentially adds a long term interest differential to the flexi-price model) and a Hooper–Morton model (which adds a wealth term and a risk premium to the Dornbusch–Frankel model)... Additionally, M + R considered a wide array of univariate models as well as a vector autoregression comprising exchange rates, relative short-term interest rate, relative inflation rates and current account. The currencies studied were the dollar–pound, dollar–mark, dollar–yen and the trade-weighted dollar, and the sample period was March 1973 to November 1980, with the out-of-sample forecasts conducted over the sub-period December 1976 to November 1980.

5 Froot and Rogoff (1995) present three stages of PPP tests. The first uses the PPP as the null hypothesis, based on Cassel's suggestion (cited in Taylor and Peel, 2000) that PPP is a central tendency with temporary shocks. A second stage considers the real exchange rate as a random walk, and the third tests for cointegration. The third test did not produce any further conclusion besides those already found in the second stage.

6 Many authors have tried to estimate non-linear models that allow for a non-convergence band. For example, Taylor and Peel (2000) suggested that the speed of convergence might increase with the deviation from equilibrium when there are non-linear factors governing the cost of arbitrage.

7 Wadhwani (1999) also suggested that the UIP failure may, to some lesser extent, have come about because of the noise induced in the signal-extraction process by uninformed investors.

8 J.P. Morgan's Emerging Markets Real Exchange Rate Model (Emerging Markets Research Team, 2000) incorporates deeper factors such as productivity, the terms of trade and trade openness that might affect the equilibrium real exchange rate in its determination of the current nominal exchange rate. In the model, higher productivity, better terms of trade and less openness should all cause the real exchange rate to appreciate over time.

9 $E_t e_{t+1} - E_{t-1} e_t = \eta_t$ can follow from assuming that (a) the determinants of expected depreciation at t seen at $t - 1$ $(E_{t-1} e_{t+1} - E_{t-1} e_t)$ are white noise; and (b) the extra information from $t - 1$ to t $(E_t e_t - E_{t-1} e_{t+1})$ is also white noise.

10 We adopt the simplifying assumption that potential output is non-stochastic. Therefore, shocks in the output gap reflect only aggregate demand disturbances.

11 To simplify the notation, we will refer to variables' expectation without using $E_{t-1}(.)$.

12 There are 10 endogenous variables – π, i, e, qxb, qxs, qxm, $qkap$, $qmbc$, $qmnd$ and $qint$ – to be solved from t to $t + K$, and 1 endogenous variable – h – to be solved from $(t + 1)$ to $(t + K)$. Therefore, there are $[11(t + K) - 1]$ linear equations.

13 The appendix explains how we found the solution for this non-linear system.

14 Since the model is non-linear, we needed to try shocks of different magnitudes to evaluate the impulse response functions; they did not significantly differ from the one we present below with 1% deviations from equilibrium.

15 This supply shock should be interpreted as a cost-push shock and not as a shock in potential output. As mentioned in note 7, we made the assumption that potential output is non-stochastic (see Clarida, Galí and Gertner, 1999).

11 Uncovered interest parity and the monetary transmission mechanism

Guy Meredith

11.1 Introduction

The exchange rate is a key transmission channel for monetary policy in conventional macro models that assume flexible exchange rates. Particularly since the work of Dornbusch (1976), the link between exchange rates and monetary policy in such models has been increasingly embodied in the uncovered interest parity (UIP) condition. Under UIP, the expected change in the exchange rate equals the interest rate differential between domestic and foreign assets. This establishes a simple and transparent link between monetary policy actions – as reflected in interest rate movements – and the exchange rate.

Although attractive from a theoretical viewpoint, there are two issues that need to be addressed in implementing the conventional framework. The first is the awkward fact that the existence of UIP has been resoundingly rejected in empirical studies, as documented in a vast literature. At face value, the empirical failure of UIP calls into question the specification of the exchange rate transmission channel in conventional models. Is there a way of explaining this empirical failure that can rescue the conventional means of specification?

The second issue involves interpreting the role of the exchange rate as a monetary transmission channel, even if UIP holds. UIP specifies only the relationship between the expected future change in the exchange rate and the current interest differential between domestic and foreign assets. Holding the expected future value of the exchange rate constant, a rise in the domestic interest rate, under UIP, would lead to an appreciation of the domestic currency. This would imply a simple linear relationship between the instrument of monetary policy, i.e. the interest rate, and the spot exchange rate. There is, however, no reason to hold the expected future exchange rate constant; on the contrary, a wide class of shocks in forward-looking models will cause *larger* movements in the expected future exchange rate than in the spot rate. This fact complicates the relationship between the current interest rate and the exchange rate. The latter can move without any change in current interest rates, or can move 'perversely', depending on the behaviour of the expected exchange rate. In what circumstances is the simple view appropriate, and what does this imply for our understanding of the exchange rate as a monetary transmission channel?

This paper addresses these two issues. We argue that the empirical failure of UIP does not undermine its use as a structural relationship in macro models. In fact, it turns out that UIP is neither necessary nor sufficient to satisfy what are often regarded as tests of the hypothesis. Furthermore, it is shown that such tests would systematically reject UIP using data generated by simulations of a model with a conventional structure – including a UIP equation with a white noise error term. By implication, there is no inconsistency between using such an equation in macro models and the empirical evidence.

On the second issue of the intertemporal nature of the exchange rate as a monetary transmission channel, we illustrate how the co-movements in the contemporaneous exchange rate and interest rate are influenced by the nature of shocks to the model. Interestingly, the same general shock can generate opposite correlations in the exchange rate and the interest rate, depending on whether the shock occurs contemporaneously or is expected to occur in the future. A further interesting result is revealed when the economy is in a liquidity trap. In these circumstances, a credible commitment to a higher inflation target can cause the exchange rate to jump even in the absence of movements in interest rates. The exchange rate then becomes the *only* proximate transmission channel for monetary policy. These results underscore the need for care in making inferences about the relationship between interest rates and the exchange rate, even when the conventional model structure holds.

The paper is organised as follows. Section 11.2 discusses conceptual issues, and in particular the relationship between the UIP hypothesis and conventional tests of its validity. Section 11.3 reviews the empirical evidence, including interpretations of what the apparent failure of UIP implies, and more recent work suggesting that the failure of such tests may not be as pervasive as earlier believed. A framework for explaining the empirical evidence is presented in section 11.4, and its implications for the use of UIP-type relationships in macro models are discussed. Section 11.5 addresses intertemporal issues, analysing the co-movements of interest rates and exchange rates under various shocks in a conventionally specified macro model. The role of the exchange rate as a monetary transmission channel during a liquidity trap is assessed in section 11.6. Concluding remarks are provided in section 11.7.

11.2   Conceptual issues regarding UIP

It is useful to review the UIP hypothesis to define terminology and clarify conceptual issues. The most convenient starting point is the covered interest parity (CIP) condition. CIP follows from the assumption that risk-free arbitrage opportunities are fully exploited between spot and forward exchange markets. Then, the ratio of the forward to the spot exchange rate equals the ratio of the returns on the assets denominated in each currency:

$$F_{t,t+k}/S_t = I_{t,k}/I_{t,k}^*,\qquad(11.1)$$

where S_t is the price of foreign currency in units of domestic currency at time t, F_{t+k} is the forward value of the exchange rate for a contract expiring k periods in the future, $I_{t,k}$ is one plus the k-period zero-coupon yield on the domestic asset and $I_{t,k}^*$ is the corresponding yield on the foreign asset. Taking logarithms of both sides of equation (11.1) gives:

$$f_{t,t+k} - s_t = (i - i^*)_{t,k},\qquad(11.2)$$

where lower-case letters indicate logarithms (or, in the case of interest rates, the log of one plus the yield).

CIP can be directly tested and, as a no-risk arbitrage condition, it holds well in the data. Other relationships between the forward rate, the expected spot future rate and the ex post realisation of the spot rate are more problematic. Consider the difference between the forward rate and the expected future spot rate. This difference reflects the expected 'excess' yield on domestic assets. To the extent, for instance, that the expected future spot rate is more appreciated than the forward rate, there will be a positive expected excess return on domestic assets. Defining the expected excess return as $\rho_{t,t+k}$ and the expected k-period ahead value of the exchange rate as $s_{t,t+k}^e$ gives:

$$\rho_{t,t+k} \equiv f_{t,t+k} - s_{t,t+k}^e.\qquad(11.3)$$

The existence of expected excess returns is often justified by the assumption that investors are risk averse, and thus, in some circumstances, demand an ex ante yield premium to hold assets denominated in one currency as opposed to another. This is a specific example of what is sometimes referred to more generally as 'portfolio effects'. These include any factor that could lead assets denominated in different currencies to be imperfect substitutes in investors' portfolios. Without prejudging the nature of ρ, we will call it a 'risk premium' for the purposes of this paper (although this terminology is used only as shorthand, and the source of the expected excess return is not material to the analysis that follows).

Substituting equation (11.3) into equation (11.2) allows the expected change in the exchange rate to be expressed in terms of the interest differential and the risk premium:

$$s_{t,t+k}^e - s_t = (i - i^*)_{t,k} - \rho_{t,t+k}.\qquad(11.4)$$

UIP holds when the risk premium in equation (11.4) is zero. In this case, the expected change in the exchange rate always equals the interest differential. UIP is not directly testable, however, absent reliable data on market expectations of future exchange rates. To operationalise the concept, UIP is generally combined with the assumption of rational expectations. Then, future realisations of s will equal their rational expectation (which we denote $s^{re}_{t,t+k}$) plus a white noise error term ($\varepsilon_{t,t+k}$) that is uncorrelated with all information known at time t (including the interest differential and the spot exchange rate):

$$s_{t+k} = s^{re}_{t,t+k} + \varepsilon_{t,t+k}. \tag{11.5}$$

Finally, we introduce an error term between actual expectations and their rational counterpart that allows for the possibility that expectations are *not* fully rational:

$$s^{e}_{t,t+k} = s^{re}_{t,t+k} + \omega_{t,t+k}. \tag{11.6}$$

The 'non-rational' error term $\omega_{t,t+k}$, by definition, is correlated with information known at time t and could be predicted on the basis of this information.

Substituting equations (11.5) and (11.6) into (11.4) gives an expression for the realised change in the exchange rate in terms of the interest differential, the risk premium and the two expectations errors:

$$s_{t+k} - s_t \cong (i - i^*)_{t,k} - \rho_{t,t+k} - \omega_{t,t+k} + \varepsilon_{t,t+k}. \tag{11.7}$$

We use the quasi-identity sign in this expression because, given the definitions of the variables, this relationship must hold except to the extent that deviations from CIP exist in the data – and it is known that such deviations are small relative to the overall variance of exchange rate changes.

Consider, in light of equation (11.7), empirical tests of UIP. The conventional approach is to run regressions of the form:

$$s_{t+k} - s_t = \alpha + \beta(i - i^*)_{t,k} + u_t \tag{11.8}$$

and then to test the hypothesis that the fitted value of β (denoted $\widehat{\beta}$) equals one.[1] This is commonly referred to as a test of the 'unbiasedness' hypothesis. In essence, it tests whether the composite error term in equation (11.7) is uncorrelated with the interest differential. The absence of such a correlation is a necessary and sufficient condition for the expected value of $\widehat{\beta}$ to equal one.[2]

How does this condition relate to the other hypotheses discussed above, such as UIP and rational expectations? Consider the joint hypothesis that UIP and rational expectations both hold, which is sometimes referred to as the 'risk neutral efficient markets hypothesis' (RNEMH). Under RNEMH, it is clear that the disturbance term in equation (11.8) will reduce to the white noise rational expectations error term $\varepsilon_{t,t+k}$ in equation (11.7). By construction, $\varepsilon_{t,t+k}$ is orthogonal to the interest differential, and $E\{\hat{\beta}\}$ equals one. So RNEMH is sufficient, but not necessary, to ensure that the unbiasedness hypothesis holds.

What if the conditions for RNEMH are not satisfied? Suppose, for instance, that there is a time-varying risk premium in equation (11.4). UIP will not hold, because the expected future spot rate will not equal the forward rate. But the unbiasedness hypothesis will still hold as long as this risk premium is uncorrelated with the interest differential. Similarly, deviations from rational expectations will not undermine the unbiasedness hypothesis as long as they are uncorrelated with the interest differential.

These points have important implications for interpreting tests of UIP. In particular, tests of the unbiasedness hypothesis are *not* tests of UIP. The latter is not a necessary condition, because the existence of a risk premium in equation (11.4) is fully consistent with the unbiasedness hypothesis holding in regression (11.8). Furthermore, it is not sufficient: UIP may hold but the unbiasedness hypothesis still be rejected if there are expectations errors that are correlated with the interest differential. Ironically, then, UIP is neither necessary nor sufficient for $E\{\hat{\beta}\}$ in regression (11.8) to equal one, which is often regarded as a test of UIP.

This is important for two reasons. First, some authors have assumed that the presence of a time-varying risk premium in the UIP relationship will automatically lead to rejection of the unbiasedness hypothesis. This is not so – one must, in addition, explain why the risk premium is correlated with the interest differential. Secondly, it is commonly assumed that rejection of the unbiasedness hypothesis invalidates the use of UIP to determine the exchange rate in a structural model. Again, such an inference is unfounded. One must first understand why the error term in regression (11.8) is correlated with the interest differential before one can assess the implications for the specification of structural models.

11.3   Empirical tests of the 'unbiasedness' hypothesis

There is a vast literature on the estimation of equation (11.8). The results overwhelmingly reject the hypothesis that $\hat{\beta}$ equals one, at least for developed economies and for horizons of up to one year. A typical value for $\hat{\beta}$ found using pooled cross-country data is in the range of about -0.8 (Froot, 1990). The hypothesis that $\hat{\beta}$ must equal unity can be soundly rejected, as can the hypothesis that it equals zero. The finding that $\hat{\beta}$ is significantly negative indicates that the interest differential is a useful but 'perverse' predictor of exchange rate movements; currencies with high interest rates tend to *appreciate* in the future, not depreciate. In other words, the interest differential reinforces, rather than offsets, the impact of exchange rate movements on the holding period yield.

Yet, the fit of these regressions is poor, with adjusted R^2 statistics of close to zero, so the information content in the interest differential is very small relative to the overall variance of exchange rate movements.

These results clearly indicate either that there must be substantial ex ante differences in expected yields between currencies, or that expectations are systematically non-rational, or both. And, whichever of these explanations is valid, the source of the failure must be correlated with the interest differential.

11.3.1 Fama's puzzles

Fama (1984) was influential in shaping subsequent thinking on the apparent failure of UIP. His work represented the first attempt to explore the implications of rejection of the unbiasedness hypothesis in terms of the implied covariance between the risk premium and the expected change in the exchange rate. Expressing his analysis using the above notation, Fama assumed that exchange rate expectations were rational, so the 'non-rational' expectations error term $(\omega_{t,t+k})$ in equation (11.7) was zero. Observing that the UIP equation (11.4) can be rearranged to yield

$$(i - i^*)_{t,k} = \left(s_{t+k}^{e} - s_t\right) + \rho_{t,t+k}, \tag{11.9}$$

Fama then substituted out for the interest differential on the right-hand side of equation (11.7), and expressed the sample value of $\widehat{\beta}$ in equation (11.8) as

$$\widehat{\beta} = \frac{\text{var}\left(s_{t+k}^{e} - s_t\right) + \text{cov}\left(s_{t+k}^{e} - s_t, \rho_{t,t+k}\right)}{\text{var}(\rho_{t,t+k}) + \text{var}\left(s_{t+k}^{e} - s_t\right) + 2 \cdot \text{cov}\left(s_{t+k}^{e} - s_t, \rho_{t,t+k}\right)}. \tag{11.10}$$

Inspection of equation (11.10) indicates that, for $\widehat{\beta}$ to be negative, (a) the covariance of the expected change in the exchange rate and the risk premium must be negative and (b) the magnitude of the (negative) covariance must exceed the variance of the expected change in the exchange rate (because the denominator must be positive). Fama regarded both of these conditions as puzzling, in particular the implication that currencies regarded as being risky would be expected to appreciate. Furthermore, he interpreted the deviation in $\widehat{\beta}$ from unity as being a direct measure of the variance in the risk premium, presumably based on the presence of this term in the denominator on the right-hand side. Subsequent acceptance of these interpretations led to the widespread belief that the risk premium, in some sense, had to exhibit 'strange' properties to be the source of the failure of tests of the unbiasedness hypothesis.[3] The view that the variance of the risk premium was directly related to the deviation between $\widehat{\beta}$ and unity may also have contributed to the perception that the existence of a risk premium was a sufficient condition for the unbiasedness hypothesis to fail.

These interpretations are misleading. Consider again the UIP equation in the presence of a risk premium:

$$s^e_{t,t+k} - s_t = (i - i^*)_{t,k} - \rho_{t,t+k}. \tag{11.4}$$

It is obvious that the covariance between the risk premium and the expected change in the exchange rate *must* be negative, unless the covariance between the interest differential and the risk premium is positive and exceeds the variance of the risk premium itself. This, in turn, would require that the variance of the interest differential exceed that of the risk premium. These properties seem much more unlikely than those found puzzling by Fama. Looked at in economic terms, a rise in the risk premium on domestic currency assets would have to result in a *more than* one-for-one contemporaneous rise in the interest differential between domestic and foreign assets to avoid a negative correlation between the risk premium and the expected exchange rate change.

Furthermore, it is evident that one cannot infer anything about the variance in the risk premium by looking only at the deviation of $\widehat{\beta}$ from unity. It is also necessary to know the covariance of the risk premium and the expected change in the exchange rate. If, for instance

$$\text{cov}\{(i - i^*)_{t,k}, \rho_{t,t+k}\} = 0,$$

then

$$\text{cov}\left(s^e_{t+k} - s_t, \rho_{t,t+k}\right) = -\text{var}(\rho_{t,t+k})$$

and thus

$$E\{\widehat{\beta}\} = 1,$$

regardless of the variance of the risk premium.

This underscores the point that the unbiasedness hypothesis will hold whatever the variance of the risk premium, as long as the risk premium is uncorrelated with the interest differential. This point can be seen clearly by rewriting expression (11.10) in a way that focuses on the interaction between the interest differential and the risk premium:

$$\widehat{\beta} = 1 - \text{corr}\{(i - i^*)_{t,k}, \rho_{t+k}\}\left\{\frac{\text{var}(\rho_{t,t+k})}{\text{var}(i - i^*)_t}\right\}^{\frac{1}{2}}. \tag{11.11}$$

Expression (11.11) shows that the deviation in $\widehat{\beta}$ from unity depends on two factors: (i) the correlation of the interest differential and the risk premium and (ii) the ratio of the variance of the risk premium to the variance of the interest differential. The correlation coefficient of the interest differential and the risk premium has a maximum value of one. For $\widehat{\beta}$ to be negative, then, the variance of the risk premium must exceed that of the interest differential. It is noteworthy, though, that the variance of the risk premium itself does not have to be large for $\hat{\beta}$ to be negative – it needs only to be large *relative to* the variance in the interest differential.

This leads to an important point that has been overlooked in much of the discussion of the empirical evidence on UIP. Understanding the failure of the unbiasedness hypothesis depends on understanding how interest rate differentials are determined, and more specifically why they are positively correlated with the risk premium – an issue not addressed in Fama's analysis. Conventional models generally specify the short-term interest rate as the policy instrument of the monetary authorities. The question, then, is why the instrument of monetary policy should respond positively to the risk premium. This issue is addressed in section 11.4.

11.3.2 Recent evidence on UIP

Before explaining the correlation of interest rates and the risk premium, it is useful to review some other stylised facts about UIP. One recent finding is that the rejection of the unbiasedness hypothesis appears to be confined to relatively short-horizon data – i.e. up to about 12 months. The exclusive use of short-horizon data in earlier studies appears to be due to at least two reasons: the limited length of the period of floating exchange rates after 1973 and the difficulty of obtaining comparable data on long-term bond yields across the G-7 countries to use as regressors in equation (11.8).

To examine the evidence on long-horizon UIP, Meredith and Chinn (1998) use various sources for long-term bond yields for the industrial countries, including benchmark government bond yields and constant-maturity yields obtained from interpolating yield curves for government securities. The general finding is that the slope coefficients in UIP regressions using long-horizon data are distinctly different from those obtained using short-horizon data. In particular, the $\hat{\beta}$s are all significantly positive using pooled data for the G-7 countries. Although in most cases it is possible to reject the hypothesis that the slope coefficient equals unity, the magnitude of the coefficient appears to get closer to this value as better-quality data are used for bond yields.

These results are summarised in table 11.1, which shows values for $\hat{\beta}$ obtained using different data sets and sample periods. The parameters are obtained from regressions using pooled data for the G-6 countries, with the United States serving as the base country; the standard errors have been corrected for the moving-average process induced by the use of overlapping observations. Using generic 'long-term' bond yields from the IMF's International Financial Statistics, a slope parameter of 0.44 is obtained. The maturity of these bonds is not well defined, however, and generally varies across time and countries. Using 10-year benchmark yields for government bonds across the G-7 countries, the slope coefficient rises to 0.64. For selected countries, constant-maturity yields

Table 11.1 *Results of long-horizon UIP regressions*

Yield definition	$\hat{\beta}$	Standard error	Sample
IFS 'long-term' yields	0.44	0.07	1983(Q1)–98(Q1)
10-year benchmark yields	0.64	0.11	1985(Q1)–97(Q4)
10-year constant-maturity yields	0.71	0.09	1985(Q1)–97(Q4)
5-year constant-maturity yields	1.01	0.35	1986(Q1)–97(Q4)

Source: Meredith and Chinn (1998).

are available. Using 10-year yields generates a value of $\hat{\beta}$ of 0.71, and using 5-year yields generates 1.01. In the latter case, the hypothesis that $\hat{\beta}$ equals unity cannot be rejected.

Other long-horizon studies have found similar results. For instance, Alexius (1998) reports results using constructed bond durations for several industrial countries, and finds that the slope coefficients are all positive and, in many cases, not significantly different from the value of unity implied by the unbiasedness hypothesis. Flood and Taylor (1997) regress three-year changes in exchange rates on annual average data on medium-term government bonds using pooled data for a sample of 21 countries, finding a slope coefficient of roughly 0.6 with a standard error of 0.2. Again, this result is much more favourable to the unbiasedness hypothesis than are the short-horizon estimates.

Another apparent regularity has been uncovered by Bansal (1997): the extent to which the unbiasedness hypothesis is violated depends on the sign of the interest differential. In particular, cases where the interest differential is positive tend to be more supportive of the unbiasedness hypothesis. In a related study, Bansal and Dahlquist (2000) find that the unbiasedness hypothesis is better supported using data for emerging market economies. Because interest differentials between emerging market and developed economies are typically positive, this finding is consistent with the stylised fact found earlier for developed economies.

Finally, there is the issue of the persistence of the forward discount. Whereas the actual exchange rate can be approximated by a random walk, indicating that there is little persistence in its first differences, the forward premium is generally found to have significant persistence. This issue is examined, for instance, in Maynard and Phillips (2000), who use a fractionally integrated model of the forward premium to explain from a statistical viewpoint the failure of tests of the unbiasedness hypothesis. Other evidence on the degree of persistence in the forward premium is mixed, but it generally indicates greater persistence in the forward premium than in the change in the spot rate.[4] In any event, it would appear that an explanation of the failure of tests of the unbiasedness hypothesis should also be capable of explaining the persistence in the forward premium.

11.4   Explaining the failure of UIP

11.4.1   McCallum's model

The critical issue of the link between the risk premium and the interest rate was addressed by McCallum (1994). He used a two-equation model to generate the positive correlation between the risk premium and the interest rate required for the unbiasedness hypothesis to be rejected. His model consists of an uncovered interest parity relationship with a risk premium, and a monetary reaction function:

$$s^e_{t,t+1} - s_t = i_t - \rho_t \tag{11.12}$$

$$i_t = \lambda(s_t - s_{t-1}) + \sigma i_{t-1} + \psi_t, \tag{11.13}$$

where McCallum's notation has been changed slightly to be consistent with that used above: i_t is the interest rate, ρ_t is a stochastic shock to the UIP condition, and ψ_t is an interest rate shock. The monetary reaction function causes the interest rate to rise in response to exchange rate depreciation according to parameter λ; there is some inertia in interest rate movements, as implied by the presence of the lagged rate with parameter σ. McCallum solves this model to show that the parameter on the interest rate in the reduced-form expression for the change in the next-period exchange rate is σ/λ, which will be negative given assumed parameter values.[5] This model, then, can explain a negative value for $\widehat{\beta}$.

Some observers did not find McCallum's result interesting, because they viewed the failure of the unbiasedness hypothesis as already being explained by the presence of an error term in the UIP equation, perhaps influenced by the Fama interpretation. In this view, McCallum simply discovered something that he had already assumed by incorporating an error in the UIP equation. This inference, as discussed above, was inappropriate. At a technical level, the realism of McCallum's interest rate reaction function was criticised by Mark and Wu (1996), who found a value for λ that is small and insignificant for Germany, Japan and the United Kingdom. More generally, McCallum's reaction function does not incorporate variables that are usually believed to be of concern to policy-makers, such as inflation and output. In this sense, his model does not provide a full characterisation of the interaction between the exchange rate and interest rates, but serves the narrower purpose of illustrating how a negative correlation between the interest rate and the UIP disturbance can be generated in a consistent framework.

11.4.2   An extended model

Meredith and Chinn (1998) subsequently extended McCallum's model to make it more general and to allow a richer interaction between interest rates and

Table 11.2 *Simulation model*

Uncovered interest parity	$s_{t+1}^e - s_t = i_t - \rho_t$
Monetary reaction function	$i_t - \pi_t = 0.5(\pi_t + y_t)$
Inflation equation	$\pi_t = 0.6 \cdot \pi_{t-1} + (1 - 0.6) \cdot \pi_{t,t+1}^e + 0.20 \cdot y_t$
	$+ 0.10 \cdot (\Delta s_t - \pi_t) + v_t$
Output equation	$y_t = 0.1 \cdot (s_t - p_t) - 0.5 \cdot \left(i_t^{l,e} - \pi_t^{l,e}\right)$
	$+ 0.5 \cdot y_{t-1} + \theta_t$
Price-level identity	$p_t = p_{t-1} + \pi_t$
Long-term expected interest rate	$i_t^{l,e} = 0.2 \cdot \left(i_t + i_{t,t+1}^e + i_{t,t+2}^e + i_{t,t+3}^e + i_{t,t+4}^e\right) + \tau_t$
Long-term expected inflation rate	$\pi_t^{l,e} = 0.2 \cdot \left(\pi_t + \pi_{t,t+1}^e + \pi_{t,t+2}^e + \pi_{t,t+3}^e + \pi_{t,t+4}^e\right)$

exchange rates. This generalised model includes equations for output and inflation; these variables then drive monetary policy and interest rates using the familiar Taylor rule (Taylor, 1993). To the extent that output and inflation are affected by the exchange rate, interest rates still respond to disturbances to the UIP relationship, but through a different channel than specified by McCallum.

The model is described in table 11.2, where the variables are defined relative to those in the partner country against which the exchange rate is measured. The frequency is assumed to be annual, and all variables are expressed at annual rates. The inflation equation is an expectations-augmented Phillips curve: current-period inflation adjusts in response to past inflation, expected future inflation, the current output gap and the current change in the real exchange rate.[6] The theoretical justification for such a specification is discussed in Chadha, Masson and Meredith (1992); similar specifications are widely used in current empirical models. Parameter values have been chosen to be broadly consistent with the empirical evidence, using panel data for the G-7 countries.

The output equation is a standard open economy IS curve, where output responds to the real exchange rate, the expected long-term real interest rate and lagged output. The parameters imply that a 10% appreciation in the real exchange rate reduces output by 1% in the first year and by 2% in the long run; a one percentage point rise in the real interest rate lowers output by 0.5% in the first year and 1% in the long run.[7] The long-term interest rate is determined as the average of the current short-term interest rate and its expected value over the four subsequent periods – thus, the long-term rate can be thought of as a five-year bond yield that is determined by the expectations theory of the term structure. Expected long-term inflation is defined similarly in constructing the real long-term interest rate.

Stochastic elements are introduced via four processes, all of which are white noise: risk premium shocks (ρ_t), inflation shocks (v_t), output shocks (θ_t) and term structure shocks (τ_t).[8] We solve the model numerically using the stacked-time algorithm described in Armstrong et al. (1998). Along the solution path, expectations are consistent with the model's prediction for future values of the endogenous variables, based on information available at the time the expectations are formed. As the innovation terms ρ_t, ν_t, θ_t and τ_t are assumed to be i.i.d., the relevant information set consists of the contemporaneous innovations and the lagged values of the endogenous variables.[9] Agents lack perfect foresight, because they cannot anticipate the future innovations that will determine the realisations of the endogenous variables. Because the innovations are white noise and the model is linear, the associated rational expectations errors are also white noise.

The only other information needed to solve the model is the relative variance of the shocks. The shocks used were chosen to yield simulated variances for the endogenous variables that are consistent with the stylised facts for the G-7 countries. Experimentation indicated that the following standard deviations were appropriate: 10.0 percentage points for the risk premium shock, 0.9 percentage points for the inflation shock, 1.6 percentage points for the output shock and 0.8 percentage points for the term-structure shock.[10] The consistency of variances in the simulated and historical data, given these values, is discussed below.

The model's deterministic properties are described in Meredith and Chinn (1998). To summarise, a temporary positive innovation in the risk premium causes the exchange rate to depreciate on impact, raising inflation and output. Interest rates also rise given the presence of inflation and output in the monetary reaction function. In the second period the shock unwinds and the exchange rate appreciates. The exchange rate appreciation in the second period occurs in spite of a higher lagged short-term interest rate – contradicting UIP – which reflects the role of the change in the risk premium. Over the longer run, the temporary risk premium shock shows little persistence in terms of its effect on the endogenous variables.

An inflation shock also causes the short-term interest rate to rise, but the exchange rate appreciates instead of depreciates. The exchange rate subsequently depreciates back to its baseline value, consistent with UIP (because there is no shock to the risk premium, UIP must hold). The dynamics induced by the inflation shock are more persistent, however, and take much longer to decay than in the case of the risk premium shock. This difference is important, because it implies that the model generates co-movements in interest rates and exchange rates that are UIP consistent at longer rather than shorter horizons. The effects of an output shock are qualitatively similar: inflation and interest rates rise on impact, and the exchange rate appreciates. The exchange rate then depreciates back to baseline consistent with UIP. Again, the model responses are more persistent than in the case of an exchange risk premium shock. A term structure shock

Table 11.3 *Standard deviations of actual and simulated data (percentage points)*

Data	Annual change	
	Actual	Simulated
Exchange rate	12.75	12.80
Short-term interest rate	2.61	2.94
5-year bond yield	1.64	1.53
Inflation	1.74	1.73
Output	1.96	1.87

Note: The actual data are averages of 1980–98 values, defined as the difference between the values for the G-6 countries and the United States. Exchange rates and interest rates are end-of-period values; inflation is defined as the log change in the GDP deflator; and output is defined as the log of the ratio of real GDP to estimated potential (IMF estimates).

causes output and prices to fall on impact; the short-term interest rate also falls, and the exchange rate depreciates. The persistence of the effects of this shock lies in between that of the risk premium shock and the inflation and output shocks.

To replicate tests of the unbiasedness hypothesis using model-generated data, stochastic simulations were performed. Each was run over a 140-year horizon, with the first and last 30 years being discarded to avoid contamination from beginning- and end-point considerations. This yielded a 'sample' of 80 observations for each simulation. This process was repeated 50 times to generate a hypothetical population of 50 such samples.

The results of these stochastic simulations replicate closely the observed volatility in the actual data for the G-7 countries, as shown in table 11.3.[11] The exchange rate is by far the most volatile variable, with a standard deviation of over 12% in terms of annual changes. In the case of the exchange rate and output, the standard deviations of the actual and simulated data moderately exceed those of the shocks in their respective equations, reflecting the propagation of shocks elsewhere in the model. For inflation, the standard deviation is significantly greater than that of the inflation shock itself, owing to the more persistent dynamics of the process. It is interesting to note that changes in short-term interest rates are actually more volatile in the simulations than in the observed data, even though no explicit monetary policy shock is incorporated in the model. Thus, in the context of this model, interest rate volatility can be more than explained by the influence of output and inflation shocks in the monetary reaction function. This finding suggests that monetary shocks per se may not be an important cause of the volatility in the observed data.[12]

Table 11.4 *Results of synthetic UIP regressions*

	Regression horizon		
Statistic	1 year	5 years	10 years
Estimated slope coefficient ($\widehat{\beta}$)	−0.714	0.772	0.519
Standard error of $\widehat{\beta}$	0.463	0.172	0.131
$\overline{R}^2$	.015	.240	.170

Another of the stylised facts about the forward premium discussed previously is its persistence. This persistence can be summarised in terms of the coefficient in a regression of the interest differential on its lagged value. Pooling actual annual data for 1980–98 for the G-6 countries relative to the United States yields the following results for this regression:

$$(i - i^*)_t = \alpha_0 + 0.580(i - i^*)_{t-1}. \tag{11.14}$$
$$(7.57)$$

The parameter on the lagged interest differential of 0.580 indicates considerable serial correlation, although perhaps somewhat less than has been found using higher-frequency, e.g. monthly, data. The coefficient obtained by performing the same regression on the data generated by the model simulations is 0.555, with a t-statistic of 5.92. Thus, the persistence in the forward premium is very similar in the simulations to that in the actual data, in spite of the fact that an 'interest rate smoothing' term is not included in the reaction function, and that the model's innovations are serially uncorrelated. The persistence in the differential is purely a result of the intrinsic dynamics of the model, and in particular the inertia generated by the lagged dependent variables in the inflation and output equations.[13]

To perform 'synthetic' UIP tests, regression (11.8) was run on the simulated data using horizons varying from 1 to 10 years. The results of the 1-year and 5-year regressions for a representative population of 50 simulations are shown in table 11.4. For the 1-year horizon regressions, the average slope parameter of −0.71 is typical of the actual estimation results discussed above. With a standard error of 0.46, the hypothesis that $\widehat{\beta}$ equals unity is easily rejected. For the 5-year regression, the average value of $\widehat{\beta}$ is dramatically different at 0.77, with a standard error of only 0.17. Thus, one could reject the hypothesis that $\widehat{\beta}$ equals zero at conventional confidence levels, but not that it equals unity. For the 10-year regression, the value of $\widehat{\beta}$ of 0.52 is somewhat below that in the 5-year regression. This divergence appears to result, at least in part, from two factors: real output in the model is specified as a function of the 5-year real interest rate, creating a stronger link between it and the model's 'fundamentals'; and the shocks to the term structure relationship are assumed to be larger for the 10-year rate, making it inherently more volatile and thus 'noisy' as a regressor.[14] Even when the 10-year rate is used in the output equation and the term structure shocks are scaled identically, however, the coefficient in the 10-year regression is lower. This phenomenon, then, appears to reflect a reversal in the relative persistence of the risk premium shock compared with the other shocks beyond five years.

These estimation results using the synthetic data are consistent with the regressions using actual long-horizon data reported above. In particular, the short-horizon parameter is strongly negative, while the long-horizon parameters are between one half and one. The adjusted R^2 statistics are also of interest. The average value in the 1-year regressions is only .015, indicating a virtually complete lack of explanatory power, similar to regressions using actual data. For the 5-year regressions, in contrast, the average value rises to .24. Again, this is consistent with the stylised facts from the actual long-horizon regressions. In either case, interest differentials do not explain much of the variance in exchange rate movements over either short or long horizons. This is consistent with the rest of the literature on exchange rate regressions, and reflects the influence of future innovations that are inherently unpredictable in affecting the future exchange rate path.

It is interesting to note that the long-horizon coefficients are somewhat below the value of unity implied by the unbiasedness hypothesis. This reflects the diminishing, but persistent, role that exchange market shocks continue to play at longer horizons. The implication is that it may be unrealistic to expect to find coefficients centred on unity in UIP tests at any horizon, even in the absence of measurement errors in the data. These results are consistent with those obtained using actual long-horizon data. The 5-year results found by Meredith and Chinn (1998) are actually somewhat more favourable to UIP than are the synthetic regressions, but the coefficients differ by less than one standard deviation of the value estimated in the latter. The 10-year results are similar to the synthetic value.

As discussed above, the value of $\widehat{\beta}$ equals the correlation coefficient of the risk premium and the interest differential multiplied by the square root of their relative variance (equation (11.11)). What do the stochastic simulations imply in terms of this decomposition of $\widehat{\beta}$? Table 11.5 shows that the short-horizon correlation of the interest differential and the risk premium of 0.58 is much larger than the long-horizon value – indeed, there is almost no correlation at the five-year horizon. In contrast, the ratio of the variance of the risk premium to that in the interest differential is actually lower at the short horizon than at the long horizon, which would otherwise tend to push the parameter towards unity. So the 'correlation effect' more than offsets the 'relative variance effect' at the short horizon, explaining why $\widehat{\beta}$ is significantly negative.

Table 11.5 *Decomposition of $\widehat{\beta}$ from synthetic regressions*

	Horizon	
Statistic	1 year	5 year
$\widehat{\beta}$	−0.71	0.77
Correlation[$(i - i^*), \rho$]	0.58	0.05
$[\text{var}(\rho)/\text{var}(i - i^*)]^{\frac{1}{2}}$	2.99	4.67
Equation: $\widehat{\beta} = 1 - \text{corr}\{(i - i^*), \rho\} \left\{ \dfrac{\text{var}(\rho)}{\text{var}(i - i^*)} \right\}^{\frac{1}{2}}$		

We can also decompose the variance of the ex post movements of the exchange rate in the simulations into its contributing factors. As an identity, the change in the exchange rate equals the sum of the interest differential, the risk premium and future movements that result from unanticipated innovations in the model's disturbances:

$$s_{t,t+1} - s_t = (i - i^*)_{t,1} - \rho_{t,t+1} + \varepsilon_{t,t+1}. \tag{11.15}$$

Of course, the interest differential is influenced by the risk premium in the simulated data, and the induced correlation must be taken into account in decomposing the variance of the left-hand side of equation (11.15). Alternatively, the variance can be decomposed in terms of the model's reduced form, where the change in the exchange rate is a function of all four of the (orthogonal) disturbance terms in periods t and $t + 1$:

$$s_{t,t+1} - s_t = f\{\rho_t, \rho_{t+1}, \nu_t, \nu_{t+1}, \theta_t, \theta_{t+1}, \tau_t, \tau_{t+1}\}. \tag{11.16}$$

Both decompositions are shown in table 11.6. The 'structural' decomposition at the one-year horizon shows that 59% of the variance of changes in the exchange rate are due to the direct impact of risk premium shocks, while 54% are due to unanticipated future disturbances. The over-explanation of the variance in the exchange rate reflects the positive correlation of the interest differential and the risk premium. Taking this into account lowers the net contribution of risk premium shocks to 41%. Only 5% of exchange rate variance is due to the impact on interest rates of the other three shocks in the model.

The reduced-form decomposition attributes the rational expectations errors to their source in the form of future innovations in each of the four disturbances. Current and future risk premium shocks explain 93% of the variance in one-year changes in exchange rates, while the other factors explain only 7%. At the five-year horizon the mix changes substantially, with the relative

Table 11.6 *Decomposing simulated exchange rate variance (percentage contribution)*

Structural decomposition	1-year change	
Interest differential ($i - i^*$)	−13	
of which:		
Monetary policy shocks	0	
Inflation, output and term structure shocks	5	
Induced effect from risk premium shocks	−18	
Risk premium	59	
Rational expectations errors	54	
Reduced-form decomposition	**1-year change**	**5-year change**
Inflation shocks	4	27
Output shocks	3	11
Term structure shocks	0	2
Risk premium shocks	93	60

contributions changing to 60% versus 40%. These decompositions indicate that 'fundamentals' in the form of shocks to output, inflation and the term structure play very little role in explaining short-term exchange rate movements. Even at the five-year horizon, they explain less than half of the variance in changes in the exchange rate.

11.4.3   Implications for monetary transmission

It is evident that a small, forward-looking model with a conventional structure is capable of explaining the important stylised facts relating to tests of UIP. Most importantly, the unbiasedness hypothesis is soundly rejected using the simulated data, reflecting the endogeneity of interest rates in the face of risk premium shocks. Over the longer term, in contrast, the model's 'fundamentals' are more important, and interest differentials are better predictors of future exchange rate movements.[15] Only a small proportion of short-term exchange rate volatility can be explained by innovations in the model that originate outside of the exchange market. This suggests that attempts to rationalise exchange rate movements as reflecting the transmission of shocks to economic fundamentals are generally misguided. Even at the five-year horizon, shocks to output, prices and the term structure have an influence that is collectively less important than that of shocks to the risk premium.

Regarding the specification of the exchange rate in macro models, the key implication of the above model is that it is the nature of the *shocks*, not the model *structure*, that undermines the unbiasedness hypothesis in real-world data. Shocks to the model that originate from other relationships will be consistent with the conventional UIP specification and the monetary transmission channel associated with it. Deterministic simulations of structural shocks in such models will yield appropriate results, providing that such shocks are independent of movements in the exchange risk premium. In contrast, to the extent that structural shocks *cause* movements in the risk premium, this orthogonality assumption would not be appropriate, and the risk premium would need to be modelled explicitly. However, the literature on trying to 'explain' the risk premium in terms of other macroeconomic variables has not been very successful, so there is no obvious basis on which to endogenise the risk premium in macroeconomic models.

The UIP puzzle illustrates a more general point. Perceived anomalies in macroeconomic data are often attributed to problems in the structure of the underlying models. Yet the models are often not made explicit. There is a tendency to consider only one structural equation at a time, or to think in terms of reduced-form models. When the structure of the overall model is taken into consideration, such problems can often be resolved. Anomalies are then seen to arise because the propagation of shocks through the model structure leads to correlations between the disturbances and the endogenous variables that are not evident from inspection of individual equations. This is true even when the shocks are 'well behaved', as are the i.i.d. shocks we assume in the simulations discussed previously.

Two caveats to the defence of the use of UIP equations in structural models are in order. First, as discussed above, the possibility must be considered that it is not the risk premium that drives the correlation with interest differentials, as the framework used here assumes, but the reverse. In particular, for reasons not explained by the conventional model structure, shocks that lead to higher interest rates could themselves drive up an (endogenous) risk premium. The second caveat is that the disturbance in the exchange market required to explain the failure of the unbiasedness hypothesis could result from expectations errors as opposed to risk premiums. The implications of this possibility are more difficult to explore in the above framework, given the complications involved with introducing systematic expectations errors into models that are designed around the assumption of rational expectations. Although it seems plausible that a consistent treatment of 'non-rational' expectations errors would lead to results similar to those for risk premium shocks, this remains to be demonstrated. And, again, there is the issue of whether expectations errors could be generated by movements in the interest differentials, as opposed to the converse.

Finally, we do not pretend to explain in this framework a deeper puzzle: what could cause shocks to expected excess returns in exchange markets of the magnitude assumed in these simulations? It is well known that consumption-based asset-pricing models are unable to generate risk premiums large enough to explain observed price fluctuations, not only in exchange markets but in almost all financial markets. More recent analyses based on 'first-order' risk aversion, such as Bekaert, Hodrick and Marshall (1997), also generate risk premiums that are far smaller than the shocks consistent with the data. Beyond this, it has also proved difficult to relate ex post exchange risk premiums to macro-economic factors. Of course, the alternative explanation is that the exchange market shocks reflect systematic expectations errors. Yet a persuasive model that explains why large, systematic expectations errors of this type could persist over time also remains to be developed.

What is inescapable is the fact that the exchange market shock, whatever its origins, must have a large variance – on the order of six times that of the interest differential – to be consistent with the stylised facts. Thus far, no plausible models have been derived that can explain the cause of such a variance, in terms of either risk premium shock or systematic expectational errors. It appears, then, that alternative theoretical approaches may be needed to explain the observed volatility in excess returns or systematic expectations errors.

11.5   Future exchange rates, UIP and monetary transmission

The other issue raised in the introduction involves how changes in expected future exchange rates affect the pattern of co-movements of the current interest rate and the exchange rate. A naive view of the exchange rate as a 'transmission channel' for monetary policy might suppose there is a monotonic relationship between the current interest differential and the exchange rate: when the interest differential increases (decreases), the exchange rate appreciates (depreciates). Indeed, much common discourse on co-movements in interest rates and exchange rates regards this outcome as the theoretically 'correct' result, and other outcomes as violating conventional laws of economics. At the other extreme, financial market participants often employ ad hoc rationalisations for any pattern of co-movement in interest rates and exchange rates. A common view in markets, for instance, is that higher interest rates undermine economic growth, worsening 'fundamentals' and causing the exchange rate to depreciate.[16]

UIP, of course, does not determine a unique relationship between the level of the interest rate and the exchange rate, because it relates only the expected *change* in the exchange rate to the interest rate. What happens to the *level* of the exchange rate depends on how its expected next-period value is affected by shocks. This effect, in turn, depends on the expected interest differential in the next period, as well as expectations for the exchange rate in the subsequent period, and so on. Iterating forward, it is evident that the current level of the exchange rate depends on the expected path of the interest differential many periods into the future. Assuming that the analytical horizon is finite, the exchange rate level will also depend on some 'terminal' expected value for the exchange rate that presumably will be consistent with the economy's equilibrium growth path at that time. Because the expected future path for the interest differential is affected by both current and all expected future shocks, and the expected terminal value for the exchange rate depends on the determinants of the equilibrium growth path, the exchange rate is a highly forward-looking variable – the 'most' forward-looking variable, generally speaking, in rational expectations models. It is not surprising, then, that the relationship between the current interest rate and the exchange rate depends significantly on complex intertemporal factors.

These ideas can be made more concrete by looking again at the UIP equation (absent a risk premium):

$$E\{s_{t+1}\} - s_t = (i - i^*)_t \tag{11.17}$$

Conventional algorithms solve for the expected value of the exchange rate in period $t + 1$ as the model solution for that period. That value, in turn, depends on the model solution for the $t + 1$ interest differential and for the exchange rate in $t + 2$. This process is iterated forward until some terminal date set for the simulation. To obtain a more fundamental implicit expression for the period-t level of the exchange rate we can repeatedly substitute the expression for $E\{s_{t+1}\}$ into equation (11.17), yielding:

$$s_t = -(i - i^*)_t - \sum_{j=t+1}^{T-1} (i - i^*)_j + E\{s_t\}, \tag{11.18}$$

where $E\{s_T\}$ is exogenous to the simulation. The right-hand side of equation (11.18) decomposes the level of the exchange rate into three factors: (i) the current interest differential, (ii) the expected future path for the interest differential and (iii) the terminal value for the exchange rate, determined by the equilibrium growth path.[17] Shocks in forward-looking models can affect all three terms in potentially offsetting ways, leading to an ambiguous net effect on the period-t exchange rate.

To illustrate alternative interest rate and exchange rate responses, a variety of shocks were performed on a relatively standard rational expectations model. For this purpose, the model for Japan described in Meredith (1999) was used. The structure of the model is based closely on that of a representative country bloc in the Mark II version of the IMF's macroeconomic simulation model, MULTIMOD, as documented in Masson et al. (1990).[18] As in the small model described in the previous section, financial market behaviour is fully forward looking in that expectations are based on the model's solution for future values of the endogenous variables.[19]

Table 11.7 *First-year impact of various shocks on interest rates and exchange rates*

Model shock:	Nominal short-term interest rate	Exchange rate[a]	Real long-term interest rate	Real effective exchange rate[a]
5% of GDP rise in government spending	2.5	12.8	2.3	16.1
2% target inflation	−0.1	−6.1	−0.7	−5.2
2% expected target inflation	0.7	−4.0	−0.3	−3.5
5% productivity level	0.7	−4.4	0.9	−3.8
1.5% productivity growth	0.3	7.1	1.6	7.7
1% point exchange risk premium	0.2	−8.7	0.4	−7.8

[a]The nominal and real exchange rates have been defined here such that positive values indicate appreciations.

The shocks are chosen to reflect both demand- and supply-side disturbances to the economy; all of the shocks are assumed to be permanent. On the demand side, three shocks are imposed: a rise in the ratio of government spending to GDP, a rise in the target inflation rate of the monetary authority and an *expected future* rise in the target inflation rate (assumed to reflect a shock to policy credibility). On the supply side, the shocks consist of both a rise in the level of productivity and an increase in the productivity growth rate. Finally, a shock to the exchange risk premium is applied.

The results of these simulations are summarised in table 11.7 in terms of the impact in the first year on four variables: the nominal short-term interest rate, the nominal exchange rate of the yen versus the US dollar, the real long-term interest rate and the real effective exchange rate. The first two variables, of course, are related via equation (11.17). The latter two are included to give a broader perspective on the decomposition of exchange rate movements implied by equation (11.18). In particular, the nominal relationship in equation (11.18) can be transformed into one relating the level of the real exchange rate to the expected long-term real interest differential and the terminal value of the real exchange rate.[20] To the extent that this terminal value is relatively insensitive to model shocks, the conventional relationship between the interest differential and the exchange rate should be more apparent using the real exchange rate and the real long-term interest rate.

Shaded observations in the table indicate co-movements in interest rates and exchange rates that contradict the conventional view that higher interest rates imply exchange rate appreciation (exchange rates have been defined such that appreciations are indicated by increases). The results for the short-term nominal interest rate and the nominal exchange rate are mixed. For the government spending shock, the productivity growth shock and the inflation target shock, all the results are conventional, with higher interest rates coinciding with exchange rate appreciation. For the other three shocks, the exchange rate depreciates on impact, while the short-term interest rate rises.

The conventional view is somewhat better supported by the results for the long-term real interest rate and the real exchange rate, with four of the six shocks generating positive co-movements. Even using these more theoretically robust variables, however, the productivity-level shock and the risk premium shock generate 'perverse' results.

What explains the differences across the shocks? The results for the government spending shock are standard. A demand-side shock of this nature has little effect on the long-run nominal or real exchange rate; thus changes in $E\{s_T\}$ are negligible. Nominal and real interest rates rise by similar amounts (because longer-term inflation expectations are stable), and they increase for an extended period. The decomposition in equation (11.18), then, is dominated by the interest rate effect, leading to the expected result.

In the case of the two inflation target shocks, the results depend on whether the shock occurs immediately or is expected to occur in the future. In either case, an increase in the inflation target causes expected inflation to rise, which puts upward pressure on nominal interest rates. Similarly, in both cases, higher price levels due to higher inflation lead to a more depreciated nominal exchange rate, but the terminal value of the *real* exchange rate is little affected by the nominal shock. The main difference is in terms of the immediate effect on the nominal interest rate via the monetary reaction function when the inflation target is raised immediately. The liquidity effects of this easing in policy more than offset the effect on the nominal interest rate of higher inflation expectations, leading to a (slight) decline in the first period. When the inflation target is expected to be raised in the future, in contrast, there is no immediate liquidity effect, and the nominal interest rate rises owing to higher expected inflation. In both cases, the exchange rate depreciates on impact, reflecting a forward-looking assessment of monetary easing. This is reflected in the immediate decline in the real long-term interest rate under both scenarios. This example shows how a subtle change in the timing of the same shock can have different implications for co-movements in interest rates and exchange rates.

The two productivity shocks also have different implications for the co-movements of interest rates and exchange rates. In this case, however, the differences are equally apparent in the real and the nominal relationships, with a productivity growth shock leading to the conventional result, while a productivity level shock gives a perverse result. Real and nominal interest rates rise in both cases, because the increase in productivity boosts investment and consumption – with the latter rising in response to higher discounted future income. In both cases, the terminal value of the real exchange rate depreciates. This is because domestic output is not a perfect substitute for foreign output in the model, so a greater supply of domestic output in the long run requires a real exchange rate depreciation to equate supply and demand. This effect is much greater over time in the growth rate shock, as the cumulative effect on the supply of domestic output is larger. After 70 years, for instance, the real exchange rate declines to about one half its original value in the growth rate shock scenario, versus a drop of only 3% in the level shock.

Taken at face value, one might expect that the larger decline in the terminal value of the real exchange rate in the productivity growth shock would cause the initial value to decline by more. But the terminal-value effect is more than offset by a much more prolonged rise in the real interest rate, reflecting the extended effect on aggregate demand. After 10 years, for instance, the real long-term interest rate is still about two percentage points above its baseline value in this shock, whereas it has fallen half a percentage point below baseline in the level shock. So forward-looking expectations of higher real interest rates dominate for the growth shock, while the expected decline in the terminal value of the exchange rate dominates for the level shock. Again, this shows how differences in the nature of similar shocks can affect the interest rate/exchange rate nexus.

As for the risk premium shock, the results are not surprising in light of the earlier discussion. For both the nominal and real variables, the effects are perverse, as a 'wedge' is driven into the UIP equation; interest rates rise while the exchange rate depreciates. In the short run, interest rates rise by less than the increase in the risk premium, because the latter is also offset by expected future exchange rate appreciation from the initial depreciated level. In the long run, the increase in the interest rate equals that in the exchange risk premium. The steady-state value of the exchange rate actually *appreciates*, as domestic saving is boosted by higher interest rates, causing an accumulation of foreign assets and thus higher international investment income.

These examples indicate that is difficult to make generalisations about co-movements in interest rates and the exchange rate, even when using a standard model with uncovered interest parity. Seemingly minor differences in the nature and timing of generic shocks – such as in the case of 'inflation target' shocks or 'productivity' shocks – can reverse the conventional relationship. Explaining observed market behaviour on the basis of economic 'fundamentals' requires recognition of these subtleties to arrive at robust interpretations. These subtleties also influence the role of the exchange rate as a 'transmission channel' for monetary policy. Clearly, it is not the case that the exchange rate will appreciate every time interest rates rise, regardless of the precise definitions of the variables.

11.6   UIP and the liquidity trap

The examples above illustrate how the relationship between interest rates and the exchange rate can be sensitive to intertemporal factors. Another interesting case arises when there is no room for current interest rates to move in response to economic shocks. This could arise, for instance, in the case of an economy in a liquidity trap. With nominal interest rates already at a lower bound of zero, there would be no scope for declines in current interest rates even if there are negative shocks to demand or attempts by policy-makers to implement expansionary monetary policy. How does the exchange rate respond under these conditions, and how does the response of the exchange rate affect the future path of interest rates after the economy has exited the liquidity trap?

We analyse these issues using the model for Japan discussed in section 11.5. For this purpose, we use a non-linear monetary policy reaction function that prevents the nominal short-term interest rate from becoming negative, even if the determinants of the reaction function would normally imply negative interest rates (the functional form and other details are described in Meredith, 1999). The model is calibrated around a baseline solution path that reflects actual economic developments up to 1999, by which time the Bank of Japan (BoJ) had implemented the well-known 'zero interest rate' policy. The model variables are projected for 2000 and beyond, holding the residuals in the stochastic equations constant at recent historical values.

The model's solution path is calculated for two scenarios. In the first, it is assumed that the public expects the BoJ to pursue a long-term monetary policy consistent with a zero target rate of inflation. This conditions the public's expectations of the future path of the policy instrument – the short-term interest rate – based on its assumed knowledge of the central bank's reaction function. In the second scenario, it is supposed that the BoJ can credibly commit to a long-term inflation target of 2% instead of the baseline value of zero. There has been an extensive debate on the feasibility of making such a commitment in the absence of an immediate policy lever that can be credibly used to achieve it. Suggestions for signalling such a policy have involved 'quantitative easing', in the form of an expansion of central bank liabilities; unsterilised exchange market intervention; massive purchases of assets such as stocks and land; and changes to the Bank of Japan Law that would obligate the BoJ to pursue such a policy.

Channels through which such actions can directly affect expectations do not exist in the model used here. Instead, it is simply assumed that, through one form or another, the BoJ is able to commit credibly to the higher inflation target. The effects on some of the model's key variables are shown in figure 11.1. Panel (a) shows the behaviour of the monetary policy lever – the nominal short-term interest rate. The commitment to the higher inflation target begins in year 1, but the

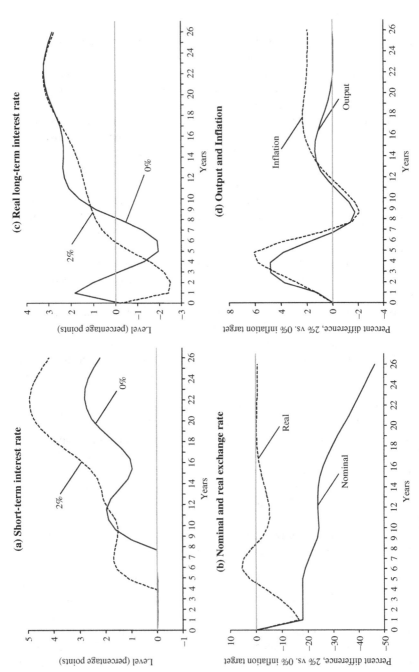

Figure 11.1 Alternative liquidity trap scenario.

interest rate remains constrained by the lower bound of zero in the initial years of the simulation in both scenarios, reflecting initial deflation and the large negative starting point for the output gap.[21] When the inflation target is believed to be zero, the economy remains in the liquidity trap for seven years. The eventual escape is triggered primarily by stock adjustment processes, as past weak investment raises the marginal productivity of new capital and external surpluses boost net foreign assets, leading to increased spending through wealth effects.

In the simulation where the inflation target is raised to 2%, the standard policy rule causes the central bank to raise interest rates four years *earlier* than would be the case under the lower target. This is paradoxical, because much of the discussion of committing to a higher inflation target has assumed that doing so would imply keeping the policy lever at an easier setting for longer. If this were the case, it would imply a clear correspondence between the policy lever and the target that would help in communicating the policy to the public and committing to it in terms of future policy actions. The fact that the policy rule causes the lever to be tightened sooner under the scenario with the more expansionary target obviously complicates this strategy.

The behaviour of the exchange rate is key to this paradox. Both the nominal and real exchange rate depreciate by over 15% at the time the expected target inflation rate is raised (see panel (b)), in spite of the fact that nominal interest rates are unchanged. The exchange rate depreciates because expected real interest rates fall substantially, as shown in panel (c). Under the 2% inflation target scenario, the long-term real rate becomes significantly negative in the first years of the simulation, as opposed to rising to positive values in the 0% scenario. The depreciation in the exchange rate, then, is consistent with the 'real' version of equation (11.18).

Both the weaker exchange rate and lower real interest rates provide a powerful boost to aggregate demand, as shown by the difference in the behaviour of real GDP in panel (d). Higher output, in turn, leads to higher inflation, validating the expectations of higher target inflation that initially set the chain of events in motion. These increases in output and inflation explain why the policy lever needs to be tightened earlier in the scenario of a more expansionary monetary policy. Indeed, under a 2% inflation target, the nominal interest rate is higher throughout virtually the whole simulation, with the exception of a brief period in years 10 and 11.

This, then, is an interesting case where the exchange rate is the *only* proximate channel for transmitting monetary policy owing to the constraint imposed by the liquidity trap.[22] Although nominal interest rates do not change, forward-looking expectations of higher inflation and its effect on future exchange rates under UIP lead to exchange rate depreciation. Indeed, the behaviour of the exchange rate could be a useful indicator of whether the higher inflation target is in fact credible. When it is, the exchange rate effect is so powerful that the actual policy lever does not need to be used in the future to create expansionary monetary conditions. In a sense, the credibility of the commitment is all that is needed – the policy lever does not need to be used to back up the commitment.

This paradox creates its own problems in terms of the time-consistency of the strategy the authorities might use to commit credibly to a higher inflation target. Holding the long-term inflation expectations of the public constant at their baseline value of zero, the authorities would want to keep interest rates lower for a longer period to raise inflation to the desired level of 2%. But if they reveal this rule to the public, and the public believes them, then the same policy rule will indicate that interest rates should be raised *earlier* than would be the case under the 0% inflation target. This creates an obvious incentive for the authorities to renege on any commitment they have made to keep rates exceptionally low, because sticking with such a commitment would imply suboptimal monetary policy in the future. This problem provides some support for reservations that the BoJ has about its ability credibly and concretely to signal a commitment to a higher inflation target.[23]

11.7   Concluding remarks

This paper has examined two issues that are central to the use of uncovered interest parity in linking monetary policy and the exchange rate. The first is the common view that UIP is rejected by the empirical evidence. In fact, it is not UIP that has been rejected, but the unbiasedness hypothesis for the coefficient on the interest differential in exchange rate regressions. This hypothesis will be rejected in the presence of either risk premiums or expectations errors that are correlated with the interest rate differential. Structural models are likely to generate such a correlation through the impact of exchange rate movements on prices and output, and the subsequent response of monetary policy to these developments. So it is not surprising that the unbiasedness hypothesis fails empirically. At the same time, its failure does not undermine the value of using of UIP equations in structural models. They remain appropriate for modelling the transmission of monetary policy via the exchange rate in the case of shocks that arise elsewhere in the model.

Forecasting exchange rates using UIP raises different issues. The relationship between the unbiased expectation of the future change in the exchange rate and the interest differential will depend on the nature of the shocks that explain the interest differential. At short horizons, the evidence is that these shocks are dominated either by risk premiums or by systematic expectations errors. The expected movement in the exchange rate will then be inversely related to that predicted by UIP. At longer horizons, it appears that the role of shocks specific to the exchange market declines, and economic 'fundamentals' play a greater role. UIP may then be a more useful guide to expected exchange rate movements. In either case, however, the proportion of the variance in ex post exchange rate movements that can be explained by these factors is low.

The other issue is the role of forward-looking expectations and their impact on current exchange rates under UIP. Common shocks can lead to situations in which interest rates will rise on impact, yet the exchange rate will depreciate. And this pattern of co-movements is quite sensitive to minor changes in the nature and timing of the shocks. As a result, common inferences about the 'normal' relationship between interest rates and the exchange rate under UIP can be misleading. Forward-looking expectations are shown to play a key role under a liquidity trap, where a credible commitment to higher inflation can lead to a sharp exchange rate depreciation, even though there is no room for the interest rate to decline. The effect on output and inflation can be so great that the interest rate need never be lowered to achieve the inflation target, leading to a problem of the time-consistency of the policy commitment.

Notes

1 Deviations in α from the value of zero suggested by equation (11.7) are often attributed to the presence of non-time-varying risk premiums, or to the effect of Jensen's inequality (although the latter is not an issue given the definitions of the data used here).

2 More trivially, the interest differential must also have positive variance.

3 This is not to say the Fama's interpretations went unchallenged. Hodrick and Srivastava (1986), for instance, showed that the empirical regularities found by Fama were consistent with both theoretical models and intuition.

4 See, for instance, Hai, Mark and Wu (1997).

5 He also allows for first-order autocorrelation in ρ. In this case, the parameter on the interest rate becomes $(\mu - \sigma)/\lambda$, where μ is the autocorrelation coefficient, which McCallum argues will also be negative for plausible parameter values.

6 Equivalently, the equation can be rewritten in terms of the change in the nominal exchange rate by bringing the inflation term (π_t) to the left-hand side and dividing through the other parameters by $(1 + 0.1)$.

7 These responses are broadly consistent with the average values for the G-7 countries used in MULTIMOD, the IMF's macroeconomic simulation model (Masson, Symansky and Meredith, 1990).

8 The shock in the exchange rate equation could also be considered a 'non-rational' expectations error, except that the non-rationality of expectations would have to be incorporated consistently throughout the model, a practice raising difficult issues that we have not attempted to address here.

9 At any point in time, the conditional expectation of the future values of the innovations is zero, given that they are white noise.

10 Given that the model variables are defined as the differences between the values in the home country and the United States, these shocks can be interpreted as the difference between the shocks in the two countries – except, of course, for the risk premium, where a single shock influences the exchange rate between the two countries.

11 The G-7 data are measured as values for the G-6 countries relative to United States values.

12 Alternatively, it may be the case that the actual monetary policy rule followed in some of these countries may have smoothed the instrument (interest rates) by more than the Taylor rule would have predicted over this period, leading to smoother actual data than the model would predict.

13 This contrasts with McCallum's model, which requires the assumption of serially correlated exchange market shocks to generate serial correlation in interest rates.

14 In particular, the size of the term structure shock was scaled linearly according to the horizon of the interest rate, and thus was twice as large for the 10-year rate as for the 5-year rate.

15 This is consistent with the finding in Mark (1995) that short-horizon movements in exchange rate are dominated by noise, whereas longer-term movements can be related to economic fundamentals.

16 This argument has been used, for instance, to explain why monetary tightening in the euro region has contributed to the weakness of the euro since its introduction.

17 The implied unit root in the dynamics of this equation stands in contrast to other forward-looking relationships, which generally have more stable intrinsic dynamics. Given the unit root, the determinacy of the exchange rate path associated with equation (11.18) will depend on the other equations in the model, and in particular on model dynamics that lead to a positive correlation of future expected exchange rates and the interest differential.

18 This version of the model linearises some key relationships to make it typical of a 'generic' industrial country bloc.

19 The model's terminal conditions, including that for the exchange rate, are determined by solution to a steady-state version of the dynamic model. This procedure is discussed in Meredith (1999).

20 This transformation involves subtracting expected inflation from both sides of equation (11.17) to express the UIP equation in real terms, giving the 'real' version of equation (11.18) described in the text.

21 The BoJ actually raised interest rates slightly in mid-2000, but this action was not indicated by the model's policy rule under either inflation target scenario.

22 We use the term 'proximate', because one could also argue that the expected real interest rate is another channel. But, because inflation expectations are not directly observable, the exchange rate is the only channel that is directly revealed by market forces.

23 This is only one of the reasons, and perhaps not the major one, that the BoJ has advanced for not pursuing this route.

Bibliography

Adams, C. and Coe, D.T. (1990), 'A systems approach to estimating the natural rate of unemployment and potential output for the United States', *International Monetary Fund Staff Papers* 37(2): 232–93, June.

Alexius, A. (1998), 'Uncovered interest parity revisited', Sveriges Riksbank Working Paper No. 53, May.

Allsopp, C.A. and Vines, D. (2001), 'The assessment: macroeconomic policy', *Oxford Review of Economic Policy* 16(4).

Almeida, A. and Goodhart, C.A.E. (1996), 'Does the adoption of inflation targets affect central bank behaviour?' London School of Economics: Financial Markets Group Working Paper, July.

Alogoskoufis, G. S. and Smith, R. (1991), 'The Phillips curve, the persistence of inflation, and the Lucas critique: evidence from exchange-rate regimes', *American Economic Review* 81(5): 1254–75.

Amato, J.D. and Gerlach, S. (2001), 'Modelling the transmission mechanism of monetary policy in emerging market countries using prior information', Bank for International Settlements, Papers No. 8 (part 12), November.

Andersen, T.M. (1994), *Price rigidity: causes and macroeconomic implications*, Oxford: Clarendon Press.

Andrews, D.K. (1993), 'Tests for parameter instability and structural change with unknown change point', *Econometrica* 61: 821–56.

Armstrong, J., Black, D., Laxton, D. and Rose, D. (1998), 'A robust method for simulating forward-looking models', *Journal of Economic Dynamics and Control* 22(4): 489–501.

Artis, M., Krolzig, H.-M., and Toro, J. (1999), 'The European business cycle', Centre for Economic Policy Research Discussion Paper 2242.

Astley, M.S. and Yates, A. (1999), 'Inflation and real disequilibria', Bank of England Working Paper No. 103, December.

Backus, D.K., Kehoe, P.J. and Kydland, F.E. (1994), 'Dynamics of the trade balance and the terms of trade: the J-curve?' *American Economic Review* 84: 84–103.

Ball, L. (1999a), 'Aggregate demand and long-run unemployment', *Brookings Papers on Economic Activity* No. 2: 189–236.

(1999b), 'Policy rules for open economies', in J.B. Taylor (ed.), *Monetary policy rules*, Chicago: University of Chicago Press, 127–44.

Ball, L. and Mankiw, G.N. (1994), 'Asymmetric price adjustment and economic fluctuations', *Economic Journal* 104(423): 247–61.

Ball, L. and Romer, D. (1991), 'Real rigidities and the nonneutrality of money', in N.G. Mankiw and D. Romer (eds.), *New Keynesian economics*, vol. 1, *Imperfect competition and sticky prices*, Cambridge, Mass.: MIT Press Readings in Economics.

Baltagi, B.H. and Griffin, J.M. (1997), 'Pooled estimators versus their heterogeneous counterparts in the context of dynamic demand for gasoline', *Journal of Econometrics* 77: 303–27.

Banerjee, A., Hendry, D.F. and Mizon, G.E. (1996), 'The econometric analysis of economic policy', *Oxford Bulletin of Economics and Statistics* 58(4): 573–600.

Bank of England (1984), *The development and operation of monetary policy, 1960–1983*, London: Bank of England.

(1995), *Inflation report*, August.

(1999a), 'The transmission mechanism of monetary policy', *Bank of England Quarterly Bulletin* 39(2): 161–70.

(1999b), *Economic models at the Bank of England*, London, April.

(2000), *Economic models at the Bank of England: September 2000 update*, London.

Bansal, R. (1997), 'An exploration of the forward premium puzzle in currency markets', *Review of Financial Studies* 10(2): 369–403.

Bansal, R. and Dahlquist, M. (2000), 'The forward premium puzzle: different tales from developed and emerging economies', *Journal of International Economics* 51.

Barker, T. and Pesaran, M.H. (eds.) (1990), *Disaggregation in econometric modelling*, London: Routledge.

Barro, R.J. (1999), 'Notes on growth accounting', *Journal of Economic Growth* 4(2): 119–37.

Barro, R.J. and Gordon, D.B. (1983), 'A positive theory of monetary policy in a natural rate model', *Journal of Political Economy* 91(1): 589–610.

Basu, S. (1996), 'Cyclical productivity: increasing returns or cyclical utilisation', *Quarterly Journal of Economics* 111: 719–51.

Basu, S. and Fernald, J. (2000), 'Why is productivity pro-cyclical? Why do we care?' National Bureau of Economic Research Working Paper 7940.

Basu, S. and Taylor, A.M. (1999), 'Business cycles in international historical perspective', *Journal of Economic Perspectives* 13(2): 45–68.

Batini, N. and Haldane, A.G. (1999), 'Forward-looking rules for monetary policy', in J.B. Taylor (ed.), *Monetary policy rules*, Chicago: University of Chicago Press.

Batini, N. and Nelson, E. (2000), 'Optimal Horizons for Inflation Targeting', Bank of England Working Paper No. 119, July.

Batini, N., Jackson, B. and Nickell, S. (2000), 'Inflation dynamics and the labour share in the U.K.', Bank of England Monetary Policy Unit Discussion Paper No. 2, November.

Baxter, M. (1995), 'International trade and business cycles', in M. Grossman, and K. Rogoff, (eds.), *Handbook of International Economics*, vol. 3, Amsterdam: North-Holland.

Baxter, M. and King, R.G. (1999), 'Approximate bandpass filters for economic time series', *Review of Economics and Statistics* 81: 575–93.

Bean, C.R. (1998), 'The new U.K. monetary arrangements: a view from the literature', *Economic Journal* 108(451): 1795–1809.

Bean, C.R., and Symons, J.S.V. (1989), 'Ten years of Mrs. T', in O.J. Blanchard and S. Fischer (eds.), *NBER Macroeconomics Annual 1989*, Cambridge, Mass.: MIT Press, 13–60.

Beechey, M., Bharucha, N., Cagliarini, A., Gruen, D. and Thompson, C. (2000), 'A small model of the Australian macroeconomy', Reserve Bank of Australia Research Discussion Paper No. 2000–5.

Bekaert, G., Hodrick, R.J. and Marshall, D.A. (1997), 'The implications of first-order risk aversion for asset market risk premiums', *Journal of Monetary Economics* 40: 3–39.

Bernanke, B.S. and Gertler, M. (1989), 'Agency costs, net worth and business cycle fluctuations', *American Economic Review* 79(1).

(1995), 'Inside the black box: the credit channel of monetary policy transmission', *Journal of Economic Perspectives* 9(4): 27–48.

Bernanke, B.S. and Mihov, I. (1998), 'Measuring monetary policy', *Quarterly Journal of Economics* 113(3): 869–902.

Bernanke, B.S. and Woodford, M. (1997), 'Inflation forecasts and monetary policy', *Journal of Money, Credit and Banking* 29: 653–84.

Bernanke, B.S., Laubach, T., Mishkin, F.S. and Posen, A.S. (1999), *Inflation targeting: lessons from the international experience*, Princeton, N.J.: Princeton University Press.

Black, R.D., Laxton, D., Rose, D. and Tetlow, R. (1994), 'The steady-state model: SSQPM, Part 1 of the Bank of Canada's New Quarterly Projection', Bank of Canada Technical Report No. 72.

Black, R., Cassino, V., Drew, A., Hansen, E., Hunt, B., Rose, D. and Scott, A. (1997), 'The forecasting and policy system: the core model', Reserve Bank of New Zealand Research Paper No. 43.

Blanchard, O.J. (1985), 'Debts, deficits and finite horizons', *Journal of Political Economy* 93: 223–47.

Blanchard, O.J. and Kahn, C. (1980), 'The solution of linear difference models under rational expectations', *Econometrica* 48: 1305–12.

Blanchard, O.J. and Quah, D. (1989), 'The dynamic effects of aggregate demand and supply disturbances', *American Economic Review* 79(4): 655–73.

Blinder, A.S. (1998), *Central banking in theory and practice, Lionel Robbins Lectures*, Cambridge, Mass.: MIT Press.

Bogdanski, J., Tombini, A.A. and Werlang, S. R. da Costa (2000), 'Implementing inflation targeting in Brazil', Banco Central do Brasil Working Paper Series No. 1, July.

Boskin, M.J., Dulberger, E.R., Gordon, R.J., Griliches, Z. and Jorgenson, D.W. (1998), 'Consumer prices, the consumer price index, and the cost of living', *Journal of Economic Perspectives* 12(1): 3–26.

Boyd, D.A.C. and Smith, R.P. (1999), 'Testing for purchasing power parity: econometric issues and an application to developing countries', *The Manchester School* 67: 287–303.

Boyd, D.A.C., Caporale, G.M. and Smith, R.P. (2000), 'Real exchange rate effects on the balance of trade: cointegration and the Marshall–Lerner condition', Birkbeck Discussion Paper in Economics 25/2000.

Brayton, F., Roberts, J.M. and Williams, J.C. (1999), 'What's happened to the Phillips curve?' Finance and Economics Discussion Series Paper No. 1999–2049, Federal Reserve Board.

Brigden, A. and Mizen, P.D. (1999), 'Money, credit and investment in the UK company sector', Bank of England Working Paper Series No. 100, September.

Britton, E.M., Fisher, P.G. and Whitley, J.D. (1998), 'The Inflation Report projections: understanding the fan chart', *Bank of England Quarterly Bulletin* 38(1).

Browning, P. (1986), *The Treasury and economic policy 1964–1985*, London: Longman.

Budd, A. (1998), 'The role and operations of the Bank of England Monetary Policy Committee', *Economic Journal* 108(451): 1783–95.

Burnside, C., Eichenbaum, M. and Rebelo, S.T. (1995), 'Capital utilisation and returns to scale', *National Bureau of Economic Research Macroeconomics Annual*, Cambridge, Mass.: MIT Press.

Butler, D. (1989), *British general elections since 1945*, Oxford: Blackwell.

Callaghan, J. (1987), *Time and Chance*, London: HarperCollins.

Campbell, J.Y. (1987), 'Does saving anticipate declining labor income: an alternative test of the permanent income hypothesis', *Econometrica* 55: 1249–73.

Campbell, J. (1993), *Edward Heath: a biography*, London: Jonathan Cape.

(2000), *Margaret Thatcher: volume 1, the grocer's daughter*, London: Jonathan Cape.

Cardia, E. (1991), 'The dynamics of a small open economy in response to monetary, fiscal and productivity shocks', *Journal of Monetary Economics* 28(3): 411–34.

Cecchetti, S.G. (2000), 'Making monetary policy: objectives and rules', *Oxford Review of Economic Policy* 16(4): 43–59.

Chadha, B., Masson, P.R. and Meredith, G. (1992), 'Models of inflation and the costs of disinflation', *International Monetary Fund Staff Papers* 39(2): 395–431.

Chadha, J.S. and Dimsdale, N. (1999), 'A long view of real rates', *Oxford Review of Economic Policy* 15(2): 17–45.

Chadha, J.S. and Perlman, M. (2000), 'Was the Gibson paradox for real? A Wicksellian study of interest rates and prices', mimeo, LSE.

Chadha, J.S., Janssen, N. and Nolan, C. (2000), 'An examination of UK business cycle fluctuations: 1871–1997', Department of Applied Economics Working Paper 0024, University of Cambridge.

(2001), 'Productivity and preferences in a small open economy', *The Manchester School* 69: 57–80.

Chinn, M.D. and Meredith, G. (1998), 'Long-horizon uncovered interest rate parity', National Bureau of Economic Research Working Paper 6797, November.

Chortareas, G., Stasavage, D. and Sterne, G. (2001), 'Does it pay to be transparent: international evidence of central bank forecasts', Bank of England Working Paper No. 143, November.

Christiano, L.J. and Eichenbaum, M.S. (1986), 'Temporal aggregation and structural inference in macroeconomics', National Bureau of Economic Research Technical Paper 60.

Christiano, L.J. and Gust, C.J. (2000), 'The expectations trap hypothesis', National Bureau of Economic Research Working Paper No. 7809.

Christiano, L.J., Eichenbaum, M. and Evans, C.L. (1999), 'Monetary policy shocks: what have we learned and to what end?', in J.B. Taylor and M. Woodford (eds.), *Handbook of macroeconomics*, vol. 1a, Amsterdam: North-Holland.

Chrystal, K.A. and Mizen, P.D. (2001a), 'Consumption, money and lending: a joint model for the UK household sector', Bank of England Working Paper No. 134, May.

(2001b), 'Other financial corporations: Cinderella or ugly sister of monetary economics?' Bank of England Working Paper No. 151, December.

Clarida, R. and Gertler, M. (1997), 'How the Bundesbank conducts monetary policy', in *Reducing inflation: motivation and strategy*, National Bureau of Economic Research, Chicago: University of Chicago Press.

Clarida, R., Gali, J. and Gertler, M. (1998), 'Monetary policy rules in practice: some international evidence', *European Economic Review* 42(6): 1033–67.

(1999), 'The science of monetary policy: a New Keynesian perspective', *Journal of Economic Literature* 37(4): 1661–1707; also National Bureau of Economic Research Working Paper No. 7147.

Clements, M.P. and Hendry, D.F. (1998), *Forecasting economic time series*, Cambridge: Cambridge University Press.

(1999), *Forecasting non-stationary economic time series*, Zeuthen Lecture Book Series, Cambridge, Mass.: MIT Press.

Clower, R.W. (1984), 'A reconsideration of the microfoundations of monetary theory', in D.A. Walker (ed.), *Money and markets: essays by Robert W. Clower*, Cambridge: Cambridge University Press.

Coe, D.T. and McDermott, J.C. (1996), 'Does the gap model work in Asia?' International Monetary Fund Working Paper No. 69 July.

Cogley, T. and Sargent, T.J. (2000), 'Evolving post-World War II U.S. inflation dynamics', manuscript, Stanford University.

Cooley, T.F. (ed.) (1995), *Frontiers of business cycle research*, Princeton, N.J.: Princeton University Press.

Crafts, N. (2000), 'The Solow productivity paradox in historical perspective', mimeo, LSE.

Cross, R. (ed.) (1995), *The natural rate of unemployment: reflections on 25 years of the hypothesis*, Cambridge: Cambridge University Press.

Cukierman, A. (1992), *Central bank strategy, credibility, and independence: theory and evidence*, Cambridge, Mass.: MIT Press.

(2000), *Accountability, credibility, transparency and stabilization policy in the Eurosystem*, Tel-Aviv University.

Cukierman, A. and Meltzer, A.H. (1986), 'A theory of ambiguity, credibility, and inflation under discretion and asymmetric information', *Econometrica* 54(5): 1099–1128.

Dell, E. (1996), *The Chancellors: A history of the Chancellors of the Exchequer, 1945–90*, London: HarperCollins.

Den Butter, F.A.G. and Morgan, M.S. (eds.) (2000), *Empirical models and policy-making: interaction and institutions*, London: Routledge.

Dhar, S. and Millard, S.P. (2000), 'A limited participation model of the monetary transmission mechanism in the United Kingdom', Bank of England Working Paper
No. 117, June.

Diebold, F.X. (1998), 'The past, present, and future of macroeconomic forecasting',
Journal of Economic Perspectives 12(2): 175–92.

Doan, T., Litterman, R. and Sims, C. (1984), 'Forecasting and conditional projection
under realistic prior distributions', *Econometric Reviews* 3: 1–100.

Dolado, J. and Maria-Dolores, R. (1999), 'An empirical study of the cyclical effects
of monetary policy in Spain (1977–1997)', Centre for Economic Policy Research
Discussion Paper 2193.

Dornbush, R. (1976), 'Expectations and exchange rate dynamics', *Journal of Political
Economy* 84: 1161–76.

Dotsey, M., King, R.G. and Wolman, A.L. (1999), 'State-dependent pricing and
the general equilibrium dynamics of money and output', *Quarterly Journal of
Economics* 114: 655–90.

Drew, A. and Hunt, B. (1998), 'The forecasting and policy system: preparing economic
projections', Reserve Bank of New Zealand Working Paper G98/7.

Driver, R.L., Greenslade, J. and Pierse, R. (2000), 'Goldilocks and new paradigm economics: the role of expectations in fairytales', manuscript, Bank of England.

Eichenbaum, M. and Evans, C.L. (1995), 'Some empirical evidence on the effects of
shocks to monetary policy on exchange rates', *Quarterly Journal of Economics*
110(4): 975–1009.

Emerging Markets Research Team (2000), 'An introduction to J. P. Morgan's Emerging
Markets Real Exchange Rate Model: theory and econometrics', mimeo.

Enders, W. (1995), *Applied econometric time series*, New York: John Wiley.

Engle, R.F. and Hendry, D.F. (1993), 'Testing superexogeneity and invariance in regression models', *Journal of Econometrics* 56: 119–39.

Erceg, C.J., Henderson, D.W. and Levin, A.T. (1999), 'Optimal monetary policy with
staggered wage and price contracts', International Finance Discussion Paper 1999–
640, Federal Reserve Board.

Ericsson, N.R. (ed.) (1994), 'Testing exogeneity: an introduction', in N.R. Ericsson
and J.S. Iron, *Testing exogeneity. Advanced texts in econometrics*, Oxford: Oxford
University Press.

Estrella, A. and Fuhrer, J.C. (2000), 'Dynamic inconsistencies: counterfactual implications of a class of rational expectations models', manuscript, Federal Reserve Bank
of Boston.

Fama, E.F. (1984), 'Forward and spot exchange rates', *Journal of Monetary Economics*
14(3): 319–38.

(1985), 'What's different about banks?' *Journal of Monetary Economics* 15(1): 29–39.

Faust, J. and Svensson, L.E.O. (1998), 'Transparency and credibility: monetary policy
with unobservable goals', National Bureau of Economic Research Working Paper
6452.

(1999), 'The equilibrium degree of transparency and control in monetary policy',
Board of Governors of the Federal Reserve System: International Finance Discussion Papers 651: 24, November.

Favero, C. and Hendry, D.F. (1990), 'Testing the Lucas critique: a review', *Econometric Reviews* 11(3).

Favero, C. and Rovelli, R. (1999), 'Modelling and identifying central banks' preferences', Centre for Economic Policy Research Discussion Paper No. 2178.

Fischer, S. (1972), 'Keynes–Wicksell and neoclassical models of money and growth', *American Economic Review* 62(5): 880–90.

Fisher, P. and Salmon, M. (1986), 'On evaluating the importance of nonlinearity in large macroeconometric models', *International Economic Review* 27(3): 625–46.

Flood, R.P. and Rose, A.K. (1996), 'Fixes: of the forward discount puzzle', *Review of Economics and Statistics*: 78(4): 748–52.

Flood, R.P. and Taylor, M.P. (1997), 'Exchange rate economics: what's wrong with the conventional macro approach?', in J.A. Frankel, G. Galí and A. Giovannini (eds.), *The microstructure of foreign exchange markets*, National Bureau of Economic Research Conference Report Series, Chicago: University of Chicago Press, 261–94.

Freeman, R.T. and Willis, J.L. (1995), 'Targeting inflation in the 1990s: recent challenges', Board of Governors of the Federal Reserve: International Finance Discussion Papers No. 525.

Freitas, P.S. de and Muinhos, M.K. (2001), 'A simple model for inflation targeting in Brazil', Banco Central do Brasil Working Paper Series No. 18, April.

Frenkel, J.A. and Razin, A. (1992), *Fiscal policies and the world economy*, 2nd edn, Cambridge, Mass.: MIT Press.

Friedman, B.M. and Kuttner, K. (1993), 'Economic activity and short term credit markets: an analysis of prices and quantities', *Brookings Papers on Economic Activity* No. 2: 193–283.

Friedman, M. (1966), 'Comments', in G.P. Shultz and R.Z. Aliber, *Guidelines: informal controls and the market place*, Chicago: University of Chicago Press, 55–61.

(1968), 'The role of monetary policy', *American Economic Review* 58: 1–17.

(1979), 'Inflation and jobs', *Newsweek*, 12 November. Reprinted in W.R. Allen (ed.), *Bright promises, dismal performance: an economist's protest*, New York: Harcourt Brace Jovanovich (1983), 201–5.

Friedman, M. and Schwartz, A.J. (1963), 'Money and business cycles', *Review of Economics and Statistics* 45: 32–64.

Froot, K.A. (1990), 'On the efficiency of foreign exchange markets', mimeo, 16 November.

Froot, K. and Rogoff, K. (1995), 'Perspectives on PPP and long-run real exchange rates', in G. Grossman and K. Rogoff (eds.), *Handbook of international economics*, vol. 3, Amsterdam: Elsevier.

Fry, M., Julius, D., Mahadeva, L., Roger, S. and Sterne, G. (2000), 'Key issues in the choice of monetary policy framework', in L. Mahadeva and G. Sterne (eds.), *Monetary frameworks in a global context*, London: Routledge.

Galí, J. (2000), 'The return of the Phillips curve and other recent developments in business cycle theory', *Spanish Economic Review* 2(1): 1–10.

Galí, J. and Gertler, M. (1999), 'Inflation dynamics: a structural econometric analysis', *Journal of Monetary Economics* 44(2): 195–222.

Garcia, R. and Schaller, H. (1995), 'Are the effects of monetary policy asymmetric?' *CIRANO Scientific Series*, 95s–6.

Geraats, P.M. (2001), 'Why adopt transparency? The publication of central bank forecasts', European Central Bank Working Paper Series No. 41.

Goodfriend, M. (2000), 'Financial stability, deflation, and monetary policy', Ninth International Conference at the Institute of Monetary and Economic Studies, Bank of Japan.

Goodfriend, M. and King, R.G. (1997), 'The new neoclassical synthesis and the role of monetary policy', in B.S. Bernanke and J.J. Rotemberg (eds.), *National Bureau of Economic Research Macroeconomics Annual, 1997*, Cambridge, Mass.: MIT Press, 231–83.

Goodhart, C.A.E. (1989), 'The conduct of monetary policy', *Economic Journal* 99: 293–346.

(1997), 'Whither now?', *Banca Nazionale del Lavoro Quarterly Review* 50: 385–430.

(1999), 'Central bankers and uncertainty', *Bank of England Quarterly Bulletin* 39(1).

Goodhart, C.A.E. and Hofmann, B. (2000), 'Asset prices and the conduct of monetary policy', manuscript, London School of Economics.

Gordon, R. (1997), 'The time-varying NAIRU and its implications for monetary policy', *Journal of Economic Perspectives* 11: 11–32.

Griliches, Z. (1996), 'The discovery of the residual: an historical note', *Journal of Economic Literature* 34(3): 1324–30.

Groeneveld, H., Koedijk, K.G. and Kool, C.J.M. (1996), 'Inflation dynamics and monetary strategies: evidence from six industrialised countries', mimeo, University of Limburg, April.

Hai, W., Mark, N. and Wu, Y. (1997), 'Understanding spot and forward exchange rate regressions', *Journal of Applied Econometrics* 12: 715–34.

Haldane, A.G. and Batini, B. (1998), 'Forward-looking rules for monetary policy', National Bureau of Economic Research Working Paper No. 6543.

Hall, S., Salmon, C., Yates, A. and Batini, N. (1999), 'Uncertainty and simple monetary policy rules: an illustration for the United Kingdom', Bank of England Working Paper No 96, June.

Hamilton, J. (1989), 'A new approach to the economic analysis of nonstationary time series and the business cycle', *Econometrica* 57: 357–84.

(1994), *Time series analysis*, Princeton, N.J.: Princeton University Press.

Hamilton, J. and Perez-Quiros, G. (1996), 'What do the leading indicators lead?' *Journal of Business* 69(1): 27–49.

Harvey, A.C. (1989), *Forecasting, structural time series models and the Kalman filter*, Cambridge: Cambridge University Press.

Harvey, A. and Jaeger, A. (1993), 'Detrending, stylised facts and the business cycle', *Journal of Applied Econometrics* 8: 231–47.

Hayakawa, H. and Maeda, E. (2000), 'Understanding Japan's financial and economic developments since autumn 1997', Working Paper 00–1, Research and Statistics Department, Bank of Japan.

Hendry, D.F. (1995), *Dynamic econometrics*, Oxford: Oxford University Press.

(2000), 'Does money determine inflation over the long run?' in R. Backhouse and A. Salanti (eds.), *Macroeconomics and the real world*, Oxford: Oxford University Press.

Hendry, D.F. and Doornik, J.A. (1997), 'The implications for econometric modelling of forecast failure', *Scottish Journal of Political Economy* 44(4): 437–61.

Hendry, D.F. and Mizon, G.E. (1993), 'Evaluating dynamic models by encompassing the VAR', in *Models, methods and applications of econometrics: essays in honour of A.R. Bergstrom*, ed. Phillips, PCB, Oxford: Blackwell.

Hennessy, P. (2000), *The Prime Minister: the office and its holders since 1945*, London: Penguin.

Hetzel, R.L. (1998), 'Arthur Burns and inflation', *Federal Reserve Bank of Richmond Economic Quarterly* 84(1): 21–44.

HM Treasury (1990), *Financial Statement and Budget Report, 1990/91*, London: HMSO.

Hodrick, R.J. and Srivastava, S. (1986), 'The covariance of risk premiums and expected future spot exchange rates', *Journal of International Money and Finance* 5: 5–21.

Hoffman, D.L. and Rasche, R.H. (1996), *Aggregate money demand functions*, Boston: Kluwer Academic Press.

Horne, A. (1989), *Macmillan, 1957–1986: Volume II of the official biography*, London: Macmillan.

Hsiao, C., Pesaran, M.H. and Tahmiscioglu, A.K. (1999), 'Bayes estimation of short-run coefficients in dynamic panel data models', in C. Hsiao, K. Lahiri, L.-F. Lee and M.H. Pesaran (eds.), *Analysis of panels and limited dependent variable models: a volume in honour of G.S. Maddala*, Cambridge: Cambridge University Press.

Hutchison, M.M. and Walsh, C.E. (1998), 'The output–inflation trade-off and central bank reform: evidence from New Zealand', *Economic Journal* 108: 703–25.

IBRD (International Bank for Reconstruction and Development) (1998), *World development indicators, 1998_CD*, Washington D.C.: World Bank.

IMF (International Monetary Fund) (1993), *International financial statistics yearbook, 1993*, Washington D.C.: IMF.

(1996), *Financial programming and policy: the case of Sri Lanka*, Washington D.C.: IMF Institute.

(1998), *International financial statistics CD*, IFS_1298.cd, Washington D.C.: IMF.

(1999), *International financial statistics yearbook, 1999*, Washington D.C.: IMF.

Ireland, P.N. (2000), 'Money's role in the monetary business cycle', manuscript, Boston College.

Isard, P. (2000), 'The role of MULTIMOD in the IMF's policy analysis', International Monetary Fund Policy Discussion Paper No. 5.

Jensen, H. (2001), 'Optimal degrees of transparency in monetary policymaking', Working Paper 01–01, University of Copenhagen.

Johansen, S. (1996), *Likelihood-based inference in cointegrated vector autoregressive models*, Oxford: Oxford University Press.

Jondeau, E., Le Bihan, H. and Sédillot, F. (1999), 'Modelling and forecasting the French consumer price index components', Banque de France Working Paper No. 68.

Kakes, J. (2000), 'Monetary policy and business cycle asymmetry in Germany', *Kredit und Kapital* 33(2): 182–97.

Kaldor, N. (1971), 'Conflicts in national economic objectives', *Economic Journal* 81: 1–16. Reprinted in F. Targetti and A.P. Thirlwall (eds.) *The essential Kaldor*, London: Duckworth (1989), 495–515.

(1972), 'The irrelevance of equilibrium economics', *Economic Journal* 82: 1237–55. Reprinted in F. Targetti and A.P. Thirlwall (eds.) *The essential Kaldor*, London: Duckworth (1989), 373–98.

Kao, C. (1999), 'Spurious regression and residuals based tests for cointegration in panel data', *Journal of Econometrics* 90: 1–44.

Kiley, M.T. (1998), 'Monetary policy under neoclassical and New-Keynesian Phillips curves, with an application to price level and inflation targeting', Finance and Economics Discussion Series No. 1998–27, Federal Reserve Board.

King, M.A. (1995), 'Credibility and monetary policy: theory and evidence', *Scottish Journal of Political Economy* 42: 1–19.

(1996), 'How should central banks reduce inflation – conceptual issues', *Bank of England Quarterly Bulletin* 36(4).

King, R.G. and Rebelo, S. (1999), 'Resuscitating real business cycles', in M. Woodford and J.B. Taylor (eds.), *Handbook of macroeconomics*, Amsterdam: North-Holland.

King, R.G. and Watson, M. (1995), 'Systems reduction and solution algorithms for singular linear difference systems under rational expectations', Working Paper, University of Virginia.

(1996), 'Money, prices, interest rates and the business cycle', *Review of Economics and Statistics* 78(1): 35–53.

King, R.G., Plosser, C.I. and Rebelo, S.T. (1988a), 'Production, growth and business cycles: I. The basic neoclassical model', *Journal of Monetary Economics* 21(2/3): 195–232.

(1988b), 'Production, growth and business cycles: II. New directions', *Journal of Monetary Economics* 21(2/3): 309–41.

Kohn, D.L. (2000), *Report to the non-executive directors of the Court of the Bank of England on monetary policy processes and the work of monetary analysis*, available at www.bankofengland.co.uk.

Kuttner, K.N. (1994), 'Estimating potential output as a latent variable', *Journal of Business and Economic Statistics* 12(3): 361–8.

Kydland, F.E. and Prescott, E.C. (1982), 'Time to build and aggregate fluctuations', *Econometrica* 50: 1345–70.

Laidler, D., and Parkin, M. (1975), 'Inflation: a survey', *Economic Journal* 85: 741–809.

Layard, R., Nickell, S. and Jackman, R. (1991), *Unemployment: macroeconomic performance and the labour market*, Oxford: Oxford University Press.

Lee, K.C., Pesaran, M.H. and Pierse, R.G. (1990), 'Testing for aggregation bias in linear models', *Economic Journal* 100(400), Supplement: 137–50.

Lee, K., Pesaran, M.H. and Smith, R.P. (1997), 'Growth and convergence in a multi-country empirical stochastic Solow model', *Journal of Applied Econometrics* 12: 357–92.

Leeper, E.M. and Zha, T. (2000), 'Assessing simple policy rules: a view from a complete macro model', manuscript, Indiana University.

Leeson, R. (1998), 'Early doubts about the Phillips curve trade-off', *Journal of the History of Economic Thought* 20: 83–102.

Levtchenkova, S., Pagan, A. and Robertson, J. (1998), 'Shocking stories', *Journal of Economic Surveys* 12(5): 507–32. Reprinted in L. Oxley and M. McAleer (eds.), *Practical issues in cointegration analysis*, Oxford: Blackwell (1999).

Long, J.B. and Plosser, C.I. (1983), 'Real business cycles', *Journal of Political Economy* 91: 39–69.

Lucas, R.E. (1973), 'Some international evidence on output–inflation trade-offs', *American Economic Review* 63: 326–34.

——— (1976), 'Macroeconomic policy evaluation: a critique', *Journal of Monetary Economics* 1(2): 19–46.

Lütkepohl, H. (1991), *Introduction to multiple time series analysis*, Berlin: Springer.

McCallum, B.T. (1994), 'A reconsideration of the uncovered interest parity relationship', *Journal of Monetary Economics* 33: 105–32.

——— (2000a), 'Should monetary policy respond strongly to output gaps?' National Bureau of Economic Research Working Paper No. 8226.

——— (2000b), 'Comments on Eric Swanson's paper, "On signal extraction and non-certainity equivalence in optimal monetary policy rules"', available on B.T. McCallum's website, http://wpweb2k.gsia.cmu.edu/faculty/mccallum/mccallum. html.

——— (2000c), 'Alternative monetary policy rules: a comparison with historical settings for the United States, the United Kingdom, and Japan', National Bureau of Economic Research Working Paper No. 7725.

McCallum, B.T. and Nelson, E. (1999a), 'Performance of operational policy rules in an estimated semi-classical structural model', in J.B. Taylor (ed.), *Monetary policy rules*, Chicago: University of Chicago Press: 15–54.

——— (1999b), 'Nominal income targeting in an open-economy optimising model', *Journal of Monetary Economics* 43: 553–78.

MacDonald, R. (1999), 'Exchange rate behaviour: are fundamentals important?' *Economic Journal* 109: F672–91.

McKibbin, W.J. and Vines, D. (2001), 'Modelling reality: the need for both intertemporal optimization and stickiness in models for policy-making', *Oxford Review of Economic Policy* 16(4).

Mankiw, N.G. and Romer, D. (eds.) (1991a), *New Keynesian economics*, vol. 1, *Imperfect competition and sticky prices*, Cambridge, Mass.: MIT Press Readings in Economics.

——— (1991b), *New Keynesian economics*, vol. 2, *Coordination failures and real rigidities*, Cambridge, Mass.: MIT Press Readings in Economics.

Mark, N. (1995), 'Exchange rates and fundamentals: evidence on long-horizon predictability', *American Economic Review* 85(1): 201–18.

Mark, N.C. and Wu, Y. (1996), 'Risk, policy rules, and noise: rethinking deviations from uncovered interest parity', mimeo, June.

Masson, P., Symansky, S. and Meredith, G. (1990), 'MULTIMOD Mark II: a revised and extended model', International Monetary Fund Occasional Paper 71, July.

Maynard, A. and Phillips, P.C.B. (2000), 'Rethinking an old empirical puzzle: econometric evidence on the forward discount anomaly', unpublished manuscript, April.

Meese, R. and Rogoff, K. (1983), 'Empirical exchange rate models of the seventies: do they fit out of sample', *Journal of International Economics* 14: 3–24.

(1988), 'Was it real? The exchange rate–interest differential relation over the modern floating-rate period', *Journal of Finance* 43.

Meltzer, A.H. (1980), 'Discussion of Robert J. Gordon, "A consistent characterisation of a near-century of price behaviour"', *American Economic Review (Papers and Proceedings)* 70: 258–9.

(1995), 'Monetary, credit and (other) transmission processes: a monetarist perspective', *Journal of Economic Perspectives* 9(4): 49–72.

(1999), 'The transmission process', in Deutsche Bundesbank, *The monetary transmission process: recent developments and lessons for Europe*, London: Macmillan.

Meredith, G.M. (1999), 'REPMOD: a smaller sibling for MULTIMOD', International Monetary Fund Working Paper No. 8, January.

Meredith, G.M. and Chinn, M.D. (1998), 'Long-horizon uncovered interest rate parity', National Bureau of Economic Research Working Paper 6797, November.

Meyer, L. (2000), 'Structural changes and monetary policy', paper presented at a conference jointly sponsored by the Federal Reserve Bank of San Francisco and Stanford Institute for Economic Policy Research, San Francisco, 3–4 March; available at http://www.federalreserve.gov/boarddocs/speeches/2000/20000303.html.

Meyer, L.H. and Varvares, C. (1981), 'A comparison of the St. Louis model and two variations: predictive performance and policy implications', *Federal Reserve Bank of St Louis Review* 63, 13–25.

Millard, S., Scott, A. and Sensier, M. (1997), 'The labour market over the business cycle: can theory fit the facts?' *Oxford Review of Economic Policy* 13(3): 70–92.

Minford, P. (1993), 'Monetary policy in the other G-7 countries: the United Kingdom', in M.U. Fratianni and D. Salvatore (eds.), *Monetary policy in developed economies (Handbook of comparative economic policies, vol. 3)*, Amsterdam: North-Holland, 405–31.

Mishkin, F.S. (1995), 'Symposium on the monetary transmission mechanism', *Journal of Economic Perspectives* 9(4): 3–10.

Mishkin, F.S. and Posen, A.S. (1997), 'Inflation targeting: lessons from four countries', National Bureau of Economic Research Working Paper 6126, August.

Muinhos, M. (2001), 'Inflation targeting in an open financially integrated emerging economy: the case of Brazil', mimeo, Banco Central do Brasil.

Muscatelli, V.A. and Tirelli, P. (1996), 'Institutional change, inflation targets and the stability of interest rate functions in OECD economies', University of Glasgow Discussion Paper No. 9606.

Muscatelli, V.A. and Trecroci, C. (2000), 'Central bank goals, institutional change, and monetary policy: evidence from the U.S. and U.K.', manuscript, University of Glasgow.

Muscatelli, V.A., Tirelli, P. and Trecroci, C. (1999), 'Does institutional change really matter? Inflation targets, central bank reform and interest rate policy in the OECD countries', University of Glasgow Discussion Paper No. 9920.

Neiss, K.S. and Nelson, E. (2000), 'The real interest rate gap as an inflation indicator', manuscript, Bank of England.

Nelson, E. (2000a), 'U.K. monetary policy 1972–1997: a guide using Taylor rules', Bank of England Working Paper No. 120, July.

(2000b), 'Direct effects of base money on aggregate demand: theory and evidence', Bank of England Working Paper No. 122, October.

Nelson, E. and Nikolov, K. (2001), 'Alternative explanations for the Great Inflation: evidence from the United Kingdom', manuscript, Bank of England.

Nickell, S. (1996), 'Inflation and the UK labour market', in T. Jenkinson (ed.), *Readings in macroeconomics*, Oxford: Oxford University Press, 141–8.

Obstfeld, M. and Rogoff, K. (1996), *Foundations of international macroeconomics*, Cambridge, Mass.: MIT Press.

Onatski, A. and Stock, J.H. (2000), 'Robust monetary policy under model uncertainty in a small model of the US economy', National Bureau of Economic Research Working Paper No. 7490.

Orphanides, A. (2000), 'The quest for prosperity without inflation', European Central Bank Working Paper No. 15.

Orphanides, A., Porter, R.D., Reifschneider, D., Tetlow, R. and Finan, F. (1999), 'Errors in the measurement of the output gap and the design of monetary policy', Federal Reserve Board Finance and Economics Discussion Series No. 1999–2045, August.

Osterwald-Lenum, M. (1992), 'A note with quantiles of the asymptotic distribution of the maximum likelihood cointegration rank test statistics', *Oxford Bulletin of Economics and Statistics* 54(3): 461–72.

Papademos, L. and Modigliani, F. (1990), 'The supply of money and the control of nominal income', in B.M. Friedman and F.H. Hahn, *Handbook of monetary economics*, vol. 1, New York: Elsevier Science Publishers.

Patel, N. (ed.) (2001), *Financial Statistics Explanatory Handbook*, London: The Stationery Office.

Peersman, G. and Smets, F. (2000a), 'The monetary transmission mechanism in the Euro area: more evidence from VAR analysis', mimeo, European Central Bank.

(2000b), 'Cyclical and industry effects of monetary policy in the Euro area', work in progress.

Perry, G.L. (1978), 'Slowing the wage–price spiral: the macroeconomic view', *Brookings Papers on Economic Activity* 2: 259–91.

Pesaran, M.H. and Smith, R.P. (1995), 'Estimating long-run relationships from dynamic heterogeneous panels', *Journal of Econometrics* 68: 79–113.

(1998), 'Structural analysis of cointegrating VARs', *Journal of Economic Surveys* 12: 471–506. Reprinted in L. Oxley and M. McAleer (eds.), *Practical issues in cointegration analysis*, Oxford: Blackwell.

Pesaran, M.H., Pierse, R.G. and Lee, K.C. (1994), 'Choice between disaggregate and aggregate specifications estimated by instrumental variables methods', *Journal of Business and Economic Statistics* 12(1): 11–21.

Pesaran, M.H., Shin, Y. and Smith, R.J. (1999), 'Bounds testing approaches to the analysis of long-run relationships', University of Cambridge DAE Working Paper 9907; available on http://www.econ.cam.ac.uk/faculty/pesaran/.

Pesaran, M.H., Shin, Y. and Smith, R.P. (1999), 'Pooled mean group estimation of dynamic heterogeneous panels', *Journal of the American Statistical Association* 94: 621–34.

Phelps, E.S. (1967), 'Phillips curves, expectations of inflation and optimal unemployment over time', *Economica* 34: 254–81.

Phillips, A.W. (1958), 'The relationship between unemployment and the rate of change of money wages in the United Kingdom, 1861–1957', *Economica* 25: 283–99.

Phillips, P.C.B. and Moon, H.R. (1999), 'Linear regression limit theory for nonstationary panel data', *Econometrica* 67: 1057–1112.

Polak, J.J. (1998), 'The IMF monetary model at 40', *Economic Modelling* 15(3): 395–410.

Prasad, E.S. (1999), 'International trade and the business cycle', *Economic Journal* 109: 588–606.

Quah, D. (1992), 'The relative importance of permanent and transitory components: identification and some theoretical bounds', *Econometrica* 60(1): 107–18.

(1994), 'One business cycle and one trend from (many,) many disaggregates', *European Economic Review* 38(3–4): 605–13.

Reifschneider, D. and Williams, J. (1999), 'Three lessons for monetary policy in a low inflation era', Federal Reserve Board.

Ritschl, A. and Woitek, U. (2000), 'Did monetary forces cause the great depression? A Bayesian VAR analysis for the US economy', mimeo, University of Glasgow.

Robbins, L. (1960), 'Monetary theory and the Radcliffe Report'. Reprinted in *Money, trade and international relations*, London: Macmillan (1971), 90–119.

Roberts, J.M. (1995), 'New Keynesian economics and the Phillips curve', *Journal of Money, Credit, and Banking* 27: 975–84.

Rogoff, K. (1996), 'The purchasing power parity puzzle' *Journal of Economic Literature* 44: 1–19.

Rotemberg, J.J. and Woodford, M. (1999), 'Interest rate rules in an estimated sticky price model', in J.B. Taylor (ed.), *Monetary policy rules*, Chicago: University of Chicago Press, 57–119.

Rudebusch, G.D. (1998), 'Do measures of monetary policy in a VAR make sense?' *International Economic Review* 39: 907–31.

(2000), 'Assessing nominal income rules for monetary policy with model and data uncertainty', Federal Reserve Bank of San Francisco Working Paper 2000–03, February.

Rudebusch, G.D. and Svensson, L.E.O. (1999), 'Policy rules for inflation targeting', in J.B. Taylor (ed.), *Monetary policy rules*, Chicago: University of Chicago Press, 203–46.

(2000), 'Eurosystem monetary targeting: lessons from U.S. data', *European Economic Review*, forthcoming; also available on G.D. Rudebusch's website at http://www.frbsf.org/economics/economists/grudebusch/index.html.

Sack, B. (1998), 'Uncertainty, learning, and gradual monetary policy', Board of Governors of the Federal Reserve System: Finance and Economics Discussion Paper Series 98/34.

Sargent, T.J. (1999), *The conquest of American inflation*, Princeton, N.J.: Princeton University Press.

Sbordone, A. (1998), 'Prices and unit labour costs: a new test of price stickiness', manuscript, Rutgers University.

Sims, C.A. (1980), 'Macroeconomics and reality', *Econometrica* 48(1): 1–48.

Smith, R. (1998), 'Emergent policy-making with macroeconometric models', *Economic Modelling* 15(3): 429–42.

Solow, R.M. (1969), *Price expectations and the behaviour of the price level*, Manchester: Manchester University Press.

Srour, G. (1999), 'Inflation targeting under uncertainty', Bank of Canada Technical Report No. 85.

Sterne, G. (2000), 'Inflation targets in a global context', prepared for the fourth annual conference at the Central Bank of Chile: '10 years of inflation targeting: design, performance, challenges', Santiago, Chile, November.

Stuart, A. (1996), 'Simple monetary policy rules', *Bank of England Quarterly Bulletin* 36(3): 281–7.

Svensson, L.E.O. (1997), 'Inflation targeting: some extensions', National Bureau of Economic Research Working Paper No. 5962.

(1999), 'Inflation targeting as a monetary policy rule', *Journal of Monetary Economics* 43: 607–54.

(2001), 'Independent review of the operation of monetary policy in New Zealand', Report to the Minister of Finance, February.

Swamy, P.A.V.B. (1970), 'Efficient inference in a random coefficient regression model', *Econometrica* 38: 311–23.

Tarkka, J. and Mayes, D. (1999), 'The value of publishing official central bank forecasts', Bank of Finland Discussion Papers No. 22/99.

Taylor, J.B. (1993), 'Discretion versus policy rules in practice', *Carnegie-Rochester Conference Series on Public Policy* 39: 195–214.

(1995), 'The monetary transmission mechanism: an empirical framework', *Journal of Economic Perspectives* 9(4): 11–26.

(1997), 'Comment on "America's peacetime inflation: the 1970s"', in C.D. Romer and D.H. Romer, (eds.), *Reducing inflation: motivation and strategy*, Chicago: University of Chicago Press, 276–80.

(1999) (ed.), *Monetary policy rules*, Chicago: University of Chicago Press.

(2000), 'Low inflation, pass-through, and the pricing power of firms', *European Economic Review* 44(7): 1389–1408.

Taylor, M.P. (1995), 'The economics of exchange rate', *Journal of Economic Literature* 33: 13–47.

Taylor, M.P. and Peel, D.A. (2000), 'Non linear adjustment, long-run equilibrium and exchange rate fundamentals', *Journal of International Money and Finance* 19(1): 33–54.

The Banker (1971), 'Time for reflation', March: 237–8.

Thomas, R.S.J. (1997a), 'The demand for M4: sectoral analysis. Part 1 – the personal sector', Bank of England Working Paper Series No. 61, June.

(1997b), 'The demand for M4: sectoral analysis. Part 2 – the company sector', Bank of England Working Paper Series No. 62, June.

Tinsley, P. (1999), 'Short rate expectations, term premiums, and central bank use of derivatives to reduce policy uncertainty', Finance and Economics Discussion Series 1999–14, Federal Reserve Board.

Treasury and Civil Service Committee (1988), *Report on the 1988 autumn statement*, London: HMSO.

Turner, D. and Seghezza, E. (1999), 'Testing for a common OECD Phillips curve', Economics Department Working Paper No. 219, OECD.

Vickers, J. (1998), 'Inflation targeting in practice: the U.K. experience', *Bank of England Quarterly Bulletin* 38(4).

—— (1999), 'Economic models and monetary policy', Speech to the governors of the NIESR, 18 March.

—— (2000), 'Monetary policy and the supply side', Society of Business Economists symposium, London, 15 March; *Bank of England Quarterly Bulletin* 40(2).

Wadhwani, S. (1999), 'Sterling's puzzling behaviour', *Bank of England Quarterly Bulletin* 39(4).

—— (2000), 'Monetary challenges in a new economy', Hong Kong & Shanghai Banking Corporate Global Seminar.

Wallis, K.F. (1989), 'Macroeconomic forecasting: a survey', *Economic Journal* 99(394): 28–61.

Wallis, K.F. and Whitley, J.D. (1995), 'Sources of error in forecasts and expectations: U.K. economic models, 1984–8', in K.F. Wallis, *Time series analysis and macroeconometric modelling: the collected papers of Kenneth F. Wallis*. Economists of the Twentieth Century series. Aldershot, UK: Elgar, 267–89. Previously published 1991.

Walsh, C.E. (1998), *Monetary theory and policy*, Cambridge, Mass.: MIT Press.

Westaway, P.F. (1995), 'The role of macroeconomic models in the policy design process', *National Institute Economic Review* 151: 53–64.

Whitley, J.D. (1997), 'Economic models and policy-making', *Bank of England Quarterly Bulletin* 37(2).

Wickens, M.R. and Motto, R. (2000), 'Estimating shocks and impulse response functions', mimeo, University of York.

Williams, D., Goodhart, C.A.E. and Gowland, D.H. (1976), 'Money, income and causality: the U.K. experience', *American Economic Review* 66: 417–23.

Williamson, J. and Wood, G.E. (1976), 'The British inflation: indigenous or imported?' *American Economic Review* 66: 520–31.

Wilson, H. (1979), *Final term: the Labour government 1974–1976*, London: Weidenfeld & Nicolson.

Woodford, M. (1994), 'Nonstandard indicators for monetary policy: can their usefulness be judged from forecasting regressions?' in G.N. Mankiw (ed.), *Monetary policy*, Chicago: University of Chicago Press, 95–115.

—— (1997), 'Doing without money: controlling inflation in a post-monetary world', National Bureau of Economic Research Working Paper 6188, September.

—— (1999a), 'Commentary: how should monetary policy be conducted in an era of price stability?' Kansas City Federal Reserve Bank conference.

—— (1999b), 'Revolution and evolution in twentieth-century macroeconomics', in P. Gifford, (ed.), *Frontiers of the mind in the twenty-first century*, Cambridge, Mass.: Harvard University Press.

—— (2000a), 'A neo-Wicksellian framework for the analysis of monetary policy', mimeo, Princeton University.

(2000b), 'Pitfalls of forward-looking monetary policy', *American Economic Review* 90(2): 100–4.

Yaari, M.E. (1965), 'Uncertain lifetime, life insurance and the theory of the consumer', *Review of Economic Studies* 32: 137–50.

Zarnowitz, V. (1992), 'Business cycles: theory, history, indicators, and forecasting', National Bureau of Economic Research Studies in Business Cycles, vol. 27.

Index

Printed in the United States
By Bookmasters